Higher National in Computing

A Pearson Custom Publication

Higher National in Computing

Compiled from:

Computers Information Technology in Perspective 12th Edition
by Larry Long and Nancy Long

Systems Analysis and Design 2nd Edition
by Donald Yeates and Tony Wakefield

Problem Solving and Programming Concepts 6th Edition
by Maureen Sprankle

Modern Systems Analysis and Design 4th Edition
by Jeffrey A. Hoffer, Joey F. George and Joseph S. Valacich

Computer Networks 4th Edition
by Andrew S. Tanenbaum

PEARSON
Custom
Publishing

Pearson Education Limited
Edinburgh Gate
Harlow
Essex CM20 2JE

And associated companies throughout the world

Visit us on the World Wide Web at:
www.pearsoned.co.uk

First published 2005, Reprinted 2005

This Custom Book Edition © 2005 Published by Pearson Education Limited

Taken from:

Computers Information Technology in Perspective 12th Edition
by Larry Long and Nancy Long
ISBN 0 13 143235 4
Copyright © 2005 by Pearson Education, Inc.,
Upper Saddle River, New Jersey, 07458

Systems Analysis and Design 2nd Edition
by Donald Yeates and Tony Wakefield
ISBN 0 273 65536 1
Copyright © Pearson Education Limited 1994, 2004

Problem Solving and Programming Concepts 6th Edition
by Maureen Sprankle
ISBN 0 13 048268 4
Copyright © 2003, 2001, 1998, 1995, 1992 by Pearson Education, Inc.,
Upper Saddle River, New Jersey, 07458

Modern Systems Analysis and Design 4th Edition
by Jeffrey A. Hoffer, Joey F. George and Joseph S. Valacich
ISBN 0 13 145461 7
Copyright © 2005, 2002 by Pearson Education, Inc.,
Upper Saddle River, New Jersey, 07458

Computer Networks 4th Edition
by Andrew S. Tanenbaum
ISBN 0 13 066102 3
Copyright © 2003 by Pearson Education, Inc., Publishing as Prentice Hall PTR
Upper Saddle River, New Jersey, 07458

ISBN-10: 1-84479-242-0
ISBN-13: 978-1-84479-242-9

Printed and bound in Great Britain by Hobbs the Printers Limited, Totton, Hants

Contents

Preface to HN course companions

This course companion to the Higher National in Computing is designed to offer the learner some resource material for some of the most commonly taught units in the specification. For each unit, it provides a relevant chapter taken from a previously published work, the learning outcomes and assessment criteria.

The material selected has been chosen because it either covers a key aspect of the unit or acts as an introduction or stimulus for the unit. It is not intended that this companion should be the sole teaching resource for the units or for the material provided to address every learning outcome of the unit.

Unit 1: Computer Platforms

Learning hours: 60

NQF level 4: BTEC Higher National — H1

Content Selected: Long and Long, Computers 12th Edition, Chapter 5

Introduction from the Qualification Leader

This chapter offers a good starting point for the unit particularly the learning outcome "investigation of computer systems".

It initially looks at storage devices and tries to capture the complexity of such undertakings with good supporting illustrations. This is followed by the development of input and output devices. Examples and supporting illustrations are used throughout to ensure that readers appreciate the broader practical aspects of solving real-life IT problems.

To reinforce the learning experience, the chapters concludes with a chapter review that includes a chapter summary, key terms, chapter self-check, IT ethics and issues and discussion and problem solving.

Description of unit

This unit is aimed at IT practitioners who need sufficient knowledge of computer architecture to make rational and commercial decisions on the selection and specification of systems. Learners will learn how to evaluate operating systems in order to create their own operating environment. Many IT practitioners communicate with specialist technical support staff during the specification and planning of systems implementation. This unit aims to give learners the confidence to communicate with technical and non-technical specialists to justify their recommendations.

It is expected that centres will use current personal computer and networking resources. Learners should be encouraged to read current journals to investigate and evaluate new hardware and software developments.

Summary of learning outcomes

To achieve this unit a learner must:

1   Investigate **computer systems**

2   Investigate **operating systems**

3   **Design a computer system**

4   **Test your computer system.**

Content

1 **Computer systems**

Processor: description of components (Von-Neuman architecture), terminology (eg bits, bytes, kilobytes etc), identification of factors affecting performance (eg millions of instructions per second (MIPS), floating point operations per second (FLOPS), clock speed, computed performance indexes, bus architectures, pipelining)

Backing store: identification of types (disc, CD, CD-R, CD-RW, DVD-RW, DVD-RAM etc), performance factors (eg data transfer rate, seek times, capacity)

Peripherals: description of available peripherals (displays, printers etc), understanding of performance factors (eg displays — performance, resolution, colour depth, video RAM, refresh rate, interlacing, slot pitch, etc, printer — speed, resolution, image quality, software requirements, postscript, PCL and associated printer control)

Computer selection: specification of requirements, performance of the selected system, costs, user benefits

2 **Operating systems**

Operating system functions: overview of functions (eg user interface, machine and peripheral management etc), comparison between functions of different types of operating system (personal computer, network, mainframe etc)

Computer operations: proprietary operating systems, creation of environment and systems for a computer user (file/directory structures, tailoring of screen interface, backup systems etc), user profile

3 **Design a computer system**

Selection: processor (eg speed, special characteristics), memory, storage devices, display, peripherals, specialised components (eg sound cards, video cards, datalogging interfaces), bus system, network readiness/adaptability

User needs: costs, productivity, particular requirements (eg power, display, special needs), training needs

4 **Test your computer system**

Test plan: software testing (eg: black box, white box), hardware testing methodologies, documentation, health and safety issues (eg compliance)

User support planning: identifying user training needs, producing a training schedule, functions of a help desk/help line/help software.

Security: physical and logical security measures, backup and recovery, hacking, encryption, levels of access rights

Outcomes and assessment criteria

Outcomes	Assessment criteria for pass **To achieve each outcome a learner must demonstrate the ability to:**
1 Investigate **computer systems**	• select machine components or sub-systems appropriate to given tasks • evaluate the performance of the selected system
2 Investigate **operating systems**	• contrast the functions and features of different types of operating systems • understand how to customise operating systems
3 **Design a computer system**	• investigate and identify the key components for a computer system for a particular user • specify a complete computer system to suit a given task
4 **Test a computer system**	• produce a plan that checks the main hardware and software components, using standard techniques • produce user documentation for your system • produce a security policy for your system. • demonstrate that the system meets health and safety requirements

STORAGE AND INPUT/OUTPUT DEVICES

LEARNING OBJECTIVES

Once you have read and studied this chapter, you will be able to:

- Understand the various types of magnetic disk storage devices and media, including their organization, principles of operation, maintenance, and performance considerations (Section 5-1).

- Understand the operational capabilities and applications for the various types of optical laser disc storage (Section 5-2).

- Describe the operation and application of common input devices (Section 5-3).

- Describe the operation and application of common output devices (Section 5-4).

Not too long ago, we stored things in file drawers, family photo albums, notebooks, recipe boxes, keepsake boxes, calendars, bookshelves, Rolodex name and address files, and many other places. Most of us still store things in these same places, but to a far lesser extent. The family photo album may be scanned and stored on a rewritable CD-ROM. Personal information software is rapidly replacing the Rolodex file. Encyclopedias are pressed into a CD-ROM rather than printed as a 20-volume set. Music is now available from many electronic sources. Much of what used to be physical and tangible is now stored permanently in electronic form on various storage media.

This chapter should help you sort out the storage options and give you some insight as to what (and how much) to buy. Plus, it will help you to know when and how to use various storage alternatives.

When PCs arrived as a viable consumer product in the late 1970s, choices for input/output were limited. Input was mostly via the standard QWERTY keyboard. Output was a small low-resolution monitor, a really slow printer, and a tiny little speaker that made annoying sounds when you tapped the wrong key. Now we have ergonomic keyboards and even speech-recognition software that lets you talk to your PC. Monitors come in many different shapes, sizes, and qualities. All-in-one devices offer fast photo-quality color printing, along with copying, scanning, and faxing capabilities. There is a broad array of input/output devices you can connect to a PC for what seems to be an infinite number of applications.

When it comes to buying PC related hardware, you are generally on your own. Realistically, you cannot depend on salespeople or friends to make these important decisions for you. It takes personal knowledge and research. This chapter should help you get exactly what you want and need in input and output devices, and ultimately, the biggest bang for your PC buck.

5-1 MAGNETIC DISK STORAGE

Why this section is important to you.

We buy them; we entrust our precious documents, images, and information to them; and we protect them to ensure the integrity of their valuable content. Pound for pound, magnetic disks may be among your most important material possessions.

Did you ever stop to think about what happens behind the scenes when you...

- Request a telephone number through directory assistance?
- Draw money from your checking account at an ATM?
- Check out at a supermarket?
- Download a file from the Internet?

Needed information—such as telephone numbers, account balances, item prices, or stock summary files on the Internet—is retrieved from rapidly rotating disk-storage media and loaded to random-access memory (RAM) for processing. Untold terabytes (trillions of bytes) of information, representing millions of applications, are stored *permanently* for periodic retrieval in magnetic (such as hard disk) and opti-

Higher National in Computing

6

cal (such as DVD+RW) storage media. There they can be retrieved in milliseconds. For example, as soon as the directory assistance operator keys in the desired name, the full name and number are retrieved from disk storage and displayed. Moments later, a digitized version of voice recordings of numbers is accessed from disk storage and played in response to the caller's request: "The number is five, zero, one, five, five, five, two, two, four, nine."

STORAGE TECHNOLOGIES

Within a computer system, programs and information in all forms (text, image, audio, and video) are stored in both *RAM* and permanent **mass storage,** such as *magnetic disk and rewritable optical laser disc* (see Figure 5-1). Programs and information are retrieved from mass storage and stored *temporarily* in high-speed RAM for processing.

Over the years, manufacturers have developed a variety of permanent mass storage devices and media. Today the various types of **magnetic disk drives** and their respective storage media are the state of the art for permanent storage. **Optical laser disc,** such as CD-ROM and DVD±RW, continues to emerge as a means of mass storage. Note that *disk* is spelled with a "k" for magnetic disk media and with a "c" for optical disc media. **Magnetic tape drives** complement disk/disc storage by providing inexpensive *backup* capability and *archival* storage, primarily for the business environment. The tape "data cartridge" is similar in appearance to the audio cassette tape. The focus of this section is magnetic disk storage. Optical laser discs are covered in the next section. Magnetic tape, which seldom is used in personal computing, is including in the backup discussion in Chapter 8.

Random and Sequential Access

Magnetic disks have *random-* or *direct-access* capabilities. You are quite familiar with these access concepts, but you may not realize it. Suppose you have Paul Simon's classic album, *The Rhythm of the Saints,* on both CD and cassette tape. To play the third song on the cassette, "The Coast," you would have to wind the tape forward and search for it sequentially. To play "The Coast" on the CD, all you would have to do is select track number 3. This simple analogy demonstrates the two fundamental methods of storing and accessing data— *random* and *sequential.*

Types of Magnetic Disks: Interchangeable and Fixed

Magnetic disks are very fast, able to seek and retrieve information quicker than a blink of an eye (in milliseconds). This direct-access flexibility and speed have made magnetic disk storage the overwhelming choice of computer users, for all types of computers and all

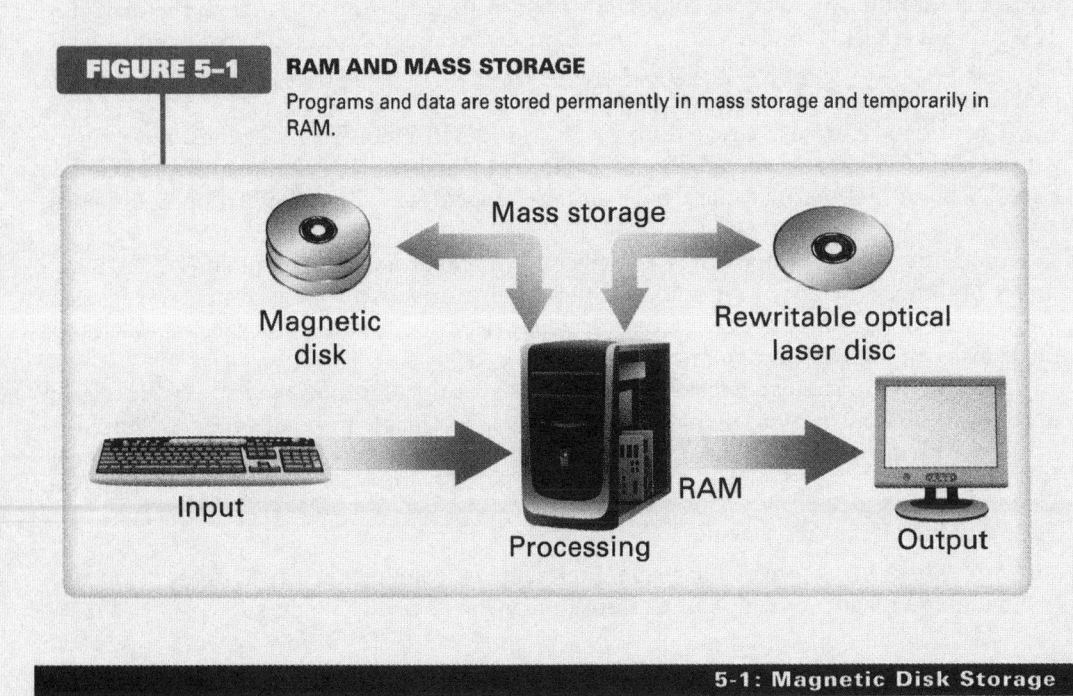

FIGURE 5-1 **RAM AND MASS STORAGE**
Programs and data are stored permanently in mass storage and temporarily in RAM.

Mass storage

Magnetic disk

Rewritable optical laser disc

Input

Processing

RAM

Output

Higher National in Computing

FIGURE 5-2

INFORMATION ON MAGNETIC DISK

Today, most readily accessible information is stored on hard disk. The information provided by these interactive ATMs and kiosks is stored on disk and all transactions are recorded on disk.

Courtesy of Diebold, Incorporated

types of applications (see Figure 5-2). A variety of magnetic disk drives, the *hardware device,* and magnetic disks, the *medium* (the actual surface on which the information is stored), are manufactured for different business requirements and are discussed in the following sections.

Generally, magnetic disks are classified as *interchangeable* or *fixed.*

- *Interchangeable disks.* The classic "floppy" diskette is an example of an **interchangeable disk.** These types of disks can be stored offline and loaded to the magnetic disk drives as they are needed. A disk or device is **offline** if it is not accessible to and under the control of a computer system.

- *Fixed disks.* **Fixed disks,** also called **hard disks,** usually are permanently installed. Typically, the hard disk is a fixed part of a computer system and is **online** at all times; that is, the disk and its information are under the control of the computer system. All hard disks are rigid and usually made of aluminum with a surface coating of easily magnetized elements, such as iron, cobalt, chromium, and nickel.

Figure 5-3 shows some of the different types of interchangeable disks and fixed disks. The type you (or a company) should use depends on the volume of data you have and the frequency with which those data are accessed.

Interchangeable Disks

Three types of interchangeable disk drives are commonly used on PCs—the traditional *floppy disk* and the newer high-capacity *SuperDisk* and *Zip disk*. These disk drives accept interchangeable disks.

The traditional 3.5-inch **floppy disk** is a thin, Mylar disk that is permanently enclosed in a rigid plastic jacket. The widely used standard for traditional "floppies," also called *diskettes,* permits only 1.44 MB of storage, not much in the modern era in which 4-MB images and 30-MB programs are commonplace. A newer version, called a **SuperDisk,** can store 120 MB of information. The diskette and the SuperDisk are the same size but have different disk densities. **Disk density** refers to the number of bits that can be stored per unit of area on the disk-face surface. In contrast to a hard disk, the diskette and the SuperDisk are set in motion only when a command is issued to read from or write to the disk. The 120-MB SuperDisk combines floppy and hard disk technology to read from and write to specially formatted floppy-size disks. The SuperDisk drive reads from and writes to the traditional diskette, as well.

The original **Zip®** drive reads and writes to 100-MB **Zip® disks.** The most recent innovation, a 750-MB Zip drive, handles all versions of Zip disks (100, 250, and 750 MB). The SuperDisk and 750-MB Zip disk have storage capacities of 70 and 521 floppy diskettes, respectively.

Soon, the 3.5-inch floppy may become a historical artifact. Many major PC manufacturers no longer include the traditional floppy disk drive with their computers. Instead, they rely on DVD±RW/CD-RW drives, local area networks, and the Internet as vehicles for the transfer of information and programs.

A blank interchangeable disk has a very modest value. But once you save your files on it, its value, at least to you, increases greatly. Such a valuable piece of property should be handled with great care. Here are a few commonsense guidelines for handling interchangeable disks.

- Avoid temperature extremes.
- Store disks in a protected location, preferably in a storage tray away from direct sunlight and magnetic fields (for example, magnetic paperclip holders).

Higher National in Computing

8

FIGURE 5-3   DISK DRIVES AND MEDIA

SUPERDISK

This illustration compares the capacity of a 120-MB SuperDisk (right) to the traditional floppy disk. The SuperDisk drive is compatible with the traditional 1.44-MB diskette.

Courtesy of Imation Corporation

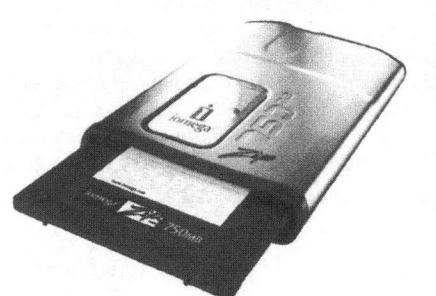
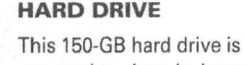

ZIP DISK

An alternative high-capacity interchangeable disk is the 100-, 250-, or 750-MB Zip disk (shown here) with an external Zip drive.

Courtesy of Iomega Corporation

HARD DRIVE

This 150-GB hard drive is exposed to show its inner workings (2 platters with 4 read/write heads).

Courtesy of Seagate Technology

MICRODRIVE

IBM unveiled the world's smallest and lightest hard-disk drive with a disk platter that will fit into an egg. The IBM Microdrive, which weighs less than an AA battery and holds 340 MB, is designed for use in PDAs and palmtop PCs.

Courtesy of International Business Machines Corporation. Unauthorized use not permitted.

PORTABLE HARD DISK

The external portable hard disk lets you take your files with you and access them on any PC with a USB port.

Courtesy of Iomega Corporation

* Remove disks from disk drives before you turn off the computer, but only when the "drive active" light is off.
* Use an interchangeable drive cleaning kit periodically.
* Avoid force when inserting or removing a disk, as there should be little or no resistance.
* Don't touch the disk surface.

Higher National in Computing

9

The Hard Disk

Hard disk manufacturers are working continuously to achieve two objectives: (1) to put more information in less disk space and (2) to enable a more rapid transfer of that information to/from RAM. Consequently, hard-disk storage technology is forever changing. There are two types of hard disks in common use—those that are permanently installed and those that are portable.

Generally, the 1- to 5.25-inch (diameter of disk) hard disks have storage capacities from about 40 GB (gigabytes) to over 300 GB. A 300-GB hard disk stores about the same amount of data as 63 DVDs or 462 CD-ROMs.

A hard disk contains up to 12 disk platters stacked on a single rotating spindle. PC-based hard disks will normally have from one to four platters. Data are stored on all *recording surfaces*. For a disk with four platters, there are eight recording surfaces on which data can be stored (see Figure 5-4). The disks spin continuously at a high speed (from 7,200 to 15,000 revolutions per minute) within a sealed enclosure. The enclosure keeps the disk-face surfaces free from contaminants (see Figure 5-5), such as dust and cigarette smoke. This contaminant-free environment allows hard disks to have greater density of data storage than the interchangeable diskettes.

The rotation of a magnetic disk passes all data under or over a **read/write head,** thereby making all data available for access on each revolution of the disk (see Figure 5-4). A fixed disk will have at least one read/write head for each recording surface. The heads are mounted on **access arms** that move together and literally float on a cushion of air over (or under) the spinning recording surfaces.

The **portable hard disk** is an external device that is connected easily to any personal computer via a USB port or FireWire port. Portable hard disks are popular in the business world where knowledge workers can take their user files with them to their home office or to a PowerPoint presentation in San Francisco. Portable hard disk capacities are similar to those of fixed hard disks and they weigh from .5 to 2 pounds.

One of the most frequently asked questions is "How much hard drive capacity do I need?" The answer you hear most is "As much as you can afford." Disk space is like closet space—you never seem to have enough. If it's there, you tend to fill it with some-

---

FIGURE 5-4   **FIXED HARD DISK WITH FOUR PLATTERS AND EIGHT RECORDING SURFACES**

A cylinder refers to similarly numbered concentric tracks on the disk-face surfaces. In the illustration, the read/write heads are positioned over Cylinder 0012. At this position, the data on any one of the eight tracks numbered 0012 are accessible to the computer on each revolution of the disk. The read/write heads must be moved to access data on other tracks/cylinders. Next to the illustration is a highly magnified area of a magnetic disk-face surface shows elongated information bits recorded serially along 8 of the disk's 1774 concentric tracks.

Courtesy of International Business Machines Corporation. Unauthorized use not permitted.

Access arm

Track 0012, Disk-Face Surface 1

Cylinder 0012

Track 0012, Disk-Face Surface 7

Read/write heads positioned at Cylinder 0012

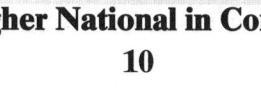

Higher National in Computing

FIGURE 5-5

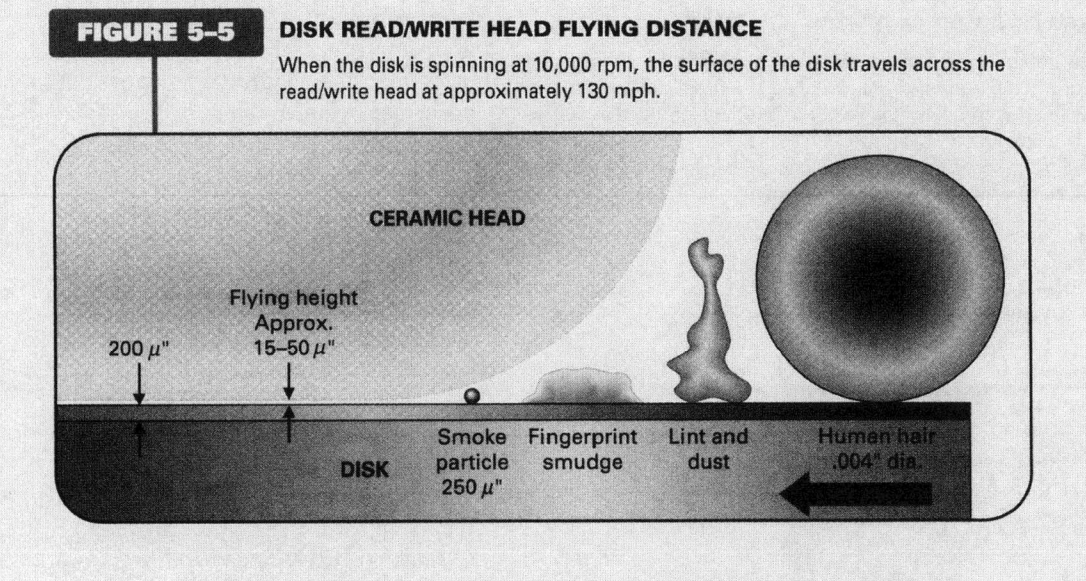

DISK READ/WRITE HEAD FLYING DISTANCE

When the disk is spinning at 10,000 rpm, the surface of the disk travels across the read/write head at approximately 130 mph.

CERAMIC HEAD

Flying height
Approx.
15–50 μ"

200 μ"

DISK

Smoke
particle
250 μ"

Fingerprint
smudge

Lint and
dust

Human hair
.004" dia.

thing. If you don't, the software vendors will. The original MS-DOS operating system was 160 KB, Windows 3.1 was 10 MB, and Windows XP is over 100 MB—over 600 times the size of MS-DOS.

techtv
CAR STEREOS WITH
HARD DRIVES

DISK ORGANIZATION

Typically, the PC owner maintains his or her own hard disk—that, probably, would be you. To keep your disk running at peak performance and to understand warnings and error messages that pertain to your hard disk, you will need to understand the fundamentals of disk organization.

The way in which data and programs are stored and accessed is similar for all disks. Conceptually, a floppy disk looks like a hard disk with a single platter. Both media have a thin film coating of one of the easily magnetized elements (cobalt, for example). The thin film coating on the disk can be magnetized electronically by the read/write head to represent the absence or presence of a bit (0 or 1).

Tracks, Sectors, and Clusters

Data are stored in concentric **tracks** by magnetizing the surface to represent bit configurations (see Figure 5-6). Bits are recorded using *serial representation;* that is, bits are aligned in a row in the track. The number of tracks varies greatly between disks, from as few as 80 on a diskette to thousands on high-capacity hard disks. The spacing of tracks is measured in **tracks per inch,** or **TPI.** The 3.5-inch floppies are rated at 135 TPI. The TPI for hard disks can be in the thousands. The *track density,* which is measured in TPI, tells only part of the story. The *recording density* tells the rest. Recording density, which is measured in *megabits per inch,* refers to the number of bits (1s and 0s) that can be stored per linear inch of track. High-density hard disks have densities in excess of 3 megabits per inch.

PC disks use **sector organization** to store and retrieve data. In sector organization, the recording surface is divided into pie-shaped **sectors** (see Figure 5-6). The number of sectors depends on the density of the disk. A hard disk may have hundreds of sectors. Typically, the storage capacity of each sector on a particular track is 512 bytes, regardless of the number of sectors per track. Adjacent sectors are combined to form **clusters,** the capacity of which is a multiple of 512. Typically, clusters range in size from 4,096 bytes up to 32,768 bytes (that's 8 up to 64 sectors). The cluster is the smallest unit of disk space that can be allocated to a file, so every file saved to disk takes up one or more clusters.

Each disk cluster is numbered, and the number of the first cluster in a file comprises the **disk address** on a particular file. The disk address represents the physical location of a particular file or set of data on a disk. To read from or write to a disk, an access arm containing the

Higher National in Computing

FIGURE 5-6

CUTAWAY OF A DISKETTE

The access arm on this 3.5-inch disk drive is positioned at a particular track (Track 2 in the example). Data are read or written serially in tracks within a given sector. Below, the flexible 3.5-inch recording disk spins between two soft liners when accessed. The recording surface is sandwiched in a rigid plastic jacket for protection. When inserted, the metal shutter slides to reveal the recording window.

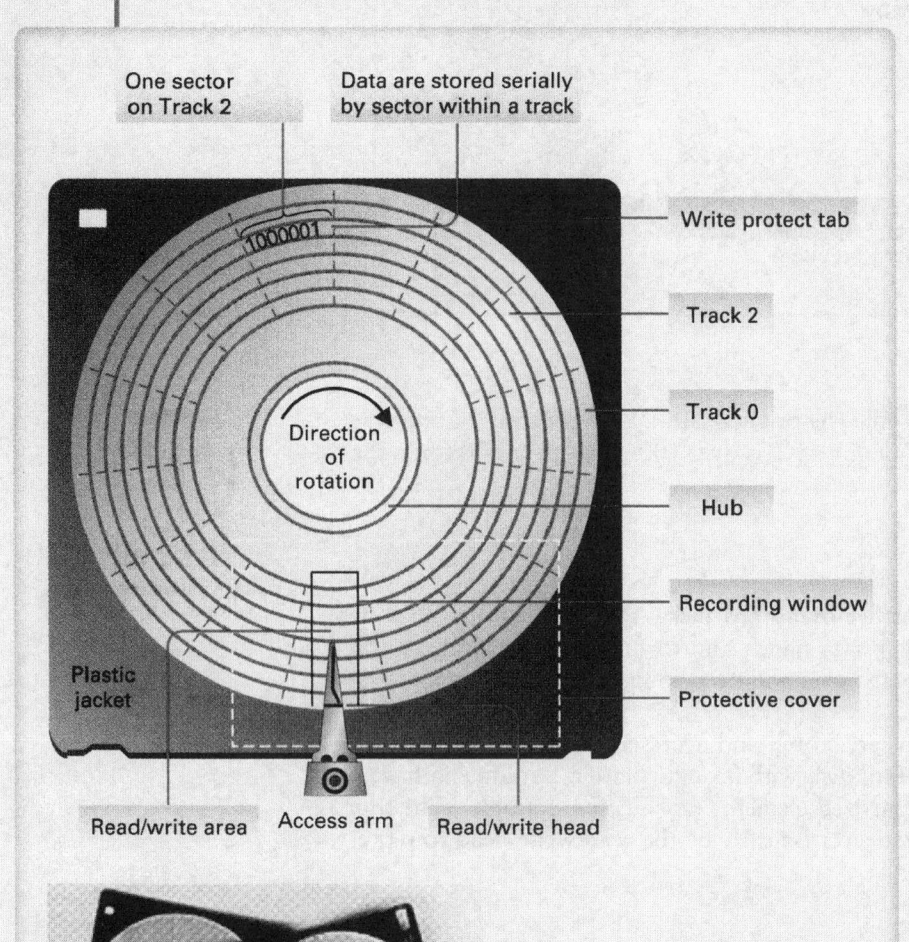

One sector on Track 2

Data are stored serially by sector within a track

1000001

Write protect tab

Track 2

Track 0

Direction of rotation

Hub

Recording window

Plastic jacket

Protective cover

Read/write area

Access arm

Read/write head

read/write head is moved, under program control, to the appropriate *track* or *cylinder* (see Figures 5-4 and 5-6). A particular **cylinder** refers to the same-numbered tracks on each recording surface (for example, Track 0012 on each recording surface; see Figure 5-4). When reading from or writing to a hard disk, all access arms are moved to the appropriate *cylinder*. For example, each recording surface has a track numbered 0012, so the disk has a cylinder numbered 0012. If the data to be accessed are on Recording Surface 01, Track 0012, then the access arms and the read/write heads for all eight recording surfaces are moved to Cylinder 0012. When the cluster containing the desired data passes under or over the read/write head, the data are read or written. Fortunately, software automatically monitors the location, or address, of our files and programs. We need only enter the name of the file to retrieve it for processing.

One of the major limitations of traditional sector organization is that recording space is wasted on the outer tracks. To overcome this limitation, some high-performance disk manufacturers employ a technique called **zoned recording**. In zoned recording, tracks are grouped into zones and all tracks in a particular zone have the same number of sectors (see Figure 5-7). A zone contains a greater number of sectors per track as you move from the innermost zone to the outermost zone. This approach to disk organization enables a more efficient use of available disk space.

The File Allocation Table

Each disk used in the Windows environment has a **Virtual File Allocation Table** (VFAT) in which information about the clusters is stored (it was a FAT in early operating systems). The table includes an entry for each cluster that describes where on the disk it can be found and how it is used (for example, whether the file is open or not). Here's what happens when you or a program on your PC makes a request for a particular file.

1. The operating system searches the VFAT to find the physical address of the first cluster of the file.

2. The read/write heads are moved over the track/cylinder containing the first cluster.

3. The rapidly rotating disk passes the cluster under/over the read/write head, and the information in the first cluster is read and transmitted to RAM for processing.

Higher National in Computing

12

4. The operating system checks an entry within the initial cluster that indicates whether the file consists of further clusters, and if so, where on the disk they are located.

5. The operating system directs that clusters continue to be read and their information transmitted to RAM until the last cluster in the chain is read (no further chaining is indicated).

The trade-off between system performance and efficient use of disk space is a major consideration during the disk design process. A 100-KB file being stored on a disk with 32,768 byte clusters would require four clusters (three clusters will store only 98,304 bytes). Most of the space in the fourth cluster is wasted disk space. Large clusters may improve overall system performance, but, because of their size, they tend to make more space inaccessible.

Eventually your PC will give you a "lost clusters found" message, indicating that the hard disk has orphan clusters that don't belong to a file. Typically, lost clusters are the result of an unexpected interruption of file activity, perhaps a system crash or loss of power. Periodically Windows users should run the **ScanDisk** utility program, a program that periodically "scans" the disk for lost clusters and, if any are found, lets the user return them to the available pool of usable clusters.

Defragmenting the Disk to Enhance Performance

Ideally, all files would be stored on disk in contiguous clusters, but such is not the case with computing. Over time, files are added, deleted, and modified such that, eventually, files must be stored in noncontiguous clusters. When clusters that make up a particular file are scattered, the read/write heads must move many times across the surface of a disk to access a single file. This excess mechanical movement slows down the PC because it takes longer to load a file to RAM for processing.

In fact, the mechanical movement of the disk read/write heads is the most vulnerable part of a PC system—the greater the fragmentation of files, the slower the PC. Fortunately, we can periodically reorganize the disk such that files are stored in contiguous clusters. This process, appropriately called **defragmentation**, is done with a handy utility program (see Figure 5-8) called a **disk defragmenter**. The program consolidates files into contiguous clusters; that is, the clusters for each file are chained together on the same or adjacent tracks (see Figure 5-9), thereby minimizing the movement of the read/write head. After running the program, each file stored on a disk is a single cluster or a chain of clusters.

How often you run a "defrag" program depends on how much you use your PC. The fragmentation problem and the defragmentation solution are illustrated in Figure 5-9. In the example, five files are loaded to a disk, each in contiguous clusters. A file is modified, another is deleted, and another is added, resulting in fragmentation of several files and a need for defragmentation. The defragmentation process rewrites fragmented files into contiguous clusters (see Figure 5-9).

Formatting: Preparing a Disk for Use

A new disk is coated with a surface that can be magnetized easily to represent data. However, before the disk can be used, it must be **formatted**. The formatting procedure causes the disk to be initialized with a recording format for your operating system. Specifically, it

- Creates sectors and tracks into which data are stored.
- Sets up an area for the virtual file allocation table.

| FIGURE 5-7 | ZONED RECORDING ON A HARD DISK |

Zoned recording groups tracks into concentric zones (three of them in the illustration) such that the number of sectors in each track increases as the zones spread to the outer edge of the disk (9, 12, 16), thus enabling a more efficient use of storage space on the disk space surface.

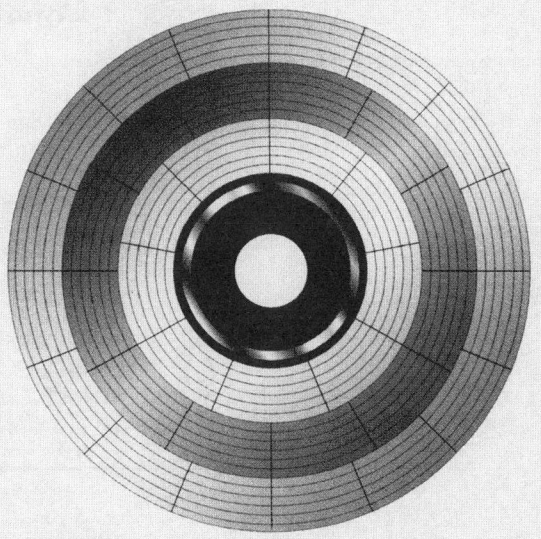

Characteristics of a Magnetic Disk

- Media
  - Fixed (hard) and interchangeable disks
- Type access
  - Direct (random) or sequential
- Data representation
  - Serial
- Storage scheme
  - Clusters on tracks

Higher National in Computing

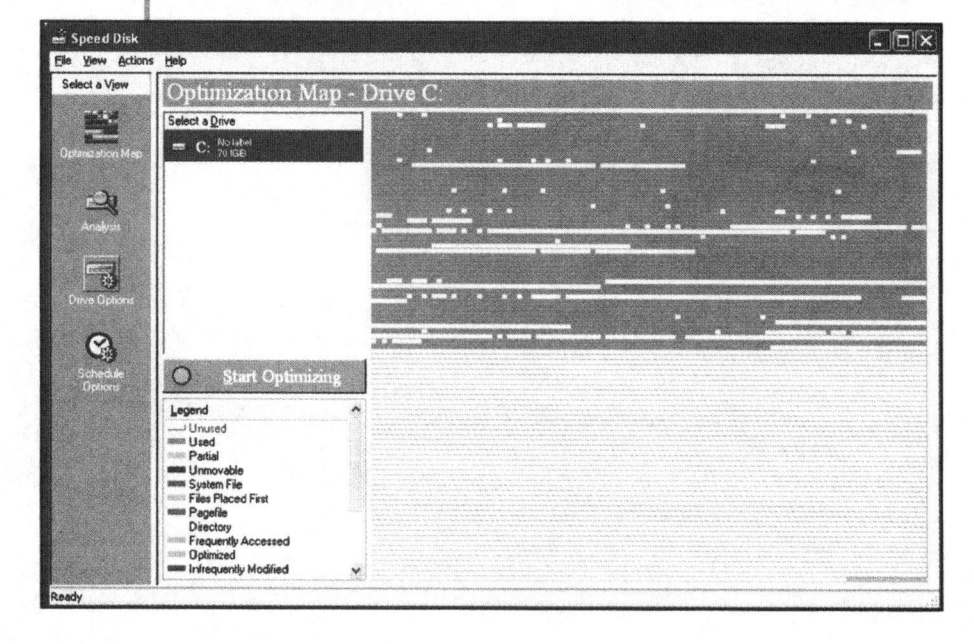

FIGURE 5-8 **DEFRAG SUMMARY**

The Speed Disk utility program within Symantec's Norton SystemWorks optimizes the disk by performing the defragmentation process. During the process, the utility program gives a visual overview of the status of each cluster, with colors indicating cluster status (used, bad, frequent access, applications, and so on).

If you purchased a PC today, the hard disk probably would be formatted and ready for use. However, if you added a hard disk or upgraded your existing hard disk, the new disk would need to be formatted.

DISK SPEED

Data access from RAM is performed at electronic speeds—approximately the speed of light. But the access of data from disk storage depends on the movement of mechanical apparatus (read/write heads and spinning disks) and can take from 4 to 8 milliseconds—still very slow when compared with the microsecond-to-nanosecond internal processing speeds of computers. The disk engineer's quest in life is to improve disk performance by reducing *access time* and increasing the *data transfer rate*.

Access time is the interval between the instant a computer makes a request for the transfer of data from a disk-storage device to RAM and the instant this operation is completed. The read/write heads on the access arm in the illustration of Figure 5-4 move together. Some hard disks have multiple access arms, some with two read/write heads per disk-face surface. Having multiple access arms and read/write heads results in less mechanical movement and faster access times.

The **data transfer rate** is the rate at which data are read from mass storage to RAM or written from RAM to mass storage. Even though the data transfer rate from magnetic disk to RAM may be 400 million bytes per second, the rate of transfer from one part of RAM to another is much faster. **Disk caching** (pronounced *"cashing"*) is a technique that improves system speed by taking advantage of the greater transfer rate of data within RAM. With disk caching, programs and data that are *likely* to be called into use are moved from a disk into a separate disk caching area of RAM. For example, if you close the Internet Explorer browser, the browser program might remain in unused RAM ready for immediate reload in case you decide to open it again. When an application program calls for the data or programs in the disk cache area, the data are transferred directly from RAM rather than from the slower disk. Updated data or programs in the disk cache area eventually must be transferred to a disk for permanent storage. All modern PCs take full advantage of disk caching to improve overall system performance.

Higher National in Computing

FIGURE 5-9

DISK DEFRAGMENTATION

(a) Initially, five files are stored ideally in contiguous clusters. (b) The user adds a few objects to a graphics file (blue), increasing its size and the number of clusters needed to store it. Note that file clusters are no longer contiguous. Then, a file (green) is deleted. (c) A new file (orange) is stored in noncontiguous clusters. (d) The disk is defragmented, resaving all files in contiguous clusters.

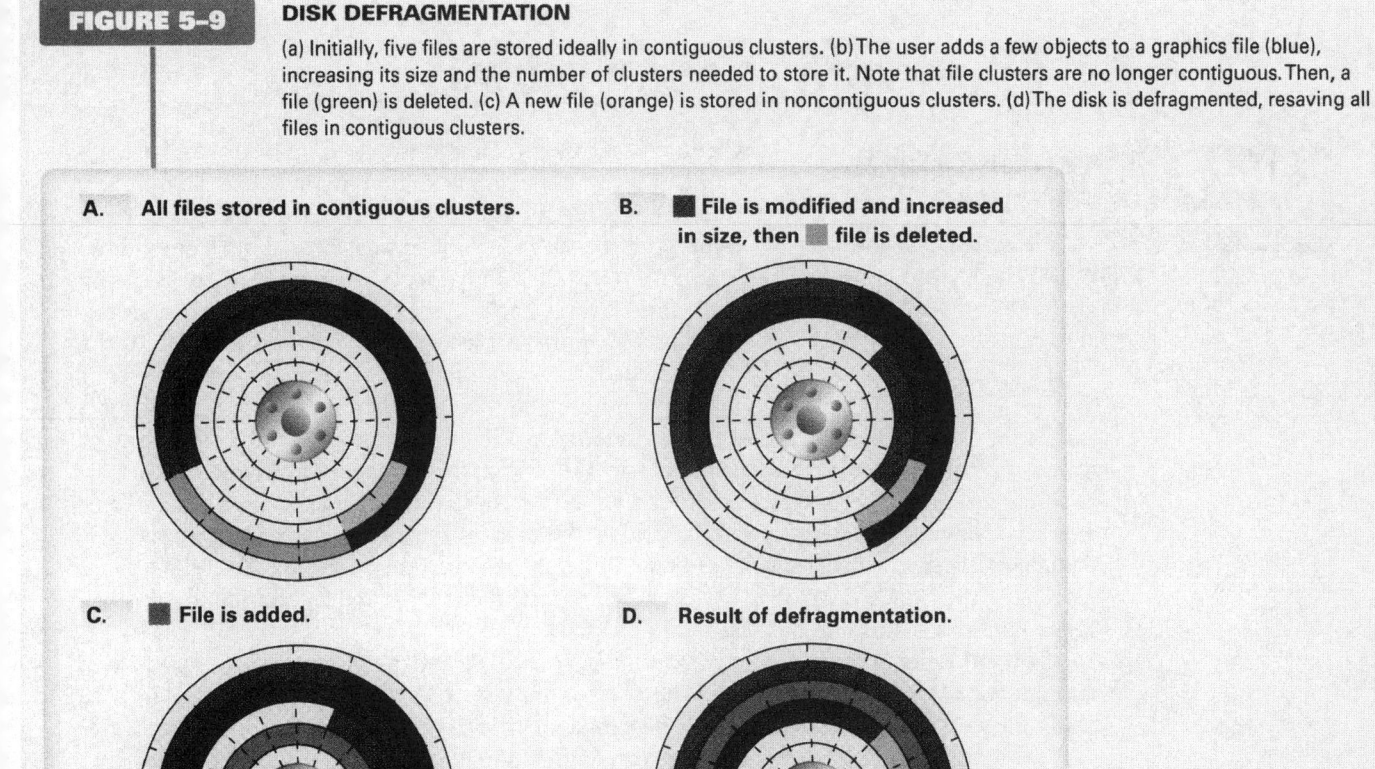

A. **All files stored in contiguous clusters.**

B. ■ **File is modified and increased in size, then** ■ **file is deleted.**

C. ■ **File is added.**

D. **Result of defragmentation.**

VIRTUAL MEMORY: DISK IMITATING RAM

RAM is a critical factor in determining a computer system's performance because all data and programs must be resident in RAM to be processed. Once RAM is full, no more programs can be executed until a portion of RAM is made available. **Virtual memory** effectively expands the capacity of RAM through the use of software and hard disk storage. The amount of virtual memory (hard disk capacity) you set aside as virtual memory is a user option in the Windows environment. In most personal computing situations, increasing the amount of disk space allocated for virtual memory can improve overall system performance, especially when running multiple applications.

The principle behind virtual memory is quite simple. Remember, a program is executed sequentially—one instruction after another. The operating system breaks programs into *pages* so only those pages of the program being executed are resident in RAM. The rest of the program is on disk storage. The pages are transferred into RAM from disk storage as they are needed to continue execution of the program.

1 Data are retrieved from temporary disk storage and stored permanently in RAM. (T/F)

2 The capacity of a floppy disk is about that of a portable hard disk. (T/F)

3 Which has the greatest storage capacity: (a) the traditional floppy, (b) the latest Zip disk, (c) the SuperDisk, (d) or the 3.5-inch diskette?

4 The defragmentation process rewrites fragmented files into: (a) contiguous clusters, (b) continuous clusters, (c) circular clusters, or (d) Cretan clusters.

5 The rate at which data are read from disk to RAM is the: (a) TPI, (b) caching rate, (c) data transfer rate, or (d) streaming velocity.

SELF-CHECK

SECTION

Higher National in Computing

15

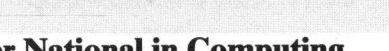

5-2 OPTICAL LASER DISCS

Why this section is important to you.

CD, CD-ROM, CD-R, CD-RW, DVD-audio, DVD-video, DVD-ROM, DVD-R, DVD-RAM, DVD+RW, DVD-RW, and DVD±RW. Life will be less confusing when you are able to sort out these optical laser disc options.

Optical laser disc technology (see Figure 5-10) complements hard disk storage in that it provides a compact, interchangeable, high-capacity alternative for the permanent storage of programs and data. The tremendous amount of low-cost direct-access storage made possible by optical laser discs has opened the door to many new applications. The most visible application for optical discs is the DVD movie that you can buy or rent and play on your DVD player or your PC. Another very visible application is that they have emerged as the media-of-choice for the distribution of software. Many of the thousands of commercially produced CD-ROM/DVD discs contain reference material, such as encyclopedias and dictionaries. The books that traditionally lined the walls of attorneys have given way to disk-based law libraries that can be easily updated as laws change in cases are added. Businesses periodically back up their data to DVD±RW discs. Companies produce their own CD-ROM-based procedures manuals and individuals burn their own audio and video discs.

Optical laser disc technology continues to evolve and may never slow down long enough for a standard to emerge. The read-only audio CD, the data CD-ROM, and the DVD movie were our only options 10 years ago. Now, we have many more optical laser disc options, including rewritable discs (see Figure 5-10).

FIGURE 5–10   **OPTICAL LASER DISC TECHNOLOGIES**

APPLICATION	CD Formats (650 MB)	DVD Formats (4.7 GB or 9.4 GB for double sided)
Audio/video consumer products	CD audio	DVD audio DVD video (movies)
Commercially distributed content (*software, reference material, and so on*)	CD-ROM	DVD-ROM
CD or DVD burner (*write once, read many times*)	CD-R	DVD-R DVD+R
CD and/or DVD burner plus CD and/or DVD rewritable applications (*write many times, read many times*)	CD-RW	DVD-RW DVD+RW (plus CD-RW capability)

Higher National in Computing

16

CD-ROM AND DVD-ROM

CD-ROM and DVD-ROM technologies have had a dramatic impact on personal computing and IT during the past decade because these technologies continue to provide ever-increasing storage capacity at ever-decreasing cost.

CD-ROM History

Introduced in 1980 for stereo buffs, the *CD*, or *compact disc,* is an optical laser disc designed to enhance the reproduction of recorded music. To make a CD recording, the analog sounds of music are digitized and stored on a plastic 4.72-inch optical laser disc about 1 millimeter thick. Seventy-four minutes of music can be recorded on each disc in digital format in 2 billion bits. With its tremendous storage capacity per square inch, computer industry entrepreneurs immediately recognized the potential of optical laser disc technology. In effect, anything that can be digitized can be stored on optical laser disc: data, text, voice, still pictures, music, graphics, and motion video.

CD-ROM and DVD-ROM Technology

CD-ROM, a spin off of audio CD technology, stands for *compact disc–read-only memory.* The name implies its application. Once inserted into the *CD-ROM drive,* the text, video images, and so on can be read into RAM for processing or display. However, the data on the disc are fixed—*they cannot be altered.* This is in contrast, of course, to the read/write capability of magnetic disks.

The capacity of a single CD-ROM is up to 650 MB. To put the density of CD-ROM into perspective, the words in every book ever written could be stored on a hypothetical CD-ROM that is 8 feet in diameter.

Magnetic disks store data in concentric tracks, each of which is divided into sectors (see Figure 5-6). In contrast, CD-ROMs store data in a single track that spirals from the center to the outside edge (see Figure 5-11). The ultra thin track spirals around the disc thousands of times.

With optical laser disc, two lasers replace the mechanical read/write head used in magnetic storage. One laser beam writes to the recording surface by scoring microscopic *pits* in the disc, and another laser reads the data from the light-sensitive recording surface. A bit is represented by the presence of a pit or a *land,* the flat area separating the pits (see

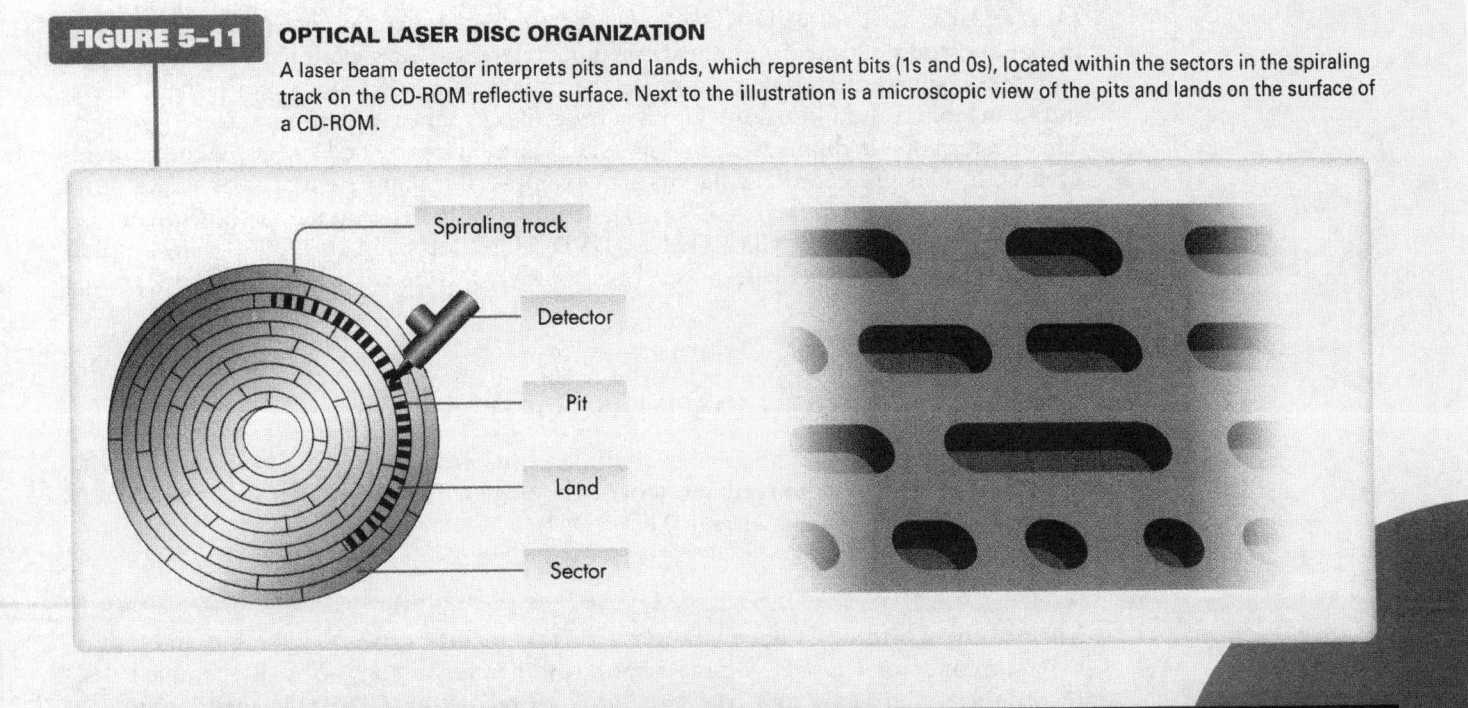

FIGURE 5-11 **OPTICAL LASER DISC ORGANIZATION**

A laser beam detector interprets pits and lands, which represent bits (1s and 0s), located within the sectors in the spiraling track on the CD-ROM reflective surface. Next to the illustration is a microscopic view of the pits and lands on the surface of a CD-ROM.

Spiraling track

Detector

Pit

Land

Sector

Higher National in Computing

17

Figure 5-11). Together they record binary (1s and 0s) information that can be interpreted by the computer as text, audio, images, and so on.

Popular CD-ROM drives are classified simply as 32X, 40X, or 75X. These spin at 32, 40, and 75 times the speed of the original CD standard. The faster the spin rate, the faster data are transferred to RAM for processing. The slower speeds may cause program/image load delays and the video can be choppy. The original 1X CD-ROM data transfer rate was 150 KB per second, so the 75X CD-ROM data transfer rate is 75 times that, or 11.25 MB per second. The speed at which a given CD-ROM spins depends on the physical location of the data being read. The data pass over the movable laser detector at the same rate, no matter where the data are read. Therefore, the CD-ROM must spin more quickly when accessing data near the center (about 450 rpm) and more slowly for data near the edge (about 250 rpm). Listen carefully and you can hear the spin motor adjusting the spin rate of the CD-ROM during read operations.

The laser detector is analogous to the magnetic disk's read/write head. The relatively slow spin rates make the CD-ROM access time much slower than that of its magnetic cousins. A CD-ROM drive may take 10 to 50 times longer to ready itself to read the information. Once ready to read, the transfer rate also is much slower.

Just as CD-ROMs have become mainstream equipment, DVD-ROMs with much greater capacities are poised to replace them. DVD stands for *digital video disc*. The DVD-ROM has the same physical dimensions as the CD and the CD-ROM, but it can store from 7 to 14 times as much information. The pits and lands are more densely packed on *DVD-ROM*, enabling 4.7 GB of storage. A *double-sided* DVD-ROM has a 9.4 GB capacity. Because data are packed more densely on a DVD-ROM, the data transfer rate is nine times that of a CD-ROM spinning at the same rate. For example, an 8X DVD-ROM drive transfers data at about the same rate as a 75X CD-ROM.

DVD-ROM drives are *backward compatible;* that is, they can play all of your CD-ROMs and CDs. They can read or play other DVD formats, too, including *DVD-video* and *DVD-audio*, which are expected to make videotapes and traditional CDs obsolete in a few years. This home entertainment version of DVD-ROM usually is shortened to simply DVD.

Creating CD-ROMs and DVD-ROMs for Mass Distribution

Most CD-ROMs and DVD-ROMs are created by commercial enterprises and sold to the public for multimedia applications and reference. Application developers gather and create source material, then write the programs needed to integrate the material into a meaningful application. The resulting files are then sent to a mastering facility. The master copy is duplicated, or "pressed," at the factory, and the copies are distributed with their prerecorded contents (for example, the complete works of Shakespeare or the movie, *Gone with the Wind*). Depending on the run quantity, the cost of producing and packaging a CD-ROM or DVD-ROM for sale can be less than a dollar apiece. These media provide a very inexpensive way to distribute applications and information.

REWRITABLE OPTICAL LASER DISC OPTIONS

Optical laser technologies are now in transition from write-only technologies, such as CD-ROM and DVD-ROM, to read and write technologies. This means that we, the end users, can make our own CD-ROMs and DVD-ROMs.

CD-R and CD-RW

Most of the world's PCs have CD-ROM or DVD-ROM drives. This rapid and universal acceptance of CD-ROM gave rise to another technology—CD-R (compact disc-recordable). Ten years ago, the capability to record on CD-ROM media cost over

Higher National in Computing

18

$100,000. CD-R drives, at less than $100, brought that capability to any PC owner. While people were celebrating the arrival of CD-R, another more flexible CD technology was introduced—**CD-RW** (CD-ReWritable). This technology goes one step further, allowing users to rewrite to the CD-sized media, just as is done on magnetic disk media. With the cost of CD-R and CD-RW technologies converging, CD-R drives have disappeared from the optical drive landscape. CD-RW discs can be inserted and read on modern CD-ROM drives, but they will not work with the older models.

PERSONAL COMPUTING

Sharing Peripheral Devices

Modern operating systems make it easy for us to set up a network in our home or in a dormitory suite. There is no reason for every PC to be configured with a dedicated printer, scanner, and/or DVD burner. Printers can be shared and files are transferred easily between networked computers; so, if you do not mind walking to another room to pick up your printout or scan a photo, consider the economics of peripheral sharing.

DVD+RW and DVD-RW

Like CD-ROM technology, recordable and read/write capabilities are emerging for DVD technology as well. **DVD+R** and **DVD-R** are like CD-R but with the recording density of DVD-ROM. **DVD+RW** and **DVD-RW** are like CD-RW, giving us rewritable capabilities for high-capacity DVD technology. DVD-RW (DVD-R) and DVD+RW (DVD+R) are competing technologies, with the most recent technology, DVD+RW (DVD+R), appearing to emerge as the technology of choice for most PC vendors. DVD rewritable alternatives are more costly than CD-RW, but as the price drops, DVD rewritable drives might become a standard storage device on new PCs.

State-of-the-art DVD rewritable drives can read all DVD and CD-ROM formats. The DVD±RW drive can read and write to either DVD format. All rewritable DVD drives have CD-RW capability, as well. You can rewrite to rewritable discs thousands of times.

OPTICAL DISCS IN YOUR PC

The typical PC will have one or two optical drives. At a minimum, users want a PC with a DVD-ROM drive so they have full optical read capability and can enjoy all CD-ROM and DVD applications, including playing DVD movies. One of the most popular optical storage options is the *DVD-ROM/CD-RW combination drive* which gives users the flexibility to read CD-ROM and DVD-ROM format discs (including audio CDs and DVD movies) and to burn their own audio and video CDs, to burn discs for data transfer, and to provide read/write backup of user files. Some people choose to configure their PCs with both a DVD-ROM drive and a DVD-ROM/CD-RW combination drive to enable easy duplication of optical media.

Those users with a few extra dollars to spend and expanded application needs are choosing a *DVD±RW/CD-RW combination drive*. You can use it to store original videos on DVD disc or archive up to 4.7 GB of data to a DVD+RW or a DVD+RW disc. People who spend the money on this high-end rewritable disk combo drive will usually add a DVD-ROM drive as well, to facilitate duplication tasks.

Optical storage technology has experienced many changes in the past decade. It's inevitable that we will continue to see new optical storage technologies that offer greater capacities and faster access times (see Figure 5-12).

WHAT'S THE BEST MIX OF STORAGE OPTIONS?

The choice of which technologies to choose for a system or an application is often a trade-off between storage capacity, cost (dollars per megabyte), and speed (access time). You can never really compare apples to apples when comparing storage media because one might have an advantage in access time, portability, random access, nonvolatility, and so on. Solid-state storage (RAM) is the fastest and most expensive (about $0.10 per MB), but it's volatile. Hard disk offers fast, permanent storage for a hundredth the cost of RAM. You can get 1 MB of interchangeable DVD±RW storage for slightly more than the cost of hard disk storage, but it is relatively slow. A well-designed system will have a mix of storage options. Each time you purchase a PC, you should spend a little extra time assessing your application and backup needs so you can configure your system with an optimum mix of storage options.

FIGURE 5-12

AN EVOLVING OPTICAL LASER DISC TECHNOLOGY: FMD-ROM

A single FMD-ROM disc, an emerging new optical storage technology, can store an amount of printed documentation that, if stacked, would stretch almost two miles into the sky.

Courtesy of Constellation 3D

Higher National in Computing

FIGURE 5-13 SOLID STATE STORAGE

THE MINI USB DRIVE

About the size of a car key, the solid-state, flash memory Iomega® Mini USB drive is a portable solution for transporting and sharing 128 MB of data.

Courtesy of Iomega Corporation

SOLID-STATE STORAGE APPLICATIONS

This RCA eBook uses solid state flash memory, rather than disk, to hold more than 5,000 pages of material. Popular magazines, novels, and periodicals are readily available for downloading and viewing on the eBook.

Photo courtesy of RCA Corporation

Rotating storage media may go the way of the steam engine when low-cost nonvolatile, solid-state memory, such as *flash memory*, can store as much in less space. Already, flash memory chips, such as the Mini USB drive, are being developed that will have many times more storage capacity than the largest flash chips currently available (see Figure 5-13). Plug the thumb-size Mini USB drive it into any computer's USB port and it is immediately recognized as an active storage drive, enabling applications to be launched and run directly from the drive. Flash memory is also already the basis for e-book (electronic book) readers that hold many books, magazines, and so on (see Figure 5-13). Perhaps someday the only moving part on PCs will be the cooling fan.

What does being able to store more information in less space mean to you? It means videophones that can be worn like wristwatches. It means that you can carry a floppy-sized reader and all your college "textbooks" in your front pocket. Each new leap in storage technology seems to change much of what we do and how we do it.

SECTION

1 CD-ROM is read-only. (T/F)
2 A double-sided DVD-ROM has a capacity of 22 GB. (T/F)
3 DVD+RW technology is: (a) rewritable, (b) read-only, (c) write-only, or (d) nonwritable.
4 Which of these is poised to replace the CD-ROM: (a) VVV, (b) jukebox, (c) CD-R, or (d) DVD-ROM?
5 Which disc drive offers the PC user the greatest flexibility: (a) DVD±RW/CD-RW, (b) DVD-ROM, (c) DVD-ROM/CD-RW, or (d) CD-R?

5-3 INPUT DEVICES

Why this section is important to you.

Computers work in binary, bits and bytes; but we don't, so we need input devices to communicate our data and wishes to computers. The more you know about the variety of available input devices, the easier it is for you to enter information to your PC.

Even people who have never sat in front of a PC communicate with computers. Perhaps you have had one of these experiences.

Have you ever been hungry and short of cash? No problem. Just stop at an automatic teller machine (ATM) and ask for some "lunch money." The ATM's keyboard and monitor enable you to hold an interactive conversation with the bank's computer. The ATM's printer provides you with a hard copy of your transactions when you leave. Some ATMs talk to you as well.

Have you ever called a mail-order merchandiser and been greeted by a message like this: "Thank you for calling BrassCo Enterprises Customer Service. If you wish to place an order, press one. If you wish to inquire about the status of an order, press

Higher National in Computing

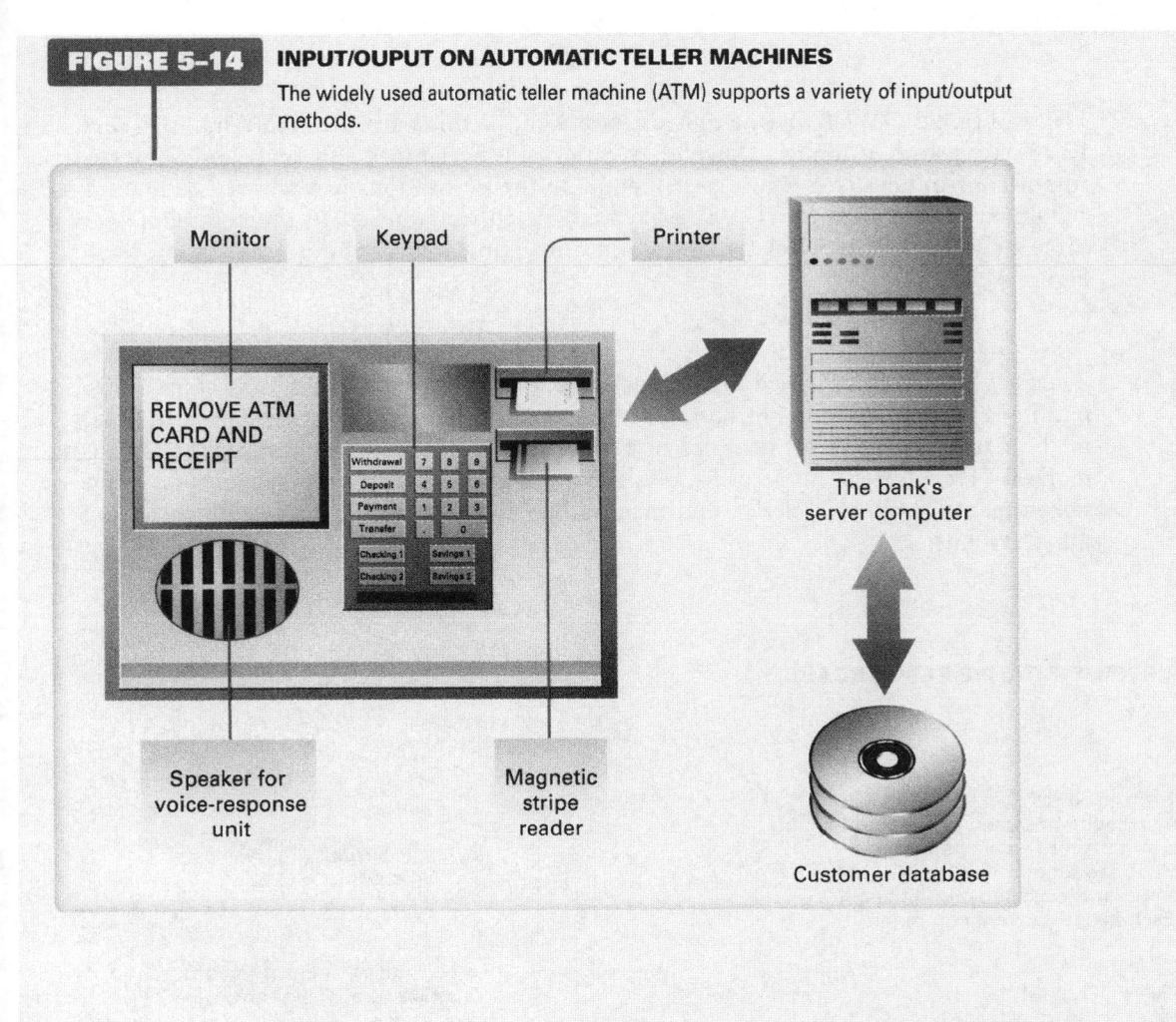

FIGURE 5-14 *INPUT/OUPUT ON AUTOMATIC TELLER MACHINES*

The widely used automatic teller machine (ATM) supports a variety of input/output methods.

Monitor — Keypad — Printer

REMOVE ATM CARD AND RECEIPT

Withdrawal · Deposit · Payment · Transfer · Checking 1 · Savings 1 · Checking 2 · Savings 2

The bank's server computer

Speaker for voice-response unit

Magnetic stripe reader

Customer database

two." The message is produced by a computer-based voice-response system, which responds to the buttons you press on your telephone keypad.

We routinely communicate directly or indirectly with these computers through input/output devices. *Input devices* translate our data and communications into a form that the computer can understand. The computer then processes these data, and an *output device* translates them back into a form we can understand. In our two examples, the ATM's keypad, touch screen monitor, and the telephone keypad serve as input devices, and the ATM's monitor, printer, and the voice-response system serve as output devices (see Figure 5-14).

Input/output devices are quietly playing an increasingly significant role in our lives. The number and variety of I/O devices are expanding even as you read this, and some of these devices are fairly exotic (see Figure 5-15). For example, there is an electronic nose that can measure and digitally record smells. It's used to analyze aroma in the food, drink, and perfume industries. Commuters enjoy another benefit of I/O as they drive through toll plazas at highway speeds. For each passing car, toll road computers grab the customer number from a credit card-sized transmitter mounted on the car windshield, then process the transaction and flash a "Thank You" message.

This part of the chapter is about I/O devices. This first section is on input devices, and we will begin with the *keyboard* and the *mouse*, the most popular input devices.

THE KEYBOARD

Every notebook and desktop PC comes with a keyboard. There are two basic types of keyboards: alphanumeric keyboards and special-function keyboards.

FIGURE 5-15

INNOVATIONS IN INPUT/OUTPUT

This PC is evolutionary in its approach to user interaction in that it provides a variety of I/O options and is converted easily from a notebook PC to a tablet PC—just twist the screen and close.

Photo courtesy of Intel Corporation

Higher National in Computing

The traditional *QWERTY* (the first six letters on the third row) keyboard has 101 keys, 12 function keys, a numeric keypad, a variety of special-function keys, and dedicated cursor-control keys (see Figure 5-16). Some of the innovations in keyboard technology are illustrated in Figure 5-17. The keyboard is either attached to the computer by a cable or linked via a wireless connection (either infrared or radio wave as shown in Figure 5-18).

Special-Function Keyboards

Some keyboards are designed for specific applications. For example, the cash-register-like terminals at most fast-food restaurants have special-purpose keyboards. Rather than key in the name and price of an order of French fries, attendants need only press the key marked "French fries" to record the sale. Such keyboards help shop supervisors, airline ticket agents, retail salesclerks, and many others interact more quickly with their computer systems.

FIGURE 5-16   A REPRESENTATIVE PC KEYBOARD

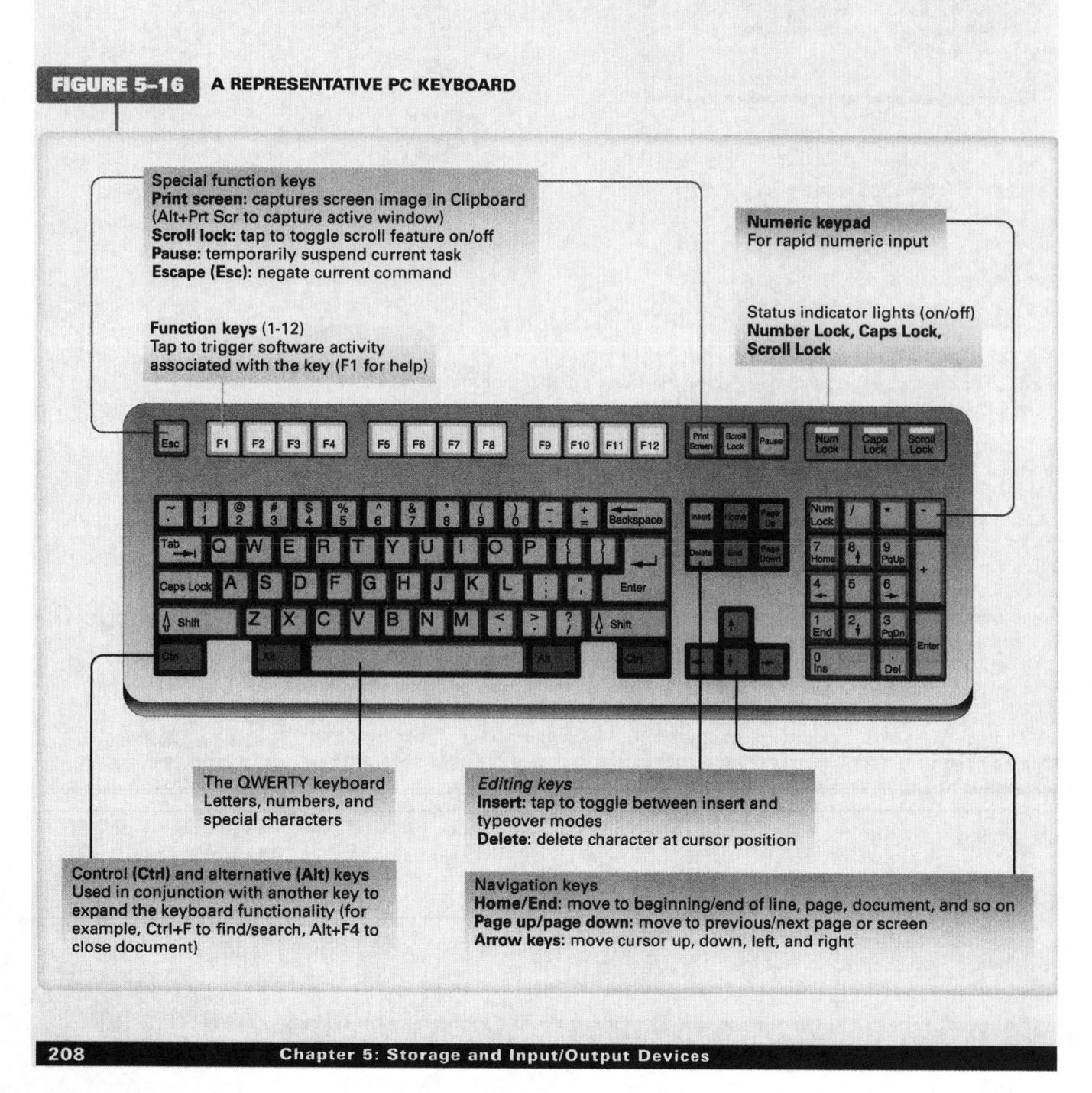

Special function keys
Print screen: captures screen image in Clipboard
(Alt+Prt Scr to capture active window)
Scroll lock: tap to toggle scroll feature on/off
Pause: temporarily suspend current task
Escape (Esc): negate current command

Function keys (1-12)
Tap to trigger software activity
associated with the key (F1 for help)

Numeric keypad
For rapid numeric input

Status indicator lights (on/off)
**Number Lock, Caps Lock,
Scroll Lock**

The QWERTY keyboard
Letters, numbers, and
special characters

Editing keys
Insert: tap to toggle between insert and
typeover modes
Delete: delete character at cursor position

Control **(Ctrl)** and alternative **(Alt)** keys
Used in conjunction with another key to
expand the keyboard functionality (for
example, Ctrl+F to find/search, Alt+F4 to
close document)

Navigation keys
Home/End: move to beginning/end of line, page, document, and so on
Page up/page down: move to previous/next page or screen
Arrow keys: move cursor up, down, left, and right

Higher National in Computing

22

FIGURE 5-17 KEYBOARD INNOVATIONS

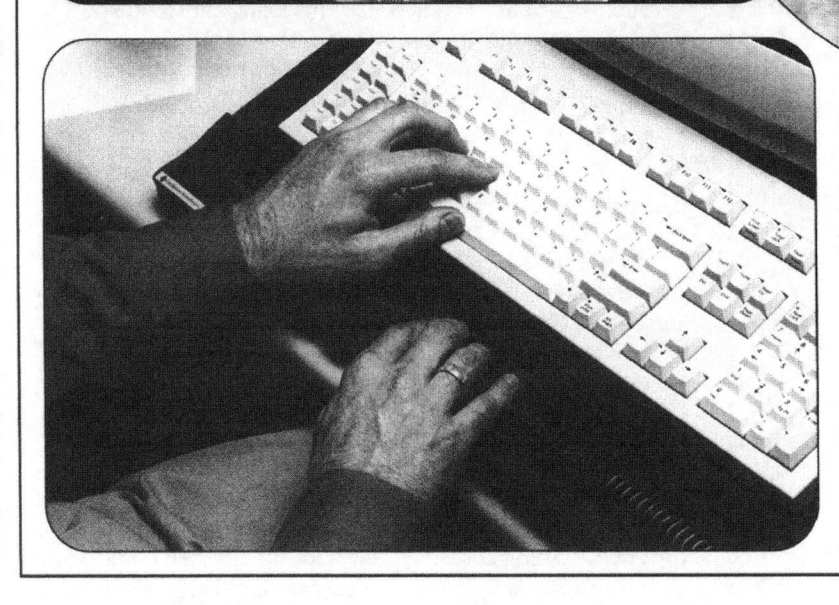

ALTERNATIVE KEYBOARD

The DataHand System is designed ergonomically as two independent units molded to fit the shape of the human hand such that fingers move no more than .1 inch, 88% less travel than on a standard keyboard.

Courtesy of DataHand

FOLDUP KEYBOARD FOR HANDHELDS

This ultra slim keyboard is designed for use with handheld PCs. It folds into a 5 oz. package that can easily slip into a shirt pocket.

Courtesy of Logitech

KEYBOARD INPUT AND BRAILLE OUTPUT

Special input/output devices, called assistive technology, are available for disabled people. This traditional keyboard is used in conjunction with an electronic Braille display enabling this blind man real-time two-way interaction with his PC.

Courtesy of Sun Microsystems, Inc.

THE MOUSE AND OTHER POINT-AND-DRAW DEVICES

A point-and-draw device, such as a mouse, complements the keyboard in a *graphical user interface* (GUI), allowing users to *point* to and select (click) a particular user option quickly and efficiently. Also, such devices can be used to *draw*.

When the mouse, which can be wireless or tethered via a cable (its tail), is moved across a desktop, the *mouse pointer* on the display moves accordingly. The mouse pointer is displayed as an arrow, a crosshair, or a variety of other symbols, depending on the current application and its position on the screen. Figure 5-19 illustrates several of the many mouse pointer schemes available to users. The text cursor and mouse pointer may be dis-

Higher National in Computing

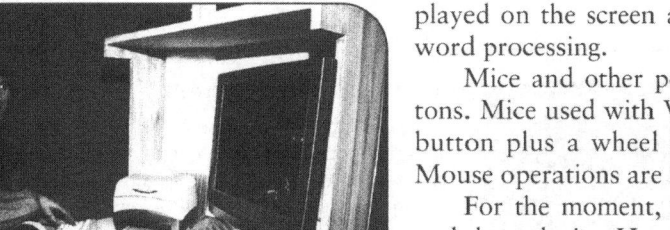

FIGURE 5-18

WIRELESS PC

This PC is wireless—the mouse, keyboard, and monitor are no longer tethered to the system unit by wires.

Photo courtesy of Intel Corporation

FIGURE 5-19   **MOUSE POINTER SCHEMES**

This figure shows three of many predefined mouse pointer schemes available to Windows users. Each mouse pointer shape provides a visual clue showing what Windows is doing or what you can do in various situations.

Normal Select			
Help Select			
Working In Background			
Busy			
Precision Select			
Text Select			
Handwriting			
Unavailable			
Vertical Resize			
Horizontal Resize			
Diagonal Resize 1			
Diagonal Resize 2			
Move			
Alternate Select			
Link Select			

played on the screen at the same time in some programs, such as word processing.

Mice and other point-and-draw devices have one or two buttons. Mice used with Wintel PCs typically will have a left and right button plus a wheel between the buttons to facilitate scrolling. Mouse operations are introduced in Chapter 2.

For the moment, the mouse remains the most popular point-and-draw device. However, a variety of devices is available and each has its advantages and disadvantages. Here are a few of the more popular ones, all of which are illustrated in Figure 5-20.

- *Trackpad.* The **trackpad** has no moving parts and is common on notebook PCs. Simply move your finger about a small touch-sensitive pad to move the mouse pointer.
- *Trackpoint.* A **trackpoint** usually is positioned in or near a notebook's keyboard. Trackpoints function like miniature joysticks but are operated with the tip of the finger.
- *Trackball.* The **trackball** is a ball inset in a notebook PC or as a separate unit. The ball is rolled with the fingers to move the mouse pointer.
- *Joystick.* The **joystick** is a vertical stick that moves the mouse pointer in the direction the stick is pushed.
- *Digitizer tablet and pen.* The **digitizer tablet and pen** is a pen and a pressure-sensitive tablet whose X-Y coordinates correspond with those on the computer's display screen. Some digitizing tablets also use a crosshair device instead of a pen. Digitizer tablets are used to enable drawing or sketching of images, such as X-rays, and for many other drawing and engineering applications.

SCANNERS

Scanners read and interpret information on printed matter and convert it to a format that can be stored and/or interpreted by a computer (see Figure 5-21). Some scanners automate the data entry process, such as those at the grocery store checkout counter, and some scan and digitize images, such as photographs.

Scanners for Source Data Automation

In **source data automation,** data are entered directly to a computer system at the source without the need for key entry transcription. For example, scanners read preprinted bar codes on consumer products, eliminating the need for most key entry at checkout counters in retail stores.

Two types of scanners—*contact* and *laser*—read information on labels and various types of documents. Both bounce a beam of light off an image, and then measure the reflected light to interpret the image. Contact scanners must make contact as they are brushed over the printed matter to be read. Laser-based scanners are more versatile and can read data passed near the scanning area. Scanners of both technologies can recognize printed characters and various types of codes. Generally, scanners used for source data automation are in three basic categories.

FIGURE 5-20 **POINT-AND-DRAW DEVICES**

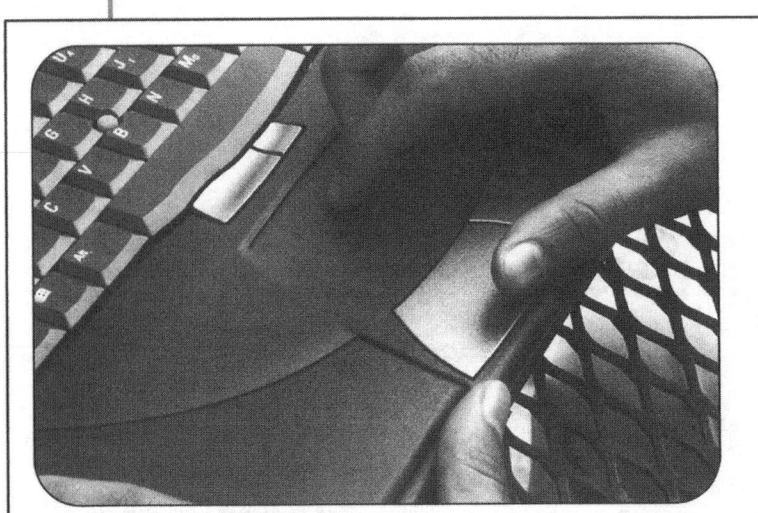

TRACKPAD AND TRACKPOINT

This notebook PC has both a trackpad and a trackpoint (between the B, G, and H keys) to enable mouse pointer movement with the tip of the finger.

Long and Associates.

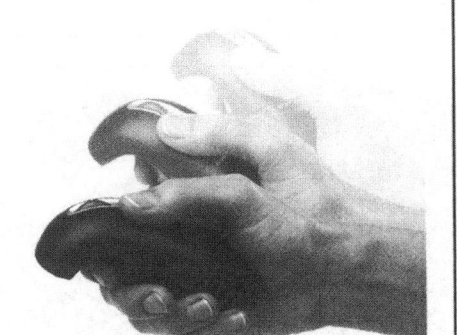

THE IN-AIR MOUSE

This wireless mouse uses gyroscopic, motion-sensing technology that lets you use it in the traditional manner or away from the desktop. The mouse's gyroscope lets you use in-air gestures to control the movement of the mouse pointer.

TRACKBALL

This cordless, optical track-ball is a mouse alternative that reduces wrist and elbow fatigue.

Courtesy of Kensington Technology Group

PEN WITH TOUCH-SENSITIVE DISPLAY

These students are using a pen with a tablet PC's touch-sensitive display to interact remotely via a wireless link to the school's server computer and the Internet.

Courtesy of Xybernaut

CROSSHAIR AND DIGITIZER

This ALTEK digitizer uses a crosshair for medical imaging. The backlighting system enables the digitizing of x-rays for such applications as radiation treatment planning.

Courtesy of ALTEK Corporation

Higher National in Computing

25

FIGURE 5–20 continued

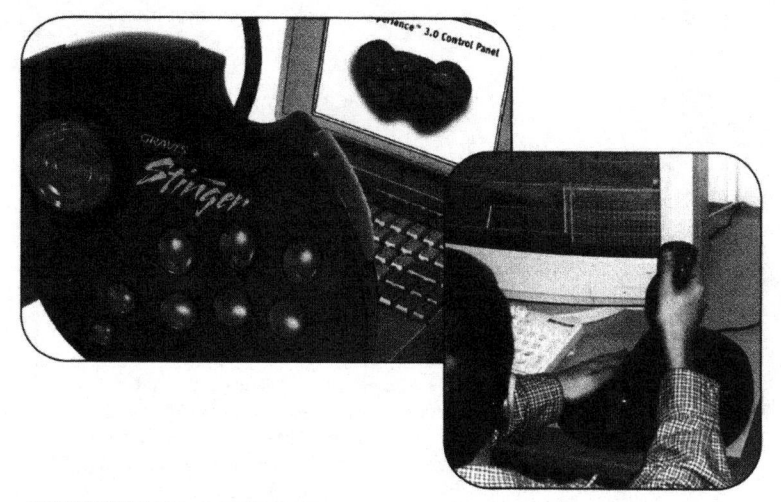

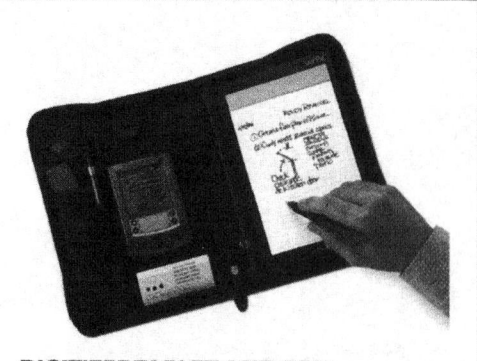

JOYSTICK AND GAME PAD

This Microsoft Sidewinder Force Feedback Pro (joystick) and the Gravis Stinger (game pad) are designed specifically for PC action games and flight simulation programs. The Sidewinder is both an input and output device in that it provides tactile feedback (vibration and pressure).

Courtesy of Advanced Gravis Computer Technology Ltd.

DIGITIZER TABLET AND PEN

Infrared technology enables handwritten notes and drawings to be transferred to Palm organizers, such as the Palm VII shown here. As users write on the notepad with the SmartPen™, their notes and drawings are instantly transferred to the Palm.

Courtesy of Seiko Instruments USA Inc.

- *Handheld label scanners.* These devices read data on price tags, shipping labels, inventory part numbers, book ISBNs, and the like. **Handheld label scanners,** sometimes called **wand scanners,** use either contact or laser technology. You have seen both types used in libraries and various retail stores.

- *Stationary label scanners.* These devices, which rely exclusively on laser technology, are used in the same types of applications as wand scanners. **Stationary scanners** are common in grocery stores and discount stores.

- *Document scanners.* **Document scanners** are capable of scanning documents of varying sizes. Document scanners read envelopes at the U.S. Postal Service, and they also read turnaround documents for utility companies. A **turnaround document** is computer-produced output that we can read and, ultimately, is returned as computer-readable input to a computer system. For example, the stub you return with your utility bill is a turnaround document.

Bar Code and OCR Technology

Bar codes represent alphanumeric data by varying the size of adjacent vertical lines. One of the most visible bar-coding systems is the Universal Product Code (**UPC**). The UPC, originally used for grocery items, is now being printed on other consumer goods. See other applications in Figure 5-21.

OCR (**optical character recognition**) technology permits the reading of coded and text information into a computer system, including reading your handwriting. The United States Postal Service relies on both OCR and bar code scanning to sort most mail. At the Postal Service, light-sensitive scanners read and interpret the ZIP code and POSTNET bar code on billions of envelopes each day. The ZIP information then is sent to computer-based sorting machines that route the envelopes to appropriate bins for distribution.

The advantage of bar codes over OCR is that the position or orientation of the code being read is not as critical to the scanner. In a grocery store, for example, the UPC can be recorded even when a bottle of ketchup is rolled over the laser scanner. Most retail

Higher National in Computing

26

FIGURE 5-21 SCANNERS AND SCANNER APPLICATIONS

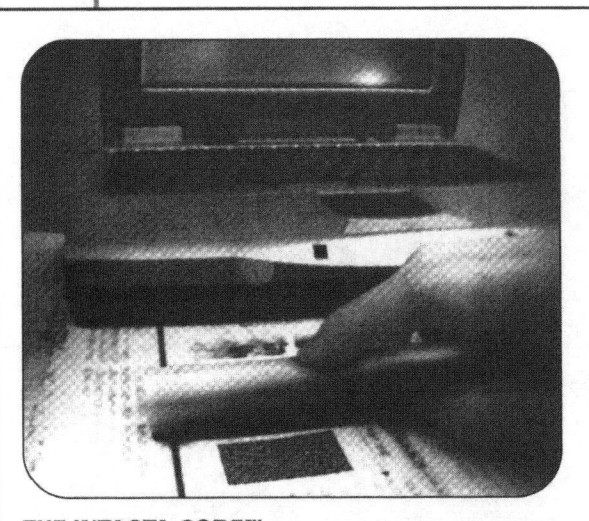

THE INTACTA.CODE™

The bar-code has taken on a new meaning with the recent invention of the INTACTA.CODE™. This print bar code is capable of storing photo images, MP3 music files, gaming software demos, or anything else that can be digitized. When newspaper or magazine readers scan the printed INTACTA.CODE™ into their computers, special software, working with standard scanners, decodes the dot pattern to the original electronic file.

Courtesy of Intacta Technologies

BAR CODES IN MANUFACTURING

Here at the Dell Computer Corporation manufacturing facility in Austin, Texas, bar codes on boxed parts are scanned as they are moved throughout the warehouse to ensure efficient inventory management, a goal of every manufacturing company.

Courtesy of Dell Computer Corp.

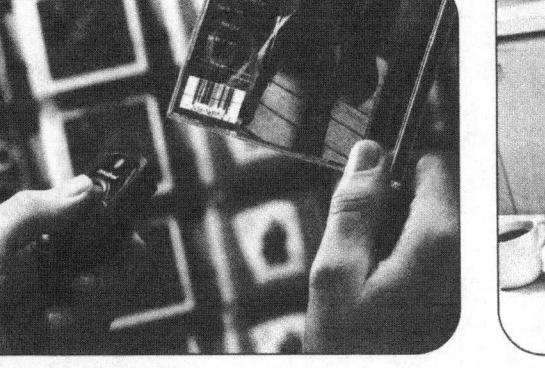

PERSONAL SCANNERS

This tiny scanner, which is small enough to hang on a keychain, allows consumers to scan products and services anywhere, anytime. Transactions such as purchases, inquiries, and payments can be made while commuting on a train or anywhere else. To retrieve the data contained in the scanner, the unit synchs up (synchronizes) with a PC, and uploads the data stored in its memory.

Courtesy of Symbol Technology, Inc.

stores and distribution warehouses, and all overnight couriers, use scanners for source data automation. Salespeople, inventory management personnel, and couriers would much prefer to wave their "magic" wands than enter data one character at a time.

Magnetic-Ink Character Recognition: Banking Exclusive

Magnetic-ink character recognition (MICR) is similar to optical character recognition and is used exclusively by the banking industry. MICR readers are used to read and sort checks and

Higher National in Computing

27

FIGURE 5-21 continued

SCANNERS IN THE SUPERMARKET: STATIONARY AND HANDHELD

Supermarket checkout systems are now an established cost-saving technology. The automated systems use stationary laser scanners to read the bar codes that identify each item (left). Price and product descriptions are retrieved from a database and recorded on the sales slip. Stockers use handheld scanners to order products and update the database (right).

Courtesy of International Business Machines Corporation

EXPEDITING THE 2000 U.S. CENSUS

One of the reasons the 2000 U.S. census went smoothly is that millions of completed mark-sense census forms were read by document scanners, thus enabling the data to be entered directly to the system for processing.

Courtesy of Lockheed Martin Corporation

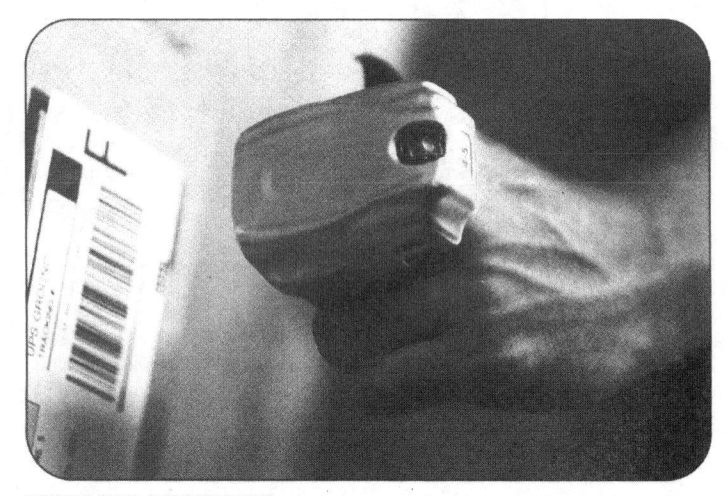

WIRELESS SCANNERS

UPS maintains a worldwide wireless network, including wireless scanners (shown here), to facilitate the movement of 13 million packages each day.

Courtesy of UPS

Higher National in Computing

deposits. You probably have noticed the *bank number,* the *account number,* and the *check number* encoded on all your checks and personalized deposit slips. The *date* of the transaction is automatically recorded for all checks processed that day; therefore, only the *amount* must be entered. The **MICR reader-sorter,** a MICR scanner especially designed to interpret MICR characters, reads the data on the checks and sorts the checks for distribution to other banks and customers or for further processing.

Optical Mark Recognition

You are probably familiar with one of the oldest scanner technologies, *optical mark recognition* (**OMR**). One of the most popular applications for these scanners is grading tests. All of us at one time or another has marked answers on a preprinted multiple-choice test answer form. The marked forms are scanned and corrected, comparing the position of the "sense marks" with those on a master to grade the test. The results of surveys and questionnaires often are tabulated with OMR technology.

Image Scanners

Image scanners can read written text and hard copy images, then translate the information into an electronic format that can be interpreted by and stored on computers. The image to be scanned can be a photograph, a drawing, an insurance form, a medical record—anything that can be digitized. Once an image has been digitized and entered into the computer system, it can be retrieved, displayed, modified, merged with text, stored, sent via data communications to one or several remote computers, and even faxed. Manipulating and managing scanned images is known as **image processing.**

Organizations everywhere are replacing space-consuming metal filing cabinets and millions of hard copy documents, from tax returns to warrantee cards, with their electronic equivalents. Image processing's space-saving incentive, along with its ease of document retrieval, are making the image scanner a must-have peripheral in the office. The same is true of the home as people begin converting their family photo albums and other archives to electronic format.

The Page and Hand Image Scanners

Image scanners are of two types: *page* and *hand*. Virtually all modern scanners can scan in both black and white images and color images.

- *Page image scanners.* **Page image scanners** work like copy machines. The scanned result is a high-resolution digitized image. Inexpensive sheet-fed page scanners weighing less than two pounds accept the document to be scanned in a slot.
- *Hand image scanners.* The **hand image scanner** is rolled manually over the image to be scanned. About five inches in width, hand image scanners are appropriate for capturing small images or portions of large images.

In addition to scanning photos and other graphic images, image scanners can also use OCR technology to scan and interpret the alphanumeric characters on regular printed pages. For applications that demand this type of print-to-word processing document translation, page scanners can minimize or eliminate the need for key entry. Today's image scanners and the accompanying OCR software are very sophisticated. Together they can read and interpret the characters from most printed material, such as a printed letter or a page from this book. They do a respectable, but less than perfect, job with handwritten material.

Image Processing: Eliminating the Paper Pile

In some organizations, paper files take up most of the floor space. Finding paper documents is always time consuming and, sometimes, you never find what you want. Image processing applications scan and index thousands, even millions, of documents (see Figure 5-22). Once scanned documents are on the computer system, they can be easily retrieved and manipulated. For example, banks use image processing to archive canceled checks and documents associated with mortgage loan servicing. Insurance companies use image processing in claims processing applications.

Higher National in Computing

FIGURE 5-22   IMAGE PROCESSING

PAGE SCANNER

Inexpensive image scanners have given rise to a variety of image processing applications. Here, a graphic artist scans an image into the system on a page scanner.

Photo courtesy of Hewlett-Packard Company

HAND SCANNER

A manager uses a hand scanner to convert text in a magazine into electronic text that can be inserted into a word processing document.

Courtesy of Caere Corporation

IMAGE PROCESSING SOFTWARE

PageKeeper image processor software helps you organize documents in your computer. The software lets you scan documents, such as this newsletter, into a folder system (bottom left). Once in the system, documents are retrieved and viewed easily (background). You also can make annotations on documents and copy contents to other documents (see the Word document on the right).

Higher National in Computing

30

A decade's worth of hospital medical records can be scanned and stored on magnetic disks in an area the size of a file cabinet drawer. The images are organized so they can be retrieved in seconds rather than minutes or hours. Medical personnel who need a hard copy can simply print one out in a matter of seconds.

The real beauty of image processing is that the digitized material can be easily manipulated. For example, any image can be faxed easily to another location (without being printed). A fax is sent and received as an image. The content on the fax or any electronic image can be manipulated in many ways. OCR software can be used to translate any text on the stored bit-mapped image to an electronic format (see Figure 5-22). For example, a doctor might wish to pull selected printed text from various patient images into a word processing document to compile a summary of a patient's condition. The doctor can even select specific graphic images (X-rays, photos, or drawings) from the patient's record for inclusion in the summary report.

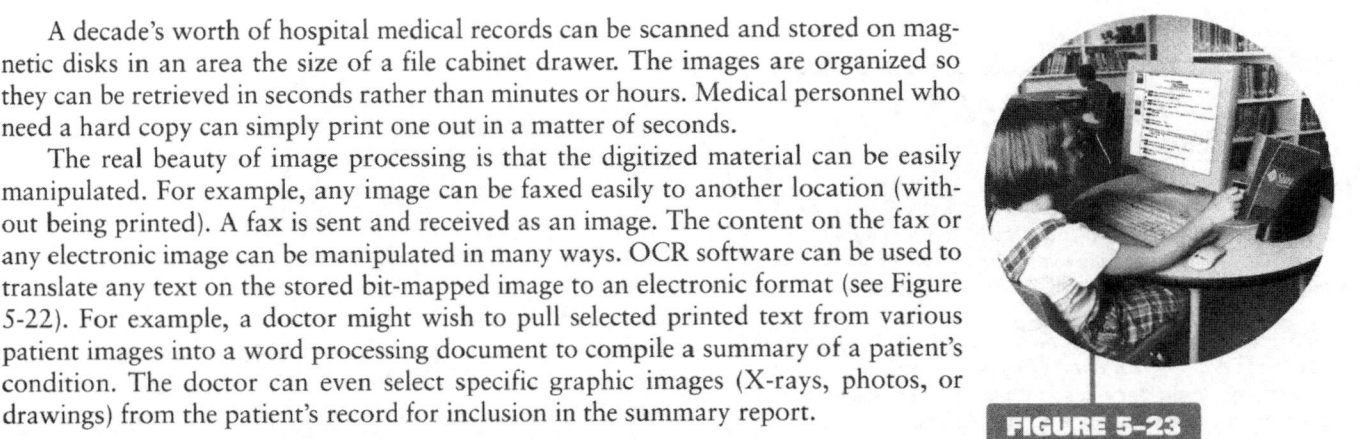

FIGURE 5-23

INTELLIGENT PLASTIC

Smart cards and magnetic stripe cards have a variety of applications, including banking, medical records, security, and more. In the photo, a girl uses her card to gain access to the library's automated resources.

Courtesy of Sun Microsystems, Inc.

MAGNETIC STRIPES AND SMART CARDS

Most of us carry this method of input with us—magnetic stripes. The magnetic stripes on the back of charge cards and badges offer another means of data entry. The magnetic stripes are encoded with data appropriate for specific applications. For example, your account number and personal identification number are encoded on a card for automatic teller machines.

Magnetic stripes contain much more data per unit of space than do printed characters or bar codes. Plus, because they cannot be read visually, they are perfect for storing confidential data, such as a personal identification number. Employee cards, security badges, and library cards (see Figure 5-23) often contain authorization data for access to physically secured areas, such as a computer center, or to protected resources, such as e-books in a library. To gain access, an employee or patron inserts a card or badge into a **badge reader,** a device that reads and checks the authorization code before permitting the individual to enter a secured area. When badge readers are linked to a central computer, that computer can maintain a chronological log of people entering or leaving secured areas.

What looks like any garden-variety credit card, but with a twist? The **smart card** has an embedded microprocessor with up to 64 KB of nonvolatile memory (see Figure 5-24). Because the smart card can hold more information, has processing capability, and is almost impossible to duplicate, smart cards may soon replace cards with magnetic stripes. Already, smart cards are gaining widespread acceptance in Europe and in the United States, especially smart cards with *stored value.* The dual-function stored-value smart card serves as a credit card and as a replacement for cash. Customers with these cards can go to automatic teller machines to transfer electronic cash from their checking or savings accounts to the card's memory. They are used like cash at the growing number of stores that accept stored-value cards. Each time the card is used, the purchase amount is deducted from the card's stored value. To reload the card with more electronic cash, the card's owner must return to an automatic teller machine. The stored-value smart card is another big step toward the inevitable elimination of cash.

SPEECH RECOGNITION

Generally, input technology has lagged behind that of output, processing, and storage, but one input area is starting to take wings: speech recognition. In fact, the power of PCs has finally caught up with speech-recognition technology. With the modern speech-recognition software and a quality microphone, the typical off-the-shelf PC is able to accept spoken words in continuous speech (as you would normally talk) at speeds of up to 125 words a minute. Speech recognition has made hands-free interaction possible for surgeons during operations and for quality control personnel who use their hands to describe defects as they are detected. Many executives now dictate, rather than keyboard, their e-mail messages. Also, speech recognition is a tremendous enabling technology for the physically challenged. The two types of speech recognition technology are speaker-dependent and speaker-independent.

techtv
TALK TO YOUR PC

Higher National in Computing

31

Talking with Computers

Although successful for many people, speech recognition remains a novelty with most PC users. Speech recognition is now a mature application on PCs and it is poised to expand into new applications. For example, it is likely that you will be able to record the text of a telephone conversation in your cellular phone's memory, should you so desire. You will be able to walk into your room, speak "Poseidon," or some other system wake-up command, and then begin your "conversation" with your computer, speaking commands and entering text. Our PCs and other electronic devices and appliances will be constantly listening for our wake-up command.

Speaker-Dependent Speech Recognition

Speaker-dependent speech-recognition systems, which usually are associated with PCs, interpret spoken words from one person at a time. A PC-based speech-recognition system consists of software, a generic vocabulary database, and a high-quality microphone with noise-canceling capabilities. Speech recognition capability is now built into modern versions of the Microsoft Office suite. Several software companies offer more sophisticated and/or application-specific speech recognition software (law, medicine, engineering, and so on). The size of the vocabulary database ranges from 30,000 words for general dictation to more than 300,000 words for legal, medical, or technical dictation.

Already, thousands of attorneys, doctors, journalists, and others who routinely rely on dictation and writing are enjoying the benefits of speech recognition. The basic steps in speech recognition are illustrated in Figure 5-25. The system will accept most of your spoken words (see Figure 5-26). However, you can *train* the system to accept virtually all of your words. It helps to train the system to recognize your unique speech patterns. We all sound different, even to a computer. To train the system, simply read to it for about an hour—the longer the better. Even if a word is said twice in succession, it will probably have a different inflection or nasal quality. The system learns your speech patterns and updates the vocabulary database accordingly. The typical speech-recognition system never stops learning, for it is always fine-tuning the vocabulary so it can recognize words with greater speed and accuracy. Each user on a given PC would need to train the system to customize his or her own vocabulary database. To further customize your personal vocabulary database, we can add words that are unique to our working environment, such as acronyms or product names (for example, QRCV or Xbox).

It is only a matter of time before we all will be communicating with our PCs in spoken English rather than through time-consuming keystrokes. Soon, one of the speech recognition options available to us, as users, would be to give our PCs a personality. What kind of personality would you give your computer: somber, serious, happy-go-lucky, polite, rude, frivolous, Valley girl, punk? The possibilities are endless.

Speaker-Independent Speech Recognition

Speaker-independent speech-recognition systems accept words spoken by anyone. Such systems typically are server-based and are restricted to accepting only a limited number of words and tasks. Today, speech-enabled applications are being implemented in all types of industries. For example, thousands of salespeople in the field can enter an order simply by calling in to the company's computer and stating the customer number, item number, and quantity. Several airline companies offer a speech-enabled airline reservation system. Telephone companies have introduced speech-enabled directory service.

FIGURE 5-24

SMART CARD PRODUCTION

Each smart card has embedded nonvolatile memory and a processor (shown here) that can be loaded with information and programmed for a wide variety of applications.

Courtesy of Sun Microsystems, Inc.

DIGITAL CAMERAS: DIGICAMS

We all know that a picture is worth 1000 words, whether at home or the office. We now have the tools to capture still and video imagery, easily and economically. Personal computing and the Net have made it easy to share these images and video with our neighbors or with friends around the world.

Digital Cameras: Digicams

Photo images are an effective way to communicate. The **digital camera** (or **digicam**), which records images digitally rather than on traditional film, has become a popular consumer item. When you take a picture with a modern digicam, a digitized image goes straight to onboard flash memory in the form of a *memory stick*. Once in the interchangeable memory cards, or "stick," it can be uploaded to a PC and manipulated (viewed, printed, modified, and so on) as you would other graphic images (see Figure 5-27).

There are many applications for digital cameras. For example, customers from all over the world make special requests to a designer jewelry store. Store personnel take photos of available merchandise from various angles, and then they e-mail the photos to the customer. An automobile repair center takes photos of all major repair jobs to show customers exactly what the problem was and for training purposes. To help them to adjust braces better, orthodontists use digital cameras to track the migration of patients' teeth. Online retailers use digital cameras when preparing product Web pages, thereby skipping the film developing and scanning process altogether. One of the most popular applications is expanding the family photo album.

PERSONAL COMPUTING
Using Digital Cameras for File Transfer

Modern digital cameras have memory sticks (flash memory) that can store hundreds of images. When a digital camera is connected to a PC via a USB port, its memory stick is treated as another disk, enabling you to upload and download information, as needed. This capability makes digital cameras a convenient alternative for transferring files between PCs.

MEMORY BITS

Input Devices
- Keyboard
- Point-and-draw devices
- Scanners
- Image scanners (*page* and *hand*)
- Badge reader (for magnetic stripes and smart cards)
- Speech-recognition systems
- Digital cameras
- Digital video cameras
- Digital camcorders
- Handheld and wearable data entry devices

FIGURE 5-25 **SPEECH RECOGNITION**

The sound waves created by the spoken word *Move* are digitized by the computer. The digitized template is matched against templates of other words in the electronic dictionary. When the computer finds a match, it displays a written version of the word.

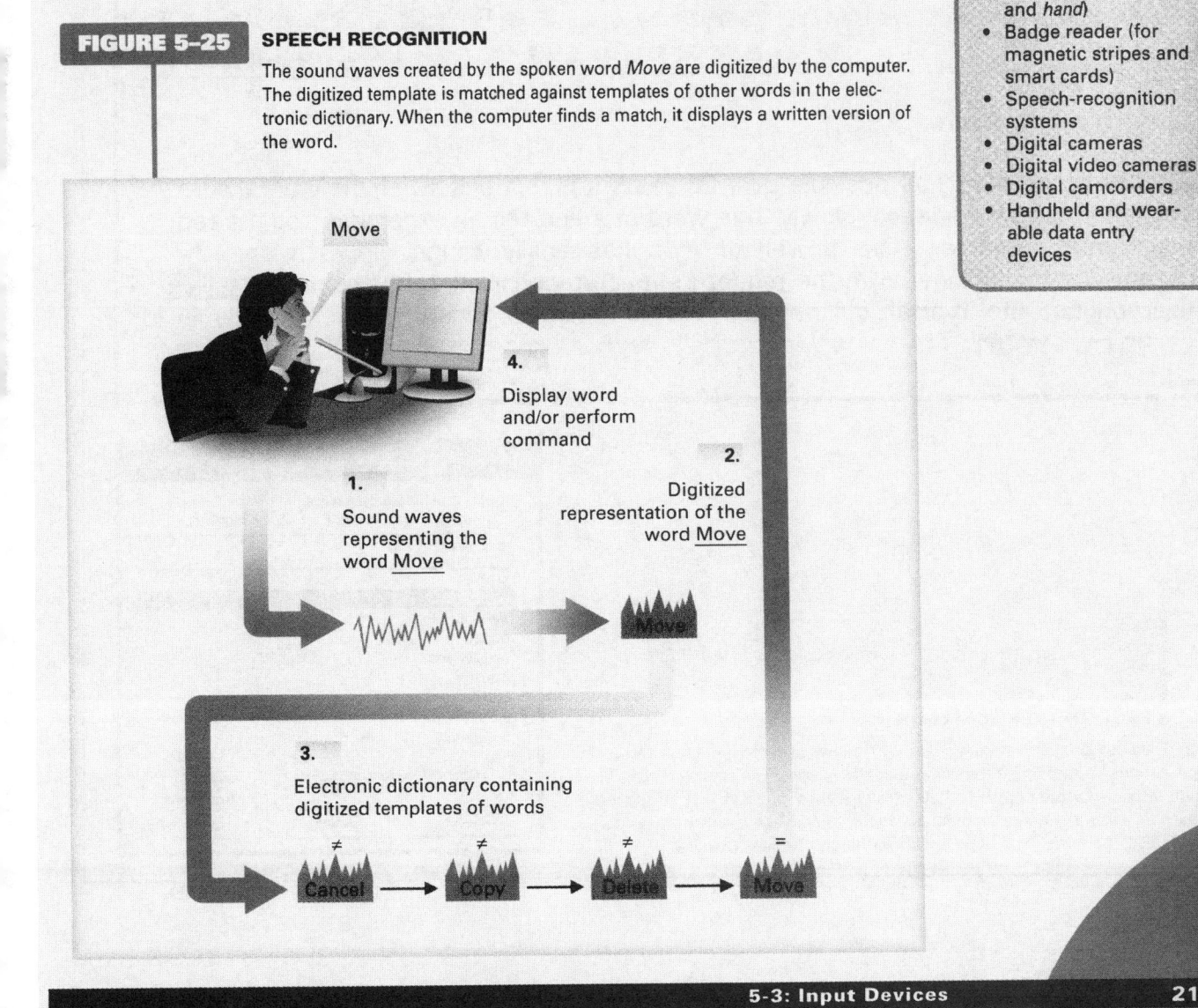

Move

4.
Display word and/or perform command

1.
Sound waves representing the word Move

2.
Digitized representation of the word Move

3.
Electronic dictionary containing digitized templates of words

Higher National in Computing

FIGURE 5-26 **TALKING TO COMPUTERS**

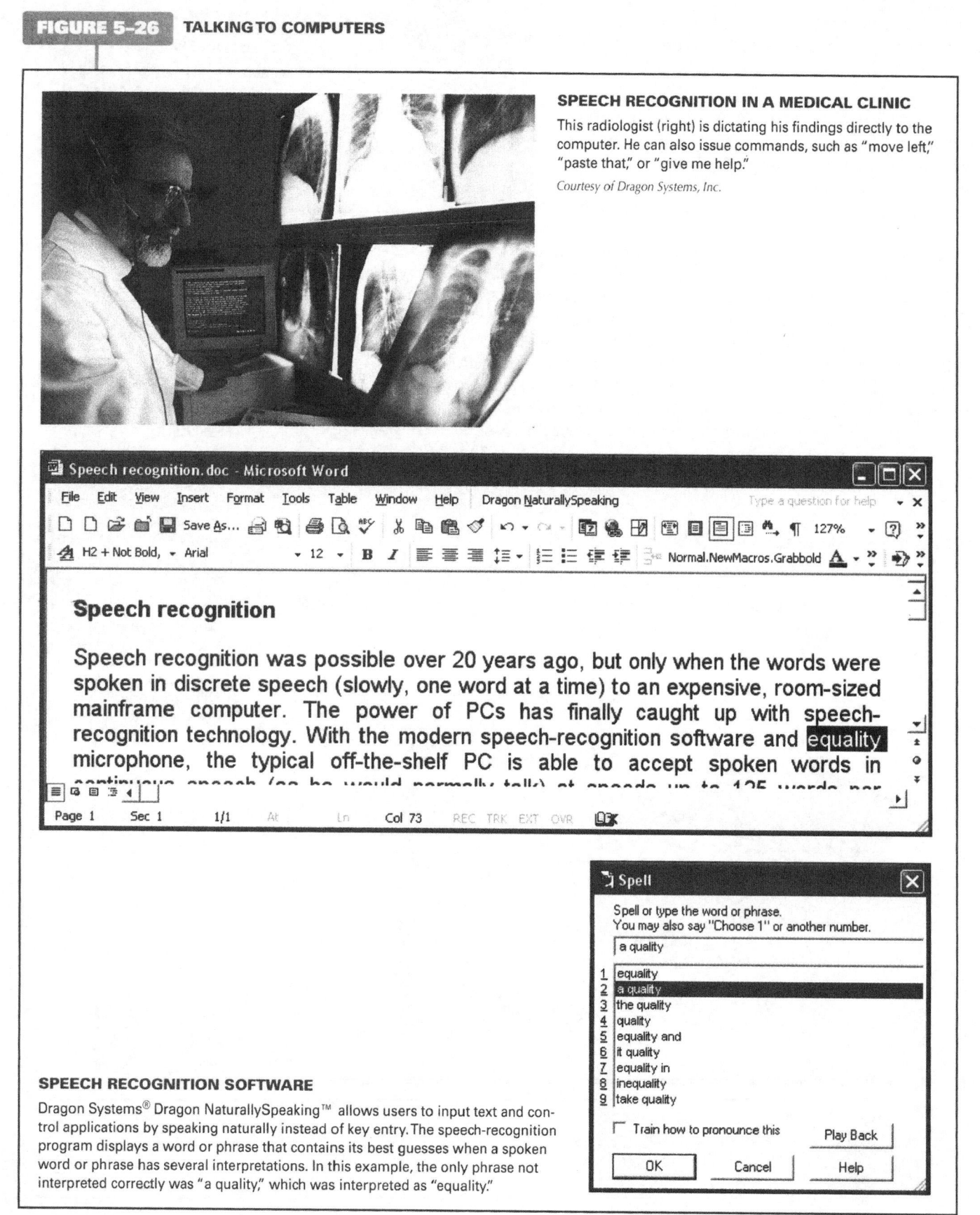

SPEECH RECOGNITION IN A MEDICAL CLINIC

This radiologist (right) is dictating his findings directly to the computer. He can also issue commands, such as "move left," "paste that," or "give me help."

Courtesy of Dragon Systems, Inc.

Speech recognition

Speech recognition was possible over 20 years ago, but only when the words were spoken in discrete speech (slowly, one word at a time) to an expensive, room-sized mainframe computer. The power of PCs has finally caught up with speech-recognition technology. With the modern speech-recognition software and equality microphone, the typical off-the-shelf PC is able to accept spoken words in

Spell

Spell or type the word or phrase.
You may also say "Choose 1" or another number.

a quality

1. equality
2. a quality
3. the quality
4. quality
5. equality and
6. it quality
7. equality in
8. inequality
9. take quality

☐ Train how to pronounce this   Play Back

OK   Cancel   Help

SPEECH RECOGNITION SOFTWARE

Dragon Systems® Dragon NaturallySpeaking™ allows users to input text and control applications by speaking naturally instead of key entry. The speech-recognition program displays a word or phrase that contains its best guesses when a spoken word or phrase has several interpretations. In this example, the only phrase not interpreted correctly was "a quality," which was interpreted as "equality."

Higher National in Computing

34

FIGURE 5-27

DIGITAL PHOTOGRAPHY

We may be entering an era of filmless photography. This image of Niagara Falls was taken with a digital camera, the one in the inset. You can capture, view, print, store, and transmit almost any image. Images are stored on interchangeable memory cards (see inset) or diskettes, then uploaded to a PC and used in countless applications, from the family photo album to training software.

Photo courtesy of Hewlett-Packard Company
Long and Associates

With the cost of high-resolution digital cameras, about that of a quality 35-mm camera, a lot more people are going digital for photography. Once you own a digital camera, the cost of photography plummets because the costly, time-consuming developing processing is eliminated. With digital cameras, you can take all the photos you want and just keep the really good ones.

Desktop Digital Video Cameras

The **desktop digital video camera** lets you capture motion video in the area of the PC. Two popular uses for these cameras are as Webcams and to capture video for real-time Internet-based videophone conversations. **Webcams** are digital video cameras that are continuously linked to the Internet, providing still and video imagery from thousands of sites, usually 24 hours a day. Webcams are located in zoos, classrooms, offices, living rooms, forests, on top of tall buildings, and just about any other place you can imagine beaming stills or video of whatever is happening into cyberspace. If you have a PC, videophone software, an Internet connection, and a digital video camera, you are set to have videophone conversations, whereby you both see and hear the other party.

Digital video cameras have many applications. They are used to create video content for Web pages. People use them to capture still images. More and more companies are opting to save the airfare and have videoconferences instead. Already the relative inexpensive digital video camera (around $70) is standard on some PCs. The emergence of low-cost rewritable optical disc storage means that you can use digital video cameras for the family video, too. Digital video imagery can eat up the megabytes on a hard disk, so people often move captured video to optical laser discs. A CD-R will hold about 15 minutes of video.

FIGURE 5-28

DIGITAL MOVIEMAKER

This digital camcorder can capture favorite scenes that can be shared with your friends and relatives. The digital video can be viewed via TV or PC.

Digital Camcorders

Handheld **digital camcorders** offer another way to capture video (see Figure 5-28). Video is stored on digital tape, but it can be

Higher National in Computing

FIGURE 5-29

WEARABLE INFORMATION RETRIEVAL AND DATA ENTRY HARDWARE

This wearable PC is worn around the head and on the waist. This U.S. Army mechanic enters data and retrieves information in a hands-free environment, eliminating the need to carry maintenance manuals during field maneuvers.

Courtesy of Xybernaut

uploaded to a PC for digital video editing. Digital video is edited easily, that is, parts can be deleted, moved, or copied to meet application needs. Digital camcorders offer greater portability and the quality of the video is higher than that of desktop cameras, but so is the price ($500 to $1,000).

Another way to capture video is to use a standard analog camcorder or VCR in conjunction with a *video capture card,* an expansion card that enables full-motion color video with audio to be captured and stored on disk. Simply plug the cable from the camera or VCR into the expansion card and hit the record or play button. The analog signal is sent to the video capture card where it is digitized for viewing, editing, and storage.

HANDHELD AND WEARABLE DATA ENTRY DEVICES

Handheld and wearable computers, introduced in Chapter 1, frequently are used as data entry devices (see Figure 5-29). Some data entry tasks still require the use of some keystrokes and are performed best on handheld data entry devices. The typical *handheld data entry device,* which is actually a small computer, has the following:

- A limited external keyboard or a soft keyboard (displayed on a touch-sensitive screen)
- A small display that may be touch sensitive
- Some kind of storage capability for the data, usually solid-state nonvolatile flash memory
- A scanning device, capable of optical character recognition

After the data have been entered, the portable data entry device is linked with a central computer, and data are *uploaded* for processing. Although most handheld data entry devices have these or similar characteristics, new innovations keep this type of handheld input device in a continual state of evolution (see Figure 5-30).

FIGURE 5-30

A NEW ERA FOR BALL POINT PENS

With the Logitech io pen, write down whatever you want—up to 40 pages at a time. When you place your pen into its cradle, your drawings, handwritten notes, or whatever you enter on the paper is digitized and transferred to your PC. The images can be integrated with such applications as Microsoft Outlook.

Courtesy of Logitech

Higher National in Computing

Stock clerks in department stores routinely use handheld devices to collect and enter reorder data. As clerks visually check the inventory level, they identify the items that need to be restocked. They first scan the price tag (which identifies the item), and then enter the number to be ordered on the keyboard.

SECTION

1 Input devices translate data into a form that can be interpreted by a computer. (T/F)

2 The wheel on the wheel mouse makes it easier to drag icons. (T/F)

3 The Universal Product Code (UPC) was used originally by which industry: (a) grocery, (b) hardware, (c) mail-order merchandising, or (d) steel?

4 Which is generally not considered a source-data automation technology: (a) digicams, (b) OCR, (c) MICR, or (d) UPC?

5 Memory on smart cards is: (a) volatile, (b) nonvolatile, (c) inert, or (d) never more than 1024 bits.

6 The Webcam is associated with all but which of the following: (a) digital video, (b) the World Wide Web, (c) touchpad input, or (d) The Internet?

5-4 OUTPUT DEVICES

Output devices translate bits and bytes into a form we can understand. There are many output devices, including monitors, printers, plotters, multimedia projectors, and voice-response systems, all presented in this section.

Why this section is important to you.

There are hundreds of output devices that provide hard copy output, video, and audio, all with different features and price tags. It's up to you to determine how big, clear, fast, or loud you want these devices to be. Familiarizing yourself with the options should help you get exactly those devices that meet your personal computing output needs.

MONITORS

Monitors are amazing in that their gray surfaces can spring to life as an artist's drawing, an engineer's design, an author's novel, and even a virtual world. Monitors come in all shapes and sizes to meet a variety of application needs (see Figure 5-31). The primary descriptors for modern monitors are the following:

- Technology
- Graphics adapter (the electronic link between the processor and the monitor)
- Size (viewable area)
- Resolution (detail of the display)

Technology: CRT and Flat-Panel

The basic technology employed in the bulky, boxy **CRT monitors** that you see used with most desktop personal computers has been around since the 1940s. These monitors offer excellent resolution at a very competitive price. However, their footprint, the amount of space they take up on a desk, remains a user concern. The alternative, the **flat-panel monitor,** which is found on all notebook PCs and with many modern desktop PCs, has a much smaller footprint. Some of the space-saving flat-panel monitors are less than 1/4-inch thick. The flat-panel monitor is becoming an increasingly viable option for the PC user as the price continues to drop toward that of the CRT. You must still pay a premium to save desk space and energy, as much as two to three times the cost per unit of viewing area. It is inevitable that the space-saving, energy-saving flat-panel displays will eventually displace the traditional CRT-type monitors for desktop PCs.

FIGURE 5–31 MONITORS

46-INCH TFT LCD PANEL DISPLAY

This 46-inch TFT LCD panel offers 1280 by 720 resolution and a 170 viewing angle in all directions.

Courtesy of Samsung Electronics Co., Ltd.

DURABLE MONITORS

In video arcades, the action takes place on large, durable monitors.

Photo courtesy of Intel Corporation

FLAT-PANEL MONITORS

Flat-panel LCD monitors may be the wave of the future for desktop PCs.

Photo courtesy of Intel Corporation

MULTIPLE-MONITOR ENVIRONMENTS

Monitors are an integral component of virtually all computer-based applications, including video editing. This one-person studio employs a variety of high-resolution CRT and flat-panel monitors.

Photo courtesy of Hewlett-Packard Company

TOUCH SCREEN MONITORS

A growing number of ATMs (shown here) and public information kiosks use touch screen monitors with input/output capabilities.

Courtesy of Diebold, Incorporated

WEARABLE MONITORS

This tiny wearable monitor is worn on a wireless headset and linked to a wearable PC, and lets this pipe fitter view a schematic of the lattice work of pipes at an oil refinery.

Courtesy of Xybernaut

Flat-panel monitors use a variety of technologies, the most common being *LCD* (liquid crystal display). LCD monitors are *active matrix* or *passive matrix*. Active matrix, which has the more brilliant display, also is known as TFT (thin film transistor) LCD monitors. Millions of transistors are needed for TFT LCD monitors. Color monitors need three transistors for each pixel: one each for red, green, and blue. Active matrix LCD displays are more expensive than passive matrix displays; therefore, these displays are usually associated with the better desktop monitors and notebook PCs.

Graphics Adapters

The **graphics adapter** is the device controller for the monitor. Some are built into the motherboard. On desktop PCs, graphics adapters usually are inserted into an *AGP bus* expansion slot on the motherboard. The monitor cable is plugged into the graphics adapter board to link the monitor with the processor. All display signals en route to the monitor pass through the graphics adapter, where the digital signals are converted to signals compatible with the monitor's display capabilities.

Most existing graphics adapters have their own RAM, called **video RAM** or **VRAM**, whereby they prepare monitor-bound images for display. The size of the video RAM is important in that it determines the number of possible colors and resolution of the display, as well as the speed at which signals can be sent to the monitor. Gamers, those who do video editing, and others who place extreme demands on graphics adapters will want to upgrade the standard graphics adapter to one with enough VRAM to handle heavy video demands.

The better graphics adapters enable *dual monitor* support; that is, two monitors can be connected to a single PC. Dual monitor support effectively expands the viewing area by an additional display. The mouse pointer and application windows can be moved seamlessly between the two displays. An application window, perhaps a wide spreadsheet, can be expanded into an adjacent screen. The use of dual monitors is popular with gamers, graphics designers, video editors, accountants, engineers, and others who routinely require extra viewing area or switch between a variety of open applications.

Monitor Size

Display screens vary in size, the viewing area, from 5 to 60 inches (measured diagonally). The monitor size for newly purchased desktop PCs has inched up from 14 inches to 17 inches and is now moving toward 19 inches. If your applications demand a large viewing area or you routinely switch between a variety of open programs, you might want to consider a 20-plus inch monitor or a dual monitor set up. The larger displays, 30 inches and up, usually are designed for viewing by two or more people.

Monitor Resolution

Monitors vary in their quality of output, or *resolution*. Resolution depends on:

- The number of pixels that can be displayed
- The number of bits used to represent each pixel
- The dot pitch of the monitor

A *pixel*, short for *picture element* (see Figure 5-32), is an addressable point on the screen, a point to which light can be directed under program control. Every computer-generated image is composed of a grid of pixels in which the pixels are so close they appear to be connected. The typical monitor is set to operate with a *screen area* of 786,432 addressable points in 1024 columns by 768 rows; however, most can have screen area up to 2000 by 1600. This setting has over three million addressable points. The higher the number of pixels, the more information you can display on your screen. Use a magnifying glass to examine the pixels and observe the pixel grid on your computer's monitor.

Each pixel can be assigned a color or, for monochrome monitors, a shade of gray. **Gray scales** refer to the number of shades of a color that can be shown on a monochrome monitor's screen. Most color monitors mix red, green, and blue to achieve a spectrum of colors,

MEMORY BITS

Output Devices
- Monitors
  - CRT
  - Flat-panel
  - Touch screen (input and output)
  - Wearable display
- Printers
  - Laser (page) printers
  - Ink-jet printers
  - Large-format ink-jet printers (plotters)
  - All-in-one multi-function devices (print, fax, scan, and copy)
- LCD projectors (screen image projection for groups)
- Sound systems (speakers and sound card)
- Voice-response systems
  - Recorded voice
  - Speech synthesis

Higher National in Computing

39

FIGURE 5-32 PIXELS

This photo of children enjoying a snow day off from school illustrates how computers use picture elements, or pixels, arranged in rows and columns to portray digital images. In the inset image, the pixels are so close together they portray continuous color.

and are called **RGB monitors.** One of the user options is the number of bits used to display each pixel, sometimes referred to as **color depth.** Differences in color depth are illustrated in Figure 5-33. In 8-bit color mode, 256 colors are possible ($2^8 = 256$). The 16-bit mode *high-color* mode yields 65,536 colors. *True color* options, either 24-bit or 32-bit mode, provide photo-quality viewing with over 16 million colors. There is a trade-off between the color depth being used and system performance. Greater depth of color demands more of the processor, leaving less capacity for other processing tasks.

Its **dot pitch,** or the distance between the centers of adjacent pixels, also affects a monitor's resolution—the lower the dot pitch number, the greater the number of pixels in the display. Any dot pitch equal to or less than .28 mm (millimeters) provides a sharp image. A dot pitch of .25 is even better, enabling 10,000 pixels per square inch.

Touch Screen Monitors

A special input/output version of the monitor is the touch screen monitor. **Touch screen monitors** have pressure-sensitive overlays that can detect pressure and the exact location of that pressure. Users simply touch the desired icon or menu item with their finger. Interactive touch screen systems are installed in shopping centers, zoos, airports, grocery stores, post offices, and many other public locations.

LCD PROJECTORS

Screen images can be displayed on a monitor or they can be projected onto a large screen to be viewed by a group of people or an audience with the aid of a **LCD projector** (see Figure 5-34). The need for overhead transparencies and 35-mm slides is beginning to fade as presenters discover the ease with which they can create dynamic multimedia presentations, then present them with LCD projectors. LCD projectors use their own built-in lens and light source to project the image on the screen.

LCD projectors are expensive, costing as much as a quality PC. Because of their high cost, they are considered business-oriented hardware. The price, however, continues to drop, and we can expect LCD projectors to eventually become a consumer item. It won't belong before we at home can splash games, DVD movies, and whatever else is on our monitor across the living room wall.

Higher National in Computing

40

PRINTERS

There is a printer to meet the hard copy output requirements of any individual or company, and almost any combination of features can be obtained (see Figure 5-35)—size (some weigh less than a pound), speed, quality of output, color requirements, and even noise level. Printers sell for as little as a pair of shoes or as much as a house. Think about these considerations as you read about various printer options. Keep in mind that additional features, such as two-sided printing, and each increment in speed and quality of output add to the cost of the printer. The most popular technologies for PC-based printers are *laser* and *ink-jet*.

Laser Printers

Nonimpact **laser printers** use laser, LED (*light-emitting d*iode), LCS (*l*iquid *cr*ystal *s*hutter), and other laser-like technologies to achieve high-speed hard copy output by printing *a page at a time*. The operation of laser printers, sometimes called *page printers,* is illustrated in Figure 5-36. Most of the laser printers in use print shades of gray; however, color laser printers are becoming increasingly popular as their price continues to drop. Economically priced laser printers have become the standard for office printing on a local area network. These printers can run through up to six feet of paper during a business day.

The resolution (quality of output) of the low-end desktop page printer is 600 *dpi* (dots per inch). High-end desktop page printers are capable of at least 1200 dpi. The dpi qualifier refers to the number of dots that can be printed per linear inch, horizontally or vertically. That is, a 600-dpi printer is capable of printing 360,000 (600 times 600) dots per square inch.

Ink-Jet Printers

To the naked eye, there is little difference between the print quality of nonimpact **ink-jet printers** and laser printers, but they print in very different ways. The ink-jet printer has a print head that moves back and forth across the paper to write text and create the image (see Figure 5-37). Several independently controlled injection chambers squirt ink droplets on the paper.

FIGURE 5-34

LCD PROJECTORS

LCD projectors are used in conjunction with presentation software, such as Microsoft PowerPoint, and notebook PCs.

Photo courtesy of Hewlett-Packard Company

FIGURE 5-33   **COLOR DEPTH**

The same Niagara Falls image is shown at three levels of color depth: 8 bit with 256 (2^8) possible colors, 16-bit *high color* with 65,536 (2^{16}) possible colors, and 32-bit *true color* with over 4 billion (2^{32}) possible colors.

Higher National in Computing

FIGURE 5-35 PRINTERS

INK-JET PRINTER

During a break in the competition, Miss America Pageant contestants Casey Preslar, Miss Oklahoma; Morgan O'Murray, Miss Colorado; and Stephanie Moore, Miss Iowa, look over photographs printed on this high-resolution ink-jet printer.

Courtesy of Epson America, Inc. Photo by Bruce Boyajian

LASER PRINTER

Laser printers, such as this, often are on a local area network and service the printing needs of all people on the LAN.

Photos courtesy of Hewlett-Packard Company

LARGE-FORMAT PRINTERS

Typical applications for this large-format ink-jet printer include point-of-sale displays, billboards, banners, backlit signs, backdrops for photography or video, and trade show graphics.

Courtesy of Xerox Corporation

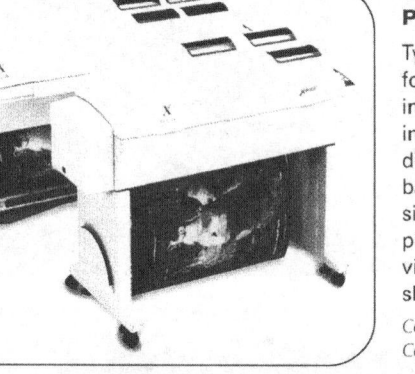

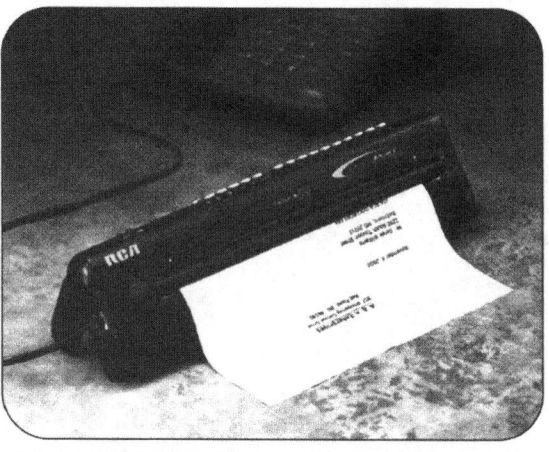

IT'S A FAX, A PRINTER, A COPIER, AND A SCANNER

This compact and lightweight all-in-one multifunction device lets road warriors take the office with them.

Photo courtesy of RCA

SPECIAL-FUNCTION PRINTERS

There is a printer for every job. This printer prints wristbands for hospital patients. The wristbands include bar-coded patient information that can be read with wand scanners.

Courtesy of Diebold, Incorporated

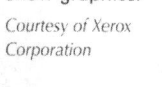

ENTERPRISE PRINTERS

Enterprise printers are designed for high-volume printing (telephone bills, financial statements, insurance coverage summaries, and so on). This IBM printer can print over 400 miles of cut sheet paper per month at 600 dpi resolution.

Courtesy of International Business Machines Corporation. Unauthorized use not permitted.

Higher National in Computing

42

FIGURE 5-36 **LASER PRINTER OPERATION**

(A) Prior to printing, a laser printer applies an electrostatic charge to a drum. Then the laser beam paths to the drum are altered by a spinning multisided mirror. The reflected beams selectively remove the electrostatic charge from the drum.

(B) Toner is deposited on those portions of the drum that were affected by the laser beams. The drum is rotated and the toner is fused to the paper to create the image.

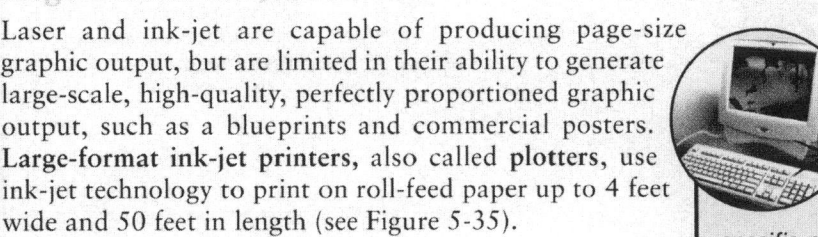

A

Prior to printing, a laser printer applies an electrostatic charge to a drum. Then laser beam paths to the drum are altered by a spinning multisided mirror. The reflected beams selectively remove the electrostatic charge from the drum.

B

Toner is deposited on those portions of the drum that were affected by the laser beams. The drum is rotated and the toner is fused to the paper to create the image.

The droplets, which dry instantly as dots, form the letters and images. Resolutions for the typical ink-jet printer are about that of laser printers, 1200 dpi for regular black and white printing and up to 4800 dpi for color printing on premium photo paper.

Large-Format Ink-Jet Printers

Laser and ink-jet are capable of producing page-size graphic output, but are limited in their ability to generate large-scale, high-quality, perfectly proportioned graphic output, such as a blueprints and commercial posters. **Large-format ink-jet printers,** also called **plotters,** use ink-jet technology to print on roll-feed paper up to 4 feet wide and 50 feet in length (see Figure 5-35).

The All-in-One Device: Print, Fax, Scan, and Copy

Traditionally, businesses and individuals with home offices have purchased separate machines to handle printing, facsimile (fax), scanning, and copying (duplicating). The considerable overlap in the technologies used in these machines has enabled manufacturers to create **all-in-one multifunction devices** that perform all of these functions (see Figure 5-35), which include both input and output. These multifunction devices are popular in the small office/home office environments and in other settings where the volume for any of their functions is relatively low. The laser all-in-one peripheral is faster and more expensive than the ink-jet all-in-one.

You can easily pay in excess of $1,000 for a printer, a scanner, a copier, and a fax machine. Many people with low volume needs are choosing the all-in-one device for 20 to 40% of the cost of separate peripherals. It's an easy choice when you consider that there is relatively little loss of functionality when compared to separate devices. The popularity of the all-in-one device has exploded since the print/scan/copy quality and the speeds of the all-in-one are

PERSONAL COMPUTING
What Input/Output Peripheral Devices Do You Need?

The I/O peripherals you select depend on your *specific needs, usage volumes,* and the *amount of money you are willing to spend.* Each increment in expenditure gets you a device that is faster, bigger, more durable, and/or provides higher quality I/O. A good mix of peripheral devices would include these devices: an all-in-one multifunction device (print, scan, fax, and copy), a *quality* keyboard and mouse (good ones last longer), a 17-inch monitor (preferably a 19-inch), surround-sound speakers, a *quality* headset with a mike (for speech recognition), and a digital Web camera (for videophone).

THE CRYSTAL BALL
The Paperless Society

Forecasters have been predicting a movement to a paperless society for 30 years. It hasn't happened. However, the forces of the economy have given this latent trend new life. The cost of producing and handling paper, whether it is a utility bill, a college textbook, or a company manual, is becoming prohibitive. Adding fuel to the trend, an increasingly IT-competent population is demanding quick and easy access to information in electronic documents. Businesses and government agencies are providing incentives for customers to opt for electronic alternatives to paper. Finally, the paperless society is on the horizon.

FIGURE 5-37   **INK-JET PRINTER OPERATION**

(A) Ink-jet printers use interchangeable cartridges with up to 100 nozzles for each of the four colors. Frequently, black has its own cartridge (left cartridge), whereas the other colors share a separate cartridge (right cartridge). Tiny droplets of ink, about one millionth the volume of a drop of water, in blue, red, yellow, or black, are positioned with great precision on the paper to form characters and images. The droplets, which are mixed to form a wide range of possible colors, are squirted from a nozzle less than the width of a human hair.

(B) Movement of the print heads and paper are coordinated under program control to squirt the dots to form the text and images. Several methods are used to squirt the droplets onto the paper. One method involves superheating ink in a tiny chamber such that it boils and the pressure forces droplets out the nozzle. The chamber cools, ink flows into the chamber, and a process is repeated every few millionths of a second. The dots of color are overlapped to increase the density and, therefore, the quality of the image.

A
Ink-jet printers use interchangeable cartridges with up to 100 nozzles for each of the four colors. Frequently, black has its own cartridge (left cartridge), whereas the other colors share a separate cartridge (right cartridge). Tiny droplets of ink, about one millionth the volume of a drop of water, in either blue, red, yellow, or black, are positioned with great precision on the paper to form characters and images. The droplets, which are mixed to form a wide range of possible colors, are squirted from a nozzle less than the width of a human hair.

B
Movement of the print heads and paper are coordinated under program control to squirt the dots to form the text and images. Several methods are used to squirt the droplets onto the paper. One method involves superheating ink in a tiny chamber such that it boils and the pressure forces droplets out the nozzle. The chamber cools, ink flows into the chamber, and a process is repeated every few millionths of a second. The dots of color are overlapped to increase the density and, therefore, the quality of the image.

now comparable to that of the separate devices. The pros and cons of laser, ink-jet, and all-in-one multifunction devices are summarized in Figure 5-38.

SOUND SYSTEMS

For the first decade of personal computing, small, tinny-sounding speakers came with PCs, primarily to "beep" users when an operation was completed or interaction was needed. Today we watch DVD movies, listen to CDs and MP3 music, play games, and do multimedia presentations on our PCs.

The two parts of a PC's sound systems are the *sound card* and the *speaker system*. As with any sound system, these components can be purchased at various levels of quality. Speaker and sound card capabilities must be compatible; that is, a high-end speaker system requires a high-end sound card. Sound systems vary from a couple of small speakers embedded in notebook PCs to sophisticated sound systems that provide 6.1 surround sound with seven channels of audio. The 6.1 sound systems, which have seven speakers (3 front, 3 rear, and a subwoofer), can provide thunderous Dolby Digital Surround audio and a true cinematic experience.

VOICE-RESPONSE SYSTEMS

Anyone who has used a telephone has heard "If you wish to speak to customer service, press 1. If you wish to speak to..." You may have driven a car that advised you to "fasten your seat belt." These are examples of talking computers that use output from a

Higher National in Computing

44

FIGURE 5-38 PRINTER SUMMARY

	Pros	Cons	Outlook
Page/laser printers	• High-resolution output • Fast (up to 32 ppm) • Quiet • Low cost per page	• High purchase price • Cut sheet only	• High-speed, high-quality page printers will remain the mainstay of office printing for the foreseeable future.
Ink-jet printers	• High-resolution output • Quiet • Small footprint • Energy-efficient	• Higher cost per page than laser • Slower than laser (up to 20 ppm) • Cut sheet only • High cost of print cartridges	• Ink-jet printers will remain the choice for any environment, home or office, with low-volume printing needs.
All-in-one (multifunction) printers	• Can function as a printer, a scanner, a copier, and a fax machine • Get four functions for the price of 1 or 2 • Functional specifications close to separate devices (output quality, speed, and so on)	• Can handle only one function at a time • Larger footprint than a comparable printer	• The all-in-one printer has emerged as the choice in the home or home office with copier, scanner, and fax needs, too.

voice-response system. A **voice-response system** is a device that enables output in the form of user-recorded words, phrases, music, alarms, and so on. There are two types of voice-response systems: One uses a *reproduction* of a human voice and other sounds, and the other uses speech synthesis.

In the first type of voice-response system, the actual analog recordings of sounds are converted into digital data, then permanently stored on disk or in a memory chip. When output occurs, a particular sound is routed to a speaker. Sound chips are mass-produced for specific applications, such as output for automatic teller machines, microwave ovens, smoke detectors, elevators, alarm clocks, automobile warning systems, video games, and vending machines, to mention only a few. When sounds are stored on disk, the user has the flexibility to update them to meet changing application needs.

Speech synthesis systems convert raw data into electronically produced speech. All you need to produce speech on a PC are a sound expansion card, speakers (or headset), and appropriate software. *Text-to-speech software* often is packaged with speech recognition software and produces speech by combining phonemes (from 50 to 60 basic sound units) to create and output words.

Despite limitations such as limited vocal inflections and phrasing, the number of speech synthesizer applications is growing. For example, a visually impaired person can use the speech synthesizer to translate printed words into spoken words. Some people use their notebook PCs to "read" their e-books to them. Translation systems offer one of the most interesting applications for speech synthesizers and speech-recognition devices. Researchers are making progress toward enabling conversations among people who are speaking different languages.

1 Ink-jet printers are nonimpact printers. (T/F)

2 The passive matrix LCD monitor provides a more brilliant display than those with active matrix technology. (T/F)

3 What type of printer would most likely be found in a busy office: (a) laser printer, (b) ink-jet printer, (c) multifunction duplicator system, or (d) glove box printer?

4 What technology converts raw data into electronically produced speech: (a) voice response, (b) reproduction analysis, (c) speech synthesis, or (d) sound duping?

5 All other things being equal on a monitor, which dot pitch would yield the best resolution: (a) .24 dot pitch, (b) .26 dot pitch, (c) .28 dot pitch, or (d) .31 dot pitch?

SELF-CHECK

SECTION

Higher National in Computing

Chapter Review

5-1 MAGNETIC DISK STORAGE

Data and programs are stored permanently in mass storage. Magnetic disk drives are popular devices for mass storage. Magnetic tape drives are used mostly for backup capability and archival storage. Optical laser disc technology continues to emerge as a mass storage medium.

Data are retrieved and manipulated either sequentially or randomly. There are two types of magnetic disks: interchangeable disks and fixed disks. Magnetic disk drives enable random- and sequential-processing capabilities.

Popular types of interchangeable disks include the 3.5-inch floppy disk, the 120-MB SuperDisk, and the 100-, 250-, or 750-MB Zip disk. The floppy disk and the SuperDisk are the same size but have different disk densities.

There are two types of hard disks—those that are permanently installed and those that are portable. Hard disks contain at least one platter and usually several disk platters stacked on a single rotating spindle. The rotation of a magnetic disk passes all data under or over read/write heads, which are mounted on access arms. The portable hard disk is an external device that is connected easily to any personal computer via a USB port or FireWire port.

The way in which data and programs are stored and accessed is similar for both hard and interchangeable disks. Data are stored via serial representation in concentric tracks on each recording surface. The spacing of tracks is measured in tracks per inch (TPI). In sector organization, the recording surface is divided into pie-shaped sectors, and each sector is assigned a number. Adjacent sectors are combined to form clusters.

Each disk cluster is numbered, and the number of the first cluster in a file comprises the disk address on a particular file. The disk address designates a file's physical location on a disk. A particular cylinder refers to every track with the same number on all recording surfaces.

Some high-performance disk manufacturers employ zoned recording where zones contain a greater number of sectors per track as you move from the innermost zone to the outermost zone.

Each disk used in the Windows environment has a Virtual File Allocation Table (VFAT) in which information about the clusters is stored. Clusters are *chained* together to store file information larger than the capacity of a single cluster. The ScanDisk utility lets you return lost clusters to the available pool of usable clusters.

The defragmentation process rewrites fragmented files into contiguous clusters. A Windows utility program called Disk Defragmenter consolidates files into contiguous clusters.

Before a disk can be used, it must be formatted. Formatting creates *sectors* and *tracks* into which data are stored and establishes an area for the VFAT.

The access time for a magnetic disk is the interval between the instant a computer makes a request for transfer of data from a disk-storage device to RAM and the instant this operation is completed. The data transfer rate is the rate at which data are read from (written to) mass storage to (from) RAM. Disk caching improves system speed.

Virtual memory effectively expands the capacity of RAM through the use of software and hard disk storage.

5-2 OPTICAL LASER DISCS

Optical laser disc storage is capable of storing vast amounts of data. The main categories of optical laser discs are CD, CD-ROM, CD-R, CD-RW, DVD-audio, DVD-video, DVD-ROM, DVD-R, DVD-RAM, DVD+RW, DVD-RW, and DVD±RW.

A CD-ROM is inserted into the CD-ROM drive for processing. Most of the commercially produced read-only CD-ROM discs contain reference material or multimedia applications.

A blank compact disc-recordable (CD-R) disc looks like a CD-ROM and once information is recorded on it, it works like a CD-ROM. CD-RW (CD-ReWritable) allows users to rewrite to the same CD media and "burn" discs, such as audio CDs.

The DVD (digital video disc) looks like the CD and the CD-ROM, but it can store up to about 17 GB. DVD drives can play CD-ROMs and CDs. DVD+R and DVD-R are like CD-R but with the recording density of DVD-ROM. DVD+RW and DVD-RW are like CD-RW, giving us rewritable capabilities for high-capacity DVD technology.

The typical PC will have at least a DVD-ROM drive and possibly another read/write disc drive. Most people who want to burn discs and use optical media for backup and transfer purposes are installing a versatile rewritable combination drive, such as the DVD±RW/CD-RW drive.

The choice of which technologies to choose for a system or an application is often a trade-off between storage capacity, cost (dollars per megabyte), and speed (access time).

5-3 INPUT DEVICES

A variety of input/output (I/O) peripheral devices provides the interface between the computer and us. There are two basic types of keyboards: traditional alphanumeric QWERTY-style keyboards and special-function keyboards, which are designed for specific applications. The mouse and its cousins enable interaction with the operating system's graphical user interface (GUI) and they help us to draw. These devices include the trackball, trackpad, joystick, trackpoint, and digitizer tablet and pen.

The trend in data entry has been toward source-data automation. A variety of scanners reads and interprets information on printed matter and converts it to a format that can be interpreted directly by a computer. Two types of scanners—*contact* and *laser*—read information on labels and various types of documents. Generally, scanners used for source data automation are in three basic categories—

handheld label scanners (called wand scanners), stationary label scanners, and document scanners (which are often used with turnaround documents).

OCR (optical character recognition) is the ability to read printed information into a computer system. Bar codes represent alphanumeric data by varying the size of adjacent vertical lines.

Bar codes, such as UPC, represent alphanumeric data by varying the size of adjacent vertical lines. OCR (optical character recognition) technology permits the reading of coded and text information into a computer system, including reading your handwriting. Two types of OCR or bar code scanners—*contact* and *laser*—read information on labels and various types of documents.

MICR scanning technology is used exclusively by the banking industry. The most popular application for optical mark recognition (OMR) is for grading sense-mark tests.

An image scanner uses laser technology to scan and digitize an image. Image scanners provide input for image processing. Image scanners are of two types: *page* and *hand*.

Magnetic stripes, smart cards, and badges provide input to badge readers.

Speech-recognition systems can be used to enter spoken words by comparing digitized representations of words to similarly formed templates in the computer system's electronic dictionary. Usually, PC-based speech-recognition systems are speaker dependent. Server-based systems that accept words spoken by anyone are speaker dependent.

Digital cameras (digicams) are used to take photos that are represented digitally (already digitized). The desktop digital video camera lets you capture motion video in the area of the PC. The Webcam is a popular application for these cameras. Handheld digital camcorders offer another way to capture video. Use a video capture card to capture video from a standard analog video camera or VCR.

Handheld and wearable data entry devices have a limited external keyboard or a soft keyboard, a small display that may be touch-sensitive, nonvolatile RAM, and often a scanning device.

5-4 OUTPUT DEVICES

Output devices translate bits and bytes into a form we can understand. Common output only devices include monitors, printers, plotters, LCD projectors, sound systems, and voice-response systems.

Monitors are defined in terms of their technology (CRT monitor or flat-panel monitor), graphics adapter (which has video RAM or VRAM), size (viewing area), and resolution (number of pixels, number of bits used to represent each pixel, and dot pitch).

Gray scales are used to refer to the number of shades of a color that can be shown on a monochrome monitor's screen. RGB monitors mix red, green, and blue to achieve a spectrum of colors. One user option is the number of bits used to display each pixel, sometimes referred to as color depth.

Flat-panel monitors are used with notebook PCs and some desktop PCs, many of which use LCD technology. Wearable displays give us freedom of movement. Touch screen monitors permit input as well as output.

The most popular technologies for PC-based printers are laser and ink-jet. Laser printers (page printers) use several technologies to achieve high-speed hard copy output by printing a page at a time. Ink-jet printers have print heads that move back and forth across the paper, squirting ink droplets to write text and create images.

Large-format ink-jet printers, also called plotters, use ink-jet technology to print on roll-feed paper up to four feet wide.

Multifunction all-in-one peripheral devices are available that handle several paper-related tasks: computer-based printing, facsimile (fax), scanning, and copying.

PC sound systems include the speakers, up to seven on seven channels, and the sound card.

Voice-response systems provide recorded or synthesized audio output (via speech synthesis). Text-to-speech software enables you to produce speech on a PC.

KEY TERMS

access arms (p. 196)
access time (p. 200)
all-in-one multifunction device (p. 229)
badge reader (p. 217)
bar code (p. 212)
CD-ROM (p. 203)
CD-R (p. 204)
CD-RW (p. 205)
cluster (p. 197)
color depth (p. 226)
CRT monitors (p. 223)
cylinder (p. 198)
data transfer rate (p. 200)
defragmentation (p. 199)

desktop digital video camera (p. 221)
digital camcorder (p. 221)
digital camera (or digicam) (p. 219)
digitizer tablet and pen (p. 210)
disk address (p. 197)
disk caching (p. 200)
disk defragmenter (p. 199)
disk density (p. 194)
document scanner (p. 212)
dot pitch (p. 226)
DVD (p. 204)
DVD+R (p. 205)
DVD+RW (p. 205)
DVD-R (p. 205)
DVD-RW (p. 205)

fixed disk (p. 194)
flat-panel monitor (p. 223)
floppy disk (p. 194)
formatted (p. 199)
graphics adapter (p. 225)
gray scales (p. 225)
GUI (p. 209)
handheld label scanner (p. 212)
hand image scanner (p. 215)
hard disk (p. 194)
image processing (p. 215)
image scanner (p. 215)
ink-jet printer (p. 227)
interchangeable disk (p. 194)
joystick (p. 210)

Higher National in Computing

large-format ink-jet printer (plotter) (p. 229)
laser printers (p. 227)
LCD projector (p. 226)
magnetic disk drive (p. 193)
magnetic tape drive (p. 193)
magnetic-ink character recognition (MICR) (p. 213)
mass storage (p. 193)
MICR reader-sorter (p. 214)
OCR (optical character recognition) (p. 212)
offline (p. 194)
OMR (p. 215)
online (p. 194)
optical laser disc (p. 193)

page image scanner (p. 215)
portable hard disk (p. 196)
read/write head (p. 196)
RGB monitors (p. 226)
ScanDisk (p. 199)
scanners (p. 210)
sector (p. 197)
sector organization (p. 197)
smart card (p. 217)
source-data automation (p. 210)
speech synthesis system (p. 231)
stationary scanner (p. 212)
SuperDisk (p. 194)
touch screen monitor (p. 226)
track (p. 197)

trackball (p. 210)
trackpad (p. 210)
trackpoint (p. 210)
tracks per inch (TPI) (p. 197)
turnaround document (p. 212)
video RAM (VRAM) (p. 225)
Virtual File Allocation Table (VFAT) (p. 198)
virtual memory (p. 201)
voice-response system (p. 231)
wand scanner (p. 212)
Webcam (p. 221)
Zip® disk (p. 194)
Zip® drive (p. 194)
zoned recording (p. 198)

MATCHING

_____ 1. fixed disk
_____ 2. LCD projector
_____ 3. zoned recording
_____ 4. disk clusters
_____ 5. mouse pointer
_____ 6. DVD+RW
_____ 7. cylinder
_____ 8. joystick
_____ 9. smart card
_____ 10. all-in-one peripheral device

a chained together
b hard disk
c gaming control
d uses disk space efficiently
e fax, copy, print, and scan
f provides screen image display for groups
g has multiple tracks
h moved with a point-and-draw device
i rewritable optical disc
j embedded processor

CHAPTER SELF-CHECK

TRUE/FALSE

1. Magnetic disks have sequential-access capabilities only. (T/F)
2. The terms hard disk and fixed disk are used interchangeably. (T/F)
3. Both the floppy disk and the SuperDisk disk are the same size but have different disk densities. (T/F)
4. Information on interchangeable disks cannot be stored offline. (T/F)
5. The capacity of clusters is based on a multiple of 521 bytes. (T/F)
6. In a disk drive, the read/write heads are mounted on an access arm. (T/F)
7. Before a disk can be used, it must be formatted. (T/F)
8. The innermost zone has fewer sectors than the outermost zone in zoned recording. (T/F)
9. CD-ROM is a spinoff of audio CD technology. (T/F)
10. Optical laser discs store data in spiraling tracks. (T/F)
11. DVD+RW technology is faster—for read and write—than hard disk storage. (T/F)

12. The primary function of I/O peripherals is to facilitate computer-to-computer data transmission. (T/F)
13. Use the keyboard's numeric keypad for rapid numeric data entry. (T/F)
14. Only those keyboards configured for notebook PCs have function keys. (T/F)
15. Speech-recognition systems can be trained to accept words not in the system's original dictionary. (T/F)
16. Desktop ink-jet printers generate graphs with greater precision than plotters. (T/F)
17. The graphics adapter is the device controller for a high-resolution speech synthesizer. (T/F)

MULTIPLE CHOICE

1. Which of these statements is *not* true: (a) the rotation of a disk passes all data under or over a read/write head; (b) the heads are mounted on access arms; (c) the standard size for PC hard disks (diameter) is 8 inches; (d) a hard disk contains several disk platters stacked on a single rotating spindle?

Higher National in Computing
48

2. The standard size for common diskettes is: (a) 3.25 inches, (b) 3.5 inches, (c) 3.75 inches, or (d) 5.25 inches.

3. The VFAT is searched by the operating system to find the physical address of the (a) first cluster of the file, (b) read/write head, (c) microprocessor, (d) midsector of the file.

4. What denotes the physical location of a particular file or set of data on a magnetic disk: (a) cylinder, (b) data compression index, (c) CD-R, or (d) disk address?

5. TPI refers to: (a) sector density, (b) cylinder overload, (c) track density, or (d) bps thickness.

6. The disk caching area is: (a) on a floppy disk, (b) in RAM, (c) on a hard disk, or (d) on the monitor's expansion board.

7. In zoned recording, tracks are grouped into: (a) sectors, (b) regions, (c) zones, or (d) partitions.

8. Using disk capacity to expand RAM capacity is called: (a) virtual memory, (b) RAM-expand, (c) actual disk, or (d) mystic RAM.

9. The CD-ROM drive specifications 32X, 40X, or 75X refer to its: (a) speed, (b) diameter, (c) number of platters, or (d) sector groupings.

10. The data transfer rate for an 8X DVD-ROM is about how many MB per second: (a) 3, (b) 6, (c) 11, or (d) 124?

11. Which optical laser disc has the greatest storage capacity: (a) double-sided DVD-ROM, (b) DVD+RW, (c) 75X CD-ROM, or (d) CD-RW?

12. Which of the following is not a point-and-draw device: (a) joystick, (b) document scanner, (c) trackpad, or (c) trackpoint?

13. Banks use which technology to scan checks: (a) OCR, (b) UPC, (c) MICR, or (d) e-commerce?

14. The enhanced version of cards with a magnetic stripe is a(n): (a) badge card, (b) intelligent badge, (c) smart card, or (d) debit card.

15. Which of these is not a type of scanner: (a) document scanner, (b) stationary label scanner, (c) wand scanner, or (d) magnetic scanner?

16. Manipulating and managing scanned images would be considered: (a) image processing, (b) parallel processing, (c) scanner management, or (d) image administration.

17. Which of the following is not true of digital cameras: (a) uses the same film as 35-mm cameras, (b) digitized images are uploaded from the camera, (c) uses flash memory to store images, or (d) can be purchased for as little as $200?

18. Which of these is not one of the capabilities of all-in-one multifunction devices: (a) duplicating, (b) faxing, (c) scanning, or (d) vision input?

19. Which of these does not play a part in determining a monitor's resolution: (a) number of colors mixed within a pixel, (b) number of pixels, (c) number of bits that represent a pixel, or (d) dot pitch?

20. Which of these would not be a pixel density option for monitors: (a) 1024 by 768, (b) 640 by 480, (c) 84 by 123, or (d) 1600 by 1200?

21. Flat-panel monitors always are used in conjunction with which computer systems: (a) server computers, (b) tower PCs, (c) notebook PCs, or (d) desktop PCs?

22. Which of these I/O devices produces hard copy output: (a) monitor, (b) printer, (c) LCD projector, or (d) voice-response system?

23. In text-to-speech technology, speech is produced by combining: (a) firmware, (b) synonyms, (c) phonemes, or (d) digitized templates.

24. Gamers looking to purchase a new PC would pay special attention to the amount of what: (a) gray scales, (b) VRAM, (c) image RAM, or (d) ppm of output?

IT ETHICS AND ISSUES

1. ASSISTIVE TECHNOLOGY IN THE IT WORKPLACE

The Americans with Disabilities Act of 1990 prohibits discrimination that might limit employment or access to public buildings and facilities. Under the law, employers cannot discriminate against any employee who can perform a job's "essential" responsibilities with "reasonable accommodations." Increasingly, these "accommodations" take the form of a personal computer with special input/output peripherals and software, called *assistive technology*. Almost 20,000 assistive technology-based products are available for the disabled. Assistive technology in its many forms has enabled people with disabilities greater freedom to work and live independently.

Discussion: Employers can easily spend from $20,000 to $50,000 on assistive technology for a single disabled employee. What is the payback to the employer? To the disabled employee?

Discussion: Surveys show that employers who provide "assistive technologies" to their employees gain highly motivated and productive workers. Discuss strategies for encouraging managers to invest in assistive technology and hire disabled workers.

2. FILE SHARING

Today's high-capacity hard disk and optical disc storage options enable PC users to storage thousands of huge files, including music and movies. The music industry, which has relied almost exclusively on CD and cassette tape media to market and distribute its products in recent years, is now confronted with millions of music-hungry people who routinely share MP3 files (via the Internet by burning CDs). In

Higher National in Computing
49

the same vein, netizens have begun to share movies, as well (over a half-million a day).

Discussion: In the eyes of the music industry, if you receive an MP3 file containing copyrighted music, then you are receiving stolen goods. Do listeners share this view? Why or why not?

Discussion: Sometimes people attend concerts and tape parts of the concerts, make MP3 files of the music, then send these MP3 files to friends. Is this practice unethical or illegal, or both? Explain.

Discussion: People routinely use digital cameras and illegally tape first-run movies at theaters. They then post the movie file to the Internet. Would you download and view an illegal movie video? Why or why not?

Discussion: Violating copyright laws is punishable by up to five years in prison and a $250,000 fine. Describe what someone would have to do to get the maximum sentence for copyright violations.

Discussion: The upside to MP3 file sharing is that an aspiring artist can place his or her music on the Internet and make it available at little or no charge. Would it be ethical

for an artist to change his or her mind and ask users to pay a fee for music that was offered previously for free?

3. THE SPYCAM

Wireless technology for peripheral devices and the proliferation of small, inexpensive, wireless video cameras has created many new applications for personal computing—some good and many bad. The video cameras can be placed within 100 feet of the host unit and can return clear streaming video images. Moreover, the camera is tiny and is hidden easily from view. You can imagine where pranksters and the lower elements of our society might have placed these cameras. Restrooms, college communal showers, conference rooms, the doctor's office, every room in the house, and so on, are now vulnerable to the spycam.

Discussion: Should those who purchase wireless video cameras be warned of the legal consequences of using this technology to "spy" on people, perhaps by a label similar to those on cigarette packaging? Explain why or why not.

Discussion: What would you do if you had a wireless video camera that could be placed discretely anywhere within 100 feet of your PC?

DISCUSSION AND PROBLEM SOLVING

1. Traditionally, personal computers have had a floppy disk drive. However, some personal computers no longer come with a floppy drive. Is the floppy drive needed anymore? Explain.

2. A program issues a "read" command for data to be retrieved from hard disk. Describe the resulting mechanical movement and the movement of data.

3. What happens during formatting? Why must hard disks and diskettes be formatted?

4. The SuperDisk and Zip disk serve similar purposes on a computer system. The SuperDisk drive is compatible with the traditional floppy diskette, but the Zip disk reads and writes data more rapidly and has a higher capacity. Costs are comparable. Which one would you choose and why?

5. What would determine the frequency with which you would need to defragment your hard drive? Explain.

6. Describe the danger of having too little hard disk capacity allocated to virtual memory. Of having too much.

7. List six content areas that are distributed commercially on CD-ROM (for example, electronic encyclopedias).

8. Describe the potential impact of optical laser disc technology on public and university libraries. On home libraries.

9. Describe at least two applications where CD-RW or DVD+RW would be preferred over a hard disk for storage.

10. The DVD+RW drive also has the capabilities of the CD-RW drive, the "CD burner." Currently the DVD+RW drive is more expensive than the CD-RW drive, but prices are converging. Speculate on when or if DVD+RW will replace CD-RW.

11. With the capability to store digital music, the audio CD has revolutionized the way we play and listen to recorded music. Now music can be downloaded over the Internet and played on PCs, solid-state MP3 players, and other electronic devices. Does this signal the beginning of the end of the audio CD? Explain.

12. The only internal mechanical movement in a typical notebook PC is associated with the disk and optical drives. Someday soon, both may be replaced with solid-state nonvolatile memory. Speculate on how this might change the appearance of notebook PCs and on how we use and what we do with them.

13. Describe two instances during the past 24 hours in which you had indirect communication with a computer; that is, something you did resulted in computer activity.

14. Describe an automated telephone system with which you are familiar that asks you to select options from a series of menus. Discuss the advantages and disadvantages of this system.

15. Name four types of point-and-draw devices. Which one do you think you would prefer? Explain your reasoning.

Higher National in Computing

16. The QWERTY keyboard, which has been the standard on typewriters and keyboards for decades, actually was designed to keep people from typing especially rapidly. Speculate on why built-in inefficiency was a design objective.

17. Today's continuous speech-recognition systems are able to interpret spoken words more accurately when the user talks in phrases. Why would this approach be more accurate than discrete speech where the user speaks one word at a time with a slight separation between words?

18. In the next generation of credit cards, the familiar magnetic stripe probably will be replaced by embedded microprocessors in smart cards. Suggest applications for this capability.

19. Some department stores use handheld label scanners, and others use stationary label scanners to interpret the bar codes printed on the price tags of merchandise. What advantages does one scanner have over the other?

20. Today, literally billions of pages of documentation are maintained in government and corporate file cabinets. Next year, the contents of millions of file cabinets will be digitized via image processing. Briefly describe at least one situation with which you are familiar that is a candidate for image processing. Explain how image processing can improve efficiency at this organization.

21. Describe how your photographic habits might change (or have changed) if you owned a digital camera.

22. Four PCs at a police precinct are networked and currently share a 5 ppm ink-jet printer. The captain has allocated money in the budget to purchase one laser printer (20 ppm) or two more 5 ppm ink-jet printers. Which option would you suggest the precinct choose and why?

23. Describe the input/output characteristics of a workstation/PC that would be desirable for engineers doing computer-aided design (CAD).

24. By purchasing 17-inch low-quality monitors rather than 19-inch high-quality monitors, a large company can save up to $300 per employee on the cost of new PCs. In the long run, however, health and overall efficiency implications of this decision may result in costs that exceed any savings. Explain.

25. In five years, forecasters are predicting flat-panel monitors less than .25-inch thick may be placed everywhere around the home and office. Speculate on how these ultra thin monitors might be used in the home. In the office.

26. Would an all-in-one multifunction device be appropriate in your home or would you prefer purchasing separate devices for the various document-handling functions (duplicating, faxing, printing, and scanning)? Explain your reasoning.

27. Describe the benefits of using a notebook PC in conjunction with an LCD projector during a formal business presentation as opposed to the traditional alternative (transparency acetates and an overhead projector).

28. Some people are calling PC-based speech-recognition software a "killer app." Why?

FOCUS ON PERSONAL COMPUTING

1. *Organizing Your Folders and Files.* The typical user's folder/file structure needs some cleanup. Set up a hierarchical file structure (on paper or on your PC) that includes specific folder categories within general areas of usage. For example, one major folder might be "State University" with subfolders for each semester. Each semester subfolder would have subfolders for your classes and perhaps a miscellaneous folder with subfolders for your extracurricular activities. Rename folders/files as needed.

2. *Hard Disk Maintenance.* If you are an active user and have not defragmented your hard disk, use a disk defragmenter utility and "defrag" your hard disk. Defragmenting the hard disk can substantially improve system performance.

3. *Customizing Preferences for I/O Devices.* Too often, we do not take time to assess and, if needed, adjust I/O features to meet our needs more effectively. Open your Control Panel and open the settings for any I/O device. Familiarize yourself with the device's features and settings and customize them as you see fit. For example, you might prefer the "nature" scheme for the mouse pointer or you might opt for a higher resolution on your display. Examine and customize all input/output devices on your system, including sound and audio devices.

4. *Exploring Available Assistive Technologies.* Modern operating systems provide a minimum level of functionality for people with disabilities. For example, one utility provides visual warnings for system-produced sounds. Another enables the keyboard to perform mouse functions. Search for "accessibility" in the Windows Help and Support Center and learn more about these capabilities. Open and experiment with the Magnifier utility and/or use your system's text-to-speech capabilities. These may not be available with all operating systems or they may need to be installed.

Higher National in Computing

51

1. The Online Study Guide (multiple choice, true/false, matching, and essay questions)
2. Internet Learning Activities
   - Magnetic Disk
   - Optical Storage
   - Input
   - Output
   - Printers
3. Serendipitous Internet Activities
   - Travel

Higher National in Computing

Unit 2: Systems Analysis

Learning hours: 60

NQF level 4: BTEC Higher National — H2

Content Selected: Yeates and Wakefield, Systems Analysis and Design, Chapter 6

Introduction from the Qualification Leader

The learning outcome "system analysis life cycle" has three assessment criteria. This neat little chapter captures the spirit of the system life cycle development and offers a good fundamental range of models to allow for comparison.

The illustrations and text provide good coverage and will support readers in achieving success in this and subsequent learning outcomes.

Description of unit

This unit will provide learners with a detailed insight into the systems analysis life cycle, modelling tools and techniques, testing procedures and the need for systems evaluation. This unit will examine the requirements of analysis for both commercial and technical applications. It will also introduce the data and functional modelling techniques which learners can be expected to use.

Summary of learning outcomes

To achieve this unit a learner must:

1 Understand the **systems analysis life cycle**

2 Use **systems analysis tools and techniques**

3 Perform a **system investigation**

4 Investigate **functional and data modelling**.

Content

1 **Systems analysis life cycle**

Systems lifecycle: the stages of a chosen cycle (eg feasibility, analysis, specification, design, detailed design, code and unit test, integrate and test, maintenance), the purpose of each stage, differentiation between validation and verification

Evaluation of other lifecycle models: comparison of a chosen model with other models (eg prototyping, dynamic systems development, waterfall, spiral, rapid applications design)

2 **Systems analysis tools and techniques**

Tools: using a variety of modelling tools, for example context diagrams, data flow diagrams and entity relationship diagrams

Techniques: using systems analysis documentation — requirements and user catalogue preparing BSOS (business systems options) and TSOS (technical systems options)

3 **System investigation**

Fact-finding techniques: interview, observation, investigation, questionnaire

Fact-recording methods and standards: current computer and paper-based fact-recording methods such as grid charts, flow diagrams, standard documentation technique

4 **Functional and data modelling**

Functional modelling: identification of system processes and functions, data flow diagrams and process modelling techniques

Data modelling: top down techniques, entity relationship modelling

Outcomes and assessment criteria

Outcomes	Assessment criteria for pass **To achieve each outcome a learner must demonstrate the ability to:**
1 Understand the **systems analysis life cycle**	• identify the functions and purpose of each stage of a systems life cycle • provide evidence to support an understanding of the lifecycle • compare different life cycle models
2 Understand **systems analysis tools and techniques**	• use data modelling techniques • create entity-relationship diagrams • use modelling documentation
3 Perform a **system investigation**	• investigate a given problem • identify system requirements • document an investigated system
4 Perform **functional and data modelling**	• identify system processes and functions • produce a functional model • perform data modelling

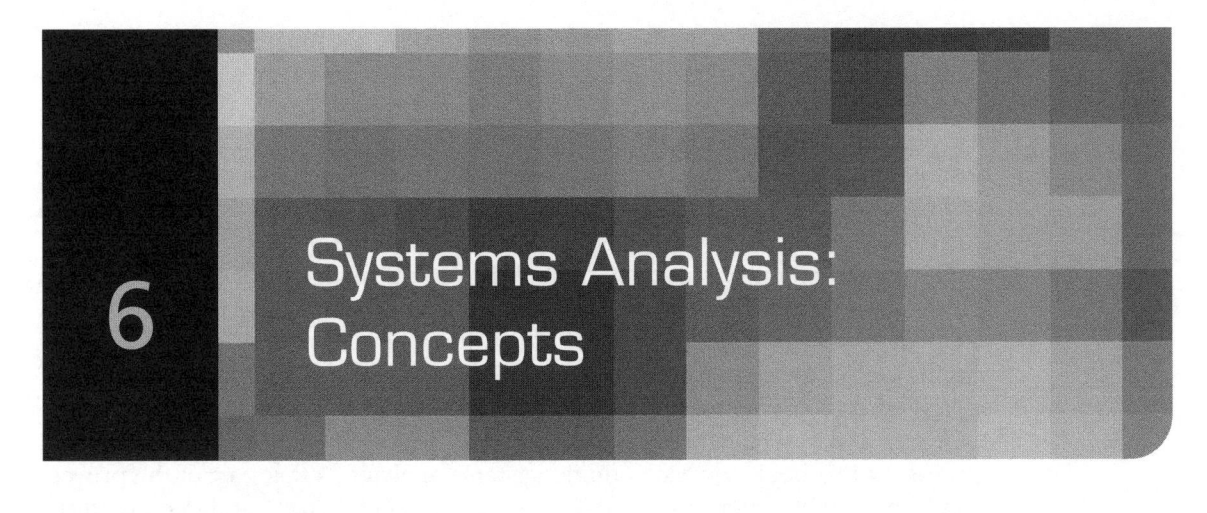

6 Systems Analysis: Concepts

6.1 Introduction

Taking a simple view, we can model systems development as shown in Figure 6.1 where analysis is represented as a discrete stage, which fits neatly between feasibility and design. The model indicates the relative position of the stages in the development process, but systems analysis cannot always be so easily compartmentalised, and there is frequently an overlap between analysis and feasibility and between analysis and design. Indeed, the time on a project at which analysis ends and design starts can often be identified only because it says so in the project plan! High-level analysis begins during feasibility, high-level design begins during analysis, and analysis continues as part of the design process. On small projects, analysis and design may be carried out by the same team of people, who have the job title analyst/designer or simply system developer.

Although it's important to appreciate this overlap between the stages of system development, for the purposes of this book we are treating analysis and design as separate processes. In this chapter we shall answer the question 'What is systems analysis?', consider a structured approach to analysis, and examine systems development life cycles.

Fig. 6.1 Stages in system development

6.2 What Is Systems Analysis?

The Oxford Dictionary defines *analysis* as follows:

> separation of a substance into parts for study and interpretation; detailed examination.

In the case of systems analysis, the 'substance' is the business system under investigation, and the parts are the various subsystems that work together to support the business. Before designing a computer system that will satisfy the information requirements of a company, it is important that the nature of the business and the way it currently operates are clearly understood. The detailed examination will then provide the design team with the specific data they require in order to ensure that all the client's requirements are fully met.

The investigation or study conducted during the analysis phase may build on the results of an initial feasibility study, and will result in the production of a document that specifies the requirements for a new system. This document is usually called the requirements specification or functional specification, and it is described it as a *target document* because it establishes goals for the rest of the project and says what the project will have to deliver in order to be considered a success. In this book, we are defining systems analysis as that part of the process of systems development that begins with the feasibility study and ends with the production of this target document.

A systems analyst will be required to perform a number of different tasks in carrying out the analysis phase of a development project. As a result of discussions with practising analysts, five areas have been identified into which these tasks can be grouped, and these are represented in Figure 6.2.

- *Investigation.* This group of tasks consists of all the fact-finding activities that an analyst may have to undertake. At the heart of these activities is the key skill of asking questions, orally or on paper, which will yield the required information. However, observing others and searching through documents can also be important tasks in gathering information.

- *Communication with customers.* Many analysts regard this as the single most important factor in ensuring a successful outcome to the analysis and producing an accurate specification of the client's requirements. It will include all the tasks that involve communicating ideas in writing, over the phone or face to face. This communication can be formal – presentations, meetings,

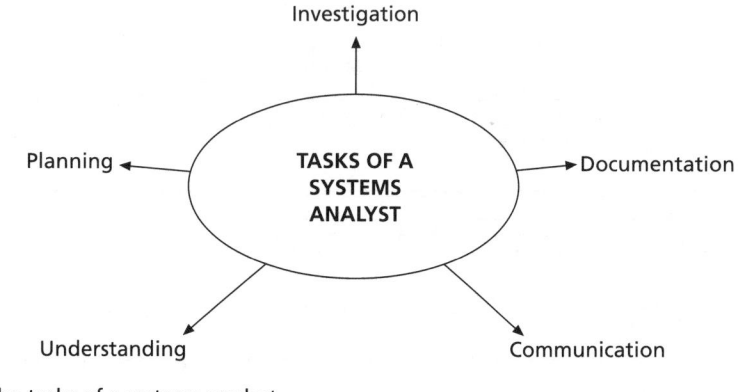

Fig. 6.2 The tasks of a systems analyst

walkthroughs and reports – or informal, but it does need to be regular and as open as possible. It may include giving explanations, providing reassurance and dealing with concerns expressed, as well as exchanging factual information. In addition this group of tasks will also include regular communication with others on the analysis team and their internal customers.

- *Documentation*. The production of documentation, like communicating with the customer, is a broad heading that encompasses many tasks. The writing of meeting minutes and interview records, the drawing of data models, the compiling of lists or catalogues of requirements and the reviewing of documents produced by others would all be included in this group. To be useful to the author and to the rest of the analysis team, any documents produced must be complete, accurate and easily accessible to those who need them. The involvement of the users in checking these documents is a useful way of ensuring accuracy, and has the added advantage of contributing to the building of a good working relationship.

- *Understanding*. This is a heading that really includes all the others, because at the heart of the analyst's job is the desire to understand the information collected, so that they can pass on this understanding to others on the project. The tasks in this group will include checking facts with the person who initially supplied them, cross-checking them where possible with others, and recording them as precisely as possible. It also involves a number of interpersonal skills, especially listening, if *real* needs are to be documented and problems are to be understood from the *users'* point of view.

- *Preparation and planning*. This group of tasks will include the planning of analysis activities, estimating how long these activities will take, and scheduling them to fit in with the project plan. Also included are the management of time and other resources, detailed preparation for interviews, and the work involved in putting together presentations and walkthroughs. Analysts agree that these activities can be time consuming, but are essential if the analysis is to proceed smoothly.

We talked in Chapter 1 about the role of the analyst. In thinking about the tasks the analyst has to perform, we can add the following guidelines, which have been identified by practising analysts:

- Check and agree the terms of reference before beginning your work.

- Involve the client as much as possible, both formally and informally, in developing your understanding of the system.

- Don't take information at face value.

- Be prepared for some resistance. The analyst is concerned with change, and this is uncomfortable for many people.

- Be aware of political issues in the client's organisation, but don't get involved.

- Remember that ownership of the system must always stay with the users.

6.3 Development Life Cycles

The model in Figure 6.1 shows analysis occurring just once in the life of a project, and then the next phases of the project follow on from this. As we suggested, this is not really true; and there are several other lifecycle models to consider. The first of these, the *b-model* of system development – devised by Birrell and Ould – shows in Figure 6.3 the whole life cycle of a system. Development is represented as a vertical straight line – similar to the horizontal path in our original model – and this leads into a maintenance cycle at the bottom. Each stage of the model is important, and no stage is independent of the others. Analysts need to be aware of all the other stages in the life cycle and not just their part of it.

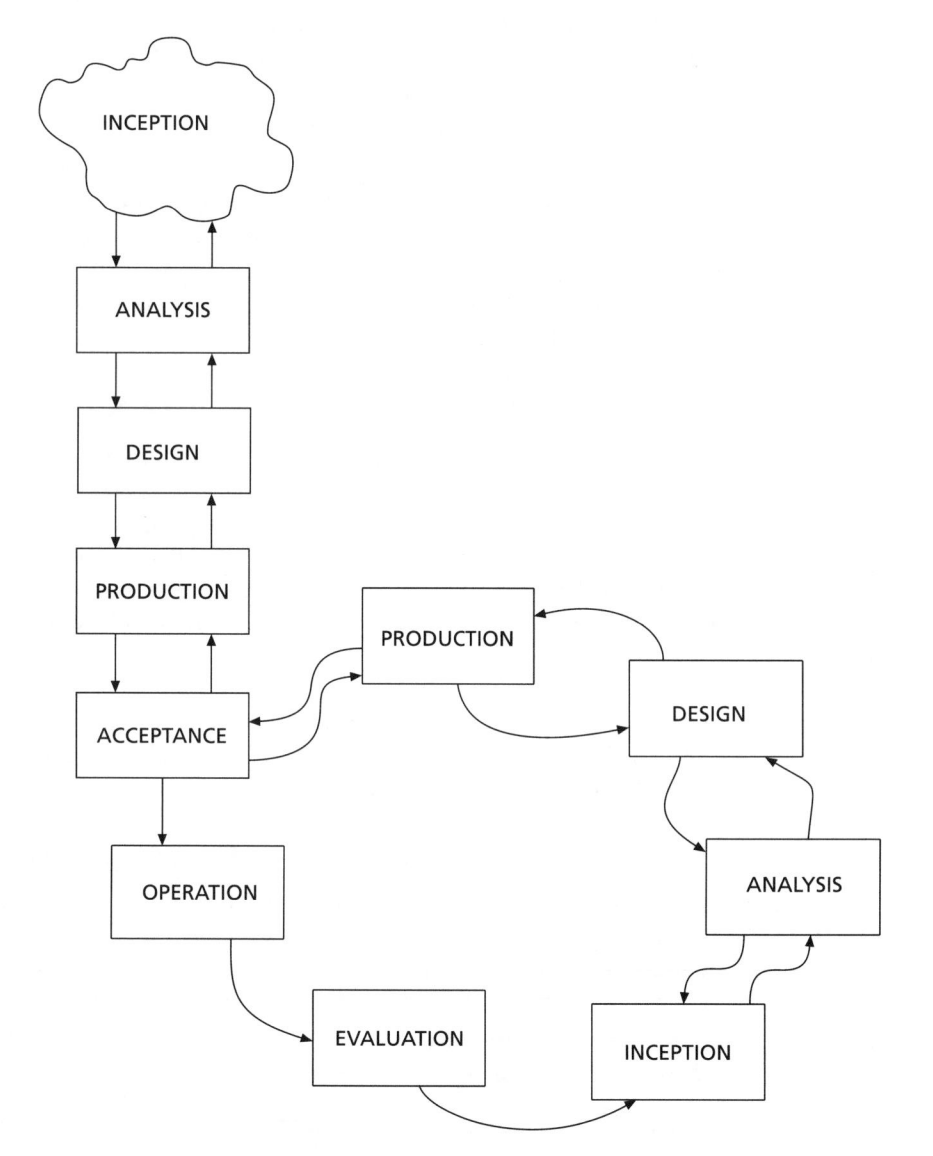

Fig. 6.3 The b-model of system development

The b-model life cycle begins with *inception*, the identification of the need for a new computer system. This leads to the *analysis* stage, the objectives of which are to define the problem, to create a detailed specification of what the system has to do, and to agree with the customer the level of service and performance required. This stage on the b-model also includes the feasibility study – an initial investigation to enable a properly informed decision to be made about whether to commit resources to the project. The next phase is *design*. The objectives of design are to define the structure and content of the system and specify how the system will be implemented. Within this phase, interfaces, dialogues, inputs and outputs are designed, and program and file or database specifications are produced as deliverables.

Once the design is complete, the *production* of the system can begin. During this phase program code is created and tested, supporting manuals and documentation are produced, and work proceeds according to the agreed development schedule. In parallel with this activity, data may be converted into a form that can be used by the new system, and training courses may be designed and implemented in preparation for handover. *Acceptance* marks the point at which the system is installed, handed over and paid for by the client. Any testing at this stage is usually conducted by the client to make sure the system does what they requested. Acceptance of the system by the client is a contractual issue and a project milestone.

Once development is complete, the system 'goes live' and is used by the client to meet the needs of the business. This is the *operation* phase. During the operation phase, there will be an *evaluation* of the system by the users, which may lead to the *inception* of ideas for changes and improvements, and the beginning of the maintenance cycle. During the maintenance cycle, the system may be modified a number of times. For each modification, there will be another analysis phase where the problems associated with the current system and the requirements for changes would need to be investigated and understood. Although this might be a much smaller piece of work than the initial analysis phase of the development project, the same principles will apply, and the same types of task will need to be completed. Maintenance may account for the bulk of the total work done on the system, and more than one change may be moving through the cycle at the same time. While a major change is moving slowly round the maintenance cycle, several smaller changes may move round it quickly.

You will notice in Figure 6.3 that there are two-way arrows between most of the boxes; it is sometimes necessary to go back a step if there is a change in the requirement or if an error introduced earlier in the development shows up only in a later phase.

Next there is the *waterfall model*, which was originally published in 1970 by Royce. In this model, system development is broken down into a number of sequential sections or stages represented by boxes, with each stage being completed before work starts on the following one. The outputs from one stage are used as inputs to the next. This is illustrated by the 'flow' from one stage to the next. For example, using Figure 6.4, the product design products are completed and accepted before being used as inputs to the work of the next stage, detailed design, and so on.

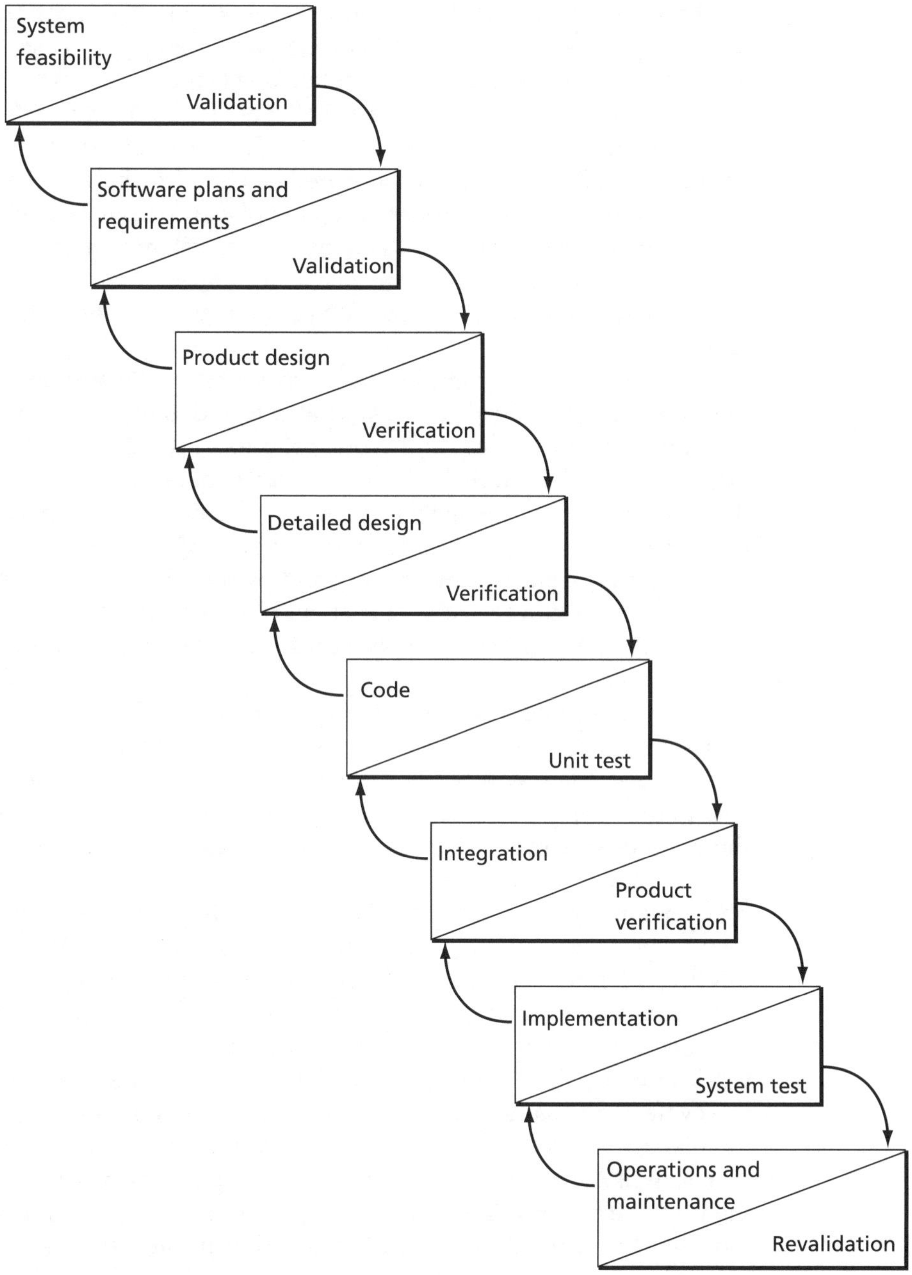

| System feasibility |
| Validation |

| Software plans and requirements |
| Validation |

| Product design |
| Verification |

| Detailed design |
| Verification |

| Code |
| Unit test |

| Integration |
| Product verification |

| Implementation |
| System test |

| Operations and maintenance |
| Revalidation |

Fig. 6.4 The waterfall model

Each stage is divided into two parts: the first part covers the actual work being carried out in the stage, and the second part covers the 'verification and validation' of that work. *Verification* is taken to mean establishing the correspondence between a product and its specification – in other words, are we building the product in the right way? *Validation*, on the other hand, is concerned with whether the product is fit for its operational mission – in other words, are we building the right product? Typically, there is a degree of iteration of work and products within a stage, but very little between stages. Rework, where necessary, is carried out in succeeding stages, and the original stage in which the product was produced is not revisited. For example, if a new requirement is identified during the detailed design stage, the project will not return to the software plans and specification stage but will incorporate the reworking within the current stage. This may mean that some of the previously delivered products need to be amended however.

Nowadays, the waterfall model is generally taken to mean any sequential model divided into consecutive stages and having the attributes of the original model. The identification and naming of the stages are not fixed, and can be modified to suit particular project characteristics.

The model has a number of good points. Apart from the sequencing of activities, it addresses elements of quality management through verification and validation, and configuration management by baselining products at the end of the stage. It does not have explicit means for exercising management control on a project, however, and planning, control and risk management are not covered. Nevertheless, the stage-by-stage nature of the waterfall model and the completion of products for the end of each stage lend themselves well to project management planning and control techniques and assist in the process of change control. Many projects still use versions of the waterfall model, generally with some of the shortcomings of the original one addressed, and the model is used as the basis for many structured methods such as SSADM. Waterfall models work best when the level of reworking of products is kept to a minimum and the products remain unchanged after completion of their 'stage'. In situations where the requirements are well understood and the business area in general is not likely to undergo significant business change, the waterfall model works well. In situations where the business requirements are not well understood and where the system is likely to undergo radical change, a different approach from that suggested by the waterfall model may be more appropriate.

A variation on the waterfall model is the *'V' model*, in which the successive stages are shown in a 'V' formation as in Figure 6.5. In the diagram, the left, downward leg of the V shows the progress from analysis to design to programming and the increasing breakdown of the system components. The right, upward leg shows the progressive assembly and testing, culminating in the delivered product. The important feature of this model is that it shows correspondence between the different stages in the project. For instance, the individual programs or modules are tested against the individual module designs, the integrated set of software is system-tested against the system design, and the final system is user acceptance-tested against the requirements specification. This model demonstrates elements of quality assurance (QA) in its treatment of this correspondence.

In contrast to the waterfall approach, the *spiral model* introduces an evolutionary or iterative approach to systems development. The waterfall model concentrates on a stage-by-stage process, with the end products from one stage being finalised before the next stage is begun. This works reasonably well where the requirements of the system are well understood by the users and the

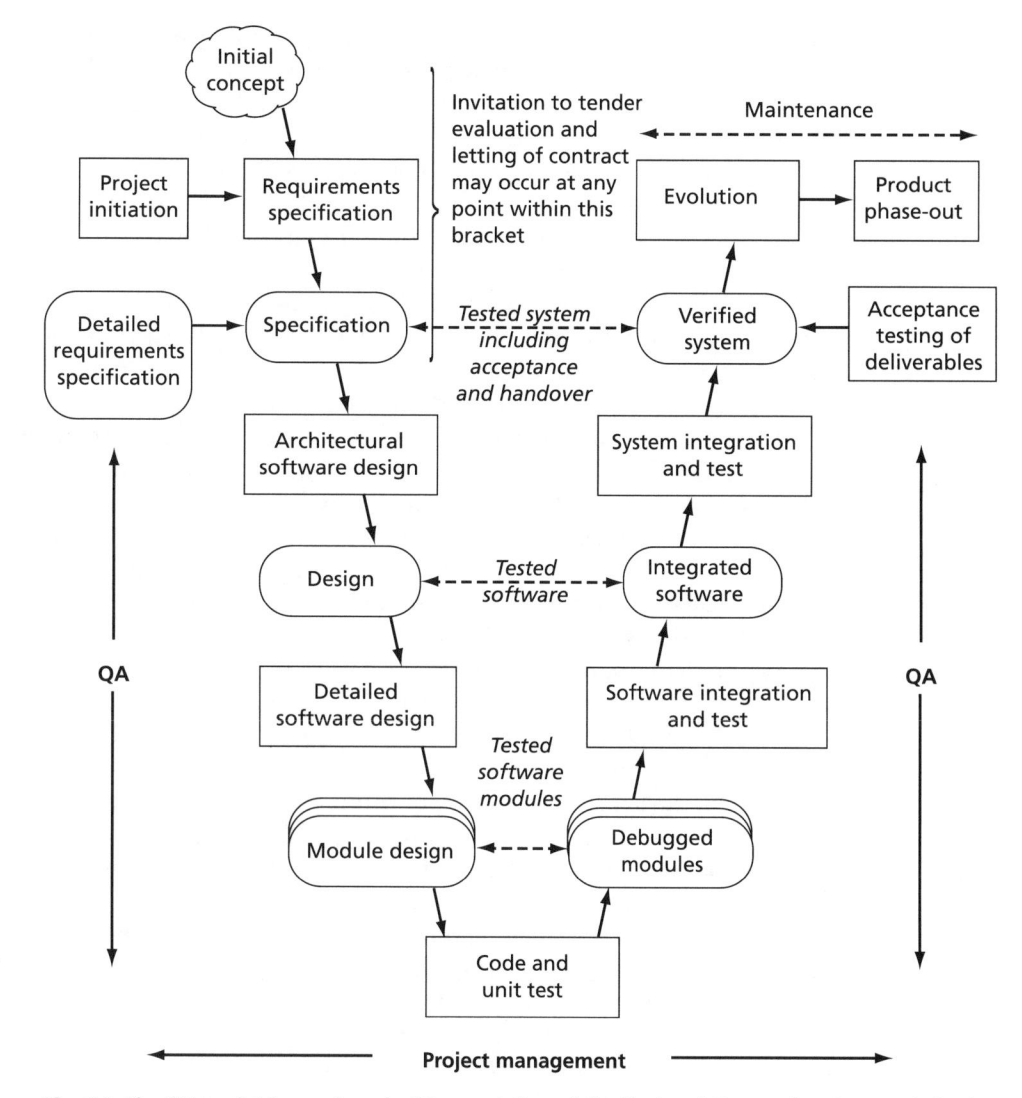

Fig. 6.5 The 'V' model (reproduced with permission of the National Computing Centre Limited from the *STARTS Guide* 1987, which was supported by the Department of Trade and Industry)

environment is stable. There are often occasions where the requirements are not well formed or understood by the users, where it is difficult to specify the requirements, or where it is difficult to determine how a proposed solution will perform in practice. In this situation, an evolutionary approach may be appropriate. This involves carrying out the same activities over a number of cycles in order to clarify the requirements, issues and solutions, and in effect amounts to repeating the development life cycle several times.

The original spiral model was developed by Barry Boehm, and it is shown in Figure 6.6. The project starts at the centre of the spiral and progresses outwards.

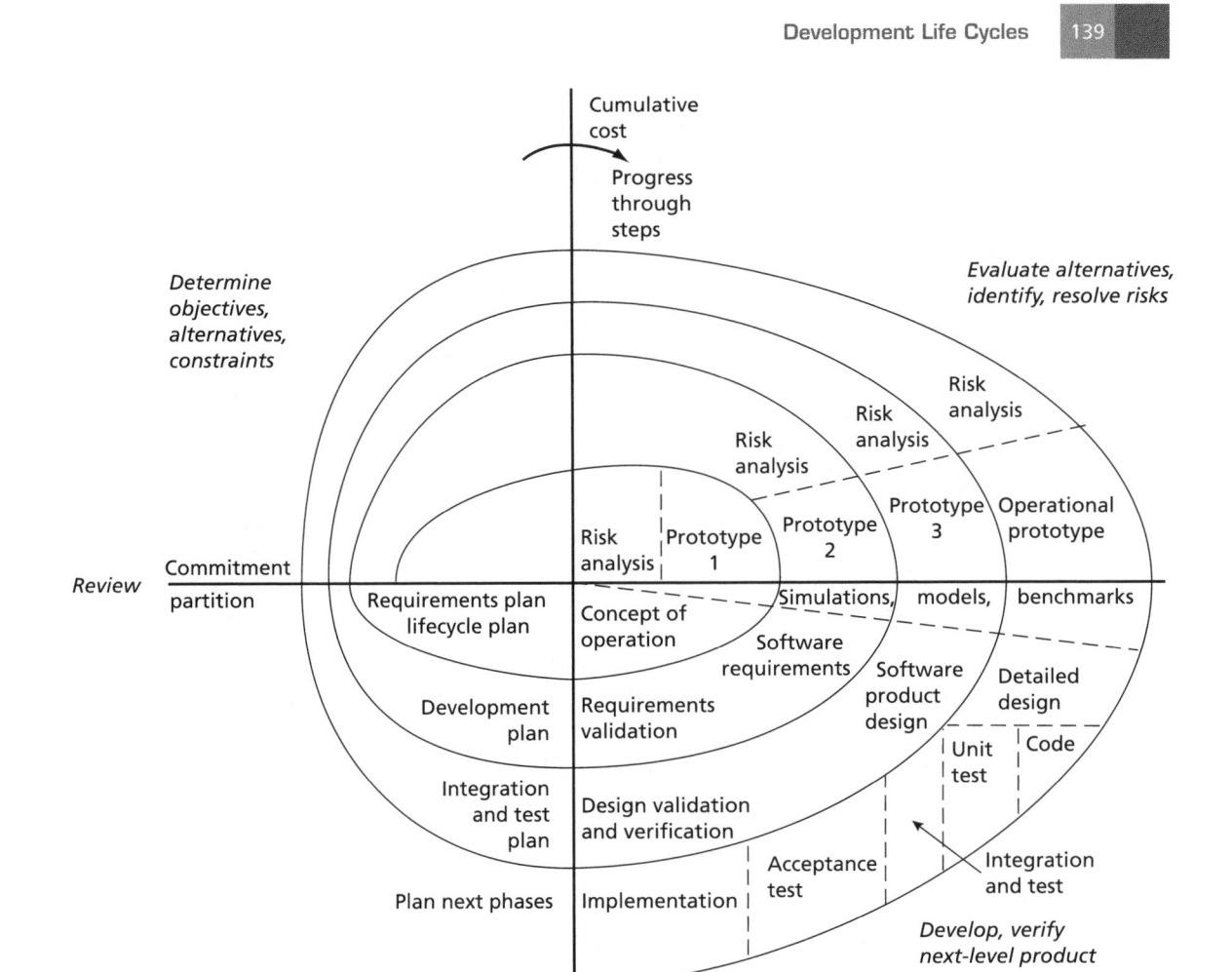

Fig. 6.6 Boehm's spiral model (*Computer*, May 1988, © IEEE)

At the centre, the requirements will be poorly understood, and they will be successively refined with each rotation around the spiral. The total cost of the project will increase as the length of the spiral increases. The model is divided into four quadrants:

- The top-left quadrant is where the objectives are determined and the alternatives and constraints identified.

- The top-right quadrant is where the alternatives are evaluated and the various risks are identified and resolved.

- The bottom-right quadrant is where the development takes place. This in effect covers the same area as the more conventional waterfall model.

- The bottom-left quadrant is where the next phase or iteration is planned.

Higher National in Computing

The Boehm spiral introduces the important concepts of objective setting, risk management and planning into the overall cycle. These are all very desirable from a project management point of view as they apply explicitly to factors that may affect the timely delivery of the system within its defined constraints.

In the *traditional approach* to systems development, 'traditional' tends to mean unstructured and somewhat non-specific, and most traditional approaches are based on variations of the waterfall model. Although the overall picture will probably be familiar, the actual methods of developing the systems are almost as numerous as the projects themselves. In a typical traditional approach, three of the stages are as follows:

- *Analyse requirements*. In this stage the analyst considers the current system and investigates any problems associated with it. The users are also interviewed to obtain their views of the problems and to get their ideas for improvements. Other sources of information about the system and the new requirements would also be investigated at this time. The output from this stage would probably be no more than a set of notes put together by the analyst.

- *Specify requirements*. In this stage the analyst considers the information that has been accumulated, and produces a requirements document. This is likely to be a mix of business requirements, functional and non-functional requirements and an overview of the proposed hardware and software. Elements of the physical specification in terms of screens and printed output reports might also be included.

- *Produce high-level design*. The designer would consider the requirements document and, on that basis, produce a high-level design for the system setting out the database design, the input and output specifications, the menu structure and the overall program design and breakdown.

6.4 A Structured Approach

Analysis can be considered to be a four-stage process, as illustrated in Figure 6.7. This process begins with the analyst investigating and understanding the *current physical system*. This will involve fact-finding activities and the recording of information about how the current system operates. As part of this process, the analyst will also be constructing models to show the data and processing within the system, as well as documenting problems and requirements described by users of the system.

The next stage requires the analyst to move away from the constraints that determine how the current system is physically implemented, and to put together a clear picture of the logical functions carried out by the system – in other words, to state exactly what the system is doing rather than how it is doing it. This view is described as the *current logical system*. To move to the *required logical system*, the customer's requirements for a new information system must be mapped onto the current logical system. This will state what the new system will do. By discussing the requirements with the users who

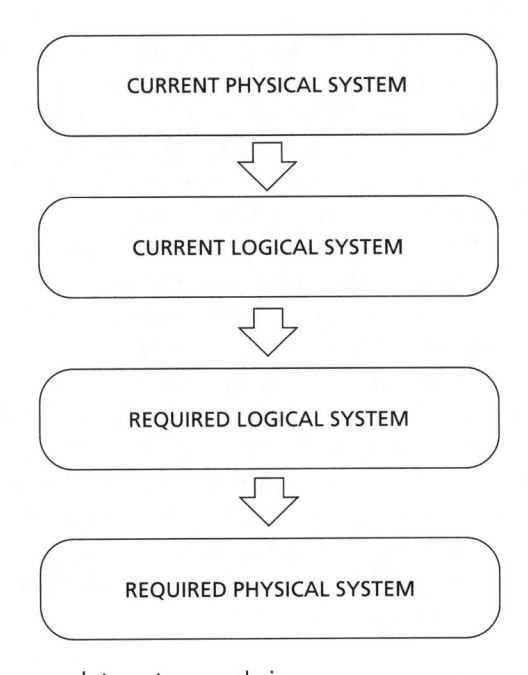

Fig. 6.7 A structured approach to systems analysis

specified them, priorities can be assigned and a number of alternative versions of the required logical system can be developed. These alternative versions can be presented to the client as part of the system proposal.

Finally, when the client has given the go-ahead to the system proposal, the *required physical system* can be developed. This involves specifying in detail exactly how the new system will work, and begins during analysis, with the high-level design included in the functional specification, and continues during the design phase of the project.

In traditional approaches to system development there was a tendency to move from a description of the current physical system to a specification of the required physical system without considering the underlying logical view. Structured techniques such as data flow diagrams and data models support the four-stage model described above and ensure continuity between analysis and design, by developing logical views of the system.

6.4.1 Structured Systems Analysis

Structured systems analysis, which is based on the four-stage model described above, also has associated with it three general principles:

- modelling;
- partitioning;
- iteration.

Modelling refers to the use of graphic models, which are employed wherever possible, in place of narrative text, to provide clear and unambiguous information about the system. They are produced to represent both the current system and data structure and the required system and data structure. They enable detailed investigation to be made of the requirements and the design before money is spent in actually producing the system.

Partitioning describes a method of breaking the system down into a number of smaller parts so that it can be more easily understood, and so that work can be allocated to the members of the project team. The system is first considered as a whole to establish the system boundaries. Once these have been agreed with the users, the system is partitioned, on a top-down basis.

Iteration: As it is unlikely that the first representation of the current system and the requirements for the new system will be completely accurate first time, structured systems analysis provides opportunities for revisiting and amending the models of the system. If this iteration of the process of analysis is carried out in close consultation with the users, it will ensure that our understanding of the existing system is correct and agreed with the client before development of the new system begins.

6.5 The PARIS Model

We have divided the process of analysis into five stages, each of which will be described in detail in subsequent chapters. The first letters of each step form the five-letter word PARIS, which is a useful mnemonic to help you remember the steps. The five steps are:

1 Planning the approach

This is the vital first stage in the PARIS model, and the success of the systems analysis phase of a project will depend on the thoroughness and care with which planning is carried out. During planning, objectives are set, constraints identified, terms of reference agreed, and preparations made for fact finding. Planning is described in Chapter 7, which also includes a section on the feasibility study.

2 Asking questions and collecting data

This includes all the fact-finding activities carried out as part of the analysis. The key technique here is interviewing, which applies many of the principles introduced in Chapter 3 on communication. Interviewing is described in detail in Chapter 8 under three headings – planning, conducting, and recording the interview – and there is also a section on difficult interviews. Other fact-finding methods described in Chapter 8 include observation, designing and sending out questionnaires, document analysis and record searching.

3 Recording the information

The third stage in the model is about recording information. The fact-finding methods, used during stage 2, yield many facts and details about the current and required systems. This information must then be recorded in a clear and unambiguous way. In structured systems analysis, a series of diagrams – or models – are drawn to represent the system, and these can be interpreted and built on by the analysis team, and may also be reviewed by the user to check that the information gathered by the analyst is complete and correct. Chapter 9 introduces two important models that are used to document the current system: the *data flow diagram* and the *data model*. Both are part of all structured methods, but we shall be concentrating on the way they are implemented in SSADM to explain how they are constructed and interpreted.

4 Interpreting the information collected

Having documented the current physical system, we need to understand the underlying logical system, and then consider how the client's requirements can be built in. Again, diagrams can be used to help analysts through this stage of the PARIS model, and Chapter 11 describes some techniques that can be used.

5 Specifying the requirement

The final stage in the model, *specifying the requirement*, is described in detail in Chapter 12. This involves the analyst in preparing a number of options, based on the models constructed earlier, for the development of the new system. These options are discussed with the client, costed, and then presented in a way that emphasises the benefits they will bring to the client's business. The analyst, during this stage, will usually be involved in writing a report, and in preparing and delivering a presentation. Once a decision has been made by the client on the way forward, a detailed functional specification will be prepared so that the designers will know exactly what the system has to do to meet the requirements.

6.6 Summary

This chapter has introduced the process of systems analysis, illustrated this with models, and explained where analysis fits into the development and maintenance life cycle. The PARIS model, which divides the job of analysis into five stages, provides the structure for five of the following chapters, and each stage of the model will now be described in detail. *Planning the approach* is described in Chapter 7; *Asking questions and collecting data* in Chapter 8; *Recording the information* in Chapter 9; *Modelling systems behaviour* in Chapter 11; and *Specifying the business requirements* in Chapter 12.

Unit 3: Programming Concepts

Learning hours: 60

NQF level 4: BTEC Higher National — H1

Content Selected: Sprankle, Problem Solving and Program Concepts, Chapter 2

Introduction from the Qualification Leader

The aim of the unit is to provide the learner with the general principles and concepts of programming. This chapter partially meets the needs of the learning outcome, "Design and develop code using structured programming methods".

The learner needs to understand the general language and meaning of terms. This chapter sets the foundations for development of the unit by providing an overview to five key areas, including:

- constants and variables
- data-types
- functions
- operators and expressions
- equations

Description of unit

An understanding of the general principles and concepts of programming should underpin some of the basic knowledge that learners need.

Learners will develop programs and although the content could be delivered from a range of languages, compilers or platforms, the unit should aim to deliver skills and knowledge that will easily transfer to other areas of the qualification life cycle.

This unit will design programs using industry techniques in order that learners will adopt good practice.

Summary of learning outcomes

To achieve this unit a learner must:

1 Design and develop code using **structured programming** methods

2 Use **modularisation** appropriate to the chosen programming language

3 Produce appropriate **documentation** for a given program application

4 Create and apply appropriate **test schedules**.

Content

1 **Structured programming**

Storage: the concepts of data storage within a computer program, using variables, constants and literals. For a third generation language, the pre-defined data types, integers, floating-point, character, Boolean (logical), strings, 1D and 2D arrays of simple types, and simple files, consequences of using these types, and the available operators within the supplied language

Control structures: identify and select appropriate iterative and selection structures when writing simple programs

Programming language syntax: the facilities and rules of the language (operators, I/0 commands etc)

Program design: employment of an algorithmic approach for the development of a solution to a problem (structure charts, pseudo code etc), producing tested programs to meet given specifications

Programming standards and practice: use of comments, code layout eg consistent indentation and descriptive identifiers

2 **Modularisation**

Use of functions/procedures: the learner should use/create functions/procedures both pre-defined and user-defined, map structured design onto a program using functions/procedures

Scope of variables: global, local, static and external variables

Parameters: passing data by value and reference, using return values

3 **Documentation**

Presentation of documentation: software applications (word processor or graphics), analysis, design and implementation documentation, professional standards, needs of industry

User documentation: user documentation for specified programming applications. Purpose and operation of the program developed

Program documentation: documentation that covers technical aspects of a given programming application, including algorithms implemented, data table, syntax (selection, iteration) structures used, user interface methods adapted

4   **Test schedules**

Error types: semantic, syntax and run-time

Test documentation: test plan and related evidence of testing (may include reading sample inputs from a file and/or writing test results to a file)

Test data and schedules: eg black box, white box, dry testing, data collection

Error detection techniques: compiler and linker error messages, debugging tools and structured walk-through

Outcomes and assessment criteria

Outcomes	Assessment criteria for pass To achieve each outcome a learner must demonstrate the ability to:
1 Design and develop code using **structured programming** methods	• identify and select appropriate pre-defined data types • use simple input/output and appropriate operators with the above • identify and use appropriate selection structures and loop structures for the given task • produce programs to desired standards
2 Use **modularisation** appropriate to the chosen programming language	• construct a program from a design and use appropriate functions/procedures • demonstrate the effect of scope and life-time of variables • pass data effectively between modules
3 Produce appropriate **documentation** for a given program application	• produce user documentation for a completed programming application including the user interface design • develop documentation for a predescribed program application
4 Create and apply appropriate **test schedules**	• demonstrate discrimination between semantic and syntax errors • produce test documentation • successfully construct and use test data and schedules to detect logic errors • use appropriate techniques for detecting errors

Chapter 2

Beginning Problem-Solving Concepts for the Computer

Overview

Constants and Variables
    Rules for Naming and Using Variables

Data Types
    Numeric Data
    Character Data—Alphanumeric Data
    Logical Data
    Other Data Types
    Rules for Data Types
    Examples of Data Types

Functions

Operators

Expressions and Equations

Objectives

When you have finished this chapter, you should be able to:

1. Differentiate between variables and constants.
2. Differentiate between character, numeric, and logical data types.
3. Identify operators, operands, and resultants.
4. Identify and use functions.
5. Identify and use operators according to their placement in the hierarchy chart.
6. Set up and evaluate expressions and equations using variables, constants, operators, and the hierarchy of operations.

Although problems that arise in daily life are of many types, problems that can be solved on computers generally consist of only three: 1) computational, problems involving some

13

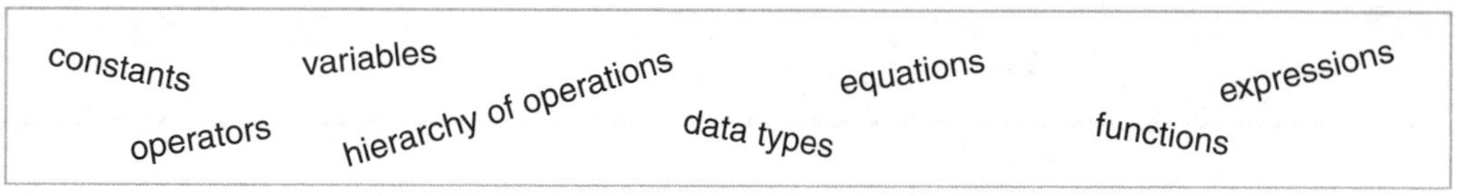

Figure 2.1 Important Concepts to Learn

kind of mathematical processing; 2) logical, problems involving relational or logical processing, the kinds of processing used in decision making on the computer; and 3) repetitive, problems involving repeating a set of mathematical and/or logical instructions. This chapter explains some computer fundamentals and demonstrates ways to set up expressions and equations to solve these types of problems on the computer. End users (users of prewritten software), as well as programmers, need to know these computer fundamentals. See Figure 2.1. In this chapter, both end users and programmers will be referred to as programmers.

Two of the most fundamental concepts that you will learn in this chapter are the constant and the variable. A programmer takes the data, the unorganized facts, and the information, the organized facts, relevant to a problem and defines them as constants or variables. They are the building blocks of the equations and expressions that ultimately make up solutions to computer problems. The programmer defines each constant and variable in a problem solution as a particular data type, such as numeric or character.

Other concepts that are essential to developing computer solutions to problems are operators and functions. Operators are the many signs and symbols that show relationships between the constant and variables in the expressions and equations that make up the solution. The programmer has to know all of the many operators and how to use them. The order in which operators are processed is determined by a hierarchy that programmers need to know as well.

Operators are combined with constants and variables to create expressions and equations. Expressions and equations are used in instructions that are the building blocks of the solution. Functions are sets of instructions that are so commonly used that they are built into a computer language or application, saving the programmer the trouble of writing them.

These are key concepts. Without an understanding of how the computer uses and defines data, without knowing what the operators are, and without knowing how to use these concepts to construct expressions and equations, a programmer or a user of applications software cannot effectively use the computer to solve problems.

When you study this chapter, it may help to keep these pointers in mind:

- Take each topic as it is presented, and learn the concepts pertaining to it.
- Understand the examples.
- Complete the questions and problems at the end of the chapter.
- Don't skip sections.
- Don't feel that something is too hard before you make an effort to understand it.
- Take each problem one step at a time.
- Don't skip steps.
- Don't assume anything.
- Don't be afraid to read a passage over again. Once may not be enough!

The computer uses constants and variables to solve problems. They are data used in processing. A **constant** is a value, that is, a specific alphabetical and/or numeric value, that never changes during the processing of all the instructions in a solution. Constants can be any type of data—numeric, alphabetical, or special symbols. (Data types are explained in more detail later.) Each constant is either part of the instructions in the solution or a piece of data (a datum) to be entered during processing. In some programming languages and applications, constants can be named. In this case, the constant is given a location in memory and a name. During the execution of the program, this constant is given a value and then is referred to by its name. Once the constant is given a value, it cannot be changed during the execution of the program. For example, because the value of PI does not change, it would be a constant and defined within the program. This constant may be given a name, but the only way to change the value of the constant is to change the program.

In contrast, the value of a **variable** may change during processing. A programmer must give a name to each variable value used in a solution. The programmer uses a variable name as a reference name for a specific value of the variable. In turn, the computer uses the name as a reference to help it find that value in its memory. The computer sets up a specific memory location to hold the value of each variable name found in a program. Variables can be any data type, just as constants can. For instance, consider the cost of a pair of shoes. This data item should be given a variable name because the cost of a pair of shoes may change during the processing of the program or during multiple executions of the program. The variable name should be consistent with what the value of the variable represents. In this case, the name of the variable is SHOE_COST because it represents the cost of the pair of shoes:

SHOE_COST

56.00

However, if the cost of the shoes changes during the next execution of the program, then the value of SHOE_COST will change but the variable name will not:

SHOE_COST

35.00

Notice in Table 2.1 that when the value of a constant or a variable contains alphanumeric data—that is, numbers and/or special symbols—it is surrounded by quotation marks. These marks indicate to the computer that the value is a datum, and not a variable name. The computer must have some way to distinguish between the two. Also notice that the variable names stand for specific data. The variable name CASH has a sum of money as its value. The variable name CITY has a city name as its value. Finally, notice that there are no blank spaces in variable names. A space indicates the end of a variable name for the computer. If you need a space in a variable name, use the underline character, for example LAST_NAME. You would not use a dash, as a dash is a subtraction symbol. The programmer decides on the variable name.

Table 2.1 Constants and Variables on the Computer

Constants	Variables

Rules:
    Constants cannot be changed.
Examples:
 	
    Value   25
 	
    Value   −1.5
 	
    Value   "ARCATA"
 	
    Value   "95521"
 	
Named Constants
Rules:
    A constant cannot be changed
        after it is initially given a value.
    Storage location given a name.
    Referred to by the given name.
Example:
        PI
        3.142857
	Rules:
	    Storage locations are
	        given names.
	    Values of the contents for
	        name variable locations
	        can be changed.
	    Referred to by variable
	        name in the instructions.
	Examples:
	    Variable Name—AGE
	      Value 25
	    Variable Name—CASH
	      Value 83.59
	    Variable Name—CITY
	      Value "EUREKA"
	    Variable Name—ZIPCODE
	      Value "95501"

In a solution that calculates payroll for a company, the name of the company would be a constant since it does not change. The employee name, the hours, and the rate of pay would be variables because the values of these items change for each employee. If there were no such thing as a variable, the programmer would have to write a separate set of instructions for each employee. It is far more efficient to have one rather than a thousand programs to process payroll for 1,000 employees.

The rules for naming variables differ from language to language and application to application. However, the general rule is to name the variable as near to its meaning as possible: PAYRATE for the rate of pay, HOURS for the number of hours worked during the pay period, and the like. Some languages and applications have character-length limitations or other restrictions for names (called reserved words), so adjustments have to be made as necessary. In this book, there will be no character-length limitations for variable names.

It is important to understand the difference between the name of a variable and the value of a variable. The *name* is the label the computer uses to find the correct memory location; the *value* is the contents of the location. The computer uses the variable name to find the location; it uses the value found at the memory location to do the processing.

It is also important to be consistent in the use of variable names because the computer will go only to the location with the specified name, whether or not it is the one intended by the user. For example, if you use HOURS for hours worked, then you must use HOURS at all times in referring to hours worked not HRS or Hours. If the computer cannot find a memory location by the specified name, it will either name a new memory location and yield an incorrect result, or it will return an error message indicating there is no location as referenced and then cease execution.

Table 2.2 Incorrect Variable Names

Data Item	Incorrect variable names	Problem	Corrected variable name
Hours Worked	Hours Worked	Space between words	Hours_Worked
Name of client	CN	Does not define data item	Client_Name
Rate of Pay	Pay-Rate	Uses a mathematical operator	Pay_Rate
Quantity per customer	Quantity/customer	Uses a mathematical operator	Quantity_Per_Customer
6% sales tax	6%_sales_tax	Starts with a number	Six_percent_sales_tax or Sales_tax
Client address	Client_address_for_client_of_ XYZ_corporation_in_California	Too long	Client_address
Variable name Introduced as Hours	Hrs	Inconsistent name	Hours
Variable name Introduced as Hours	Hours_worked	Inconsistent name	Hours

Rules for Naming and Using Variables, see Table 2.2

1. Name a variable according to what it represents, that is, HOURS for hours worked, PAYRATE for rate of pay, and so on. Create as short a name as possible but one that clearly represents the variable.
2. Do not use spaces in a variable name. If a space is needed, use the underline character.
3. Start a variable name with a letter.
4. Do not use a dash (or any other symbol that is used as a mathematical operator) in a variable name. The computer will recognize these symbols as mathematical operators, turn your variable into two or more variables, and treat your variable as a mathematical expression.
5. After you have introduced a variable name that represents a specific data item, this exact variable name must be used in all places where the data item is used. For example, if the data item *hours worked* has the variable name of HOURS, HOURS must be used consistently. You may not use HRS or HOURSWORKED to represent the same data item. If you do, the computer views these variables as new and different data items and will assign a new memory location to the new name.
6. Be consistent when using upper- and lowercase characters. In some languages HOURS is a different variable name than Hours.

Data Types

To process solutions, the computer must have data. **Data** are unorganized facts. They go into the computer as input and are processed by the program. What is returned to the user is output, or **information.** This information is printed in the form of reports. For example, when a computer calculates the balance of a checkbook, data are the checks, the deposits, and the bank charges. The information from the processing is shown on the balance sheet (see Figure 2.2).

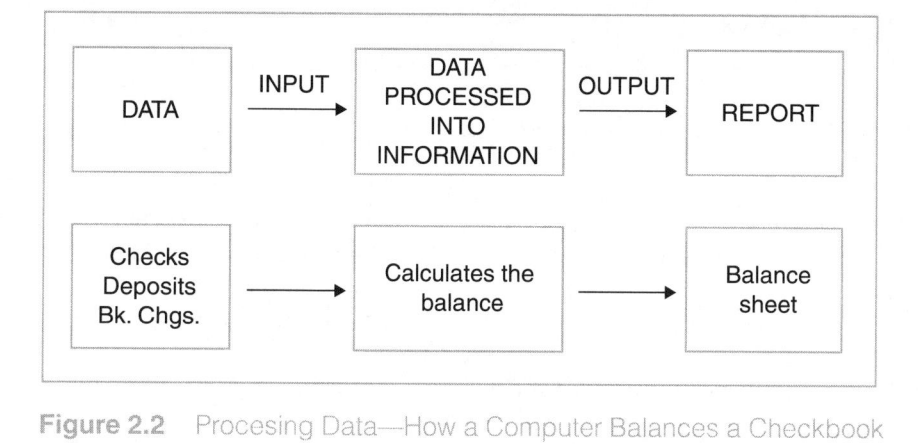

Figure 2.2 Procesing Data—How a Computer Balances a Checkbook

The data the computer uses are of many different types. Computers must be told the **data type** of each variable or constant. The most common data types are numeric, character, and logical. A few languages and applications also use the date as a data type. Other languages allow the programmer to define data types.

Numeric Data

Numeric data include all types of numbers (see Table 2.3). Numeric is the only data type that can be used in calculations. The subtypes of numeric data include *integers* and *real numbers*. Integers are whole numbers, such as 5,297 or −376. They can be positive or negative. Real numbers, or floating point numbers, are whole numbers plus decimal parts. In problem solving on the computer, programmers use integers when there is no reason for using partial numbers, as when they are designing counters, expressions used for counting things, such as inventory items or people. A real number can be expressed in scientific notation, such as 2.3E5 or 5.4E–3. In scientific notation, the *E* stands for *times 10 to the power of*. Therefore, 2.3E5 is the same number as 2.3×10^5, or

Table 2.3 Data Types and Their Data Sets

Data Type	Data Set	Examples
Numeric: INTEGER	All whole numbers	3580 −46
Numeric: REAL	All real numbers (whole + decimal)	3792.91 4739416.0 0.00246
CHARACTER (surrounded by quotation marks)	All letters, numbers, and special symbols	"A" "a" "M" "z" "k" "1" "5" "7" "8" "0" "+" "=" "(" "%" "$"
STRING (surrounded by quotation marks)	Combinations of more than one character	"Arcata" "95521" "707-444-5555"
LOGICAL	TRUE FALSE	TRUE FALSE

Higher National in Computing

80

230,000.0, and 5.4E–3 is the same number as 5.4×10^{-3}, or 0.0054. A number expressed in scientific notation is always considered a real data type. The computer does not use commas in a number during the processing of a calculation, only when the number is formatted as output for the user.

Numeric data are used in business for values, such as rate of pay, salary, tax, or price, that have calculations performed on them. Numbers such as an account number or a zip code, which would not have calculations performed on them, would not be designated by the programmer as numeric data.

Each data type has a *data set*, the set of symbols necessary to specify a datum as a particular data type. The data set for the numeric data type includes all base 10 numbers, the plus sign $(+)$, and the negative sign $(-)$. The data set for the integers includes all whole numbers within the limitations of the computer or the language, and for the real numbers, all whole numbers with decimal parts within the limitations of the computer or the language, including zero as a whole number and zero as a decimal part.

Character Data—Alphanumeric Data

The **character data** set, sometimes called alphanumeric data set, consists of all single-digit numbers, letters, and special characters available to the computer—a, A, Z, 3, #, &, and so forth—placed within quotation marks. An uppercase letter is considered a different character from a lowercase letter. The ASCII (American Standard Code for Information Interchange) character set contains 256 characters. The first 128 comprise a standard set (see Appendix C for the ASCII and EBCDIC data codes), and the second 128 differ with each computer. Characters cannot be used for calculations even if they consist of only numbers. When more than one character is put together, the computer considers this item a *string*—derived from *a string of characters*. Some languages do not differentiate between characters and strings. All character data are considered string data.

Character and string data can be compared and arranged in alphabetical order in the following way. The computer gives each character a number. This numeric representation is necessary because the computer works only with numbers. The numbers are compared to see which is larger and are then arranged in ascending numeric order. Since B has a larger number representing it than A, B is placed after A. C would follow B by the same method, and so forth. String data can be tested in the same way to alphabetize names, cities, and the like. Banana is larger than Apple because B has a larger number representing it than A. Joan is larger than James since the letter o is attributed a larger number than a. Uppercase letters have smaller numeric representations than lowercase letters. It is important to bear this difference in mind when you are comparing letters to see if they are equal. Languages and applications that differentiate between lower case and upper case are called case sensitive. When they are not case sensitive, upper and lower case letters are treated the same. You can use functions before the comparison to insure that data are not case sensitive by making all letters either upper or lower case.

Character data or string data can be joined together with the $+$ operator in an operation called **concatenation.** When two pieces of character data are joined, the concatenation results in the second being placed at the end of the first, as in "4" + "4" = "44" (not "8"). Concatenation could be used to join a first name with a last name or to join pieces of data together to make a code for an inventory item. The concatenation operator varies with each language or application.

Most data in business—names, account numbers, addresses, cities, states, telephone numbers, zip codes—are string data. As a rule, items that would not have mathematical computations performed on them should be designated string data types. There

Higher National in Computing

is another reason for designating a zip code as string data. If you are using numeric data, there is no way to hold onto leading zeros, that is, the zeros at the front of a number, such as 00987. As a result, a zip code on the East Coast could not be entered correctly as a numeric datum. The leading zeros could be preserved only with string data.

Logical Data

Logical data consist of two pieces of data in the data set—the words TRUE and FALSE. (Some languages accept *yes*, T, and Y for TRUE, and *no*, F, and N for FALSE as part of the data set.) These are used in making yes-or-no decisions. For example, logical data type might be used to check someone's credit record; TRUE would mean her credit is okay, and FALSE would mean it's not okay. A home accounting system could use logical data type for check returns; TRUE would mean the check has been returned, and FALSE would mean it has not. There are many such uses for logical data. They are discussed further in later chapters. Remember the logical data set True and False are *not* string data.

Other Data Types

There are other data types available to most programmers, such as the date data type and user-defined data types. The date data type is a number for the date that is the number of days from a certain date in the past such as the first day of the 20th century or January 1, 1940. The use of this data type for the date allows the user to subtract one date from another date to calculate the number of days between dates. This simplifies the calculation when the dates cross over years or months. The date is printed in the date format instead of a number. The date data type is a numeric data type as you can perform mathematical calculations on any date.

Programmers may define their own data types, such as data types that have as their data set soda pop brands, or types of cars, or computer components. The user must specify the items in the data set for each user-defined data type. If the data item is not contained within the data set, it is not part of the set. For example, if the programmer does not include HARD DISK as part of the data set for a user-defined data type of computer parts, then the computer does not recognize a HARD DISK as a computer part.

This book will use the date data type in a few places; however, user-defined data types will not be further discussed or used.

Rules for Data Types

1. The data that define the value of a variable or a constant will most commonly be one of three data types: numeric, character (including character string), or logical.
2. The programmer designates the data type during the programming process. The computer then associates the variable name with the designated data type.
3. Data types cannot be mixed. For example, string data cannot be placed in a variable memory location that has been designated as numeric, and vice versa. When the computer expects a certain data type, the user must use that type or the computer will return an error message.
4. Each of the data types uses what is called a *data set* (see Table 2.2). The numeric data uses the set of all base 10 numbers, the plus sign (+), and the

negative sign ($-$); the character type uses the set of all characters available to the computer; the logical data type uses the set of data consisting of the words TRUE and FALSE. The use of any data outside the data set results in an error.

5. Any numeric item that must be used in calculations resulting in a numeric result must be designated as numeric data type. All other numbers should be designated as character or character-string data types, even if data are all numbers, as in zip codes.

Examples of Data Types

Table 2.4 illustrates some common uses for numeric, character (including character string), and logical data types. Data are drawn from everyday life and business, and are

Table 2.4 Examples of Data Types

Data	Data Type	Explanation
The price of an item: 7.39, 12.98	Numeric: real	The price of an item would be used in calculations. The price is money and needs decimals.
An account number: "A2453," "2987"	Character string	An account number consists of alphanumeric or simply numeric data. It is not used for calculations.
A quantity: 12389	Numeric: integer	A quantity is used for calculations. It is an integer because it normally is a whole number.
The name of a company: "Smith Corp."	Character string	A name of something is alphabetical and therefore would be character string data type.
A credit check: TRUE, FALSE	Logical	The credit check of a customer would be a choice of two answers such as *yes,* it is ok, or *no,* it is not ok. Therefore, it should be logical data.
A zip code: "95521" "76548" "00538"	Character string	A zip code would be a character string because there are no calculations to be done on a zip code, and the leading zeros need to be retained.
A date: 01/23/87 or "03/14/87"	Date or character string	If the date data type is available then it is used; if not, then it has to be a string because it is alphanumeric.
A date: 187259	Numeric: integer	A calendar date is the number of days from a given date; such as, the first day of the 20th century. It can be used for calculations.
Social Security Number "333-33-333"	Character string	A SSN is string data because it is alphanumeric and is not used for calculations.

Higher National in Computing

83

examples of the kinds of data that are commonly used in solving various types of problems on the computer. To the right of the data examples are data types and explanations of why each type is appropriate to the data.

Functions are small sets of instructions that perform specific tasks and return values. They are usually built into a computer language or application. Functions are used as parts of instructions in a solution. Because they are basic tasks that are used repeatedly in the problem-solving process, by using them a programmer or user can shorten the problem-solving time and improve the readability of the solution. Each language or application has a set of functions within it. This set varies with the language, the application, and the computer. Most languages allow programmers to write their own functions. Libraries of functions can be added to many languages.

The form of a function is the name of the function followed by an open parenthesis, followed by the data needed to perform the function and concluded by a closed parenthesis:

functionname(data)

The value of the result of the function is returned in the name of the function.

Functions use data. These data are listed as part of the function and are called **parameters.** Functions normally do not alter the parameters. Take the square root function, SQRT(N). This function will calculate the square root of N. SQRT is the name of the function. N is the data needed to calculate the square root and, therefore, it is the parameter. Parameters are surrounded by parentheses. The maximum function, MAX(N1, N2, N3), will find which of three numbers is the largest. The name of the function is MAX. The parameters, data surrounded by parentheses and needed to do the calculation, are N1, N2, and N3. Not all functions need parameters. The function RANDOM generates or calculates a random number. No data are needed to do this calculation, so there are no parameters. A parameter can be a constant, a variable, or an expression. (An expression is a calculation, such as interest/100, which has not been given a permanent memory location in the computer.) The names of the functions may vary from language to language and from application to application. This book will give a generic name to each function and list the parameters in parentheses.

Table 2.5 lists and defines a few of the basic functions that are found in many languages. Functions are unique to each language. As a programmer you need to investigate the functions used in the language in which you are writing your solution. These functions have been divided into classes.

1. *Mathematical functions.* Often used in science and business, mathematical functions calculate such things as square root, absolute value, or a random number. Other mathematical functions used primarily for scientific purposes have not been included in the table.
2. *String functions.* These are used to manipulate string variables. For example, they copy part of the string into another variable, find the length or the number of characters in the string, and so forth.
3. *Conversion functions.* These functions are used to convert data from one data type to another. For example, since character strings cannot be used in calculations, one of these functions would convert a string value to a numeric value.

4. *Statistical functions*. These functions are used to calculate things such as maximum values, minimum values, and so forth.
5. *Utility functions*. This class is very important in business programming because most reports require some use of utility functions. They access information outside the program and the language in the computer system. Examples of these include date and time functions.

Table 2.5 Functions *(continued on page 24)*

(continued on page 24)

Function*	Definition	Example	Result
Mathematical Functions Used in Business			
SQRT(N)	Returns the square root of N.	SQRT(4)	2
ABS(N)	Returns the absolute value of N.	ABS(−3)	3
ROUND(N, n1)	Returns the rounded value of N to the n1 place.	ROUND (3.7259,2)	3.73
INTEGER(N)	Returns the closest whole number less than or equal to N.	INTEGER (5.7269)	5
RANDOM	Returns a random number between 0 and 1, but not 1. This number is mathematically generated. To find a number N between N1 and N2, inclusive, use the following formula: N = INTEGER (RANDOM * (N2 − N1 + 1)) + N1, where N1 is the smallest number and N2 is the largest number.	RANDOM	0.239768
SIGN(N)	Returns the sign of N: 1 when N is positive, 0 when N is zero, −1 when N is negative.	SIGN(7.39)	1
String Functions			
MID(S, n1, n2)	Returns a set of n2 characters starting at n1 in the string S.	MID(S, 3, 2) where S = "THOMAS"	"OM"
LEFT(S, n)	Returns a set of n characters on the left side of the string S.	LEFT(S, 3) where S = "THOMAS"	"THO"
RIGHT(S, n)	Returns a set of n characters on the right side of the string S.	RIGHT (S, 3) where S = "THOMAS"	"MAS"
LENGTH(S)	Returns the number of characters in the string S.	LENGTH(S) where S = "THOMAS"	6

*Definitions of symbols:

N is a numeric value—a constant, a variable, or an expression

S is a string value—a constant, a variable, or an expression

n, n1, n2 are integer values—a constant, a variable, or an expression

Higher National in Computing

Table 2.5   *(continued from page 23)*

Function	Definition	Example	Result
Conversion Functions (change data type)			
VALUE(S)	Changes a string value into a numeric value.	VALUE ("57.39")	+57.39
STRING(N)	Changes a numeric value into a string value.	STRING (+57.39)	"57.39"
Statistical Functions			
AVERAGE(list)	Returns the average of a list of numbers.	AVERAGE (5, 3, 8, 6)	5.5
MAX(list)	Returns the maximum value from a list of numbers.	MAX (5, 3, 8, 6)	8
MIN(list)	Returns the minimum value from a list of numbers.	MIN (5, 3, 8, 6)	3
SUM(list)	Returns the sum of a list of numbers.	SUM (5, 3, 8, 6)	22
Financial Functions are listed in Chapter 20.			
Utility Functions			
DATE	Returns the current date from the system. The date may be in various forms: mm/dd/yy, day only, month only, year only, or Julian calendar.	DATE	09/15/98
TIME	Returns the current time from the system, The time may be in various forms: hh:mm:ss, seconds from midnight, or minutes from midnight.	TIME	9:22:38
ERROR	Returns control to the program when a systems error occurs.		

Table 2.5 is only a partial list of functions. There are other functions that are not universal or not used very much. The programmer should check the particular language or software package to find any additional functions provided there.

Operators

The computer has to be told how to process data. This task is accomplished through the use of operators. **Operators** are the data connectors within expressions and equations. They tell the computer how to process the data. They also tell the computer what type of processing (mathematical, logical, or whatever) needs to be done. The types of operators used in calculations and problem solving include mathematical, relational, and logical operators. Without these operators very little processing can be done.

The *operand* and the *resultant* are two concepts related to the operator. Operands are the data that the operator connects and processes. The resultant is the answer that results when the operation is completed. For example, in the expression 5 + 7, the + is the operator, 5 and 7 are the operands, and 12 is the resultant. Operands can be constants or variables. The data type of the operands and the resultant depends on the operator.

Mathematical operators include addition, subtraction, multiplication, division, integer division, modulo division, powers, and functions. The computer has a symbol for each of them (see Table 2.6). You are probably familiar with addition, subtraction, multiplication, division, and powers. However, you may not be familiar with integer and modulo division.

These two operations are related. In integer division, the resultant is the whole number in the quotient. In modulo division, the resultant is the whole number remainder. These two types of division are used in business to find the hours and minutes someone has worked given the total number of minutes, or the days and weeks worked given the total number of days. For example, if Jane Smith has worked 19 days during the month, then, assuming a 5-day work week, she has worked 19\5 = 3 weeks and

Table 2.6 Operators and Their Computer Symbols

Operator	Computer Symbol	Example	
Mathematical		Operation	Resultant
Addition	+	3.0 + 5.2	8.2
Subtraction	−	7.5 − 4.0	3.5
Multiplication	*	8.0 * 5.0	40.0
Division	/	9.0/4.0	2.25
Integer division	\	9\4	2
Modulo division	MOD	9 MOD 4	1
Power	^	3 ^ 2	9
Relational			
Equal to	=	5 = 7	FALSE
Less than	<	5 < 7	TRUE
Greater than	>	5 > 7	FALSE
Less than or equal to	<= (two key strokes)	5 <= 7	TRUE
Greater than or equal to	>= (two key strokes)	5 >= 7	FALSE
Not equal to	<> (two key strokes)	5 <> 7	TRUE
Logical			
Not	NOT	NOT TRUE	FALSE
And	AND	TRUE AND TRUE	TRUE
Or	OR	TRUE OR FALSE	TRUE

Higher National in Computing

19 MOD 5 = 4 days. Therefore, she has worked 3 weeks and 4 days. When dividing 19 by 5 the result is 3 with a remainder of 4. The 3 is the resultant of the integer division and the 4 is the resultant of the modulo division. If the dividend is less than the divisor, such as 28 MOD 379, then the resultant is always equal to the dividend, in this case 28. The resultant of 28 \ 379 is zero because the dividend is less than the divisor. When you divide 28 by 379 your resultant is zero with a remainder of 28.

Relational operators include the following: equal to, less than, greater than, less than or equal to, greater than or equal to, and not equal to. A programmer uses relational operators to program decisions. The operands of a relational operator can be either numberic or character (a string); however, both operands must be of the same data type. The resultant of a relational operation is logical data type TRUE or FALSE. The programmer designs one action or set of actions that will follow when a relational expression is TRUE, and another action or set of actions that will follow when the expression is FALSE. The use of relational operators is the only way for the computer to make decisions.

For example, when a credit card customer's balance is *less than $500* (TRUE), then the customer can charge another purchase. When the balance is *not less than $500* (FALSE), then he cannot charge another purchase. The expression would be set up as BALANCE < 500. The operands are BALANCE and 500; the operator is <; the resultant is either TRUE or FALSE depending on the value of the balance. The programmer would use this expression in what is called a *decision instruction*.

Relational operators are also used to control repetitive instructions called *loops*. A set of instructions to enter data for a client, which would be repeated until the data are entered for every client, is one example of a loop. When the computer processes this type of instruction, the loop repeats until the resultant changes from TRUE to FALSE, or vice versa. In the example, the resultant would change when the computer can find no more client data to enter.

Logical operators are the third type of operator (see Table 2.7). Logical operators are used to connect relational expressions (decision-making expressions) and to perform operations on logical data. For example, a store might require a driver's license or a check-cashing card on file for a customer to cash a check. When the customer has a driver's license, the check can be cashed. When he or she has a check-cashing card, the check can be cashed. The expression is written as LICENSE OR CARD. LICENSE and CARD are the operands. They are logical data; that is, the value of each is TRUE or FALSE. The operator is OR. The resultant is TRUE or FALSE depending on the values of the operands. When one or both of the operands is TRUE, then the resultant is TRUE. When both of the operands are FALSE, then the resultant is FALSE.

The OR operator is one of three logical operators. The others are AND and NOT. When the AND operator is used, the resultant is TRUE only when both of the operands are TRUE. When either or both of the operands are FALSE, the resultant is FALSE. A programmer uses AND when two requirements must be TRUE in order for an action or set of actions to take place, such as when a store requires a customer to have *both* a driver's license *and* a check-cashing card to cash a check. The NOT operator is the only logical operator that requires only one operand. The resultant of the NOT operator changes in an operand from TRUE to FALSE, or from FALSE to TRUE. A programmer uses the NOT operator to change an operand to the opposite value. This operation is sometimes called *reversing* the value of the operand.

These mathematical, relational, and logical operators have a **hierarchy,** or precedence, an order in which their operations take place (see Table 2.8). To reorder the

Table 2.7 Definitions of the Logical Operators

NOT

A	Not A	When A is		The Resultant is
T	F	NOT TRUE	IS	FALSE
F	T	NOT FALSE	IS	TRUE

AND

A	B	A AND B	When A is		When B is		The Resultant is
T	T	T	TRUE	AND	TRUE	IS	TRUE
T	F	F	TRUE	AND	FALSE	IS	FALSE
F	T	F	FALSE	AND	TRUE	IS	FALSE
F	F	F	FALSE	AND	FALSE	IS	FALSE

OR

A	B	A OR B	When A is		When B is		The Resultant is
T	T	T	TRUE	OR	TRUE	IS	TRUE
T	F	T	TRUE	OR	FALSE	IS	TRUE
F	T	T	FALSE	OR	TRUE	IS	TRUE
F	F	F	FALSE	OR	FALSE	IS	FALSE

normal processing sequence, the programmer uses parentheses. The processing of the operands (as directed by the operators) always starts with the innermost parentheses and works outward, and processes from left to right. Each level of operators within a set of parentheses requires that the computer make another pass through the parentheses, until all levels have been cleared. This hierarchy is important to the programmer because the order of the operations determines the result of the expression. If the operations are not completed in the correct order, the result of the expression may be incorrect. For example, assuming a 40-hour work week and overtime pay at 1.5 times regular pay, the expression to calculate overtime pay would subtract 40 from the hours worked and multiply the result by the regular wage times 1.5. The expression would be written as

$$(HOURS - 40) * WAGE * 1.5$$

As you can see from the hierarchy chart, multiplication is processed before subtraction, so parentheses must be added to tell the computer to do the subtraction first, before the multiplication. If the parentheses are not added, the result will be incorrect.

In this hierarchy table the integer and modulo divisions are on a separate level from real number multiplication and division. However, many languages place these four operators on the same level. When this is true, it is important to place parenthesis around the integer or modulo operations so that the integer and modulo divisions are

Table 2.8   Hierarchy of Operations

Order of Operations	Operand Data Type	Resultant Data Type
( ) Reorders the hierarchy; all operations are completed within the parentheses using the same hierarchy.		
1. Functions		
Mathematical Operators		
2. Power	Numeric	Numeric
3. \, MOD	Numeric	Numeric
4. *, /	Numeric	Numeric
5. +, −	Numeric	Numeric
Relational Operators		
6. =, <, >, <=, >=, <>	Numeric or string or character	Logical
Logical Operators		
7. NOT	Logical	Logical
8. AND	Logical	Logical
9. OR	Logical	Logical

executed before the multiplication and division. In the following example you will get two different results depending upon whether you execute the integer and modulo division on the same level or separate them with parenthesis to force different levels. Look at the equation:

$$F = 6 * 2 \setminus (6 + 2)$$

If the multiplication and integer division is on the same level the answer will be 1. When they are on different levels, where the integer division will be executed first, the answer will be 0. Remember the execution of operators on the same level is completed from left to right. To force the integer division to be executed first, resulting in a zero resultant, the equation would have to be changed to:

$$F = 6 * (2 \setminus (6 + 2))$$

Check with the language you are working with to find out whether integer and modulo divisions are on the same or different levels. In this book we will assume they are on the different levels. However, please be aware of the difference when starting to develop equations and expressions for the language you are learning.

Each type of operator requires a certain data type for operands and determines the data type of the resultant. Mathematical operators require numeric data as the operands and have numeric resultants. When any of the relational or logical operators are used (whether or not they are used in conjunction with mathematical operators), the resultant is logical data. Relational operators use numeric, character, or string data types as the operands; however, the data type of the operands of an operator must be the same. The logical operators require logical data for operands.

Expressions and Equations

A knowledge of constants and variables, of the three data types, and of operators, operands, and resultants is not very valuable until you can use these concepts to create expressions and equations. The problem you are trying to solve may be calculating pay, including tax, Social Security, and medical deductions. It may be an inventory problem with reorder quantities and cash values. It may be a problem of calculating interest or payments on a loan, or of putting a mailing list in order. These tasks all require the use of different operators, and would be written as expressions and equations in order for the computer to process the data and arrive at a result. There are very few computer problems that do not use expressions and equations in their solutions.

Expressions and equations make up part of the instructions in the solution to a computer problem. An **expression** processes data, the operands, through the use of operators. For example, to find the number of square feet in a room you would multiply the length of the room by the width in the expression

LENGTH * WIDTH

An **equation** stores the resultant of an expression in a memory location in the computer through the equal (=) sign. The expression above would be used as part of an instruction in the equation

AREA = LENGTH * WIDTH

The resultant of the expression LENGTH * WIDTH would then be stored in a memory location called AREA.

As you can see in Table 2.9, expressions use no equal sign (except as a relational operator) and are used as part of an instruction, such as part of an equation. The resultant of an expression is not stored and, therefore, is not available for use at another time. An expression can use numeric, string, character, or logical data types.

Equations are often called *assignment statements* because the variable on the left-hand side of the equal sign is assigned the value of the expression on the right-hand side. The equal sign does not mean *equals*; instead, it means *replaced by* or *is assigned the value of*. This distinction is important because it is possible to have equations on the computer that are not allowed in a mathematics class, such as N = N + 1 (one is added to the old value of N to get a new value of N). This equation is the way the computer counts. There is only one variable on the left-hand side of the equal sign. On the right-hand side of the equal sign is an expression. The right-hand side is processed before the assignment is made (see Table 2.9 and the examples that follow).

For the beginning programmer, a big part of learning to solve problems on the computer is learning how to write and evaluate expressions and equations. (Recall that to *evaluate* means to test for correctness using actual data.) The following examples illustrate how to use the concepts you've learned in this chapter to write and evaluate expressions and equations.

Table 2.9 Expressions and Equations

Expressions	Equations
A + B A and B are numeric. The resultant is numeric and is not stored.	C = A + B C, A, and B are numeric. The resultant is stored in C.
A < B A and B are numeric, character, or string. The resultant is logical and is not stored.	C = A < B A and B are numeric, character, or string. The resultant is stored in C; C is logical.
A OR B A and B are logical. The resultant is logical and is not stored.	C = A OR B C, A, and B are logical. The resultant is stored in C.

Example 1: Setting Up a Numeric Expression

A programmer will often be given an expression to use in solving a problem. Assume the programmer has to modify the following mathematical expression for computer use:

$$X(3Y + 4) - \frac{4Y}{X + 6}$$

The appropriate computer expression would be the following:

$$X * (3 * Y + 4) - 4 * Y / (X + 6)$$

All variables, constants, and operators have to be on the same line. There must be an operator between variables and/or constants. For the computer, there are no assumed multiplication signs. Parentheses are added when the hierarchy has to be reordered or when parentheses would improve readability.

Follow these steps to complete the expression:

1. Write all parentheses, operands, and operators on a single line with the dividend first, followed by the divisor:

$$X (3Y + 4) - 4Y / X + 6$$

2. Insert all implied operators. The computer does not use any implied operators as used in mathematics. These usually include multiplication and power signs.

$$X * (3 * Y + 4) - 4 * Y / X + 6$$

3. Insert all parentheses where the hierarchy needs to be reordered. X + 6 needs to be calculated before completing the division, therefore parentheses need to be inserted around the X + 6.

$$X * (3 * Y + 4) - 4 * Y / (X + 6)$$

Higher National in Computing

92

A mathematical equation might be given to the programmer in the following form:

$$Y + 3 = X(Z + 5)$$

The programmer has to modify the equation so that it is in the form of an assignment instruction:

$$Y = X * (Z + 5) - 3$$

Notice that there is only one variable (and no calculations) on the left side and an expression on the right side of the equal sign.

Follow these steps to complete the equation:

1. Write all parentheses, operands, and operators on a single line:

$$Y + 3 = X (Z + 5)$$

2. Use mathematical rules to complete the equation so that there is one variable on the left side of the equal sign. In this case, subtract 3 from each side:

$$Y + 3 - 3 = X (Z + 5) - 3$$
$$Y = X (Z + 5) - 3$$

3. Follow the steps in Example 1 to complete the equation.

$$Y = X * (Z + 5) - 3$$

Example 3: Setting Up a Relational Expression

A relational expression is used to make decisions. Given the expression

X is less than Y + 5

the programmer would change its form to the following:

$$X < Y + 5$$

Because this is a relational expression, either a variable or a mathematical expression is on either side of the operator. X and Y would be the same data type, in this case, a numeric data type. The resultant would be a logical data type—TRUE or FALSE, depending on the values of X and Y.

Example 4: Setting Up a Logical Expression

Often a computer decision is based on more than one TRUE or FALSE operand. For example, in order to cash a check a customer must have a driver's license (A) or a check-cashing card (B) on file at the store. As is the case with all logical expressions, this case would require a logical operator, A OR B. The operands, A and B, are logical data type; it is either TRUE or FALSE that the customer has a driver's license, and TRUE or FALSE that she has a check-cashing card. The resultant is also a logical type: The customer can cash a check (TRUE or FALSE).

Higher National in Computing

To find out if proposed solutions are correct, it is important for the programmer to evaluate, or test, all expressions and equations. Assume the programmer has written the-expression

$$5 * (X + Y) - 4 * Y/(Z + 6)$$

The programmer uses the following values to evaluate the expression:

$$X = 2 \qquad Y = 3 \qquad Z = 6$$

Notice the structure of the evaluation that follows. A dashed line leading to a circle indicates the operator. The solid lines indicate the operands. Following the illustration of the equation is a list of the operations and the resultant of each operation. The number of circles should equal the number of operators. Be sure the circles using other circles are below the circles they need to use, that is, 3 is lower than 1, 6 is lower than 3 and 5.

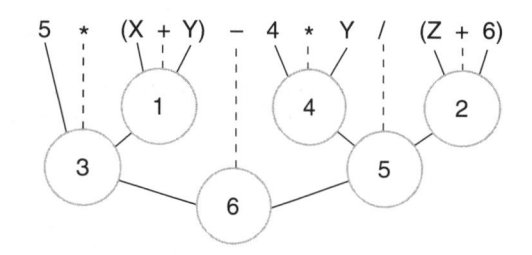

Operation	Resultant
1. X + Y	5
2. Z + 6	12
3. 5 * resultant of 1	25
4. 4 * Y	12
5. Resultant of 4 / resultant of 2	1
6. Resultant of 3 − resultant of 5	24

Illustrating the structure of the expression and listing the operations and results in this way simplifies the evaluation process for the programmer. The evaluation must be completed according to the hierarchy of operations. The operations within the parentheses would be completed first, moving from left to right—so X + Y would be completed first, and Z + 6 second. According to the hierarchy, the programmer would then complete the multiplications and the divisions from left to right. The division would be completed after the multiplications in this expression only because it is to the right. The final operation to be completed would be the subtraction.

This evaluation shows how to test a computer expression to see if it matches an equivalent mathematical expression. It gives the programmer a correct result that can be compared to the results manually calculated by the client, or by whoever requested the computer solution to the problem, so one can be sure that the solution is correct.

Assume the programmer has written the expression

$$A - 2 > B$$

The programmer uses the following values to evaluate the expression:

$$A = 6 \qquad B = 8$$

The following illustration shows the structure of the evaluation:

	Operation	Resultant
	1. A − 2	4
	2. Resultant of 1 > B	FALSE

A − 2 > B

According to the hierarchy of operations, the mathematical operation is completed first.

Example 7: Evaluating a Logical Expression

Assume the programmer has written the expression

A AND B OR C AND A

The programmer uses the following values to evaluate the expression:

$$A = \text{TRUE} \qquad B = \text{FALSE} \qquad C = \text{TRUE}$$

	Operation	Resultant
	1. A AND B	FALSE
	2. C AND A	TRUE
	3. Resultant of 1 OR resultant of 2	TRUE

A AND B OR C AND A

Example 8: Evaluating an Equation That Uses Both Relational and Logical Operators

Assume the programmer has written the following equation:

$$F = \text{NOT } (A < B) \text{ AND } (C \text{ OR } D)$$

The programmer uses the following values to evaluate the equation:

$$A = 4 \qquad B = 2 \qquad C = \text{TRUE} \qquad D = \text{FALSE}$$

The operations are completed in hierarchical order from left to right, as illustrated in the figure.

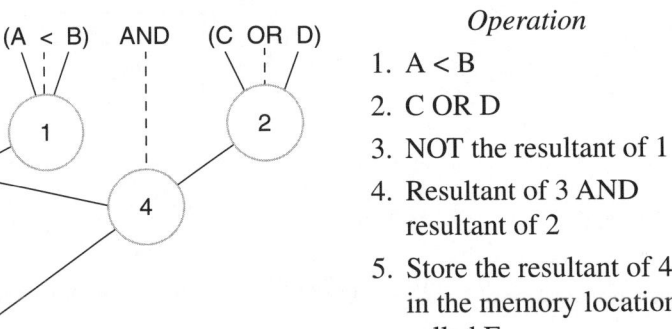

	Operation	Resultant
	1. A < B	FALSE
	2. C OR D	TRUE
	3. NOT the resultant of 1	TRUE
	4. Resultant of 3 AND resultant of 2	TRUE
	5. Store the resultant of 4 in the memory location called F.	

F = NOT (A < B) AND (C OR D)

Higher National in Computing

It is often valuable for a programmer to figure out the resultants for all of the possible combinations of values of the variables in an expression. To create a table of all possible combinations, double the number of combinations from a table with one less unknown. For example:

- One unknown—A. Two combinations: A can be either T or F.

A
T
F

- Two unknowns—A and B. Four combinations: B can be either T or F for each value of A.

A
T
F

A	B
T	T
T	F
F	T
F	F

- Three unknowns—A, B, and C. Eight combinations.

A	B
T	T
T	F
F	T
F	F

A	B	C
T	T	T
T	T	F
T	F	T
T	F	F
F	T	T
F	T	F
F	F	T
F	F	F

Given the expression

NOT A OR B

Higher National in Computing
96

the following table gives the resultants for all combinations of the values of A and B. The equation to find the number of combinations is 2^n, where n is the number of variables. For example, with two variables, A and B, there are four combinations; and with three variables, A, B, and C, there are eight combinations.

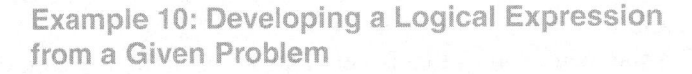

A	B	NOT A OR B
T	T	F
T	F	F
F	T	F
F	F	T

Example 10: Developing a Logical Expression from a Given Problem

Many times a programmer will be given the policies of a company and then be required to set up a logical expression from those policies. To do this, the programmer first needs to list the items on which the condition is dependent. Then the logical expression can be developed from this list.

> Problem: A large department store has its own charge card. The policy for a customer to charge an item is that the customer must have a valid charge card and either a balance of less than $500 or a charge of less than $50.

1. The first step is to list the items the charge is dependent on and their data types:
   a. the charge card (logical data type)
   b. the balance (numeric data type)
   c. the charge amount (numeric data type)
2. The second step is to write down these items as variables along with the conditions on each. Put them on one line, leaving space between, so that the logical operator can be added next. The resultant or the data type of each expression must be logical. Remember that the operators must match the data types of the operands (see Table 2.7). Do not put the logical operators in as of yet.

   CHARGE_CARD BALANCE < 500 AMOUNT < 50

3. The third step is to put in the logical operators and parentheses:

   CHARGE_CARD AND (BALANCE < 500 or AMOUNT <50)

   Because the condition between the balance and the amount is one or the other, the OR operator is needed. The condition between the charge card and the other two items is both; this calls for the AND operator. Since the AND has precedence over the OR, the parentheses are added around the OR operation.

4. You have now created the logical expression. This expression can be used in various ways:

  a. In an assignment statement:

$$\text{OKTOCHG} = \text{CHARGE\_CARD AND (BALANCE} <500 \text{ OR}$$
$$\text{AMOUNT} < 50)$$

  b. In a decision statement (this will be explained in Chapter 6, Problem Solving with Decisions):

$$\text{IF CHARGE\_CARD AND (BALANCE} < 500 \text{ OR AMOUNT} < 50)$$
$$\text{THEN PRINT "OKAY TO CHARGE"}$$
$$\text{ELSE PRINT "NOT OKAY TO CHARGE"}$$

Summary

This chapter explains fundamental concepts for solving problems on the computer, including constants, variables, data types, common functions, operators, expressions, and equations. It also shows the beginning programmer how to set up computer expressions and equations.

Constants are values that never change during processing, even if they are named constants; variables are values that do change. Constants and variables are assigned data types and are used in expressions and equations. The most common data types include numeric, character, and logical.

Expressions and equations use functions to process standard tasks. Most functions are part of the computer language. Expressions and equations use operators to process the data. These operators are of three types: mathematical, relational, and logical. By using operators and the hierarchy of operations, a programmer can design calculations and decisions, which are the key to solving problems on the computer.

New Terms

character data	information
concatenation	logical data
constant	logical operator
data	mathematical operator
data type	numeric data
equation	operator
expression	parameter
function	relational operator
hierarchy	variable

Questions

1. What is a constant? What is a variable?
2. Fill in the following table with the variable name and data type needed to solve an inventory problem for White Auto Supplies.

Data Item	Variable Name	Data Type
a. Name of vendor company		
b. Inventory item name		
c. Inventory number		
d. Quantity		
e. Price		
f. Address of company		
g. Date last ordered		
h. Reorder quantity		
i. Obsolete item (yes/no)		

3. Name the data type for each of the following constants. Explain your answer.
   a. 5.38
   b. "87654"
   c. TRUE
   d. "A"
   e. "707–434–5555"
   f. "New York"
   g. −389
   h. 2.45E6
   i. 48976.0
   j. FALSE

4. What is a function?

5. Why are functions used?

6. What is the difference between the operators /, \, and MOD? Give an example of each.

7. Find the result of the following operations:
   a. 5 + 4
   b. 10/2
   c. TRUE OR FALSE
   d. 20 MOD 3
   e. 5 < 8
   f. 25 MOD 70
   g. "A" > "H"
   h. NOT TRUE
   i. 25\70
   j. FALSE AND TRUE
   k. 20 * .5
   l. 35 < = 35
   m. 35/7
   n. FALSE OR FALSE
   o. TRUE AND TRUE
   p. 50 MOD 5

(Question 7 continued on next page)

q. $-35 < 67$

r. $4.0 \wedge 3$

s. $60 \backslash 9$

t. $35 < 35$

u. TRUE AND FALSE

8. Using the hierarchy chart (Table 2.8), list the order in which the following operations would be processed. (Remember: operations are processed left to right within a level in the hierarchy table.)

a. $+, -, *$

b. $/, \backslash, =$

c. OR, $*, <$

d. NOT, AND, $*$

e. NOT, $>, +$

f. AND, OR, NOT

g. $<$, AND, $>, +$

h. $*, \wedge, +$

i. NOT, $+, \backslash$

j. MOD, $\backslash, <$

9. Name the data type of the operands and the resultant of each of the following expressions or equations.

	Data Types of Operands	Data Types of Resultant
a. A * B		
b. D > R		
c. NOT C		
d. B AND F		
e. G = B		

10. What is the difference between an expression and an equation?

11. What does the equal sign mean in an equation? Is the meaning of the equal sign as a relational operator different from that in an assignment statement?

Problems

1. Evaluate the following equations, given the values A = 12, B = 3, C = 6, D = 2:

a. $F = A + B/C - D \wedge 2$

b. $F = (A + B)/C - D \wedge 2$

c. $F = A + B/(C - D \wedge 2)$

d. $F = (A + B) \text{MOD } C$

e. $F = (A + B) \backslash D \wedge 2$

2. Write the following equations in computer form:

a. $X = Y + 3Z - \dfrac{Z + Y}{Z - 3}$

b. $X = 5Y + \dfrac{3Z - 1}{4(3Z + 1) - Y}$

$X = (X - Y)^2$

c. $X = (X - Y)^2$

3. Is the = sign an assignment instruction or a relational operator in the following equations? Justify your answer.
   a. $A = B + 2 + C$
   b. $A - B = 2 + C$

4. Set up an equation to calculate the following (create your own variable names):
   a. The area of a room.
   b. The wall area of a room including windows and doors.
   c. The wall area of a room not including 2 windows and a door.
   d. The number of miles given a number of feet. (Use 5280 feet per mile.)
   e. The percent increase (or decrease) of a value given the beginning number and the ending number. How would the result differ between increase and decrease?
   f. The average of 5 numbers.
   g. Sale price of an item given an original price and a percentage discount.

5. Evaluate the following equations given $A = 5, B = 4, C = 3, D = 12$
   a. $E = A * B + D / C$
   b. $E = D \text{ MOD } A * B$
   c. $E = 5 * A \setminus D * (B + 1)$
   d. $E = D / B * ((A + 4)\setminus(C + 1))$

6. An employee came in to work and clocked in at MORNING_IN, clocked out at NOON_OUT for lunch, clocked back in at NOON_IN, and clocked out to go home at NIGHT_OUT (all in minutes since midnight). Set up equations to calculate the number of hours and the number of minutes the employee worked for the day. (You will develop two equations.)

7. Steve Thompson bought and charged an electric saw on DATE1 and made the first payment on DATE2. Write an equation to calculate how many days (DAYS) elapsed between the two dates.

   DAYS =

8. Eureka Lumber Company gives a 2% discount if the remaining balance is paid within 10 days of purchase. Write a logical expression to verify whether or not a customer qualifies for this discount. Use the following variable names:

   BUYING_DATE: date the customer purchased the merchandise

   PAID_DATE: date the customer made the final payment

9. A part-time employee worked 20 hours in the first week and 15 hours in the second week of a two-week pay period. He is paid a weekly salary based on a 40-hour week. What is his full-time equivalent for the two weeks based on a 40-hour week (i.e., what percentage of full-time did he work)? Write a general equation that could be used to express and store the full-time equivalent of any hours worked per week.

   FULL_TIME =

10. Evaluate the following equations, given A = FALSE, B = TRUE, C = FALSE, D = TRUE. (Include the structure of the order of processing—see page 34 for example.)
    a. R = A AND B OR C AND D
    b. R = NOT (A AND B) OR NOT (D AND C)

(Problem 10 continued on next page)

c. R = (A OR B) AND (D OR C)

d. R = NOT (A AND B OR C) AND (A OR B AND D)

e. R = C OR NOT (A AND D) AND (A OR B) OR NOT (A OR C)

11. Create a table that gives all possible answers for the following logical equations. (Include the structure of the order of processing—see page 34 for example.) Make clear how you set up the table.

a. R = A OR B

b. R = NOT A OR B

c. R = A AND B AND (B OR C)

d. R = NOT (A OR B) AND NOT (B OR C)

e. R = B AND NOT (A OR C) OR NOT (B AND C)

12. Evaluate the following for the values A = 5, B = 2, C = TRUE, D = FALSE. (Include the structure of the order of processing.)

a. R = A + 3 > B − 1 AND C OR D

b. R = NOT C OR D OR A − 3 < = B

13. Set up a logical expression for the following conditions. A company gives a bonus at the end of each fiscal year. For an employee to get a bonus, the following must be true:

a. The employee has been working at the company for more than six months with no negative reports.

b. The employee has earned more than $5,000 during the fiscal year.

14. Set up a logical expression for the following conditions. A retail store has this check-cashing policy:

a. The customer must have a driver's license.

b. When the check is for more than $50, the customer must have a check-cashing card on file.

1. What is wrong with these variable names? Can you correct them?
   a. *City Name* referencing the name of a city.
   b. *Client-name* referencing a client name.
   c. *City/State* referencing a city and state.
   d. *LN* referencing a last name.
   e. *Street address*
   f. *Q* for a quantity of books
   g. *Street_Address_for_Joe's_Hardware_Supply_Incorporated_Client*

2. The answers given are wrong. What is the correct answer and why are the answers wrong?

The answer to:	is:
a. 5 mod 255	0
b. 250\100	2.5

3. What is wrong with the following expressions? Can you correct them?
   a. "L" < 5
   b. "D" * "5"
   c. TRUE < "F"
   d. FALSE >= 5

Higher National in Computing
103

Unit 4: Database Design Concepts

Learning hours: 60

NQF level 4: BTEC Higher National — H1

Content Selected: Hoffer, Modern Systems Analysis and Design 4th Edition, Chapter 12

Introduction from the Qualification Leader

Database development is a fundamental area of work and plays a key role for many organisations. This chapter has been selected because it focuses on a key learning objective within the syllabus, designing databases.

The chapter provides guidelines for well-structured and efficient database files and logical and physical database design. It provides concise definitions for a range of key terms within the area, including the complex area of normalisation. An applied approach is used throughout with lots of examples of how to structure data and problems and exercises.

Description of unit

Databases play an integral part in both academic and commercial domains, they provide users with a tool in which to store, model and retrieve data. Database development is fundamental to the area of computing and ICT as it offers so many links to other areas such as programming, systems analysis, HCI as well as embracing issues of compatibility and end user interfacing.

This core unit introduces learners to the practical aspects of designing a database. Learners will be expected to use applications software to a prescribed level in order to design, use basic tools, develop and demonstrate a database that is fully functional.

Summary of learning outcomes

To achieve this unit a learner must:

1   Understand **database environments**

2   Use and **manipulate** appropriate **database software**

3   **Design a database**

4   **Demonstrate the database.**

Content

1 **Database environments**

Database environment: examination of the database environment and its relationship with different users, platforms, issues of compatibility

DBMS: the emergence of the DBMS, what it is, how it is structured, how it works

Database uses: examine different case studies and organisational contexts in which databases are used. Look at the contrast in database use across a range of environments eg academic, medical, industrial etc

2 **Manipulate database software**

Database software: use appropriate applications software eg Microsoft Access or database tools and functions as part of an integrated software applications tool

Tools and techniques: tables, forms, dropdown lists, check boxes etc, reports, queries, macros, validation techniques

3 **Design a database**

Normalisation: normalise a data set to third normal form prior to building a database

Methodology: adopt a framework for the database design. Ensure that the design meets the given requirements of the specified user criteria

Documentation: user manual providing a step-by-step guide on how to use the database or part of the database, draft designs, test logs, evaluations

4 **Demonstrate the database**

Format: in a formal and professional environment demonstrate the database design giving clear explanations and justifications as to the overall structure

Documentation: instruction manuals to support the designs, printed screen shots to further clarify certain design decisions made, printed examples of reports

Outcomes and assessment criteria

Outcomes	Assessment criteria for pass
	To achieve each outcome a learner must demonstrate the ability to:
1 Understand **database environments**	• provide evidence to support a knowledge and understanding of database environments • examine a range of issues that are integral to database environments such as the end user, use across different platforms and compatibility • identify the importance of DBMS in commercial and non-commercial environments
2 Use and **manipulate** appropriate **database software**	• use database or database function applications software • develop a range of sample input and output screens eg tables, forms and reports, dropdown lists, checkboxes, etc • critique the software used and state how it will be used to develop your own database design
3 **Design a database**	• apply normalisation techniques to a given data set • use a range of database tools and techniques • design a fully working database
4 **Demonstrate** the use of a **database**	• demonstrate the database design to a third party • provide clear justifications as to the structure of the database or the use of particular tools and techniques • provide supporting documentation to complement the design

Chapter 12

Designing Interfaces and Dialogues

LEARNING OBJECTIVES

After studying this chapter, you should be able to:

- Explain the process of designing interfaces and dialogues and the deliverables for their creation.

- Contrast and apply several methods for interacting with a system.

- List and describe various input devices and discuss usability issues for each in relation to performing different tasks.

- Describe and apply the general guidelines for designing interfaces and specific guidelines for layout design, structuring data entry fields, providing feedback, and system help.

- Design human–computer dialogues and understand how dialogue diagramming can be used to design dialogues.

- Design graphical user interfaces.

- Discuss guidelines for the design of interfaces and dialogues for Internet-based electronic commerce systems.

INTRODUCTION

In this chapter, you learn about system interface and dialogue design. Interface design focuses on how information is provided to and captured from users; dialogue design focuses on the sequencing of interface displays. Dialogues are analogous to a conversation between two people. The grammatical rules followed by each person during a conversation are analogous to the interface. Thus, the design of interfaces and dialogues is the process of defining the manner in which humans and computers exchange information. A good human–computer interface provides a uniform structure for finding, viewing, and invoking the different components of a system. This chapter complements Chapter 11, which addressed design guidelines for the content of forms and reports. Here, you will learn about navigation between forms, alternative ways for users to cause forms and reports to appear, and how to supplement the content of forms and reports with user help and error messages, among other topics.

We then describe the process of designing interfaces and dialogues and the deliverables produced during this activity. This is followed by a section that describes interaction methods and devices. Next, interface design is described. This discussion focuses on layout design, data entry, providing feedback, and designing help. We then examine techniques for designing human–computer dialogues. Finally, we examine the design of interfaces and dialogues within electronic commerce applications.

DESIGNING INTERFACES AND DIALOGUES

This is the third chapter that focuses on design within the systems development life cycle (see Figure 12-1). In Chapter 11, you learned about the design of forms and reports. As you will see, the guidelines for designing forms and reports also apply to the design of human–computer interfaces.

The Process of Designing Interfaces and Dialogues

Similar to designing forms and reports, the process of designing interfaces and dialogues is a user-focused activity. This means that you follow a prototyping methodology of iteratively collecting information, constructing a prototype, assessing usability, and making refinements. To design usable interfaces and dialogues, you must answer the same who, what, when, where, and how questions used to guide the design of forms and reports (see Table 11-2). Thus, this process parallels that of designing forms and reports (see Lazar, 2004; McCracken et al., 2003).

Deliverables and Outcomes

The deliverable and outcome from system interface and dialogue design is the creation of a design specification. This specification is also similar to the specification

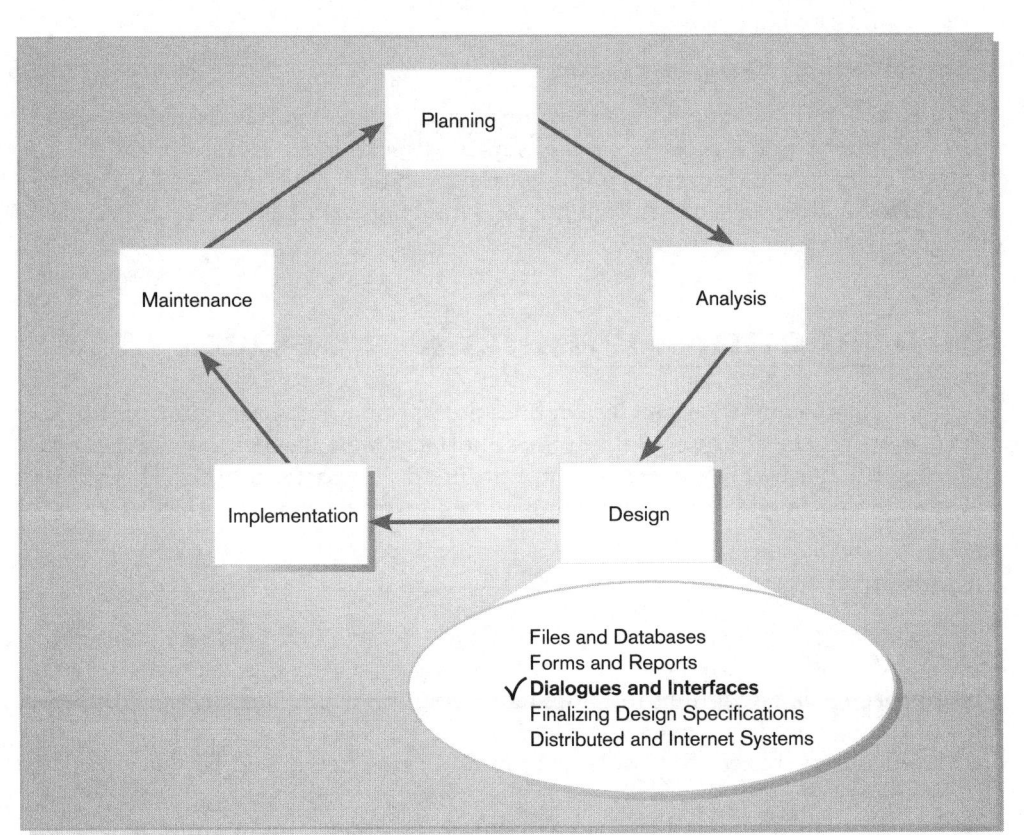

Figure 12-1
Systems development life cycle (SDLC)

Files and Databases
Forms and Reports
✓ **Dialogues and Interfaces**
Finalizing Design Specifications
Distributed and Internet Systems

Higher National in Computing

109

Figure 12-2
Specification outline for the design of interfaces and dialogues

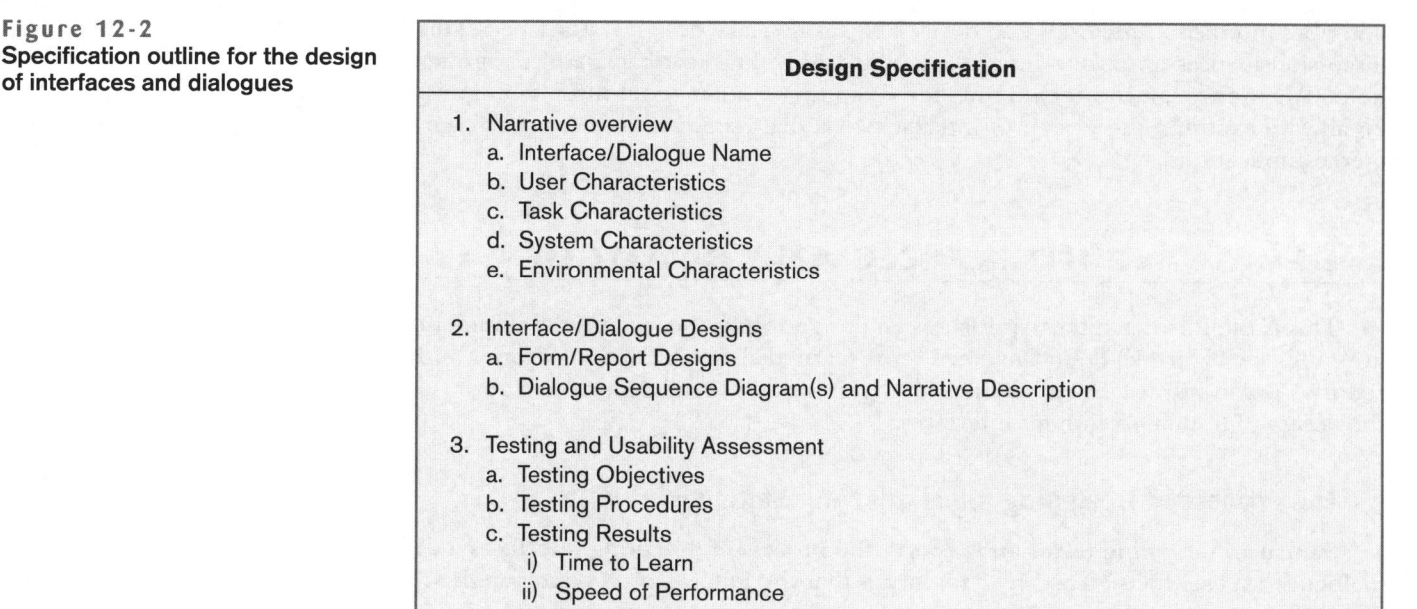

Design Specification

1. Narrative overview
   a. Interface/Dialogue Name
   b. User Characteristics
   c. Task Characteristics
   d. System Characteristics
   e. Environmental Characteristics

2. Interface/Dialogue Designs
   a. Form/Report Designs
   b. Dialogue Sequence Diagram(s) and Narrative Description

3. Testing and Usability Assessment
   a. Testing Objectives
   b. Testing Procedures
   c. Testing Results
      i) Time to Learn
      ii) Speed of Performance
      iii) Rate of Errors
      iv) Retention over Time
      v) User Satisfaction and Other Perceptions

produced for form and report designs—with one exception. Recall that the design specification document discussed in Chapter 11 had three sections (see Figure 11-4):

1. Narrative overview
2. Sample design
3. Testing and usability assessment

For interface and dialogue designs, one additional subsection is included: a section outlining the dialogue sequence—the ways a user can move from one display to another. Later in the chapter, you will learn how to design a dialogue sequence by using dialogue diagramming. An outline for a design specification for interfaces and dialogues is shown in Figure 12-2.

INTERACTION METHODS AND DEVICES

Interface: A method by which users interact with an information system.

The human–computer **interface** defines the ways in which users interact with an information system. All human–computer interfaces must have an interaction style and use some hardware device(s) for supporting this interaction. In this section, we describe various interaction methods and guidelines for designing usable interfaces.

Methods of Interacting

When designing the user interface, the most fundamental decision you make relates to the methods used to interact with the system. Given that there are numerous approaches for designing the interaction, we briefly provide a review of those most commonly used. (Readers interested in learning more about interaction methods are encouraged to see the books by Johnson [2000], Seffah and Javahery [2003], and Shneiderman and Plaisant [2004].) Our review will examine the basics of five widely used styles: command language, menu, form, object, and natural language.

We will also describe several devices for interacting, focusing primarily on their usability for various interaction activities.

Command Language Interaction In **command language interaction**, the user enters explicit statements to invoke operations within a system. This type of interaction requires users to remember command syntax and semantics. For example, to copy a file named PAPER.DOC from one storage location (C:) to another (A:) using Microsoft's disk operating system (DOS), a user would type

COPY C:PAPER.DOC A:PAPER.DOC

Command language interaction places a substantial burden on the user to remember names, syntax, and operations. Most newer or large-scale systems no longer rely entirely on a command language interface. Yet, command languages are good for experienced users, for systems with a limited command set, and for rapid interaction with the system.

A relatively simple application such as a word processor may have hundreds of commands for such operations as saving a file, deleting words, canceling the current action, finding a specific piece of data, or switching between windows. Some of the burden of assigning keys to actions has been taken off users' shoulders through the development of user interface standards such as those for the Macintosh, Microsoft Windows, or Java (Apple Computer, 1993; McKay, 1999; Sun Microsystems, 1999). For example, Figure 12-3a shows a help screen from Microsoft Word describing keyboard shortcuts, and Figure 12-3b shows the same screen for Microsoft Excel. Note how many of the same keys have been assigned the same function. Also note that designers still have great flexibility in how they interpret and implement these standards. This means that you still need to pay attention to usability factors and conduct formal assessments of designs.

Menu Interaction A significant amount of interface design research has stressed the importance of a system's ease of use and understandability. **Menu interaction** is a

Command language interaction: A human–computer interaction method whereby users enter explicit statements into a system to invoke operations.

Menu interaction: A human–computer interaction method in which a list of system options is provided and a specific command is invoked by user selection of a menu option.

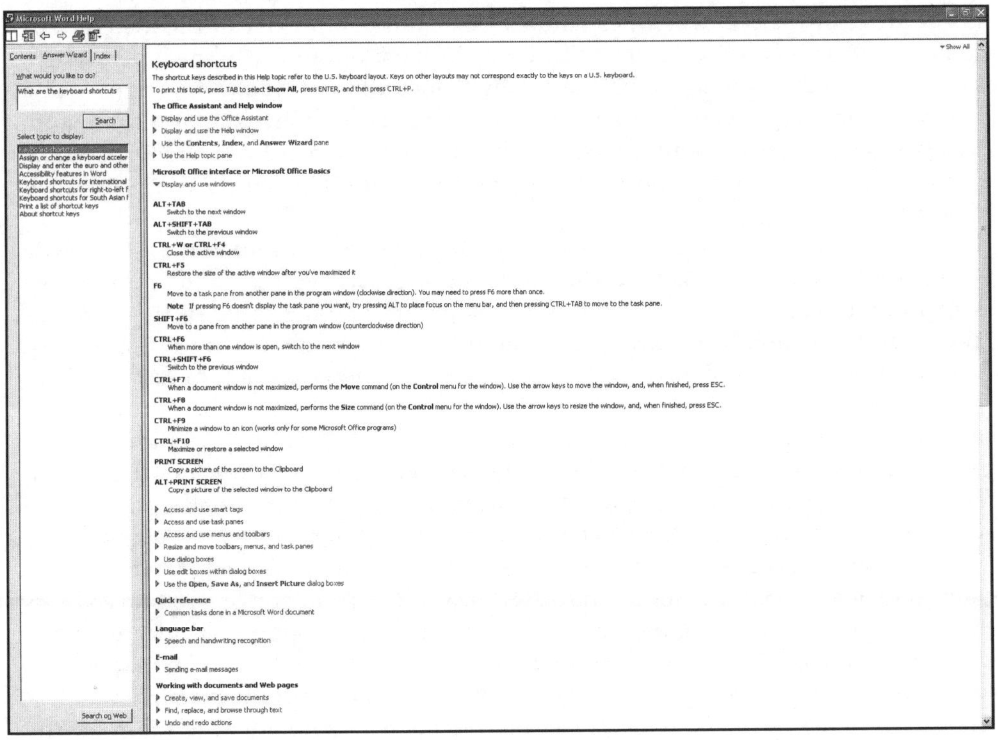

Figure 12-3
Function key assignments in Microsoft Office 97

(a) Help screen from Microsoft Word describing function key commands

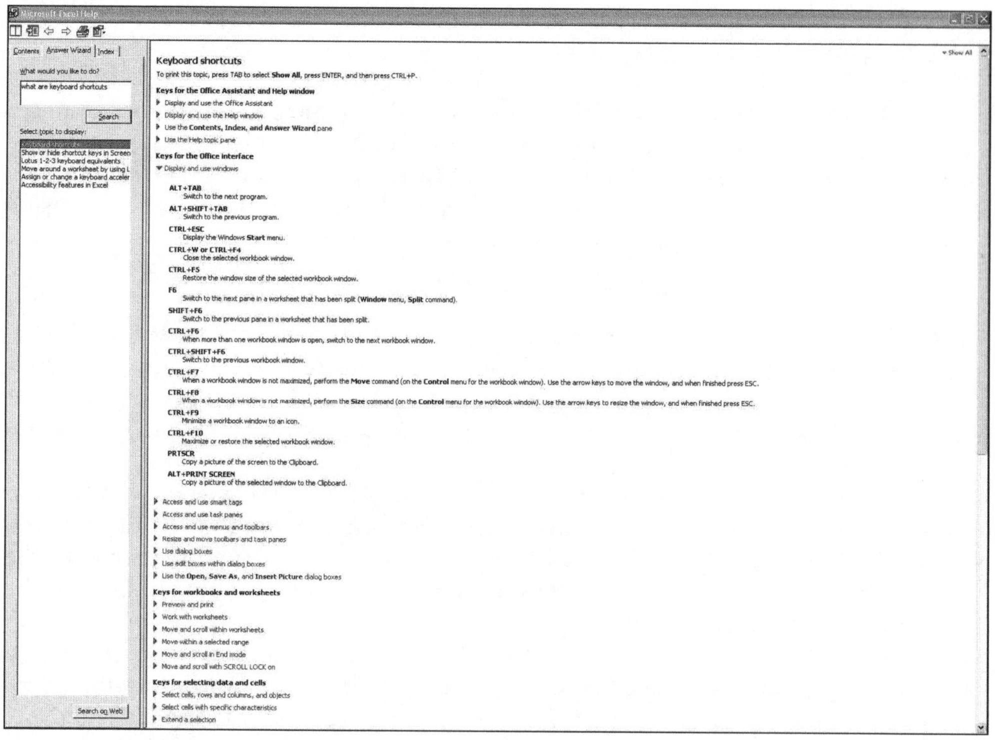

Figure 12-3 (continued)

(b) Help screen from Microsoft Excel describing function key commands

means by which many designers have accomplished this goal. A menu is simply a list of options; when an option is selected by the user, a specific command is invoked or another menu is activated. Menus have become the most widely used interface method because the user only needs to understand simple signposts and route options to effectively navigate through a system.

Menus can differ significantly in their design and complexity. The variation of their design is most often related to the capabilities of the development environment, the skills of the developer, and the size and complexity of the system. For smaller and less complex systems with limited system options, you may use a single menu or a linear sequence of menus. A single menu has obvious advantages over a command language but may provide little guidance beyond invoking the command. An example of a single menu (along the left edge of the screen) can be found on the popular screen capture program SnagIt by TechSmith Corporation, as shown in Figure 12-4.

For large and more complex systems, you can use menu hierarchies to provide navigation between menus. These hierarchies can be simple tree structures or variations wherein children menus have multiple parent menus. Some of these hierarchies may allow multilevel traversal. Variations as to how menus are arranged can greatly influence the usability of a system. Figure 12-5 shows a variety of ways in which menus can be structured and traversed. An arc on this diagram signifies the ability to move from one menu to another. Although more complex menu structures provide greater user flexibility, they may also confuse users about exactly where they are in the system. Structures with multiple parent menus also require the application to remember which path has been followed so that users can correctly backtrack.

Pop-up menu: A menu-positioning method that places a menu near the current cursor position.

There are two common methods for positioning menus. With a **pop-up menu** (also called a dialogue box), menus are displayed near the current cursor position so users don't have to move the position or their eyes to view system options (Figure 12-6a). A pop-up menu has a variety of potential uses. One is to show a list of commands relevant to the current cursor position (e.g., delete, clear, copy, or validate current field). Another is to provide a list of possible values (from a look-up table) to fill in for the

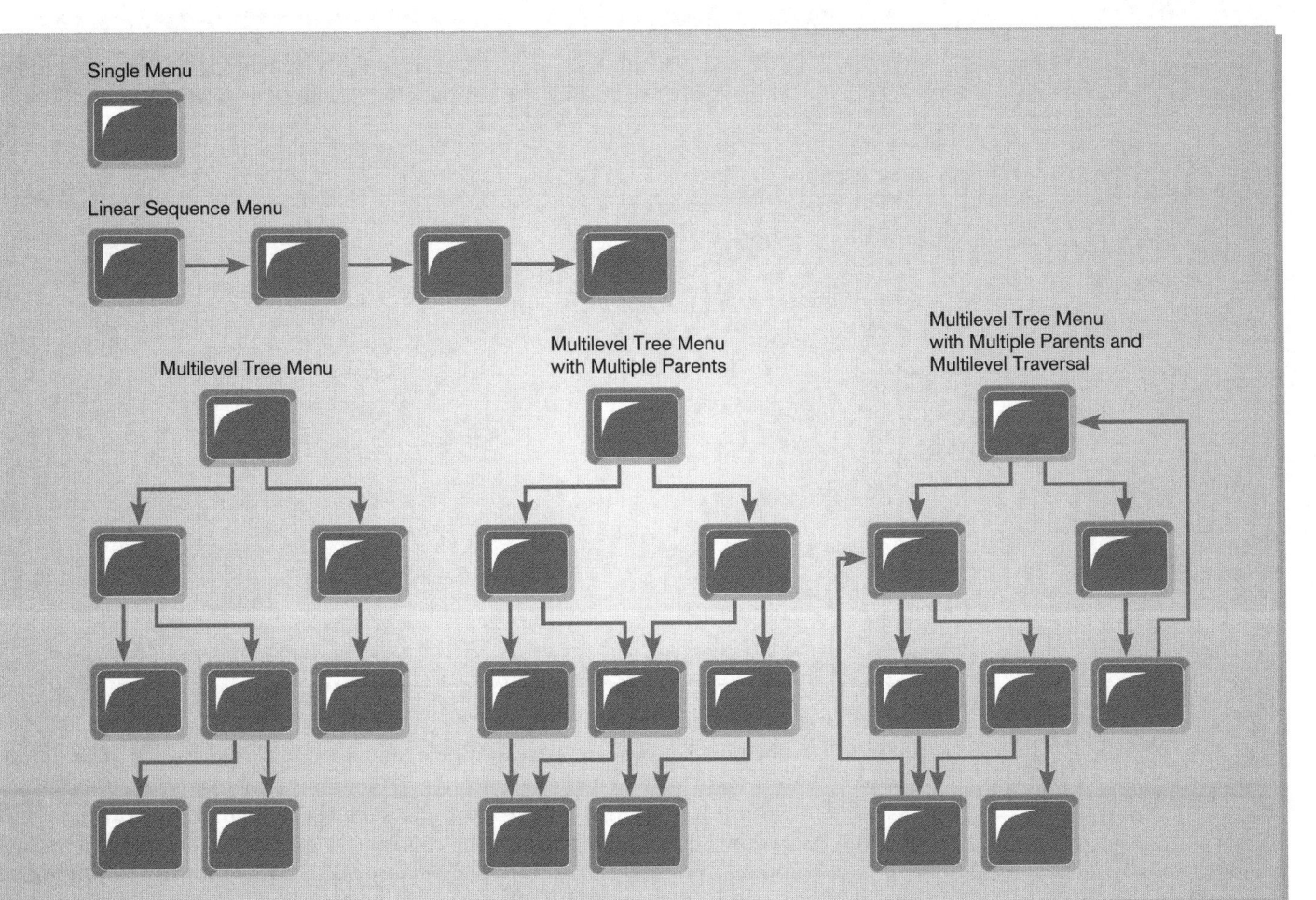

Figure 12-4
Single-level menu (along left edge of screen) from SnagIt ® by TechSmith.

Figure 12-5
Various types of menu configurations (Adapted from Schneiderman and Plaisant, 2004)

Higher National in Computing
113

Figure 12-6
Menus from Microsoft Word 2000

(a) Pop-up menu

(b) Drop-down menu

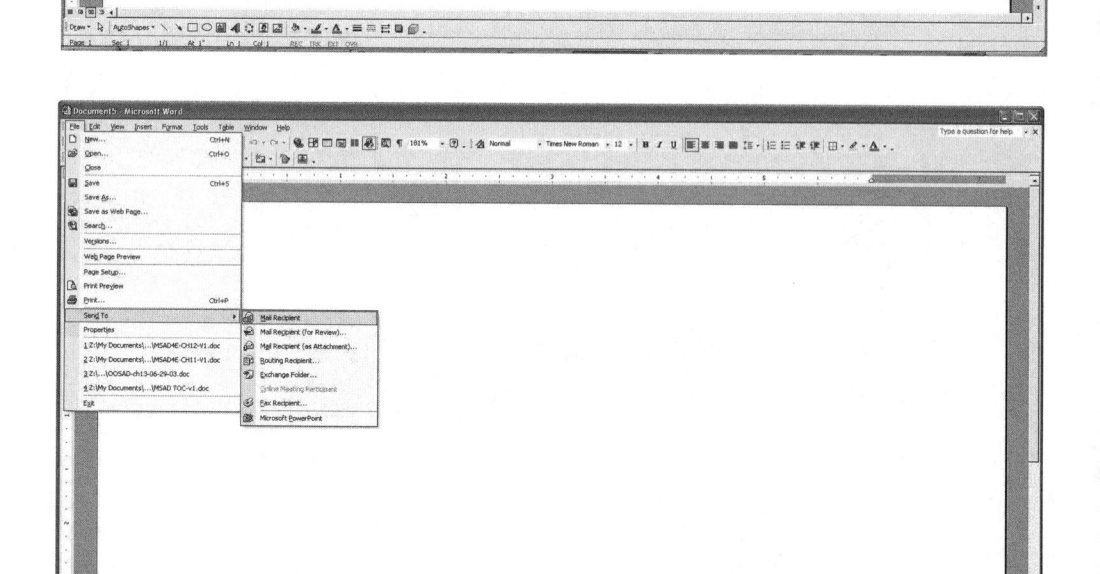

Drop-down menu: A menu-positioning method that places the access point of the menu near the top line of the display; when accessed, menus open by dropping down onto the display.

current field. For example, in a customer order form, a list of current customers could pop up next to the customer number field so the user can select the correct customer without having to know the customer's identifier. With a **drop-down menu**, menus drop down from the top line of the display (Figure 12-6b). Drop-down menus have become very popular in recent years because they provide consistency in menu location and operation among applications and efficiently use display space. Most

TABLE 12-1   Guidelines for Menu Design

Wording	• Each menu should have a meaningful title • Command verbs should clearly and specifically describe operations • Menu items should be displayed in mixed uppercase and lowercase letters and have a clear, unambiguous interpretation
Organization	• A consistent organizing principle should be used that relates to the tasks the intended users perform; for example, related options should be grouped together, and the same option should have the same wording and codes each time it appears
Length	• The number of menu choices should not exceed the length of the screen • Submenus should be used to break up exceedingly long menus
Selection	• Selection and entry methods should be consistent and reflect the size of the application and sophistication of the users • How the user is to select each option and the consequences of each option should be clear (e.g., whether another menu will appear)
Highlighting	• Highlighting should be minimized and used only to convey selected options (e.g., a check mark) or unavailable options (e.g., dimmed text)

advanced operating environments, such as Microsoft Windows or the Apple Macintosh, provide a combination of both pop-up and drop-down menus.

When designing menus, there are several general rules that should be followed, and these are summarized in Table 12-1. For example, each menu should have a meaningful title and be presented in a meaningful manner to users. A menu option of Quit, for instance, is ambiguous—does it mean return to the previous screen or exit the program? To more easily see how to apply these guidelines, Figure 12-7 contrasts a poorly designed menu with a menu that follows the menu design guidelines. Annotations on the two parts of this figure highlight poor and improved menu interface design features.

Many advanced programming environments provide powerful tools for designing menus. For example, Microsoft's Visual Basic .NET allows you to quickly design a menu structure for a system. For example, Figure 12-8 shows a design form in which a menu structure is being defined; menu items are added by selecting the "Type Here" tags and typing the words that represent each item on the menu. With the use of a few easily invoked options, you can also assign shortcut keys to menu items,

Figure 12-7
Contrasting menu designs

(a) Poor menu design

SYSTEM OPTIONS ← Vague title

01   ORDER INFO
02   ORDER STATUS ← Vague command names
03   SALESPERSON INFO
04   REPORTS
05   HELP ← All uppercase letters
06   QUIT

ENTER OPTION (01):__ ← Vague exit statement

Common options are not separated and assigned a standard key

Two-key selection

Higher National in Computing
115

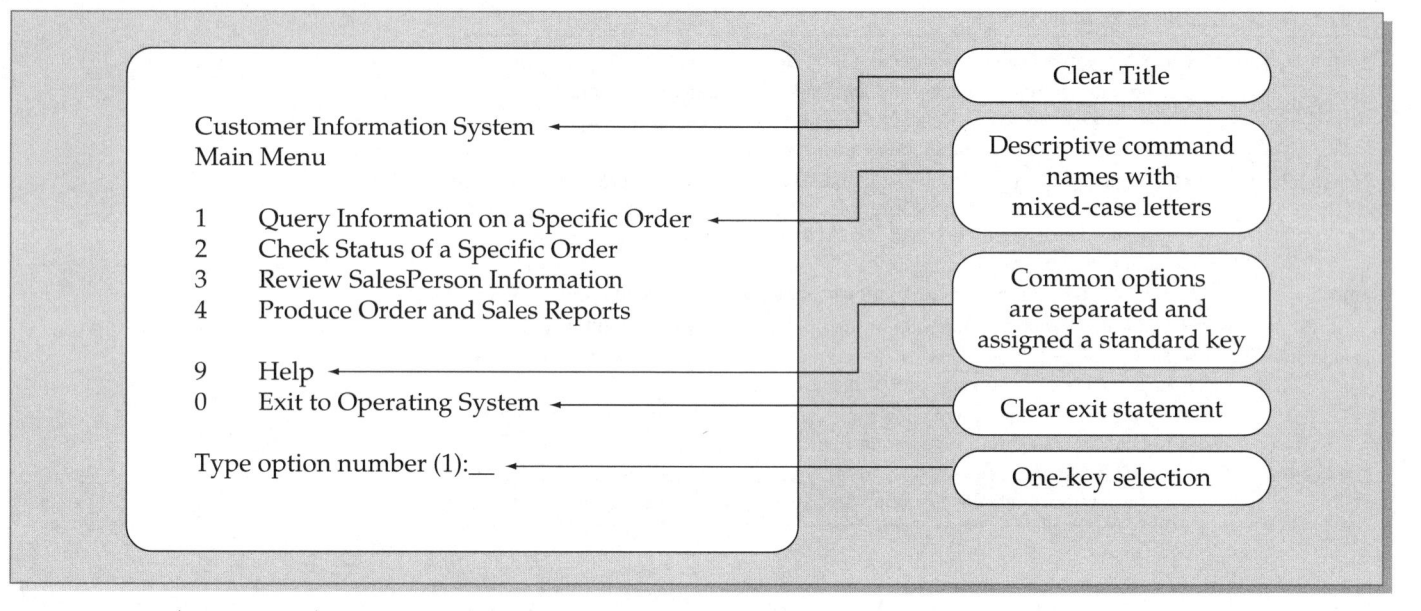

Figure 12-7 (continued)

(b) Improved menu design

connect help screens to individual menu items, define submenus, and set usage properties (see the Properties window within Figure 12-8). Usage properties, for example, include the ability to dim the color of a menu item while a program is running, indicating that a function is currently unavailable. Menu building tools allow a designer to quickly and easily prototype a design that will look exactly as it will in the final system.

Figure 12-8
Menu building with Microsoft Visual Basic. NET

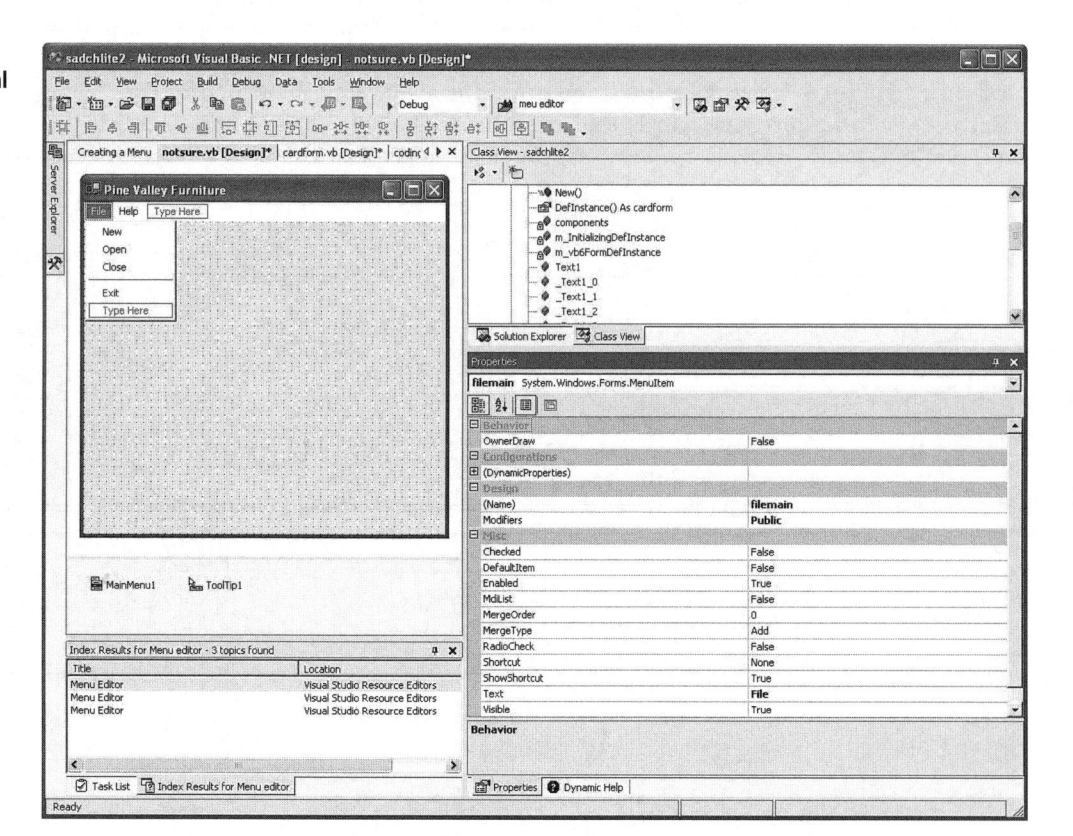

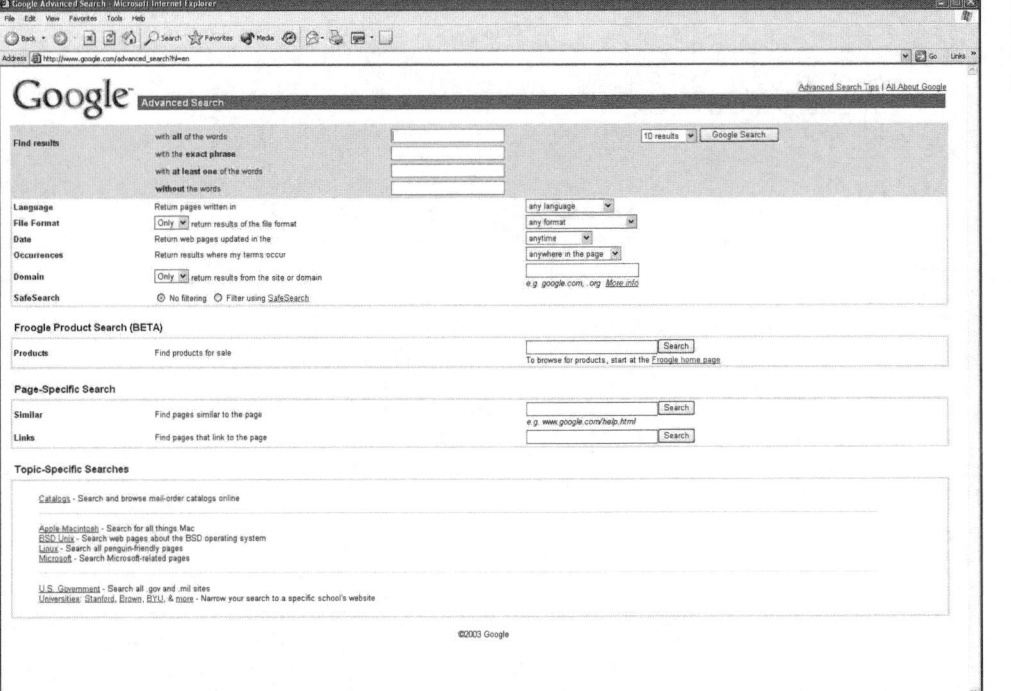

Figure 12-9
Example of form interaction from
the Google Advanced Search
Engine

Form Interaction   The premise of **form interaction** is to allow users to fill in the blanks when working with a system. Form interaction is effective for both the input and presentation of information. An effectively designed form includes a self-explanatory title and field headings, has fields organized into logical groupings with distinctive boundaries, provides default values when practical, displays data in appropriate field lengths, and minimizes the need to scroll windows (Shneiderman and Plaisant, 2004). You saw many other design guidelines for forms in Chapter 11. Form interaction is the most commonly used method for data entry and retrieval in business-based systems. Figure 12-9 shows a form from the Google Advanced Search engine. Using interactive forms, organizations can easily provide all types of information to Web surfers.

Form interaction: A highly intuitive human–computer interaction method whereby data fields are formatted in a manner similar to paper-based forms.

Object-Based Interaction   The most common method for implementing **object-based interaction** is through the use of icons. **Icons** are graphic symbols that look like the processing option they are meant to represent. Users select operations by pointing to the appropriate icon with some type of pointing device. The primary advantages to icons are that they take up little screen space and can be quickly understood by most users. An icon may also look like a button that, when selected or depressed, causes the system to take an action relevant to that form, such as cancel, save, edit a record, or ask for help. For example, Figure 12-10 illustrates an icon-based interface when entering Microsoft Visual Studio .NET.

Object-based interaction: A human–computer interaction method in which symbols are used to represent commands or functions.

Icon: Graphical pictures that represent specific functions within a system.

Natural Language Interaction   One branch of artificial intelligence research studies techniques for allowing systems to accept inputs and produce outputs in a conventional language such as English. This method of interaction is referred to as **natural language interaction.** Presently, natural language interaction is not as viable an interaction style as the other methods presented. Current implementations can be tedious, frustrating, and time-consuming for the user and are often built to accept input in narrowly constrained domains (e.g., database queries). Natural language interaction is being applied within both keyboard and voice entry systems.

Natural language interaction: A human–computer interaction method whereby inputs to and outputs from a computer-based application are in a conventional spoken language such as English.

Figure 12-10
Object-based (icon) interface from Microsoft Visual Basic .NET

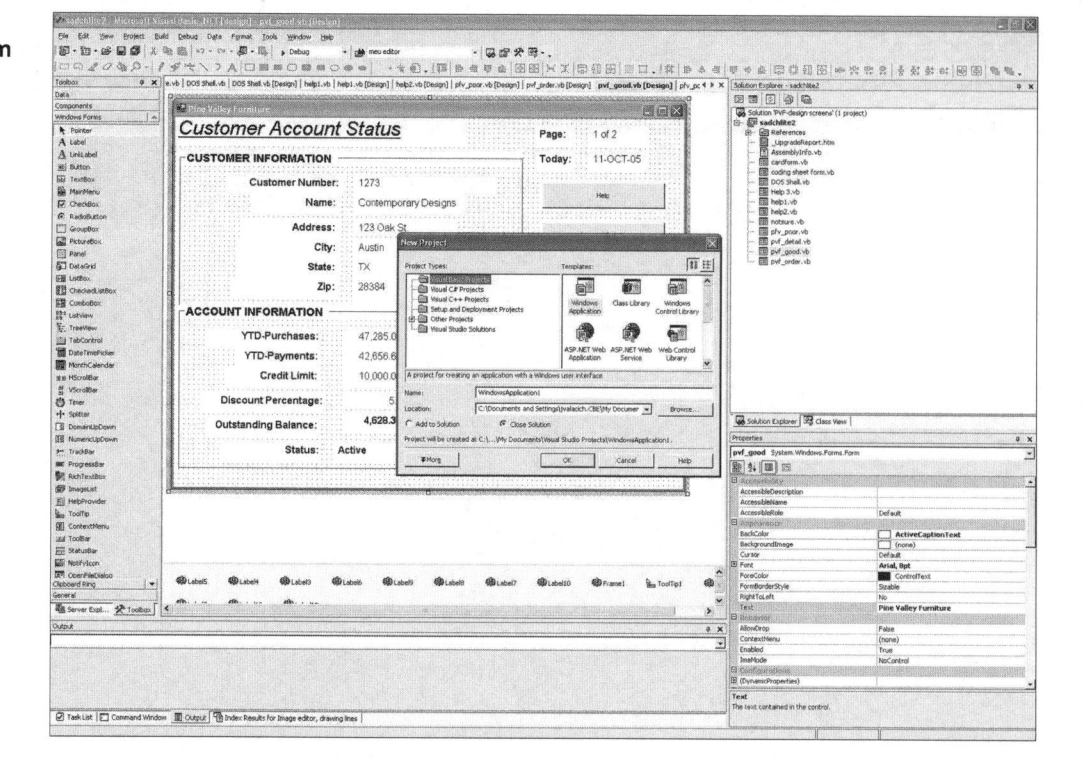

Hardware Options for System Interaction

In addition to the variety of methods used for interacting with a system, there is also a growing number of hardware devices employed to support this interaction (see Table 12-2 for a list of interaction devices along with brief descriptions of the typical usage of each). The most fundamental and widely used device is the keyboard, which is the mainstay of most computer-based applications for the entry of alphanumeric information. Keyboards vary, from the typewriter kind of keyboards used with personal computers to special-function keyboards on point-of-sale or shop-floor devices. The growth in graphical user environments, however, has spurred the broader use of pointing devices such as mice, joysticks, trackballs, and graphics tablets. The creation of notebook and pen-based computers with trackballs, joysticks, or pens attached directly to the computer has also brought renewed interest to the usability of these various devices.

Research has found that each device has its strengths and weaknesses. These strengths and weaknesses must guide your selection of the appropriate devices to aid users in their interaction with an application. The selection of an interaction device must be made during logical design, because different interfaces require different devices. Table 12-3 summarizes much of the usability assessment research by relating each device to various types of human–computer interaction problems. For example, for many applications, keyboards do not give users a precise feel for cursor movement, do not provide direct feedback on each operation, and can be a slow way to enter data (depending on the typing skill of the user). Another means to gain an understanding of device usability is to highlight which devices have been found most useful for completing specific tasks. The results of this research are summarized in Table 12-4. The rows of this table list common user–computer interaction tasks, and the columns show three criteria for evaluating the usability of the different devices. After reviewing these three tables, it should be evident that no device is perfect and that some are more appropriate for performing some tasks than others. To design the most effective interfaces for a given application, you should understand the capabilities of various interaction methods and devices.

N E T   S E A R C H

Some believed that voice interaction would become a dominant interaction method. Visit www.prenhall.com/hoffer to complete an exercise related to this topic.

TABLE 12-2   Common Devices for Interacting with an Information System

Device	Description and Primary Characteristics or Usage
Keyboard	Users push an array of small buttons that represent symbols which are then translated into words and commands. Keyboards are widely understood and provide considerable flexibility for interaction.
Mouse	A small plastic box that users push across a flat surface and whose movements are translated into cursor movement on a computer display. Buttons on the mouse tell the system when an item is selected. A mouse works well on flat desks but may not be practical in dirty or busy environments, such as a shop floor or check-out area in a retail store. Newer pen-based mice provide the user with more of the feel of a writing implement.
Joystick	A small vertical lever mounted on a base that steers the cursor on a computer display. Provides similar functionality to a mouse.
Trackball	A sphere mounted on a fixed base that steers the cursor on a computer display. A suitable replacement for a mouse when work space for a mouse is not available.
Touch Screen	Selections are made by touching a computer display. This works well in dirty environments or for users with limited dexterity or expertise.
Light Pen	Selections are made by pressing a pen-like device against the screen. A light pen works well when the user needs to have a more direct interaction with the contents of the screen.
Graphics Tablet	Moving a pen-like device across a flat tablet steers the cursor on a computer display. Selections are made by pressing a button or by pressing the pen against the tablet. This device works well for drawing and graphical applications.
Voice	Spoken words are captured and translated by the computer into text and commands. This is most appropriate for users with physical challenges or when hands need to be free to do other tasks while interacting with the application.

TABLE 12-3   Summary of Interaction Device Usability Problems

Device	Visual Blocking	User Fatigue	Movement Scaling	Durability	Adequate Feedback	Speed	Pointing Accuracy
Keyboard	□	□	■	□	■	■	□
Mouse	□	□	■	□	■	□	□
Joystick	□	□	■	□	■	□	■
Trackball	□	□	■	■	■	□	□
Touch Screen	■	■	□	■	□	□	■
Light Pen	■	■	□	□	□	□	■
Graphics Tablet	□	□	■	□	■	□	□
Voice	□	□	■	□	■	□	■

(*Source:* Adapted from Blattner & Schultz, 1988.)
Key:

□ = little or no usability problems
■ = potentially high usability problems for some applications
Visual Blocking = extent to which device blocks display when using
User Fatigue = potential for fatigue over long use
Movement Scaling = extent to which device movement translates to equivalent screen movement
Durability = lack of durability or need for maintenance (e.g., cleaning) over extended use
Adequate Feedback = extent to which device provides adequate feedback for each operation
Speed = cursor movement speed
Pointing Accuracy = ability to precisely direct cursor

Higher National in Computing
119

TABLE 12-4 Summary of General Conclusions from Experimental Comparisons of Input Devices in Relation to Specific Task Activities

Task	Most Accurate	Shortest Positioning	Most Preferred
Target Selection	trackball, graphics tablet, mouse, joystick	touch screen, light pen, mouse, graphics tablet, trackball	touch screen, light pen
Text Selection	mouse	mouse	—
Data Entry	light pen	light pen	—
Cursor Positioning	—	light pen	—
Text Correction	light pen, cursor keys	light pen	light pen
Menu Selection	touch screen	—	keyboard, touch screen

(*Source:* Adapted from Blattner & Schultz, 1988.)
Key:

Target Selection = moving the cursor to select a figure or item
Text Selection = moving the cursor to select a block of text
Data Entry = entering information of any type into a system
Cursor Positioning = moving the cursor to a specific position
Text Correction = moving the cursor to a location to make a text correction
Menu Selection = activating a menu item
— = no clear conclusion from the research

DESIGNING INTERFACES

Building on the information provided in Chapter 11 on the design of content for forms and reports, here we discuss issues related to the design of interface layouts. This discussion provides guidelines for structuring and controlling data entry fields, providing feedback, and designing online help. Effective interface design requires that you gain a thorough understanding of each of these concepts.

Designing Layouts

To ease user training and data recording, you should use standard formats for computer-based forms and reports similar to those used on paper-based forms and reports for recording or reporting information. A typical paper-based form for reporting customer sales activity is shown in Figure 12-11. This form has several general areas common to most forms:

- Header information
- Sequence and time-related information
- Instruction or formatting information
- Body or data details
- Totals or data summary
- Authorization or signatures
- Comments

In many organizations, data are often first recorded on paper-based forms and then later recorded within application systems. When designing layouts to record or display information on paper-based forms, you should try to make both as similar as possible. Additionally, data entry displays should be consistently formatted across applications to speed data entry and reduce errors. Figure 12-12 shows an equivalent computer-based form to the paper-based form shown in Figure 12-11.

Figure 12-11
Paper-based form for reporting
customer sales activity (Pine Valley
Furniture)

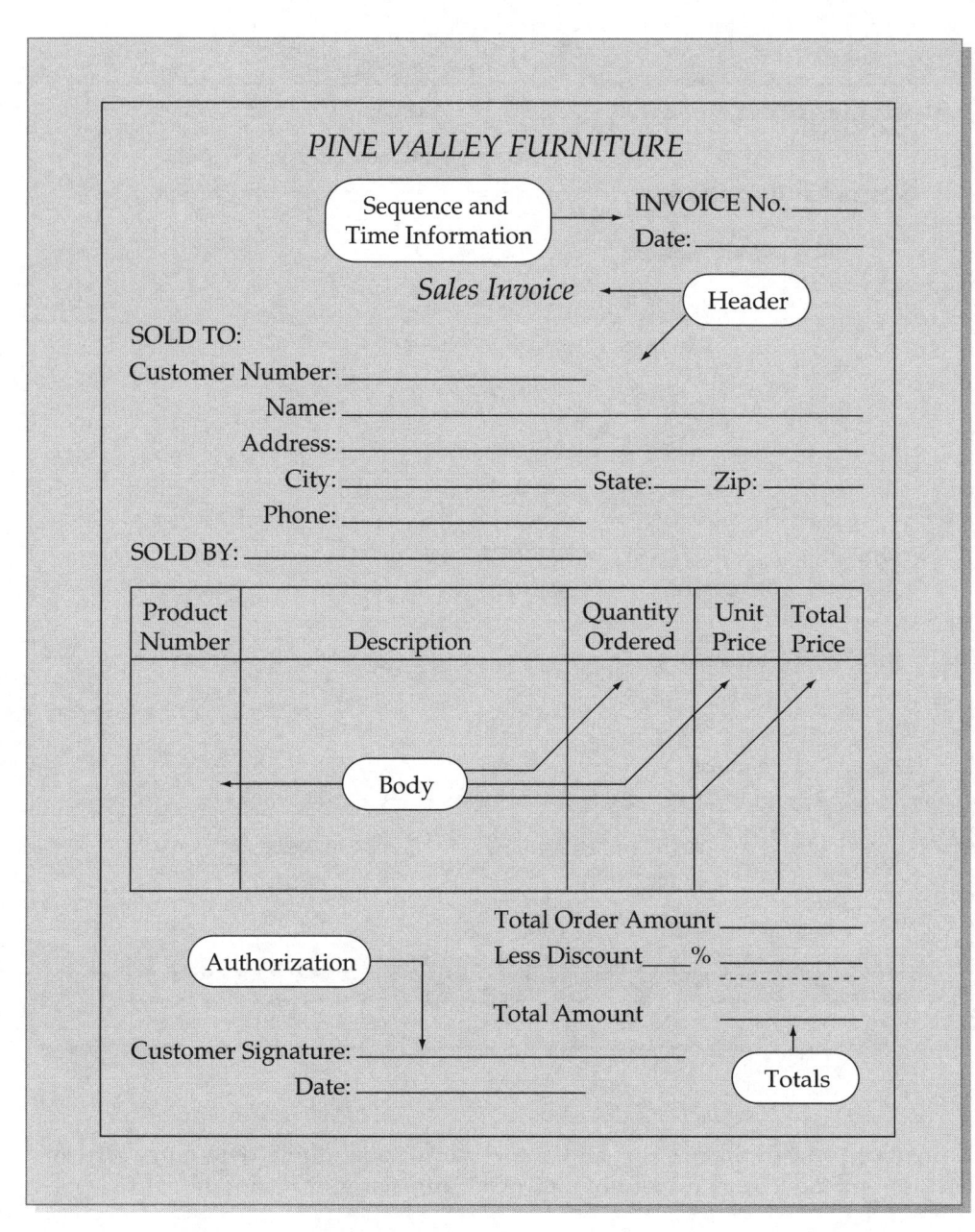

Another concern when designing the layout of computer-based forms is the design of between-field navigation. Because you can control the sequence for users to move between fields, standard screen navigation should flow from left to right and top to bottom just as when you work on paper-based forms. For example, Figure 12-13 contrasts the flow between fields on a form used to record business contacts. Figure 12-13a uses a consistent left-to-right, top-to-bottom flow. Figure 12-13b uses a flow that is nonintuitive. When appropriate, you should also group data fields into logical categories with labels describing the contents of the category. Areas of the screen not used for data entry or commands should be inaccessible to the user.

When designing the navigation procedures within your system, flexibility and consistency are primary concerns. Users should be able to freely move forward and backward or to any desired data entry fields. Users should be able to navigate each form in the same way or in as similar a manner as possible. Additionally, data should not *usually* be permanently saved by the system until the user makes an

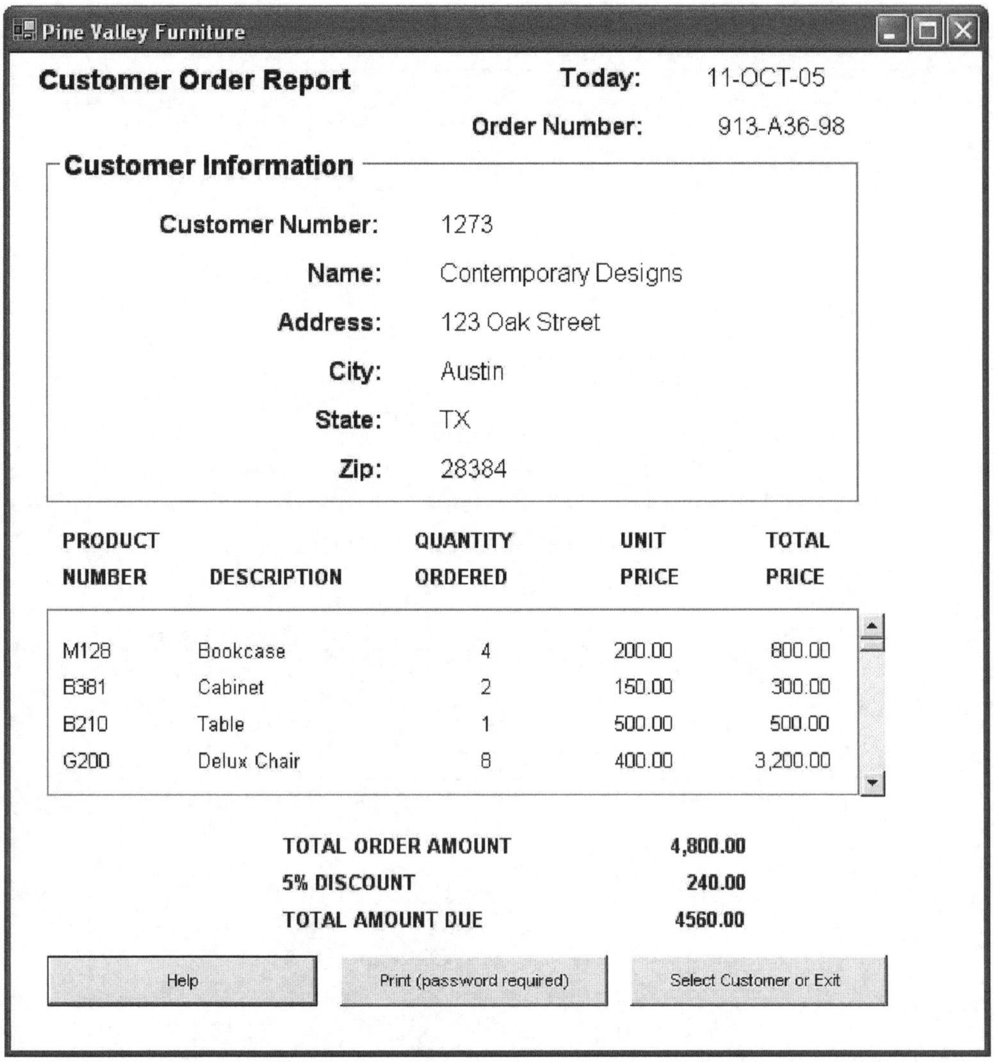

416

Figure 12-12
Computer-based form reporting customer sales activity (Pine Valley Furniture)

explicit request to do so. This allows the user to abandon a data entry screen, back up, or move forward without adversely impacting the contents of the permanent data.

Consistency extends to the selection of keys and commands. Each key or command should have only one function, and this function should be consistent throughout the entire system and across systems, if possible. Depending upon the application, various types of functional capabilities will be required to provide smooth navigation and data entry. Table 12-5 provides a list of the functional requirements for providing smooth and easy navigation within a form. For example, a functional and consistent interface will provide common ways for users to move the cursor to different places on the form, edit characters and fields, move among form displays, and obtain help. These functions may be provided by keystrokes, mouse or other pointing device operations, or menu selection or button activation. It is possible that, for a single application, all of the functional capabilities listed in Table 12-5 may not be needed in order to create a flexible and consistent user interface. Yet, the capabilities that are used should be consistently applied to provide an optimal user environment. As with other tables in Chapters 11 and 12, Table 12-5 can serve as a checklist for you to validate the usability of user interface designs.

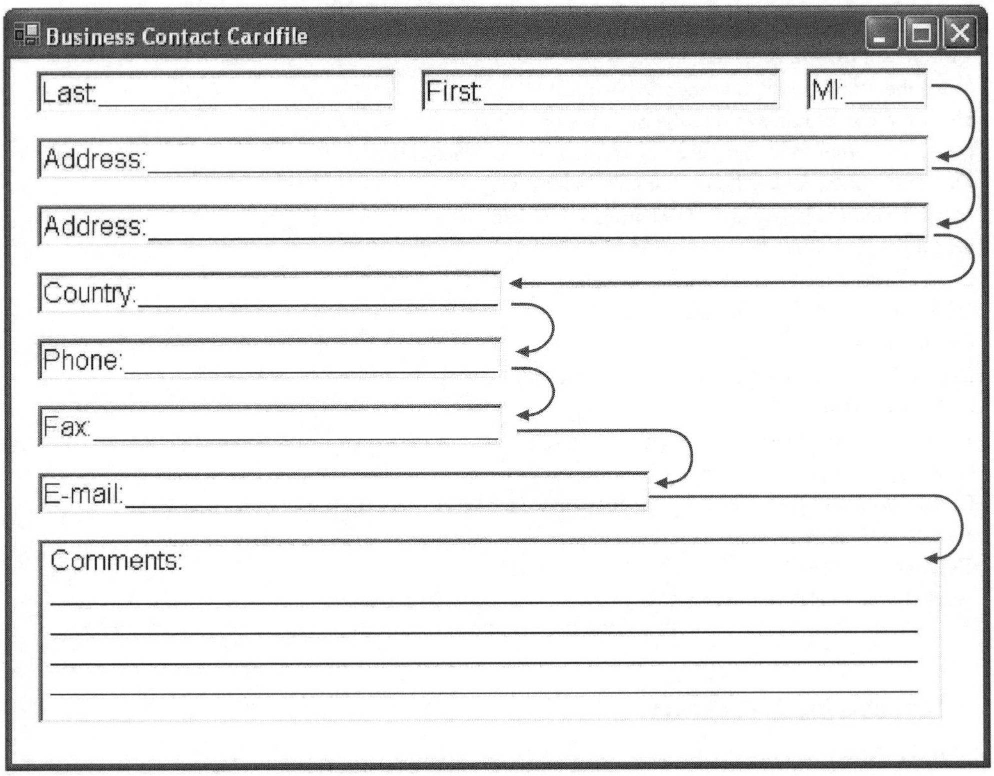

Figure 12-13
Contrasting the navigation flow within a data entry form
(a) Proper flow between data entry fields

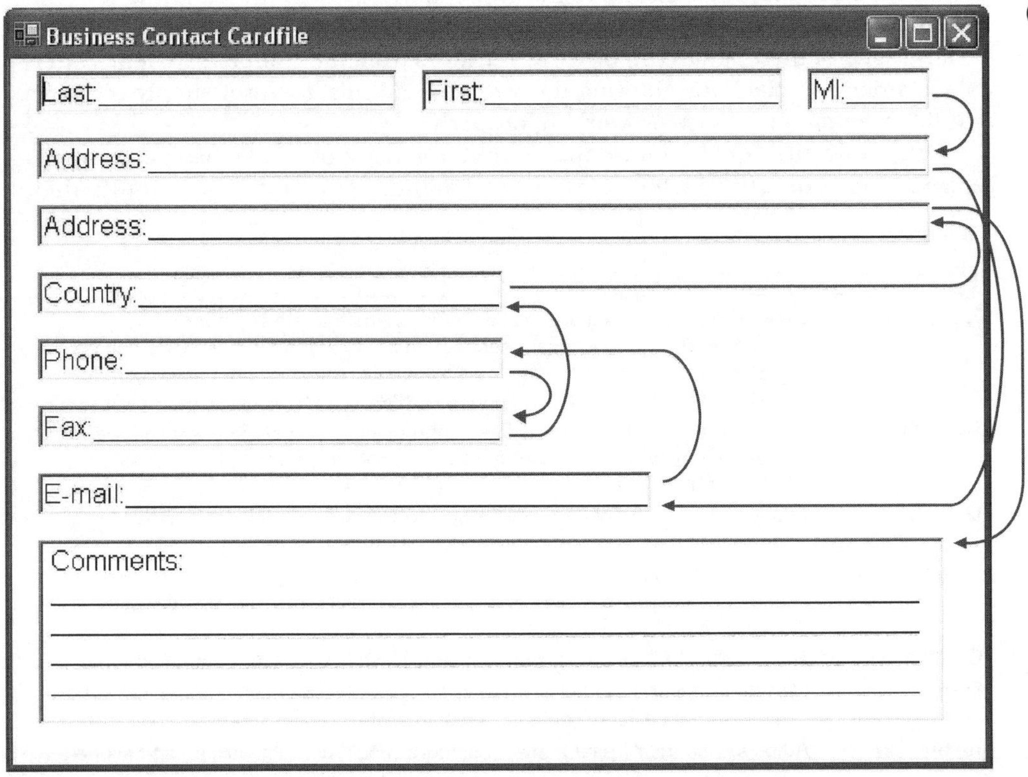

(b) Poor flow between data entry fields

TABLE 12-5   Data Entry Screen Functional Capabilities

Cursor Control Capabilities:
Move the cursor forward to the next data field
Move the cursor backward to the previous data field
Move the cursor to the first, last, or some other designated data field
Move the cursor forward one character in a field
Move the cursor backward one character in a field

Editing Capabilities:
Delete the character to the left of the cursor
Delete the character under the cursor
Delete the whole field
Delete data from the whole form (empty the form)

Exit Capabilities:
Transmit the screen to the application program
Move to another screen/form
Confirm the saving of edits or go to another screen/form

Help Capabilities:
Get help on a data field
Get help on a full screen/form

Structuring Data Entry

Several rules should be considered when structuring data entry fields on a form (see Table 12-6). The first is simple, but often violated by designers. To minimize data entry errors and user frustration, *never* require the user to enter information that is already available within the system or information that can be easily computed by the system. For example, never require the user to enter the current date and time, because each of these values can be easily retrieved from the computer system's internal calendar and clock. By allowing the system to do this, the user simply confirms that the calendar and clock are working properly.

Other rules are equally important. For example, suppose that a bank customer is repaying a loan on a fixed schedule with equal monthly payments. Each month when

TABLE 12-6   Guidelines for Structuring Data Entry Fields

Entry	Never require data that are already online or that can be computed; for example, do not enter customer data on an order form if those data can be retrieved from the database, and do not enter extended prices that can be computed from quantity sold and unit prices.
Defaults	Always provide default values when appropriate; for example, assume today's date for a new sales invoice, or use the standard product price unless overridden.
Units	Make clear the type of data units requested for entry; for example, indicate quantity in tons, dozens, pounds, etc.
Replacement	Use character replacement when appropriate; for example, allow the user to look up the value in a table or automatically fill in the value once the user enters enough significant characters.
Captioning	Always place a caption adjacent to fields; seeTable 14-7 for caption options.
Format	Provide formatting examples when appropriate; for example, automatically show standard embedded symbols, decimal points, credit symbol, or dollar sign.
Justify	Automatically justify data entries; numbers should be right justified and aligned on decimal points, and text should be left justified.
Help	Provide context-sensitive help when appropriate; for example, provide a hot key, such as the F1 key, that opens the help system on an entry that is most closely related to where the cursor is on the display.

TABLE 12-7   Options for Entering Text

Options	Example
Line caption	Phone Number ( ) -_____
Drop caption	( ) -_____ Phone Number
Boxed caption	Phone Number
Delimited characters	|(|||)|||-|||| Phone Number
Check-off boxes	Method of payment (check one) ☐ Check ☐ Cash ☐ Credit card: Type

a payment is sent to the bank, a clerk needs to record into a loan processing system that the payment has been received. Within such a system, default values for fields should be provided whenever appropriate. This means that *only* in the instances where the customer pays *more or less* than the scheduled amount should the clerk have to enter data into the system. In all other cases, the clerk would simply verify that the check is for the default amount provided by the system and press a single key to confirm the receipt of payment.

When entering data, the user should also not be required to specify the dimensional units of a particular value. For example, a user should not be required to specify that an amount is in dollars or that a weight is in tons. Field formatting and the data entry prompt should make clear the type of data being requested. In other words, a caption describing the data to be entered should be adjacent to each data field. Within this caption, it should be clear to the user what type of data is being requested. As with the display of information, all data entered onto a form should automatically justify in a standard format (e.g., date, time, money). Table 12-7 illustrates a few options appropriate for printed forms. For data entry on video display terminals, you should highlight the area in which text is entered so that the exact number of characters per line and number of lines are clearly shown. You can also use check boxes or radio buttons to allow users to choose standard textual responses. And, you can use data entry controls to ensure that the proper type of data (alphabetic or numeric, as required) are entered. Data entry controls are discussed next.

Controlling Data Input

One objective of interface design is to reduce data entry errors. As data are entered into an information system, steps must be taken to ensure that the input is valid. As a systems analyst, you must anticipate the types of errors users may make and design features into the system's interfaces to avoid, detect, and correct data entry mistakes. Several types of data errors are summarized in Table 12-8. In essence, data errors can occur from appending extra data onto a field, truncating characters off a field, transcripting the wrong characters into a field, or transposing one or more characters within a field. Systems designers have developed numerous tests and techniques for catching invalid data before saving or transmission, thus improving the likelihood that data will be valid (see Table 12-9 for a summary of these techniques). These tests and techniques are often incorporated into both data entry screens and intercomputer data transfer programs.

Practical experience has also found that it is much easier to correct erroneous data before they are permanently stored in a system. Online systems can notify a user of input problems as data are being entered. When data are processed online as

TABLE 12-8   Sources of Data Errors

Data Error	Description
Appending	Adding additional characters to a field
Truncating	Losing characters from a field
Transcripting	Entering invalid data into a field
Transposing	Reversing the sequence of one or more characters in a field

TABLE 12-9   Validation Tests and Techniques to Enhance the Validity of Data Input

Validation Test	Description
Class or Composition	Test to assure that data are of proper type (e.g., all numeric, all alphabetic, alphanumeric)
Combinations	Test to see if the value combinations of two or more data fields are appropriate or make sense (e.g., does the quantity sold make sense given the type of product?)
Expected Values	Test to see if data are what is expected (e.g., match with existing customer names, payment amount, etc.)
Missing Data	Test for existence of data items in all fields of a record (e.g., is there a quantity field on each line item of a customer order?)
Pictures/Templates	Test to assure that data conform to a standard format (e.g., are hyphens in the right places for a student ID number?)
Range	Test to assure data are within proper range of values (e.g., is a student's grade point average between 0 and 4.0?)
Reasonableness	Test to assure data are reasonable for situation (e.g., pay rate for a specific type of employee)
Self-Checking Digits	Test where an extra digit is added to a numeric field in which its value is derived using a standard formula (see Figure 12-14)
Size	Test for too few or too many characters (e.g., is social security number exactly nine digits?)
Values	Test to make sure values come from set of standard values (e.g., two-letter state codes)

events occur, it is much less likely that data validity errors will occur and not be caught. In an online system, most problems can be easily identified and resolved before permanently saving data to a storage device using many of the techniques described in Table 12-9. However, in systems where inputs are stored and entered (or transferred) in batch, the identification and notification of errors is more difficult. Batch processing systems can, however, reject invalid inputs and store them in a log file for later resolution.

Most of the tests and techniques shown in Table 12-9 are widely used and straightforward. Some of these tests can be handled by data management technologies, such as a database management system (DBMS), to ensure that they are applied for all data maintenance operations. If a DBMS cannot perform these tests, then you must design the tests into program modules. An example of one item that is a bit sophisticated, self-checking digits, is shown in Figure 12-14. The figure provides a description and an outline of how to apply the technique as well as a short example. The example shows how a check digit is added to a field before data entry or transfer. Once entered or transferred, the check digit algorithm is again applied to the field to "check" whether the check digit received obeys the calculation. If it does, it is likely (but not guaranteed, because two different values could yield the same check digit) that no data transmission or entry error occurred. If the transferred value does not equal the calculated value, then some type of error occurred.

In addition to validating the data values entered into a system, controls must be established to verify that all input records are correctly entered and that they are only processed once. A common method used to enhance the validity of entering batches of data records is to create an audit trail of the entire sequence of data entry, processing, and storage. In such an audit trail, the actual sequence, count, time, source location, human operator, and so on are recorded into a separate transaction log in the event of a data input or processing error. If an error occurs, corrections can be made by reviewing the contents of the log. Detailed logs of data inputs are not only useful for resolving batch data entry errors and system audits, but also serve as a powerful method for performing backup and recovery operations in the case of a

Figure 12-14
Using check digits to verify data correctness

Description	Techniques where extra digits are added to a field to assist in verifying its accuracy
Method	1. Multiply each digit of a numeric field by a weighting factor (e.g., 1, 2, 1, 2, _). 2. Sum the results of weighted digits. 3. Divide sum by modulus number (e.g., 10). 4. Subtract remainder of division from modulus number to determine check digit. 5. Append check digits to field.
Example	Assume a numeric part number of: 12473

Example (continued):

1-2. Multiply each digit of part number by weighting factor from right to left and sum the results of weighted digits:

$$
\begin{array}{ccccc}
1 & 2 & 4 & 7 & 3 \\
\times 1 & \times 2 & \times 1 & \times 2 & \times 1 \\
\hline
1 + & 4 + & 4 + & 14 + & 3 = 26
\end{array}
$$

3. Divide sum by modulus number.

   $26/10 = 2$ remainder 6

4. Subtract remainder from modulus number to determine check digit.

   check digit $= 10 - 6 = 4$

5. Append check digits to field.

   Field value with appended check digit $= 124734$

catastrophic system failure. These types of file and database controls are discussed further in Hoffer et al. (2005).

Providing Feedback

When talking with a friend, you would be concerned if he or she did not provide you with feedback by nodding and replying to your questions and comments. Without feedback, you would be concerned that he or she was not listening, likely resulting in a less-than-satisfactory experience. Similarly, when designing system interfaces, providing appropriate feedback is an easy method for making a user's interaction more enjoyable; not providing feedback is a sure way to frustrate and confuse. There are three types of system feedback:

1. Status information
2. Prompting cues
3. Error or warning messages

Status Information Providing status information is a simple technique for keeping users informed of what is going on within a system. For example, relevant status information such as displaying the current customer name or time, placing appropriate titles on a menu or screen, or identifying the number of screens following the current one (e.g., Screen 1 of 3) all provide needed feedback to the user. Providing status information during processing operations is especially important if the operation takes longer than a second or two. For example, when opening a file you might display "Please wait while I open the file" or, when performing a large calculation, flash the message "Working . . ." to the user. Further, it is important to tell

N E T   S E A R C H

Users have limits on how long they will patiently wait for a system to respond. Visit www.prenhall. com/hoffer to complete an exercise related to this topic.

the user that besides working, the system has accepted the user's input and that the input was in the correct form. Sometimes it is important to give the user a chance to obtain more feedback. For example, a function key could toggle between showing a "Working . . ." message and giving more specific information as each intermediate step is accomplished. Providing status information will reassure users that nothing is wrong and make them feel in command of the system, not vice versa.

Prompting Cues   A second feedback method is to display prompting cues. When prompting the user for information or action, it is useful to be specific in your request. For example, suppose a system prompted users with the following request:

READY FOR INPUT: _____

With such a prompt, the designer assumes that the user knows exactly what to enter. A better design would be specific in its request, possibly providing an example, default values, or formatting information. An improved prompting request might be as follows:

Enter the customer account number (123–456–7): ____-____-__

Errors and Warning Messages   A final method available to you for providing system feedback is using error and warning messages. Practical experience has found that a few simple guidelines can greatly improve their usefulness. First, messages should be specific and free of error codes and jargon. Additionally, messages should never scold the user and should attempt to guide the user toward a resolution. For example, a message might say "No customer record found for that Customer ID. Please verify that digits were not transposed." Messages should be in user, not computer, terms. Hence, such terms as "end of file," "disk I/O error," or "write protected" may be too technical and not helpful for many users. Multiple messages can be useful so that a user can get more detailed explanations if wanted or needed. Also, error messages should appear in roughly the same format and placement each time so that they are recognized as error messages and not as some other information. Examples of good and bad messages are provided in Table 12-10. Using these guidelines, you will be able to provide useful feedback in your designs. A special type of feedback is answering help requests from users. This important topic is described next.

N E T   S E A R C H

Standard error messages have emerged for Internet-related computing that some believe are very cryptic and difficult to understand. Visit www.prenhall.com/hoffer to complete an exercise related to this topic.

Providing Help

Designing how to provide help is one of the most important interface design issues you will face. When designing help, you need to put yourself in the user's place. When accessing help, the user likely does not know what to do next, does not understand what is being requested, or does not know how the requested information needs to be formatted. A user requesting help is much like a ship in distress

TABLE 12-10   Examples of Poor and Improved Error Messages

Poor Error Messages	Improved Error Messages
ERROR 56 OPENING FILE	The file name you typed was not found. Press F2 to list valid file names.
WRONG CHOICE	Please enter an option from the menu.
DATA ENTRY ERROR	The prior entry contains a value outside the range of acceptable values. Press F9 for list of acceptable values.
FILE CREATION ERROR	The file name you entered already exists. Press F10 if you want to overwrite it. Press F2 if you want to save it to a new name.

TABLE 12-11 Guidelines for Designing Usable Help

Guideline	Explanation
Simplicity	Use short, simple wording, common spelling, and complete sentences. Give users only what they need to know, with ability to find additional information.
Organize	Use lists to break information into manageable pieces.
Show	Provide examples of proper use and the outcomes of such use.

sending an SOS. In Table 12-11, we provide our SOS guidelines for the design of system help: simplicity, organize, and show. Our first guideline, *simplicity*, suggests that help messages should be short, to the point, and use words that enable understanding. This leads to our second guideline, *organize*, which means that help messages should be written so that information can be easily absorbed by users. Practical experience has found that long paragraphs of text are often difficult for people to understand. A better design organizes lengthy information in a manner that is easier for users to digest through the use of bulleted and ordered lists. Finally, it is often useful to explicitly *show* users how to perform an operation and the outcome of procedural steps. Figures 12-15 a and b show the contrasts between two help screen designs, one employing our guidelines and one that does not.

Many commercially available systems provide extensive system help. For example, Table 12-12 lists the range of help available in a popular electronic spreadsheet. Many systems are also designed so that users can vary the level of detail provided. Help may be provided at the system level, screen or form level, and individual field level. The ability to provide field level help is often referred to as "context-sensitive" help. For some applications, providing context-sensitive help for all system options is a tremendous undertaking that is virtually a project in itself. If you do decide to design an extensive help system with many levels of detail, you must be sure that you know exactly what the user needs help with, or your efforts may confuse users more than help them. After leaving a help screen, users should always return to where they

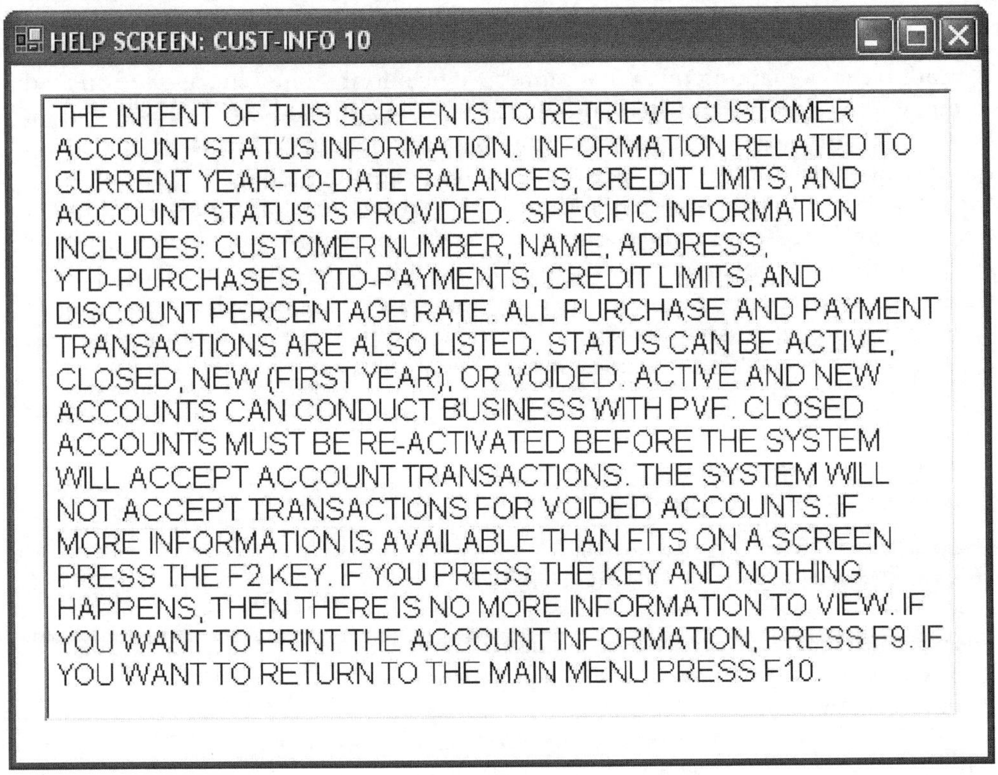

Figure 12-15
Contrasting help screens
(a) Poorly designed help display

Higher National in Computing

Figure 12-15 (continued)

(b) Improved design for help display

Help

Help Information — *Reviewing Customer Account Status*

The intent of this screen is to retrieve customer account status information. Information related to current year-to-date balances, credit limits, and account status is provided.

Field

1. Customer Number	PVF assigned customer number
2. Name / Address	full customer name and mailing address
3. YTD-Purchases	total of current-year purchases
4. YTD-Payments	total of current-year payments
5. Credit Limit	maximum outstanding balance
6. Outstanding Balance	current account balance
7. Discount Percentage	sales discount rate
8. Status	current account status

Description of Account Status:

1. Active	in good standing
2. Closed	no longer a current account; must reapply to change status to active
3. New	in good standing but a customer for < 1 year
4. Voided	not in good standing (e.g., an excessive balance)

Special Function Keys:

F1 = Help (displays this screen)
F2 = Account Details (is only displayed if > 1 page is available)
F9 = Print (prints "Customer Status Report")
F10 = Return (returns to prior screen)

were prior to requesting help. If you follow these simple guidelines, you will likely design a highly usable help system.

As with the construction of menus, many programming environments provide powerful tools for designing system help. For example, Microsoft's HTML Help environment allows you to quickly construct hypertext-based help systems. In this environment, you use a text editor to construct help pages that can be easily linked to other pages containing related or more specific information. Linkages are created by embedding special characters into the text document that make words hypertext buttons—that is, direct linkages—to additional information. HTML Help transforms the text document into a hypertext document. For example, Figure 12-16 shows a hypertext-based help screen from Microsoft's Internet Explorer. Hypertext-based help systems have become the standard for most commercial applications. This has occurred for two primary reasons. First, standardizing system help across applications eases user training. Second, hypertext allows users to selectively access the level of help they need, making it easier to provide effective help for both novice and experienced users within the same system.

TABLE 12-12   Types of Help

Type of Help	Example of Question
Help on Help	How do I get help?
Help on Concepts	What is a customer record?
Help on Procedures	How do I update a record?
Help on Messages	What does "Invalid File Name" mean?
Help on Menus	What does "Graphics" mean?
Help on Function Keys	What does each Function key do?
Help on Commands	How do I use the "Cut" and "Paste" commands?
Help on Words	What do "merge" and "sort" mean?

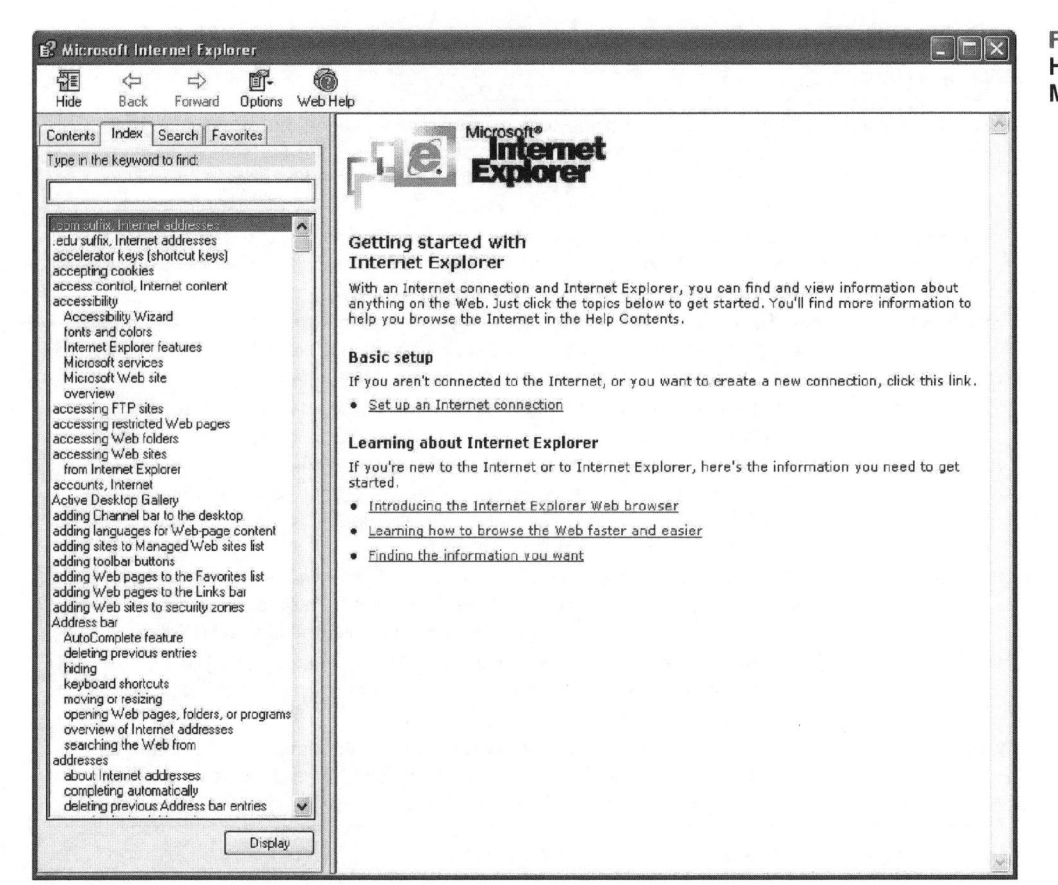

Figure 12-16
Hypertext-based help system from Microsoft's Internet Explorer

DESIGNING DIALOGUES

The process of designing the overall sequences that users follow to interact with an information system is called dialogue design. A **dialogue** is the sequence in which information is displayed to and obtained from a user. As the designer, your role is to select the most appropriate interaction methods and devices (described earlier) and to define the conditions under which information is displayed to and obtained from users. The dialogue design process consists of three major steps:

Dialogue: The sequence of interaction between a user and a system.

1. Designing the dialogue sequence
2. Building a prototype
3. Assessing usability

A few general rules that should be followed when designing a dialogue are summarized in Table 12-13. For a dialogue to have high usability, it must be consistent in form, function, and style. All other rules regarding dialogue design are mitigated by the consistency guideline. For example, the effectiveness of how well errors are handled or feedback is provided will be significantly influenced by consistency in design. If the system does not consistently handle errors, the user will often be at a loss as to why certain things happen.

One example of these guidelines concerns removing data from a database or file (see the Reversal entry in Table 12-13). It is good practice to display the information that will be deleted before making a permanent change to the file. For example, if the customer service representative wanted to remove a customer from the database, the system should ask only for the customer ID in order to retrieve the correct customer account. Once found, and before allowing the confirmation of the deletion, the system should display the account information. For actions making permanent changes to system data files and when the action is not commonly performed,

Higher National in Computing
131

TABLE 12-13 Guidelines for the Design of Human–Computer Dialogues

Guideline	Explanation
Consistency	Dialogues should be consistent in sequence of actions, keystrokes, and terminology (e.g., the same labels should be used for the same operations on all screens, and the location of the same information should be the same on all displays).
Shortcuts and Sequence	Allow advanced users to take shortcuts using special keys (e.g., CTRL-C to copy highlighted text). A natural sequence of steps should be followed (e.g., enter first name before last name, if appropriate).
Feedback	Feedback should be provided for every user action (e.g., confirm that a record has been added, rather than simply putting another blank form on the screen).
Closure	Dialogues should be logically grouped and have a beginning, middle, and end (e.g., the last in the sequence of screens should indicate that there are no more screens).
Error Handling	All errors should be detected and reported; suggestions on how to proceed should be made (e.g., suggest why such errors occur and what user can do to correct the error). Synonyms for certain responses should be accepted (e.g., accept either "t," "T," or "TRUE").
Reversal	Dialogues should, when possible, allow the user to reverse actions (e.g., undo a deletion); data should not be destroyed without confirmation (e.g., display all the data for a record the user has indicated is to be deleted).
Control	Dialogues should make the user (especially an experienced user) feel in control of the system (e.g., provide a consistent response time at a pace acceptable to the user).
Ease	It should be a simple process for users to enter information and navigate between screens (e.g., provide means to move forward, backward, and to specific screens, such as first and last).

(*Source:* Adapted from Shneiderman and Plaisant, 2004.)

many system designers use the *double-confirmation* technique. With this technique, users must confirm their intention twice before being allowed to proceed.

Designing the Dialogue Sequence

Your first step in dialogue design is to define the sequence. In other words, you must first gain an understanding of how users might interact with the system. This means that you must have a clear understanding of user, task, technological, and environmental characteristics when designing dialogues. Suppose that the marketing manager at Pine Valley Furniture wants sales and marketing personnel to be able to review the year-to-date transaction activity for any PVF customer. After talking with the manager, you both agree that a typical dialogue between a user and the Customer Information System for obtaining this information might proceed as follows:

1. Request to view individual customer information
2. Specify the customer of interest
3. Select the year-to-date transaction summary display
4. Review customer information
5. Leave system

As a designer, once you understand how a user wishes to use a system, you can then transform these activities into a formal dialogue specification.

A formal method for designing and representing dialogues is **dialogue diagramming.** Dialogue diagrams have only one symbol, a box with three sections; each box represents one display (which might be a full screen or a specific form or window) within a dialogue (see Figure 12-17). The three sections of the box are used as follows:

1. *Top*: Contains a unique display reference number used by other displays for referencing it

Dialogue diagramming: A formal method for designing and representing human–computer dialogues using box and line diagrams.

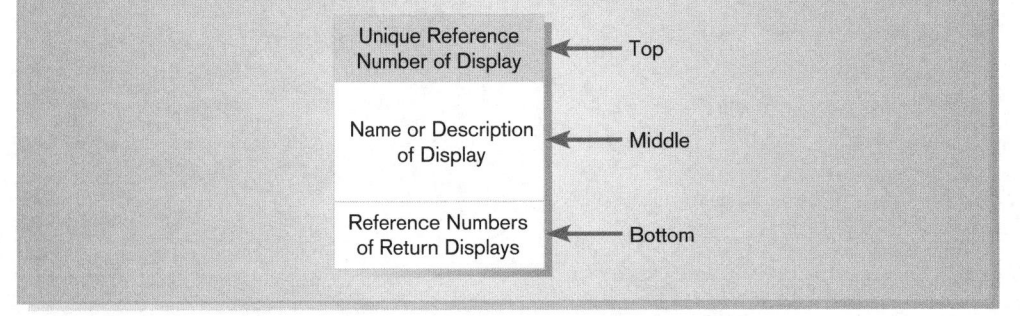

Figure 12-17
Sections of a dialogue
diagramming box

2. *Middle:* Contains the name or description of the display
3. *Bottom:* Contains display reference numbers that can be accessed from the current display

All lines connecting the boxes within dialogue diagrams are assumed to be bidirectional and thus do not need arrowheads to indicate direction. This means that users are allowed to move forward and backward between adjacent displays. If you desire only unidirectional flows within a dialogue, arrowheads should be placed on one end of the line. Within a dialogue diagram, you can easily represent the sequencing of displays, the selection of one display over another, or the repeated use of a single display (e.g., a data entry display). These three concepts—sequence, selection, and iteration—are illustrated in Figure 12-18.

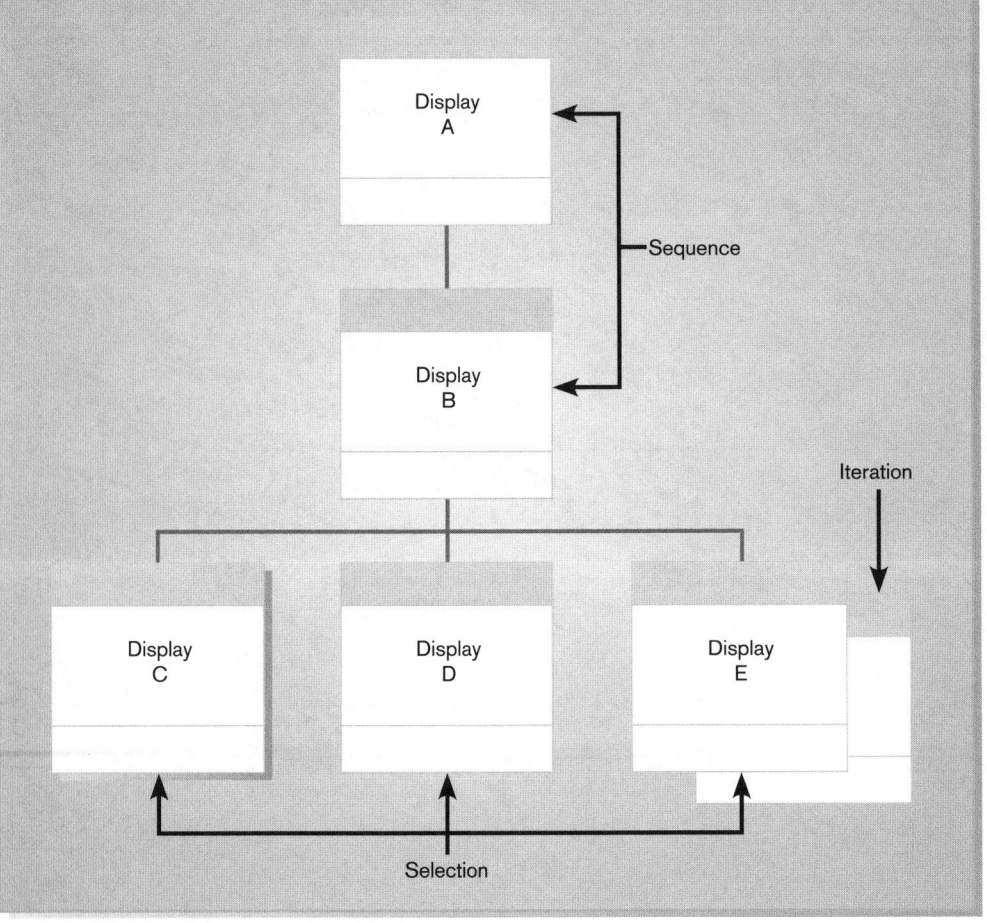

Figure 12-18
Dialogue diagram illustrating
sequence, selection, and iteration

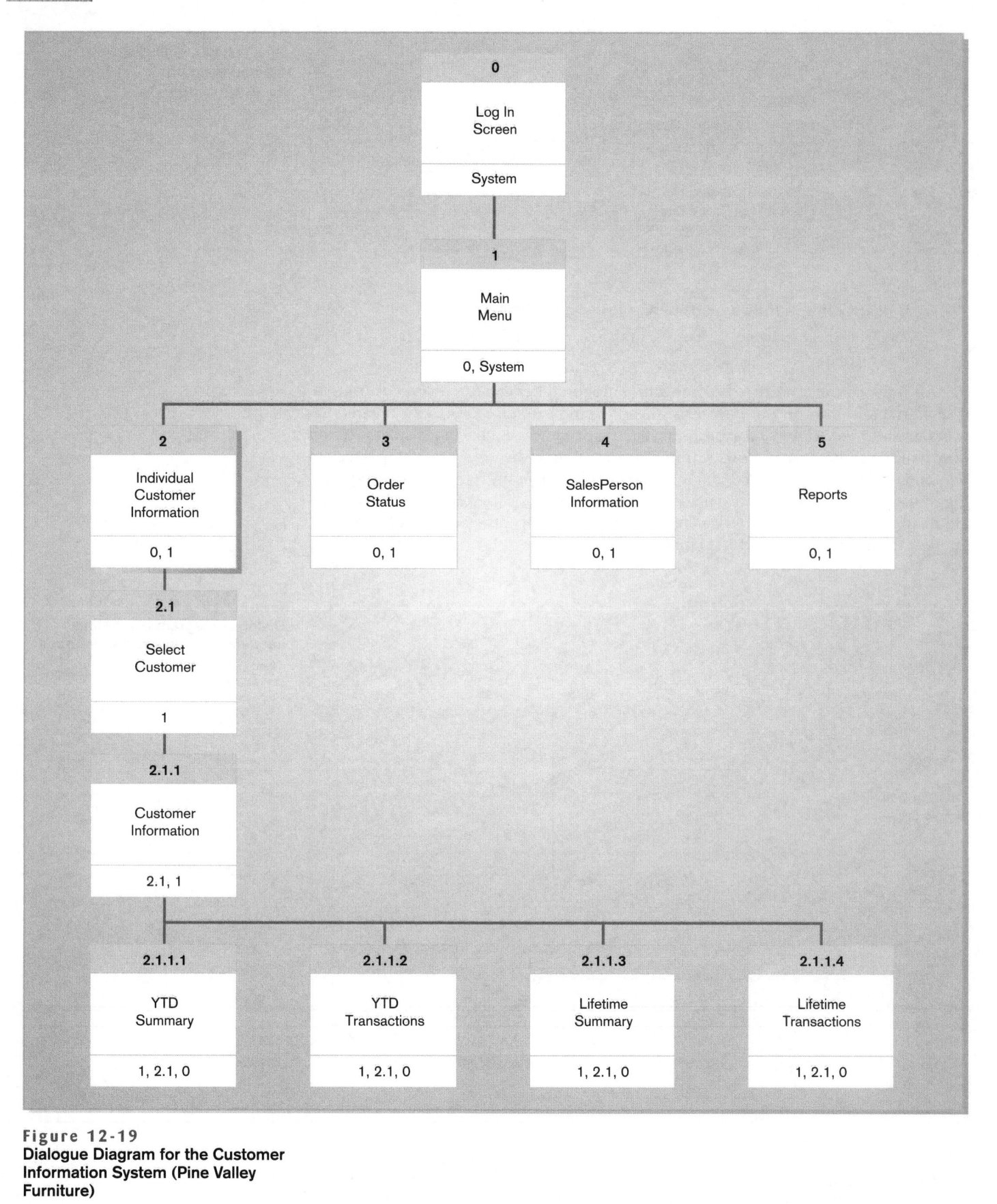

Figure 12-19
Dialogue Diagram for the Customer
Information System (Pine Valley
Furniture)

Continuing with our PVF example, Figure 12-19 shows a partial dialogue diagram for processing the marketing manager's request. In this diagram, the analyst placed the request to view year-to-date customer information within the context of the overall Customer Information System. The user must first gain access to the system through a log-on procedure (item 0). If log-on is successful, a main menu is displayed that has four items (item 1). Once the user selects the Individual Customer Information (item 2), control is transferred to the Select Customer display (item 2.1). After a customer is selected, the user is presented with an option to view customer information four different ways (item 2.1.1). Once the user views the customer's year-to-date transaction activity (item 2.1.1.2), the system will allow the user to back up to select a different customer (2.1), return to the main menu (1), or exit the system (see bottom of item 2.1.1.2).

Building Prototypes and Assessing Usability

Building dialogue prototypes and assessing usability are often optional activities. Some systems may be very simple and straightforward. Others may be more complex but are extensions to existing systems where dialogue and display standards have already been established. In either case, you may not be required to build prototypes and do a formal assessment. However, for many other systems, it is critical that you build prototype displays and then assess the dialogue; this can pay numerous dividends later in the systems development life cycle (e.g., it may be easier to implement a system or train users on a system they have already seen and used).

Building prototype displays is often a relatively easy activity if you use graphical development environments such as Microsoft's Visual Studio .NET or Borland's Enterprise Studio. Some systems development environments include easy-to-use input and output (form, report, or window) design utilities. There are also several tools called "prototypers" or "demo builders" that allow you to quickly design displays and show how an interface will work within a full system. These demo systems allow users to enter data and move through displays as if using the actual system. Such activities are not only useful for you to show how an interface will look and feel, they are also useful for assessing usability and for performing user training long before actual systems are completed. In the next section, we extend our discussion of interface and dialogue design to consider issues specific to graphical user interface environments.

DESIGNING INTERFACES AND DIALOGUES IN GRAPHICAL ENVIRONMENTS

Graphical user interface (GUI) environments have become the de facto standard for human–computer interaction. Although all of the interface and dialogue design guidelines presented previously apply to designing GUIs, additional issues that are unique to these environments must be considered. Here, we briefly discuss some of these issues.

GRAPHICAL INTERFACE DESIGN ISSUES

When designing GUIs for an operating environment such as Microsoft Windows or the Apple Macintosh, numerous factors must be considered. Some factors are common to all GUI environments, whereas others are specific to a single environment. We will not, however, discuss the subtleties and details of any single environment. Instead, our discussion will focus on a few general truths that experienced designers mention as critical to the design of usable GUIs (Cooper and Reimann,

2003; Shneiderman and Plaisant, 2004). In most discussions of GUI programming, two rules repeatedly emerge as comprising the first step to becoming an effective GUI designer:

1. *Become an expert user of the GUI environment.*

2. *Understand the available resources and how they can be used.*

The first step should be an obvious one. The greatest strength of designing within a standard operating environment is that *standards* for the behavior of most system operations have already been defined. For example, how you cut and paste, set up your default printer, design menus, or assign commands to functions have been standardized both within and across applications. This allows experienced users of one GUI-based application to easily learn a new application. Thus, in order to design effective interfaces in such environments, you must first understand how other applications have been designed so that you will adopt the established standards for "look and feel." Failure to adopt the standard conventions in a given environment will result in a system that will likely frustrate and confuse users.

The second rule—gaining an understanding of the available resources and how they can be used—is a much larger undertaking. For example, within Windows you can use menus, forms, and boxes in many ways. In fact, the flexibility with which these resources *can be used* versus the established standards for how most designers *actually use* these resources makes design especially challenging. For example, you have the ability to design menus using all uppercase text, putting multiple words on the top line of the menu, and other nonstandard conventions. Yet, the standards for menu design require that top-level menu items consist of one word and follow a specific ordering. Numerous other standards for menu design have also been established

Figure 12-20
Highlighting graphical user interface design standards

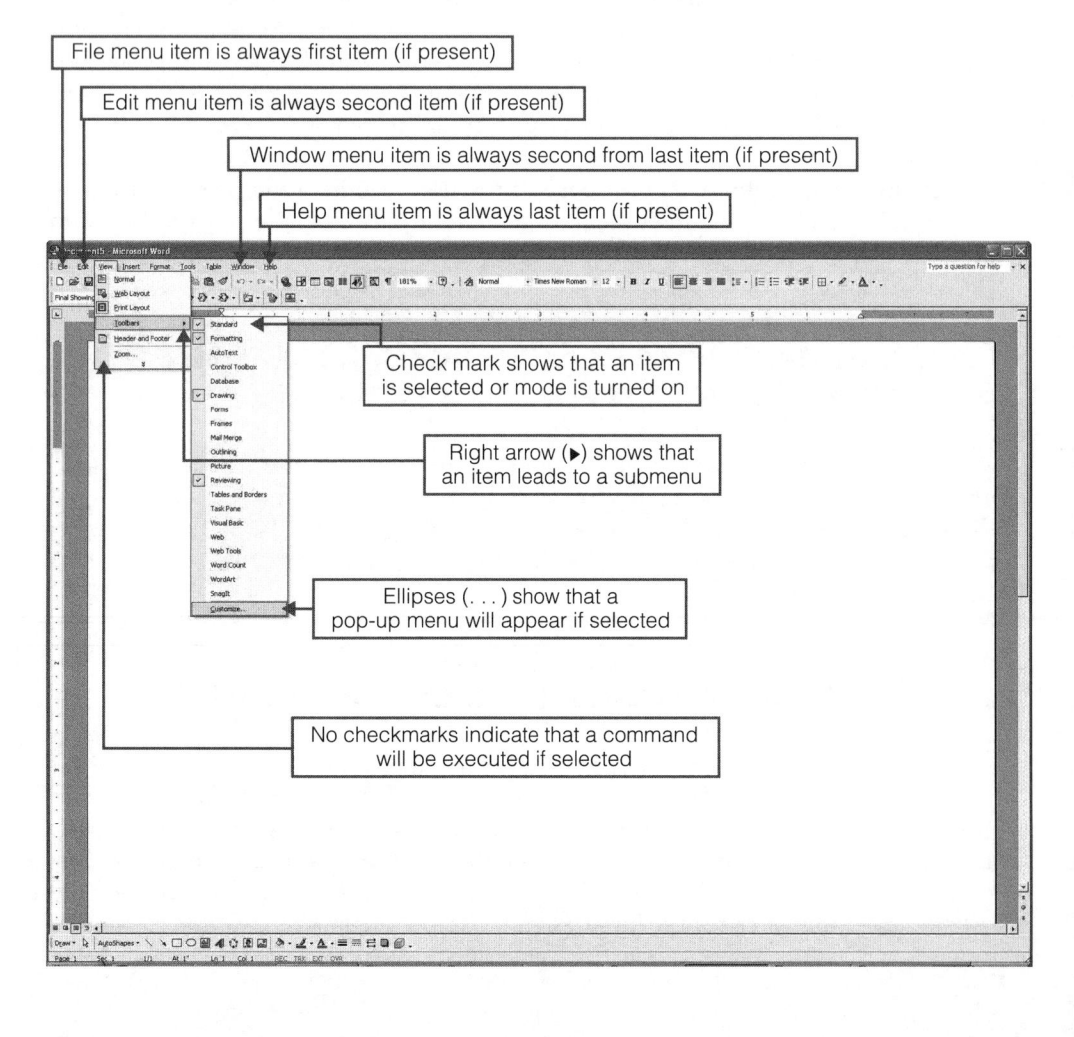

TABLE 12-14   Common Properties of Windows and Forms in a Graphical User Interface Environment That Can Be Active or Inactive

Property	Explanation
Modality	Requires users to resolve the request for information before proceeding (e.g., need to cancel or save before closing a window).
Resizable	Allows users to resize a window or form (e.g., to make room to see other windows that are also on the screen).
Movable	Allows users to move a window or form (e.g., to allow another window to be seen).
Maximize	Allows users to expand a window or form to a full-size screen (e.g., to avoid distraction from other active windows or forms).
Minimize	Allows users to shrink a window or form to an icon (e.g., to get the window out of the way while working on other active windows).
System Menu	Allows a window or form to also have a system menu to directly access system-level functions (e.g., to save or copy data).

(*Source:* Adapted from Wagner, 1994.)

(see Figure 12-20 for illustrations of many of these standards). Failure to follow standard design conventions will likely prove very confusing to users.

In GUIs, information is requested by placing a window (or form) on the visual display screen. Like menu design, forms can also have numerous properties that can be mixed and matched (see Table 12-14). For example, properties about a form determine whether a form is resizable or movable after being opened. Because properties define how users can actually work with a form, the effective application of properties is fundamental to gaining usability. This means that, in addition to designing the layout of a form, you must also define the "personality" of the form with its characteristic properties. Fortunately, numerous GUI design tools have been developed that allow you to "visually" design forms and interactively engage properties. Interactive GUI design tools have greatly facilitated the design and construction process.

In addition to the issues related to interface design, the sequencing of displays turns out to be a bit more challenging in graphical environments. This topic is discussed next.

Dialogue Design Issues in a Graphical Environment   When designing a dialogue, your goal is to establish the sequence of displays (full screens or windows) that users will encounter when working with the system. Within many GUI environments, this process can be a bit more challenging due to the GUI's ability to suspend activities (without resolving a request for information or exiting the application altogether) and switch to another application or task. For example, within Microsoft Word, the spell checker executes independently from the general word processor. This means that you can easily jump between the spell checker and word processor without exiting either one. Conversely, when selecting the print operation, you must either initiate printing or abort the request before returning to the word processor. This is an example of the concept of "modality" described in Table 12-14. Thus, Windows-type environments allow you to create forms that either *require* the user to resolve a request before proceeding (print example) or *selectively choose* to resolve a request before proceeding (the spell checker). Creating dialogues that allow the user to jump from application to application or from module to module within a given application requires that you carefully think through the design of dialogues.

One easy way to deal with the complexity of designing advanced graphical user interfaces is to require users to *always* resolve all requests for information before proceeding. For such designs, the dialogue diagramming technique is an adequate design tool. This, however, would make the system operate in a manner similar to a traditional non-GUI environment where the sequencing of displays is tightly controlled. The drawback to such an approach would be the failure to capitalize on the task-switching capabilities of these environments. Consequently, designing dialogues in environments where the sequence between displays cannot be predetermined offers significant challenges to the designer. Using tools such as dialogue diagramming helps analysts to better manage the complexity of designing graphical interfaces.

ELECTRONIC COMMERCE APPLICATION: DESIGNING INTERFACES AND DIALOGUES FOR PINE VALLEY FURNITURE'S WEBSTORE

Designing the human interface for an Internet-based electronic commerce application is a central and critical design activity. Because this is where a customer will interact with a company, much care must be put into its design. Like the process followed when designing the interface for other types of systems, a prototyping design process is most appropriate when designing the human interface for an Internet electronic commerce system. Although, the techniques and technology for building the human interface for Internet sites is rapidly evolving, several general design guidelines have emerged. In this section, we examine some of these as they apply to the design of Pine Valley Furniture's WebStore.

General Guidelines

Over the years, interaction standards have emerged for virtually all of the commonly used desktop computing environments such as Windows or Macintosh. However, some interface design experts believe that the growth of the Web has resulted in a big step backwards for interface design. One problem, as discussed in Chapter 11, is that countless nonprofessional developers are designing commercial Web applications. In addition to this, there are four other important contributing factors (Johnson, 2000):

1. The Web's single "click-to-act" method of loading static hypertext documents (i.e., most buttons on the Web do not provide click feedback)
2. Limited capabilities of most Web browsers to support finely grained user interactivity
3. Limited agreed-upon standards for encoding Web content and control mechanisms
4. Lack of maturity of Web scripting and programming languages as well as limitations in commonly used Web GUI component libraries

In addition to these contributing factors, designers of Web interfaces and dialogues are often guilty of many design errors. Although not inclusive of all possible errors, Table 12-15 summarizes those errors that are particularly troublesome. Fortunately, there are numerous excellent sources on how to avoid these and other interface and design errors (Cooper and Reimann, 2003; Johnson, 2000; Flanders and Willis, 1998; Nielson, 1999; Nielson, 2000; Seffah and Javahery, 2003; *www.useit.com*; *www.webpagesthatsuck.com*).

Designing Interfaces and Dialogues at Pine Valley Furniture

To establish design guidelines for the human–computer interface, Jim Woo and the PVF development team again reviewed many popular electronic commerce Websites. The key feature they wanted to incorporate into the design was an interface with "menu-driven navigation with cookie crumbs." In order to ensure that all team members understood what was meant by this guideline, Jim organized a design briefing to explain how this feature would be incorporated into the WebStore interface.

Menu-Driven Navigation with Cookie Crumbs

After reviewing several sites, the team concluded that menus should stay in the exact same place throughout the entire site. They concluded that placing a menu

TABLE 12-15   Common Errors When Designing the Interface and Dialogues of Websites

Error	Description
Opening New Browser Window	Avoid opening a new browser window when a user clicks on a link unless it is clearly marked that a new window will be opened; users may not see that a new window has been opened, which will complicate navigation, especially moving backwards.
Breaking or Slowing Down the Back Button	Make sure users can use the back button to return to prior pages. Avoid opening new browser windows, using an immediate redirect where, when users click the back button, they are pushed forward to an undesired location, or prevent caching such that each click of the back button requires a new trip to the server.
Complex URLs	Avoid overly long and complex URLs since it makes it more difficult for users to understand where they are and can cause problems if users want to e-mail page locations to colleagues.
Orphan Pages	Avoid having pages with no "parent" that can be reached by using a back button; requires users to "hack" the end of the URL to get back to some other prior page.
Scrolling Navigation Pages	Avoid placing navigational links below where a page opens, since many users may miss these important options that are below the opening window.
Lack of Navigation Support	Make sure your pages conform to users' expectations by providing commonly used icon links such as a site logo at the top or other major elements. Also place these elements on pages in a consistent manner.
Hidden Links	Make sure you leave a border around images that are links, don't change link colors from normal defaults, and avoid embedding links within long blocks of text.
Links That Don't Provide Enough Information	Avoid not turning off link-marking borders so that links clearly show which links users have clicked and which they have not. Make sure users know which links are internal anchor points versus external links, and indicate if a link brings up a separate browser window from those that do not. Finally, make sure link images and text provide enough information to users so that they understand the meaning of the link.
Buttons That Provide No Click Feedback	Avoid using image buttons that don't clearly change when being clicked; use Web GUI toolkit buttons, HTML form-submit buttons, or simple textual links.

in the same location on every page will help customers to more quickly become familiar with the site and therefore more rapidly navigate through it. Experienced Web developers know that the quicker customers can reach a specific destination at a site, the quicker they can purchase the product they are looking for or get the information they seek. Jim emphasized this point by stating, "These details may seem silly, but the second a user finds themselves 'lost' in our site, they're gone. One mouse click and they're no longer shopping at Pine Valley, but at one of our competitor's sites."

A second design feature, and one that is being used on many electronic commerce sites, is cookie crumbs. **Cookie crumbs** are "tabs" on a Web page that show a user where he or she is on a site and where he or she has been. These tabs are hypertext links that the user can use to quickly move backwards in the site. For example, suppose that a site is four levels deep, with the top level called "Entrance," the second called "Products," the third called "Options," and the fourth called "Order." As the user moves deeper into the site, a tab is displayed across the top of the page showing the user where he or she is, giving the user the ability to quickly jump backwards one

Cookie crumbs: The technique of placing "tabs" on a Web page that show a user where he or she is on a site and where he or she has been.

Higher National in Computing

or more levels. In other words, when first entering the store, a tab will be displayed at the top (or some other standard place) of the screen with the word "Entrance." After moving down a level, two tabs will be displayed, "Entrance" and "Products." After selecting a product on the second level, a third level is displayed where a user can choose product options. When this level is displayed, a third tab is produced with the label "Options." Finally, if the customer decides to place an order and selects this option, a fourth-level screen is displayed and a fourth tab is displayed with the label "Order." In summary:

Level 1: Entrance
Level 2: Entrance → Products
Level 3: Entrance → Products → Options
Level 4: Entrance → Products → Options → Order

By using cookie crumbs, users know exactly how far they have wandered from "home." If each tab is a link, users can quickly jump back to a broader part of the store should they not find exactly what they are looking for. Cookie crumbs serve two important purposes. First, they allow users to navigate to a point previously visited and will assure that they are not lost. Second, they clearly show users where they have been and how far they have gone from home.

Summary

In this chapter, our focus was to acquaint you with the process of designing human–computer interfaces and dialogues. It is imperative that you understand the characteristics of various interaction methods (command language, menu, form, object, natural language) and devices (keyboard, mouse, joystick, trackball, touch screen, light pen, graphics tablet, voice). No single interaction style or device is the most appropriate in all instances: Each has its strengths and weaknesses. You must consider the characteristics of the intended users, the tasks being performed, and various technical and environmental factors when making design decisions.

The chapter also reviewed design guidelines for computer-based forms. You learned that most forms have a header, sequence or time-related information, instructions, a body, summary data, authorization, and comments. Users must be able to move the cursor position, edit data, exit with different consequences, and obtain help. Techniques for structuring and controlling data entry were presented along with guidelines for providing feedback, prompts, and error messages. A simple, well-organized help function that shows examples of proper use of the system should be provided. A variety of help types were reviewed.

Next, guidelines for designing human–computer dialogues were presented. These guidelines are consistency, allowing for shortcuts, providing feedback and closure on tasks, handling errors, allowing for operations reversal, giving the user a sense of control, and ease of navigation.

We also discussed dialogue diagramming as a design tool. Assessing the usability of dialogues and procedures was also reviewed. Several interface and dialogue design issues were described within the context of designing graphical user interfaces. These included the need to follow standards to provide the capabilities of modality, resizing, moving, and maximizing and minimizing windows, and to offer a system menu choice. This discussion highlighted how concepts presented earlier in the chapter can be applied or augmented in these emerging environments. Finally, interface and dialogue design issues for Internet-based applications were discussed, and several common design errors were highlighted.

Our goal was to provide you with a foundation for building highly usable human–computer interfaces. As more and more development environments provide rapid prototyping tools for the design of interfaces and dialogues, many complying with common interface standards, the difficulty of designing usable interfaces will be reduced. However, you still need a solid understanding of the concepts presented in this chapter in order to succeed. Learning to use a computer system is like learning to use a parachute—if a person fails on the first try, odds are he or she won't try again (Blattner and Schultz, 1988). If this analogy is true, it is important that a user's first experience with a system be a positive one. By following the design guidelines outlined in this chapter, your chances of providing a positive first experience to users will be greatly enhanced.

Key Terms

1. Command language interaction
2. Cookie crumbs
3. Dialogue
4. Dialogue diagramming
5. Drop-down menu
6. Form interaction
7. Icon
8. Interface
9. Menu interaction
10. Natural language interaction
11. Object-based interaction
12. Pop-up menu

Match each of the key terms above with the definition that best fits it.

_____ A method by which users interact with information systems.

_____ A human–computer interaction method whereby users enter explicit statements into a system to invoke operations.

_____ A formal method for designing and representing human–computer dialogues using box and line diagrams.

_____ A menu-positioning method that places a menu near the current cursor position.

_____ A human–computer interaction method whereby a list of system options is provided and a specific command is invoked by user selection of a menu option.

_____ The technique of placing "tabs" on a Web page that show a user where he or she is on a site and where he or she has been.

_____ A menu-positioning method that places the access point of the menu near the top line of the display; when accessed, menus open by dropping down onto the display.

_____ A highly intuitive human–computer interaction method whereby data fields are formatted in a manner similar to paper-based forms.

_____ A human–computer interaction method whereby symbols are used to represent commands or functions.

_____ Graphical pictures that represent specific functions within a system.

_____ A human–computer interaction method whereby inputs to and outputs from a computer-based application are in a conventional speaking language such as English.

_____ The sequence of interaction between a user and a system.

Review Questions

1. Contrast the following terms:
   a. Dialogue, interface
   b. Command language interaction, form interaction, menu interaction, natural language interaction, object-based interaction
   c. Drop-down menu, pop-up menu

2. Describe the process of designing interfaces and dialogues. What deliverables are produced from this process? Are these deliverables the same for all types of system projects? Why or why not?

3. Describe five methods of interacting with a system. Is one method better than all others? Why or why not?

4. Describe several input devices for interacting with a system. Is one device better than all others? Why or why not?

5. Describe the general guidelines for the design of menus. Can you think of any instances when it would be appropriate to violate these guidelines?

6. List and describe the general sections of a typical business form. Do computer-based and paper-based forms have the same components? Why or why not?

7. List and describe the functional capabilities needed in an interface for effective entry and navigation. Which capabilities are most important? Why? Will this be the same for all systems? Why or why not?

8. Describe the general guidelines for structuring data entry fields. Can you think of any instances when it would be appropriate to violate these guidelines?

9. Describe four types of data errors.

10. Describe the methods used to enhance the validity of data input.

11. Describe the types of system feedback. Is any form of feedback more important than the others? Why or why not?

12. Describe the general guidelines for designing usable help. Can you think of any instances when it would be appropriate to violate these guidelines?

13. What steps do you need to follow when designing a dialogue? Of the guidelines for designing a dialogue, which is most important? Why?

14. Describe the properties of windows and forms in a graphical user interface environment. Which property do you feel is most important? Why?

15. List and describe the common interface and dialogue design errors found on Websites.

Problems and Exercises

1. Consider software applications that you regularly use that have menu interfaces, whether they be PC- or mainframe-based applications. Evaluate these applications in terms of the menu design guidelines outlined in Table 12-1.

2. Consider the design of a registration system for a hotel. Following the design specification items in Figure 12-2, briefly describe the relevant users, tasks, and displays involved in such a system.

3. Imagine the design of a system used to register students at a university. Discuss the user, task, system, and environmental characteristics (see Table 11-10) that should be considered when designing the interface for such a system.

4. For the three common methods of system interaction—command language, menus, and objects—recall a software package that you have used recently and list what you liked and disliked about each package with regard to the interface. What were the strengths and weaknesses of each interaction method for this particular program? Which type of interaction do you prefer for which circumstances? Which type do you believe will become most prevalent? Why?

5. Briefly describe several different business tasks that are good candidates for form-based interaction within an information system.

6. List the physical input devices described in this chapter that you have seen or used. For each device, briefly describe your experience and provide your personal evaluation. Do your personal evaluations parallel the evaluations provided in Tables 12-3 and 12-4?

7. Propose some specific settings where natural language interaction would be particularly useful and explain why.

8. Examine the help systems for some software applications that you use. Evaluate each using the general guidelines provided in Table 12-11.

9. Design one sample data entry screen for a hotel registration system using the data entry guidelines provided in this chapter (see Table 12-6). Support your design with arguments for each of the design choices you made.

10. Describe some typical dialogue scenarios between users and a hotel registration system. For hints, reread the section in this chapter that provides sample dialogue between users and the Customer Information System at Pine Valley Furniture.

11. Represent the dialogues from the previous question through the use of dialogue diagrams.

12. List four contributing factors that have acted to impede the design of high-quality interfaces and dialogues on Internet-based applications.

13. Go to the Internet and find commercial Websites that demonstrate each of the common errors listed in Table 12-15.

Field Exercises

1. Research the topic "natural language" at your library. Determine the status of applications available with natural language interaction. Forecast how long it will be before natural language capabilities are prevalent in information systems use.

2. Examine two PC-based graphical user interfaces (e.g., Microsoft's Windows and Macintosh). If you do not own these interfaces, you are likely to find them at your university or workplace, or at a computer retail store. You may want to supplement your hands-on evaluation with recent formal evaluations published on the Web. In what ways are these two interfaces similar and different? Are these interfaces intuitive? Why or why not? Is one more intuitive than the other? Why or why not? Which interface seems easier to learn? Why? What types of system requirements does each interface have? What are the costs of each interface? Which do you prefer? Why?

3. Interview a variety of people you know about the various ways they interact, in terms of inputs, with systems at their workplaces. What types of technologies and devices are used to deliver these inputs? Are the input methods and devices easy to use, and do they help these people complete their tasks effectively and efficiently? Why or why not? How could these input methods and devices be improved?

4. Interview systems analysts and programmers in an organization where graphical user interfaces are used. Describe the ways that these interfaces are developed and used. How does the use of such interfaces enhance or complicate the design of interfaces and dialogues?

References

Apple Computer. 1993. *Macintosh Human Interface Guidelines.* Reading, MA: Addison-Wesley.

Blattner, M., and E. Schultz. 1988. "User Interface Tutorial." Presented at the 1988 Hawaii International Conference on System Sciences, Kona, Hawaii, January.

Cooper, A., and R. M. Reimann. 2003. *About Face 2.0: The Essentials of Interaction Design.* New York: John Wiley & Sons.

Flanders, V., and M. Willis. 1998. *Web Pages That Suck: Learn Good Design by Looking at Bad Design.* Alameda, CA: Sybex Publishing.

Hoffer, J. A., M. B. Prescott, and F. R. McFadden. 2005. *Modern Database Management,* 7th ed. Upper Saddle River, NJ: Prentice Hall.

Johnson, J. 2000. *GUI Bloopers: Don'ts and Do's for Software Developers and Web Designers.* San Diego: Academic Press.

Lazar, J. 2004. *User-Centered Web Development: Theory into Practice.* Sudbury, MA: Jones & Bartlett.

McCracken, D. D., R. J. Wolfe, and J. M. Spoll. 2003. User-Centered Web Site Development: A Human-Computer Interaction Approach. Upper Saddle River, NJ: Prentice Hall.

McKay, E. N. 1999. Developing User Interfaces for Microsoft Windows. Redmond, WA: Microsoft Press.

Nielsen, J. 1999. "User Interface Directions for the Web." *Communications of the ACM* 42 (1): 65–71.

Nielsen, J. 2000. *Designing Web Usability: The Practice of Simplicity.* Indianapolis, IN: New Riders Publishing.

Seffah, A., and H. Javahery. 2003. *Multiple User Interfaces: Cross-Platform Applications and Context-Aware Interfaces.* New York: John Wiley & Sons.

Shneiderman, B., and C. Plaisant. 2004. *Designing the User Interface,* 4th ed. Reading, MA: Addison-Wesley.

Sun Microsystems. 1999. *Java Look and Feel Design Guidelines.* Reading, MA: Addison-Wesley.

Wagner, R. 1994. "A GUI Design Manifesto." *Paradox Informant* 5 (6): 36–42.

BROADWAY ENTERTAINMENT COMPANY, INC.

Designing the Human Interface for the Customer Relationship Management System

CASE INTRODUCTION

The students from Stillwater State University are almost ready to build a prototype of MyBroadway, the Web-based customer relationship management system for Carrie Douglass, manager of the Centerville, Ohio, Broadway Entertainment Company (BEC) store. The team has decided on the style and specific design for individual pages on the Website. Before building the prototype in Microsoft Access, the team is ready to plan the structure for the navigation between the pages of the system. For a Web-based system, the human interface is, to the customer, the system. As with the page designs, the students decide to do a pencil-and-paper prototype before development in Access. This initial prototype will be used primarily for discussion among the team members and for sharing with other teams in their information systems projects class at Stillwater.

DESIGNING THE DIALOGUE BETWEEN MYBROADWAY AND USERS

The human interfaces for MyBroadway are clearly visible from the system's context diagram (see BEC Figure 7-1 at the end of Chapter 7). The main human interfaces are data flows from and to each human external entity—customers and employees. The team has already designed one or more pages for these data flows. The team quickly realizes that these data flows are not the only human interfaces. Any Web page that is needed in a navigation path leading to these data flows is also a human interface. For example, to produce the Inventory Review output page, the customer must enter criteria for selecting which inventory items to display and must get to these pages from the welcome page.

The student team decides that the home or welcome page should contain a catchy graphic and menu selections for accessing different parts of the system. One way to categorize system functions would logically be to group all inputs, or data entry pages, together in one group and all system outputs, or form and report display pages,

together into a second group. The team decides, however, that this is a system-centric view, not a user-centric view of the system's functionality. After some brainstorming, the team decides that it would be more logical for users to understand and use the system if pages were grouped by the type of data the users want to use. There appear to be two natural data groupings: product and purchase/rental data.

BEC Figure 12-1 is a dialogue diagram that represents the relationships between system Web pages developed by the team using a data orientation for human interfaces. Page 0 is the welcome page. Besides information to introduce MyBroadway to customers, this page provides menu options or buttons for the user to indicate which data group he or she wants to use. If the user wants to work with product data, then page 1 provides the user with a way to enter the request for a new product (page 1.3, which is input 2 from BEC Figure 7-1) or to work with existing product data (pages 1.1 and 1.2). Page 1.1 guides the user either to enter a new comment on a product (page 1.1.1 for input 1) or to view existing product comments (page 1.1.2 for output 2). Therefore, page 1.1 must provide a way for the user to select or enter data to identify the product for use in subordinate pages.

In general, each system input or output is a terminal (or leaf) node of the dialogue diagram. Each superior node above a leaf is a step for guiding the user to a system input or output. Sometimes a system output can be the basis for a customer to create a system input. For example, consider pages 2.1, 2.1.1, and 2.1.1.1. Page 2.1 is the Rental Status report, output 3. The team decides that users will want to see this report before requesting an extension to a particular rental, which is done on page 2.1.1, representing input 3. Thus, page 2.1 not only displays the Rental Status report, but also provides a way for a user to select a particular outstanding rental for which to request an extension in page 2.1.1. Page 2.1.1.1 is a message page (possibly not a totally separate page, but rather a message window to overlay on top of page 2.1.1) that will say whether the extension request is accepted.

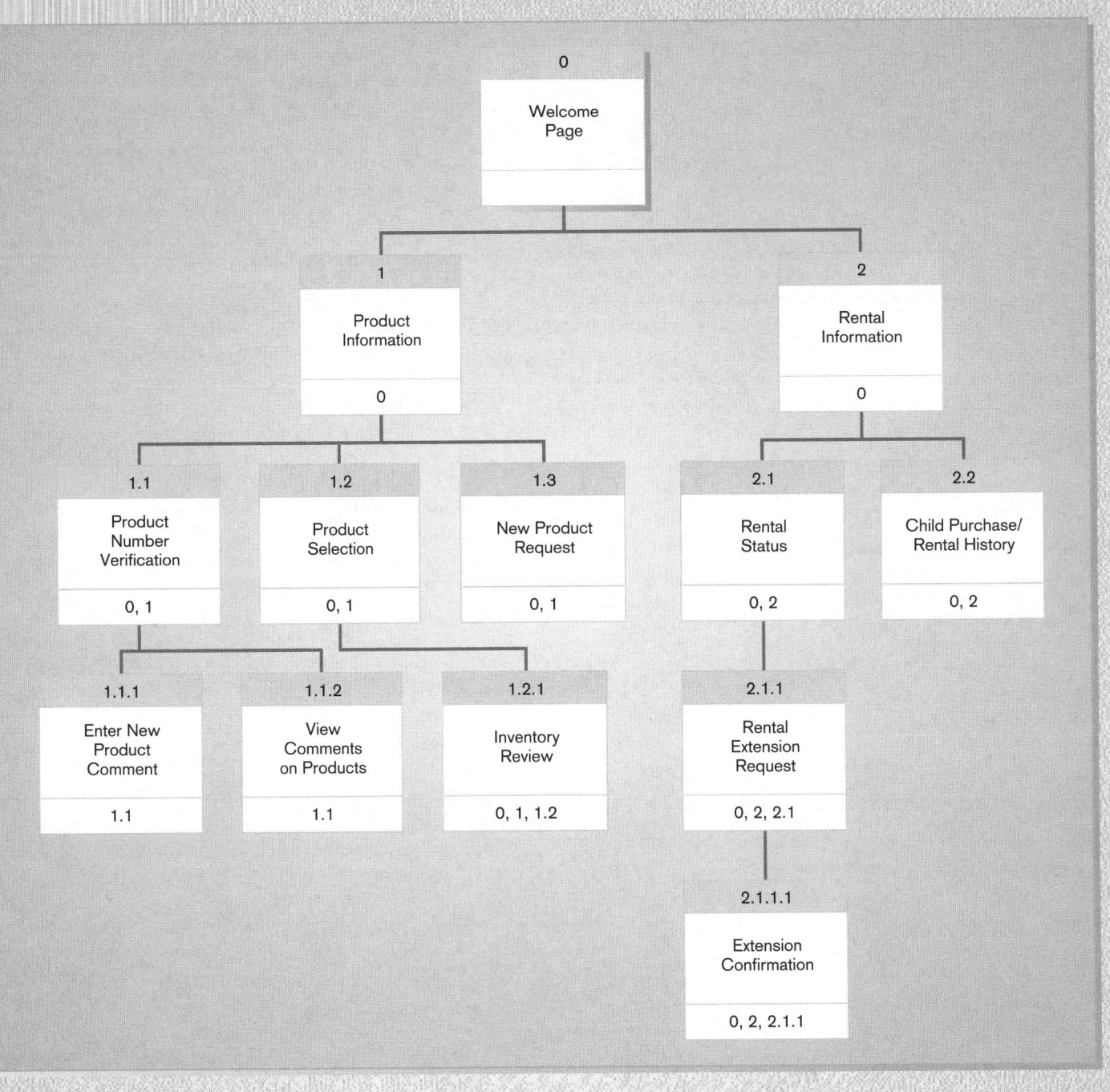

BEC Figure 12-1
Dialogue Diagram for MyBroadway

CASE SUMMARY

The student team feels that the design of the user dialogue represents a suitable project deliverable that should be reviewed by someone outside the team. Thus, they schedule a structured walkthrough of their dialogue design along with the design of pages, which they did previously (see the BEC case at the end of Chapter 11).

Because the team has not invested a great deal of time in the initial design, the team members believe they can be open to, not defensive in response to, constructive suggestions. Because other teams will also likely walk through their dialogue designs, the BEC team will see some other creative designs, which will give additional ideas for improvement.

CASE QUESTIONS

1. Using guidelines from this chapter and other sources, evaluate the usability of the dialogue design depicted in BEC Figure 12-1. Specifically, consider the overall organization, grouping of pages, navigation paths between pages, and depth of the dialogue diagram and how this depth might affect user efficiency.

2. Are there any missing pages in BEC Figure 12-1? Can you anticipate the need for additional pages in the customer interface for MyBroadway? If so, where do these pages come from if not from the list of system inputs and outputs listed in BEC Figure 7-1?

3. Chapter 12 encourages the design of a help system early in the design of the human interface. How would you incorporate help into the interface as designed by the Stillwater students?

4. The designs for pages 1.2 and 1.2.1 include a back button. Is this button necessary or desirable?

5. Are there any other possible navigation paths exiting page 1.2 that are not shown on BEC Figure 12-1? Is page 1.2.1 the only possible result of searching on the selection criteria? If not, design pages for other results and the navigation paths to these pages.

6. BEC Figure 12-1 indicates a multilevel tree menu design for MyBroadway. Do you see opportunities for other menu configurations? Explain. Do you see opportunities for interaction methods other than menus? Explain.

7. Based on the guidelines in Chapter 12 on designing interfaces, return to the page designs from the BEC case in Chapter 11 and reevaluate those page layouts. Do you now see any additional issues or do you have any specific recommendations for those pages based on the material in this chapter?

8. What types of errors might users of MyBroadway make? Design error messages and a way to display those messages. Justify your design based on guidelines in Chapter 12.

9. Now that you have studied both the form and report design and the navigation design developed by the Stillwater students for MyBroadway, evaluate the overall usability of their design. Consider the definition of usability in Chapter 11 as well as the guidelines in Chapters 11 and 12. Suggest changes to make the system more usable.

Unit 5: Networking Concepts

Learning hours: 60

NQF level 4: BTEC Higher National — H1

Content Selected: Tanenbaum, Computer Networks 4th Edition, Chapter 1

Introduction from the Qualification Leader

One of the aims of the unit is to provide a rigorous introduction to networks and this chapter offers the learner such an experience by showing the historical evolution, development of the OSI 7 layer model, ATM, wireless considerations and network standardisation. This chapter covers most of the content within the learning outcome, "Evaluate the benefits of networks."

At the end of the chapter readers are presented with a set of problems designed to test their practical application of topics covered.

Description of unit

The importance of networked solutions in the business world grows year on year. The increasingly sophisticated technologies and widening user base mean a fundamental understanding of networks is essential for many. The aim of this unit is to provide a rigorous introduction to networks, and practical experience in installing users and software on a network.

This unit will clarify the issues associated with network use and how this has developed. It will identify the architectural concepts behind networking and help develop the preliminary skills necessary to install and manage networks.

Summary of learning outcomes

To achieve this unit a learner must:

1 Evaluate the **benefit of networks**

2 Apply architectural concepts to the **design/evaluation of networks**

3 Install **network software**

4 Perform **network management** responsibilities.

Content

1   **Benefit of networks**

Network principles and applications definition of a network: evolution of network uses, from simple file and print networks, through small office computing, to client-server architectures, review of remote access, starting with email through to intranets and the internet, LANs (local area networks), WANs (wide area networks) and MANs, (metropolitan area networks), networked applications, overview of cost/benefits of network use

Network use: an overview of network resources (hardware and software), facilities of a network operating system, understanding of security implications and software licensing issues, constraints on capacity and performance (such as being asked to run video off a 10Mbit Ethernet connection)

2   **Design/evaluation of networks**

Network architecture concepts: the ISO OSI 7-layer model (and/or IEEE 802), topologies, eg bus, ring, structured, a description of communication devices, repeaters, bridges and hubs, standard connectors and wiring, functions of a network card, differences between peer to peer and server based networks, description of main protocols, ie Ethernet, ATM, token ring, IPX, SPX, and their relationship with the 7-layer model, the principles and resources required to connect LANs to WANs, TCP/IP as a WAN protocol, TCP/IP addressing and how routing works

Network design: using architectural principles and definitions to design a new network or evaluate an existing one

3   **Network software**

User factors: design and definition of users and groups, the definition of directory structures on the file server, file and directory attributes, trustee rights, IRM (inherited rights management), and setting up security

Login scripts: definition of the user environment, menu systems

Hardware and software factors: printing set-up, understanding of printing options, installation and configuration of applications on the network (including operating system constraints), file server installation and utilities

4   **Network management**

Management responsibilities: the problems of creating large numbers of accounts on a network and keeping it up-to-date, management of users, workgroup managers, network security and virus protection (elements of good practice)

Resource management: control resource usage estimation and tracing of resource usage, managing printer queues, connecting of the network to the outside world, advantages (eg internet) and disadvantages (eg hackers), firewalls

Outcomes and assessment criteria

Outcomes	Assessment criteria for pass
	To achieve each outcome a learner must demonstrate the ability to:
1 Evaluate the **benefit of networks**	a produce a coherent argument as to the advantages and disadvantages of using networks within an organisation
	b evaluate the various cost, performance, security and utility values associated with the installation of a network
	c provide an overview of a network operating system and how it works
2 Apply architectural concepts to the **design/evaluation of networks**	d design a LAN for a specific purpose or assess an existing network for fitness of purpose
	e identify the various parts (software and hardware) of a network system and relate it to the 7-layered model
	f differentiate between different kinds of network, network topologies and network operating systems
3 Install **network software**	g set up a software network environment, for example departments in an organisation
	h install a piece of network software on to a server to be used by different selected users in a group
	i configure user workstations on the network
4 Perform **network management** responsibilities	j write a report on the rights and responsibilities of the network manager and the network user
	k apply control mechanisms in a typical network for managing users
	l control printer queues and other forms of resource usage

1

INTRODUCTION

Each of the past three centuries has been dominated by a single technology. The 18th century was the era of the great mechanical systems accompanying the Industrial Revolution. The 19th century was the age of the steam engine. During the 20th century, the key technology was information gathering, processing, and distribution. Among other developments, we saw the installation of worldwide telephone networks, the invention of radio and television, the birth and unprecedented growth of the computer industry, and the launching of communication satellites.

As a result of rapid technological progress, these areas are rapidly converging and the differences between collecting, transporting, storing, and processing information are quickly disappearing. Organizations with hundreds of offices spread over a wide geographical area routinely expect to be able to examine the current status of even their most remote outpost at the push of a button. As our ability to gather, process, and distribute information grows, the demand for ever more sophisticated information processing grows even faster.

Although the computer industry is still young compared to other industries (e.g., automobiles and air transportation), computers have made spectacular progress in a short time. During the first two decades of their existence, computer systems were highly centralized, usually within a single large room. Not infrequently, this room had glass walls, through which visitors could gawk at the great electronic wonder inside. A medium-sized company or university might have had one or two computers, while large institutions had at most a few dozen. The idea

1

that within twenty years equally powerful computers smaller than postage stamps would be mass produced by the millions was pure science fiction.

The merging of computers and communications has had a profound influence on the way computer systems are organized. The concept of the "computer center" as a room with a large computer to which users bring their work for processing is now totally obsolete. The old model of a single computer serving all of the organization's computational needs has been replaced by one in which a large number of separate but interconnected computers do the job. These systems are called **computer networks**. The design and organization of these networks are the subjects of this book.

Throughout the book we will use the term "computer network" to mean a collection of autonomous computers interconnected by a single technology. Two computers are said to be interconnected if they are able to exchange information. The connection need not be via a copper wire; fiber optics, microwaves, infrared, and communication satellites can also be used. Networks come in many sizes, shapes and forms, as we will see later. Although it may sound strange to some people, neither the Internet nor the World Wide Web is a computer network. By the end of this book, it should be clear why. The quick answer is: the Internet is not a single network but a network of networks and the Web is a distributed system that runs on top of the Internet.

There is considerable confusion in the literature between a computer network and a **distributed system**. The key distinction is that in a distributed system, a collection of independent computers appears to its users as a single coherent system. Usually, it has a single model or paradigm that it presents to the users. Often a layer of software on top of the operating system, called **middleware**, is responsible for implementing this model. A well-known example of a distributed system is the **World Wide Web**, in which everything looks like a document (Web page).

In a computer network, this coherence, model, and software are absent. Users are exposed to the actual machines, without any attempt by the system to make the machines look and act in a coherent way. If the machines have different hardware and different operating systems, that is fully visible to the users. If a user wants to run a program on a remote machine, he[†] has to log onto that machine and run it there.

In effect, a distributed system is a software system built on top of a network. The software gives it a high degree of cohesiveness and transparency. Thus, the distinction between a network and a distributed system lies with the software (especially the operating system), rather than with the hardware.

Nevertheless, there is considerable overlap between the two subjects. For example, both distributed systems and computer networks need to move files around. The difference lies in who invokes the movement, the system or the user.

† "He" should be read as "he or she" throughout this book.

Although this book primarily focuses on networks, many of the topics are also important in distributed systems. For more information about distributed systems, see (Tanenbaum and Van Steen, 2002).

1.1 USES OF COMPUTER NETWORKS

Before we start to examine the technical issues in detail, it is worth devoting some time to pointing out why people are interested in computer networks and what they can be used for. After all, if nobody were interested in computer networks, few of them would be built. We will start with traditional uses at companies and for individuals and then move on to recent developments regarding mobile users and home networking.

1.1.1 Business Applications

Many companies have a substantial number of computers. For example, a company may have separate computers to monitor production, keep track of inventories, and do the payroll. Initially, each of these computers may have worked in isolation from the others, but at some point, management may have decided to connect them to be able to extract and correlate information about the entire company.

Put in slightly more general form, the issue here is **resource sharing**, and the goal is to make all programs, equipment, and especially data available to anyone on the network without regard to the physical location of the resource and the user. An obvious and widespread example is having a group of office workers share a common printer. None of the individuals really needs a private printer, and a high-volume networked printer is often cheaper, faster, and easier to maintain than a large collection of individual printers.

However, probably even more important than sharing physical resources such as printers, scanners, and CD burners, is sharing information. Every large and medium-sized company and many small companies are vitally dependent on computerized information. Most companies have customer records, inventories, accounts receivable, financial statements, tax information, and much more online. If all of its computers went down, a bank could not last more than five minutes. A modern manufacturing plant, with a computer-controlled assembly line, would not last even that long. Even a small travel agency or three-person law firm is now highly dependent on computer networks for allowing employees to access relevant information and documents instantly.

For smaller companies, all the computers are likely to be in a single office or perhaps a single building, but for larger ones, the computers and employees may be scattered over dozens of offices and plants in many countries. Nevertheless, a sales person in New York might sometimes need access to a product inventory database in Singapore. In other words, the mere fact that a user happens to be 15,000 km away from his data should not prevent him from using the data as though they were local. This goal may be summarized by saying that it is an attempt to end the "tyranny of geography."

In the simplest of terms, one can imagine a company's information system as consisting of one or more databases and some number of employees who need to access them remotely. In this model, the data are stored on powerful computers called **servers**. Often these are centrally housed and maintained by a system administrator. In contrast, the employees have simpler machines, called **clients**, on their desks, with which they access remote data, for example, to include in spreadsheets they are constructing. (Sometimes we will refer to the human user of the client machine as the "client," but it should be clear from the context whether we mean the computer or its user.) The client and server machines are connected by a network, as illustrated in Fig. 1-1. Note that we have shown the network as a simple oval, without any detail. We will use this form when we mean a network in the abstract sense. When more detail is required, it will be provided.

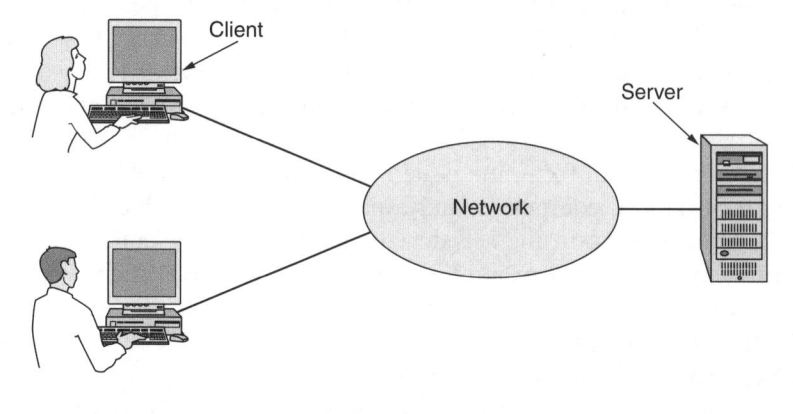

Figure 1-1. A network with two clients and one server.

This whole arrangement is called the **client-server model**. It is widely used and forms the basis of much network usage. It is applicable when the client and server are both in the same building (e.g., belong to the same company), but also when they are far apart. For example, when a person at home accesses a page on the World Wide Web, the same model is employed, with the remote Web server being the server and the user's personal computer being the client. Under most conditions, one server can handle a large number of clients.

If we look at the client-server model in detail, we see that two processes are involved, one on the client machine and one on the server machine. Communication takes the form of the client process sending a message over the network to the server process. The client process then waits for a reply message. When the server process gets the request, it performs the requested work or looks up the requested data and sends back a reply. These messages are shown in Fig. 1-2.

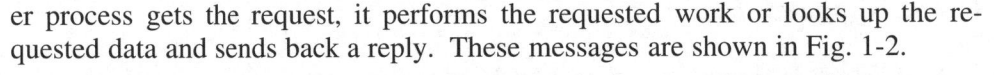
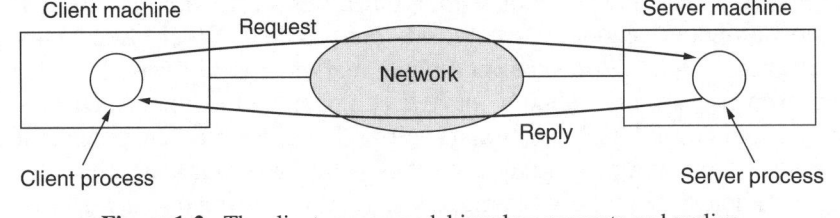

Figure 1-2. The client-server model involves requests and replies.

A second goal of setting up a computer network has to do with people rather than information or even computers. A computer network can provide a powerful **communication medium** among employees. Virtually every company that has two or more computers now has **e-mail** (**electronic mail**), which employees generally use for a great deal of daily communication. In fact, a common gripe around the water cooler is how much e-mail everyone has to deal with, much of it meaningless because bosses have discovered that they can send the same (often content-free) message to all their subordinates at the push of a button.

But e-mail is not the only form of improved communication made possible by computer networks. With a network, it is easy for two or more people who work far apart to write a report together. When one worker makes a change to an on-line document, the others can see the change immediately, instead of waiting several days for a letter. Such a speedup makes cooperation among far-flung groups of people easy where it previously had been impossible.

Yet another form of computer-assisted communication is videoconferencing. Using this technology, employees at distant locations can hold a meeting, seeing and hearing each other and even writing on a shared virtual blackboard. Videoconferencing is a powerful tool for eliminating the cost and time previously devoted to travel. It is sometimes said that communication and transportation are having a race, and whichever wins will make the other obsolete.

A third goal for increasingly many companies is doing business electronically with other companies, especially suppliers and customers. For example, manufacturers of automobiles, aircraft, and computers, among others, buy subsystems from a variety of suppliers and then assemble the parts. Using computer networks, manufacturers can place orders electronically as needed. Being able to place orders in real time (i.e., as needed) reduces the need for large inventories and enhances efficiency.

A fourth goal that is starting to become more important is doing business with consumers over the Internet. Airlines, bookstores, and music vendors have discovered that many customers like the convenience of shopping from home. Consequently, many companies provide catalogs of their goods and services on-line and take orders on-line. This sector is expected to grow quickly in the future. It is called **e-commerce** (**electronic commerce**).

1.1.2 Home Applications

In 1977, Ken Olsen was president of the Digital Equipment Corporation, then the number two computer vendor in the world (after IBM). When asked why Digital was not going after the personal computer market in a big way, he said: "There is no reason for any individual to have a computer in his home." History showed otherwise and Digital no longer exists. Why do people buy computers for home use? Initially, for word processing and games, but in recent years that picture has changed radically. Probably the biggest reason now is for Internet access. Some of the more popular uses of the Internet for home users are as follows:

1. Access to remote information.

2. Person-to-person communication.

3. Interactive entertainment.

4. Electronic commerce.

Access to remote information comes in many forms. It can be surfing the World Wide Web for information or just for fun. Information available includes the arts, business, cooking, government, health, history, hobbies, recreation, science, sports, travel, and many others. Fun comes in too many ways to mention, plus some ways that are better left unmentioned.

Many newspapers have gone on-line and can be personalized. For example, it is sometimes possible to tell a newspaper that you want everything about corrupt politicians, big fires, scandals involving celebrities, and epidemics, but no football, thank you. Sometimes it is even possible to have the selected articles downloaded to your hard disk while you sleep or printed on your printer just before breakfast. As this trend continues, it will cause massive unemployment among 12-year-old paperboys, but newspapers like it because distribution has always been the weakest link in the whole production chain.

The next step beyond newspapers (plus magazines and scientific journals) is the on-line digital library. Many professional organizations, such as the ACM (*www.acm.org*) and the IEEE Computer Society (*www.computer.org*), already have many journals and conference proceedings on-line. Other groups are following rapidly. Depending on the cost, size, and weight of book-sized notebook computers, printed books may become obsolete. Skeptics should take note of the effect the printing press had on the medieval illuminated manuscript.

All of the above applications involve interactions between a person and a remote database full of information. The second broad category of network use is person-to-person communication, basically the 21st century's answer to the 19th century's telephone. E-mail is already used on a daily basis by millions of people all over the world and its use is growing rapidly. It already routinely contains audio and video as well as text and pictures. Smell may take a while.

Any teenager worth his or her salt is addicted to **instant messaging**. This facility, derived from the UNIX *talk* program in use since around 1970, allows two people to type messages at each other in real time. A multiperson version of this idea is the **chat room**, in which a group of people can type messages for all to see.

Worldwide newsgroups, with discussions on every conceivable topic, are already commonplace among a select group of people, and this phenomenon will grow to include the population at large. These discussions, in which one person posts a message and all the other subscribers to the newsgroup can read it, run the gamut from humorous to impassioned. Unlike chat rooms, newsgroups are not real time and messages are saved so that when someone comes back from vacation, all messages that have been posted in the meanwhile are patiently waiting for reading.

Another type of person-to-person communication often goes by the name of **peer-to-peer** communication, to distinguish it from the client-server model (Parameswaran et al., 2001). In this form, individuals who form a loose group can communicate with others in the group, as shown in Fig. 1-3. Every person can, in principle, communicate with one or more other people; there is no fixed division into clients and servers.

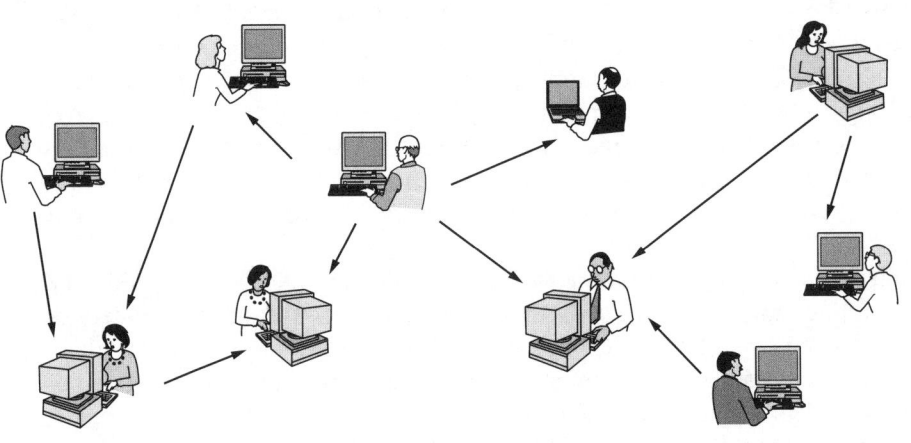

Figure 1-3. In a peer-to-peer system there are no fixed clients and servers.

Peer-to-peer communication really hit the big time around 2000 with a service called Napster, which at its peak had over 50 million music fans swapping music, in what was probably the biggest copyright infringement in all of recorded history (Lam and Tan, 2001; and Macedonia, 2000). The idea was fairly simple. Members registered the music they had on their hard disks in a central database maintained on the Napster server. If a member wanted a song, he checked the database to see who had it and went directly there to get it. By not actually keeping any music on its machines, Napster argued that it was not infringing anyone's copyright. The courts did not agree and shut it down.

However, the next generation of peer-to-peer systems eliminates the central database by having each user maintain his own database locally, as well as providing a list of other nearby people who are members of the system. A new user can then go to any existing member to see what he has and get a list of other members to inspect for more music and more names. This lookup process can be repeated indefinitely to build up a large local database of what is out there. It is an activity that would get tedious for people but is one at which computers excel.

Legal applications for peer-to-peer communication also exist. For example, fans sharing public domain music or sample tracks that new bands have released for publicity purposes, families sharing photos, movies, and genealogical information, and teenagers playing multiperson on-line games. In fact, one of the most popular Internet applications of all, e-mail, is inherently peer-to-peer. This form of communication is expected to grow considerably in the future.

Electronic crime is not restricted to copyright law. Another hot area is electronic gambling. Computers have been simulating things for decades. Why not simulate slot machines, roulette wheels, blackjack dealers, and more gambling equipment? Well, because it is illegal in a lot of places. The trouble is, gambling is legal in a lot of other places (England, for example) and casino owners there have grasped the potential for Internet gambling. What happens if the gambler and the casino are in different countries, with conflicting laws? Good question.

Other communication-oriented applications include using the Internet to carry telephone calls, video phone, and Internet radio, three rapidly growing areas. Another application is telelearning, meaning attending 8 A.M. classes without the inconvenience of having to get out of bed first. In the long run, the use of networks to enhance human-to-human communication may prove more important than any of the others.

Our third category is entertainment, which is a huge and growing industry. The killer application here (the one that may drive all the rest) is video on demand. A decade or so hence, it may be possible to select any movie or television program ever made, in any country, and have it displayed on your screen instantly. New films may become interactive, where the user is occasionally prompted for the story direction (should Macbeth murder Duncan or just bide his time?) with alternative scenarios provided for all cases. Live television may also become interactive, with the audience participating in quiz shows, choosing among contestants, and so on.

On the other hand, maybe the killer application will not be video on demand. Maybe it will be game playing. Already we have multiperson real-time simulation games, like hide-and-seek in a virtual dungeon, and flight simulators with the players on one team trying to shoot down the players on the opposing team. If games are played with goggles and three-dimensional real-time, photographic-quality moving images, we have a kind of worldwide shared virtual reality.

Our fourth category is electronic commerce in the broadest sense of the term. Home shopping is already popular and enables users to inspect the on-line catalogs of thousands of companies. Some of these catalogs will soon provide the ability to get an instant video on any product by just clicking on the product's name. After the customer buys a product electronically but cannot figure out how to use it, on-line technical support may be consulted.

Another area in which e-commerce is already happening is access to financial institutions. Many people already pay their bills, manage their bank accounts, and handle their investments electronically. This will surely grow as networks become more secure.

One area that virtually nobody foresaw is electronic flea markets (e-flea?). On-line auctions of second-hand goods have become a massive industry. Unlike traditional e-commerce, which follows the client-server model, on-line auctions are more of a peer-to-peer system, sort of consumer-to-consumer. Some of these forms of e-commerce have acquired cute little tags based on the fact that "to" and "2" are pronounced the same. The most popular ones are listed in Fig. 1-4.

Tag	Full name	Example
B2C	Business-to-consumer	Ordering books on-line
B2B	Business-to-business	Car manufacturer ordering tires from supplier
G2C	Government-to-consumer	Government distributing tax forms electronically
C2C	Consumer-to-consumer	Auctioning second-hand products on line
P2P	Peer-to-peer	File sharing

Figure 1-4. Some forms of e-commerce.

No doubt the range of uses of computer networks will grow rapidly in the future, and probably in ways no one can now foresee. After all, how many people in 1990 predicted that teenagers tediously typing short text messages on mobile phones while riding buses would be an immense money maker for telephone companies in 10 years? But short message service is very profitable.

Computer networks may become hugely important to people who are geographically challenged, giving them the same access to services as people living in the middle of a big city. Telelearning may radically affect education; universities may go national or international. Telemedicine is only now starting to catch on (e.g., remote patient monitoring) but may become much more important. But the killer application may be something mundane, like using the webcam in your refrigerator to see if you have to buy milk on the way home from work.

1.1.3 Mobile Users

Mobile computers, such as notebook computers and personal digital assistants (PDAs), are one of the fastest-growing segments of the computer industry. Many owners of these computers have desktop machines back at the office and want to be connected to their home base even when away from home or en route. Since having a wired connection is impossible in cars and airplanes, there is a lot of interest in wireless networks. In this section we will briefly look at some of the uses of wireless networks.

Why would anyone want one? A common reason is the portable office. People on the road often want to use their portable electronic equipment to send and receive telephone calls, faxes, and electronic mail, surf the Web, access remote files, and log on to remote machines. And they want to do this from anywhere on land, sea, or air. For example, at computer conferences these days, the organizers often set up a wireless network in the conference area. Anyone with a notebook computer and a wireless modem can just turn the computer on and be connected to the Internet, as though the computer were plugged into a wired network. Similarly, some universities have installed wireless networks on campus so students can sit under the trees and consult the library's card catalog or read their e-mail.

Wireless networks are of great value to fleets of trucks, taxis, delivery vehicles, and repairpersons for keeping in contact with home. For example, in many cities, taxi drivers are independent businessmen, rather than being employees of a taxi company. In some of these cities, the taxis have a display the driver can see. When a customer calls up, a central dispatcher types in the pickup and destination points. This information is displayed on the drivers' displays and a beep sounds. The first driver to hit a button on the display gets the call.

Wireless networks are also important to the military. If you have to be able to fight a war anywhere on earth on short notice, counting on using the local networking infrastructure is probably not a good idea. It is better to bring your own.

Although wireless networking and mobile computing are often related, they are not identical, as Fig. 1-5 shows. Here we see a distinction between **fixed wireless** and **mobile wireless**. Even notebook computers are sometimes wired. For example, if a traveler plugs a notebook computer into the telephone jack in a hotel room, he has mobility without a wireless network.

Wireless	Mobile	Applications
No	No	Desktop computers in offices
No	Yes	A notebook computer used in a hotel room
Yes	No	Networks in older, unwired buildings
Yes	Yes	Portable office; PDA for store inventory

Figure 1-5. Combinations of wireless networks and mobile computing.

On the other hand, some wireless computers are not mobile. An important example is a company that owns an older building lacking network cabling, and which wants to connect its computers. Installing a wireless network may require little more than buying a small box with some electronics, unpacking it, and plugging it in. This solution may be far cheaper than having workmen put in cable ducts to wire the building.

But of course, there are also the true mobile, wireless applications, ranging from the portable office to people walking around a store with a PDA doing inventory. At many busy airports, car rental return clerks work in the parking lot with wireless portable computers. They type in the license plate number of returning cars, and their portable, which has a built-in printer, calls the main computer, gets the rental information, and prints out the bill on the spot.

As wireless technology becomes more widespread, numerous other applications are likely to emerge. Let us take a quick look at some of the possibilities. Wireless parking meters have advantages for both users and city governments. The meters could accept credit or debit cards with instant verification over the wireless link. When a meter expires, it could check for the presence of a car (by bouncing a signal off it) and report the expiration to the police. It has been estimated that city governments in the U.S. alone could collect an additional $10 billion this way (Harte et al., 2000). Furthermore, better parking enforcement would help the environment, as drivers who knew their illegal parking was sure to be caught might use public transport instead.

Food, drink, and other vending machines are found everywhere. However, the food does not get into the machines by magic. Periodically, someone comes by with a truck to fill them. If the vending machines issued a wireless report once a day announcing their current inventories, the truck driver would know which machines needed servicing and how much of which product to bring. This information could lead to more efficient route planning. Of course, this information could be sent over a standard telephone line as well, but giving every vending machine a fixed telephone connection for one call a day is expensive on account of the fixed monthly charge.

Another area in which wireless could save money is utility meter reading. If electricity, gas, water, and other meters in people's homes were to report usage over a wireless network, there would be no need to send out meter readers. Similarly, wireless smoke detectors could call the fire department instead of making a big noise (which has little value if no one is home). As the cost of both the radio devices and the air time drops, more and more measurement and reporting will be done with wireless networks.

A whole different application area for wireless networks is the expected merger of cell phones and PDAs into tiny wireless computers. A first attempt was tiny wireless PDAs that could display stripped-down Web pages on their even tinier screens. This system, called **WAP 1.0 (Wireless Application Protocol)** failed, mostly due to the microscopic screens, low bandwidth, and poor service. But newer devices and services will be better with WAP 2.0.

One area in which these devices may excel is called **m-commerce (mobile-commerce)** (Senn, 2000). The driving force behind this phenomenon consists of an amalgam of wireless PDA manufacturers and network operators who are trying hard to figure out how to get a piece of the e-commerce pie. One of their hopes is to use wireless PDAs for banking and shopping. One idea is to use the wireless

PDAs as a kind of electronic wallet, authorizing payments in stores, as a replacement for cash and credit cards. The charge then appears on the mobile phone bill. From the store's point of view, this scheme may save them most of the credit card company's fee, which can be several percent. Of course, this plan may backfire, since customers in a store might use their PDAs to check out competitors' prices before buying. Worse yet, telephone companies might offer PDAs with bar code readers that allow a customer to scan a product in a store and then instantaneously get a detailed report on where else it can be purchased and at what price.

Since the network operator knows where the user is, some services are intentionally location dependent. For example, it may be possible to ask for a nearby bookstore or Chinese restaurant. Mobile maps are another candidate. So are very local weather forecasts ("When is it going to stop raining in my backyard?"). No doubt many other applications appear as these devices become more widespread.

One huge thing that m-commerce has going for it is that mobile phone users are accustomed to paying for everything (in contrast to Internet users, who expect everything to be free). If an Internet Web site charged a fee to allow its customers to pay by credit card, there would be an immense howling noise from the users. If a mobile phone operator allowed people to pay for items in a store by using the phone and then tacked on a fee for this convenience, it would probably be accepted as normal. Time will tell.

A little further out in time are personal area networks and wearable computers. IBM has developed a watch that runs Linux (including the X11 windowing system) and has wireless connectivity to the Internet for sending and receiving e-mail (Narayanaswami et al., 2002). In the future, people may exchange business cards just by exposing their watches to each other. Wearable wireless computers may give people access to secure rooms the same way magnetic stripe cards do now (possibly in combination with a PIN code or biometric measurement). These watches may also be able to retrieve information relevant to the user's current location (e.g., local restaurants). The possibilities are endless.

Smart watches with radios have been part of our mental space since their appearance in the Dick Tracy comic strip in 1946. But smart dust? Researchers at Berkeley have packed a wireless computer into a cube 1 mm on edge (Warneke et al., 2001). Potential applications include tracking inventory, packages, and even small birds, rodents, and insects.

1.1.4 Social Issues

The widespread introduction of networking has introduced new social, ethical, and political problems. Let us just briefly mention a few of them; a thorough study would require a full book, at least. A popular feature of many networks are newsgroups or bulletin boards whereby people can exchange messages with like-minded individuals. As long as the subjects are restricted to technical topics or hobbies like gardening, not too many problems will arise.

The trouble comes when newsgroups are set up on topics that people actually care about, like politics, religion, or sex. Views posted to such groups may be deeply offensive to some people. Worse yet, they may not be politically correct. Furthermore, messages need not be limited to text. High-resolution color photographs and even short video clips can now easily be transmitted over computer networks. Some people take a live-and-let-live view, but others feel that posting certain material (e.g., attacks on particular countries or religions, pornography, etc.) is simply unacceptable and must be censored. Different countries have different and conflicting laws in this area. Thus, the debate rages.

People have sued network operators, claiming that they are responsible for the contents of what they carry, just as newspapers and magazines are. The inevitable response is that a network is like a telephone company or the post office and cannot be expected to police what its users say. Stronger yet, were network operators to censor messages, they would likely delete everything containing even the slightest possibility of them being sued, and thus violate their users' rights to free speech. It is probably safe to say that this debate will go on for a while.

Another fun area is employee rights versus employer rights. Many people read and write e-mail at work. Many employers have claimed the right to read and possibly censor employee messages, including messages sent from a home computer after work. Not all employees agree with this.

Even if employers have power over employees, does this relationship also govern universities and students? How about high schools and students? In 1994, Carnegie-Mellon University decided to turn off the incoming message stream for several newsgroups dealing with sex because the university felt the material was inappropriate for minors (i.e., those few students under 18). The fallout from this event took years to settle.

Another key topic is government versus citizen. The FBI has installed a system at many Internet service providers to snoop on all incoming and outgoing e-mail for nuggets of interest to it (Blaze and Bellovin, 2000; Sobel, 2001; and Zacks, 2001). The system was originally called **Carnivore** but bad publicity caused it to be renamed to the more innocent-sounding DCS1000. But its goal is still to spy on millions of people in the hope of finding information about illegal activities. Unfortunately, the Fourth Amendment to the U.S. Constitution prohibits government searches without a search warrant. Whether these 54 words, written in the 18th century, still carry any weight in the 21st century is a matter that may keep the courts busy until the 22nd century.

The government does not have a monopoly on threatening people's privacy. The private sector does its bit too. For example, small files called cookies that Web browsers store on users' computers allow companies to track users' activities in cyberspace and also may allow credit card numbers, social security numbers, and other confidential information to leak all over the Internet (Berghel, 2001).

Computer networks offer the potential for sending anonymous messages. In some situations, this capability may be desirable. For example, it provides a way for students, soldiers, employees, and citizens to blow the whistle on illegal behavior on the part of professors, officers, superiors, and politicians without fear of reprisals. On the other hand, in the United States and most other democracies, the law specifically permits an accused person the right to confront and challenge his accuser in court. Anonymous accusations cannot be used as evidence.

In short, computer networks, like the printing press 500 years ago, allow ordinary citizens to distribute their views in different ways and to different audiences than were previously possible. This new-found freedom brings with it many unsolved social, political, and moral issues.

Along with the good comes the bad. Life seems to be like that. The Internet makes it possible to find information quickly, but a lot of it is ill-informed, misleading, or downright wrong. The medical advice you plucked from the Internet may have come from a Nobel Prize winner or from a high school dropout. Computer networks have also introduced new kinds of antisocial and criminal behavior. Electronic junk mail (spam) has become a part of life because people have collected millions of e-mail addresses and sell them on CD-ROMs to would-be marketeers. E-mail messages containing active content (basically programs or macros that execute on the receiver's machine) can contain viruses that wreak havoc.

Identity theft is becoming a serious problem as thieves collect enough information about a victim to obtain get credit cards and other documents in the victim's name. Finally, being able to transmit music and video digitally has opened the door to massive copyright violations that are hard to catch and enforce.

A lot of these problems could be solved if the computer industry took computer security seriously. If all messages were encrypted and authenticated, it would be harder to commit mischief. This technology is well established and we will study it in detail in Chap. 8. The problem is that hardware and software vendors know that putting in security features costs money and their customers are not demanding such features. In addition, a substantial number of the problems are caused by buggy software, which occurs because vendors keep adding more and more features to their programs, which inevitably means more code and thus more bugs. A tax on new features might help, but that is probably a tough sell in some quarters. A refund for defective software might be nice, except it would bankrupt the entire software industry in the first year.

1.2 NETWORK HARDWARE

It is now time to turn our attention from the applications and social aspects of networking (the fun stuff) to the technical issues involved in network design (the work stuff). There is no generally accepted taxonomy into which all computer networks fit, but two dimensions stand out as important: transmission technology and scale. We will now examine each of these in turn.

Broadly speaking, there are two types of transmission technology that are in widespread use. They are as follows:

1. Broadcast links.

2. Point-to-point links.

Broadcast networks have a single communication channel that is shared by all the machines on the network. Short messages, called **packets** in certain contexts, sent by any machine are received by all the others. An address field within the packet specifies the intended recipient. Upon receiving a packet, a machine checks the address field. If the packet is intended for the receiving machine, that machine processes the packet; if the packet is intended for some other machine, it is just ignored.

As an analogy, consider someone standing at the end of a corridor with many rooms off it and shouting "Watson, come here. I want you." Although the packet may actually be received (heard) by many people, only Watson responds. The others just ignore it. Another analogy is an airport announcement asking all flight 644 passengers to report to gate 12 for immediate boarding.

Broadcast systems generally also allow the possibility of addressing a packet to *all* destinations by using a special code in the address field. When a packet with this code is transmitted, it is received and processed by every machine on the network. This mode of operation is called **broadcasting**. Some broadcast systems also support transmission to a subset of the machines, something known as **multicasting**. One possible scheme is to reserve one bit to indicate multicasting. The remaining $n - 1$ address bits can hold a group number. Each machine can "subscribe" to any or all of the groups. When a packet is sent to a certain group, it is delivered to all machines subscribing to that group.

In contrast, **point-to-point** networks consist of many connections between individual pairs of machines. To go from the source to the destination, a packet on this type of network may have to first visit one or more intermediate machines. Often multiple routes, of different lengths, are possible, so finding good ones is important in point-to-point networks. As a general rule (although there are many exceptions), smaller, geographically localized networks tend to use broadcasting, whereas larger networks usually are point-to-point. Point-to-point transmission with one sender and one receiver is sometimes called **unicasting**.

An alternative criterion for classifying networks is their scale. In Fig. 1-6 we classify multiple processor systems by their physical size. At the top are the **personal area networks**, networks that are meant for one person. For example, a wireless network connecting a computer with its mouse, keyboard, and printer is a personal area network. Also, a PDA that controls the user's hearing aid or pacemaker fits in this category. Beyond the personal area networks come longer-range networks. These can be divided into local, metropolitan, and wide area networks. Finally, the connection of two or more networks is called an internetwork.

Interprocessor distance	Processors located in same	Example
1 m	Square meter	Personal area network
10 m	Room	} Local area network
100 m	Building	
1 km	Campus	
10 km	City	Metropolitan area network
100 km	Country	} Wide area network
1000 km	Continent	
10,000 km	Planet	The Internet

Figure 1-6. Classification of interconnected processors by scale.

The worldwide Internet is a well-known example of an internetwork. Distance is important as a classification metric because different techniques are used at different scales. In this book we will be concerned with networks at all these scales. Below we give a brief introduction to network hardware.

1.2.1 Local Area Networks

Local area networks, generally called **LANs**, are privately-owned networks within a single building or campus of up to a few kilometers in size. They are widely used to connect personal computers and workstations in company offices and factories to share resources (e.g., printers) and exchange information. LANs are distinguished from other kinds of networks by three characteristics: (1) their size, (2) their transmission technology, and (3) their topology.

LANs are restricted in size, which means that the worst-case transmission time is bounded and known in advance. Knowing this bound makes it possible to use certain kinds of designs that would not otherwise be possible. It also simplifies network management.

LANs may use a transmission technology consisting of a cable to which all the machines are attached, like the telephone company party lines once used in rural areas. Traditional LANs run at speeds of 10 Mbps to 100 Mbps, have low delay (microseconds or nanoseconds), and make very few errors. Newer LANs operate at up to 10 Gbps. In this book, we will adhere to tradition and measure line speeds in megabits/sec (1 Mbps is 1,000,000 bits/sec) and gigabits/sec (1 Gbps is 1,000,000,000 bits/sec).

Various topologies are possible for broadcast LANs. Figure 1-7 shows two of them. In a bus (i.e., a linear cable) network, at any instant at most one machine is the master and is allowed to transmit. All other machines are required to refrain from sending. An arbitration mechanism is needed to resolve conflicts when two or more machines want to transmit simultaneously. The arbitration mechanism may be centralized or distributed. IEEE 802.3, popularly called **Ethernet**, for example, is a bus-based broadcast network with decentralized control, usually operating at 10 Mbps to 10 Gbps. Computers on an Ethernet can transmit whenever they want to; if two or more packets collide, each computer just waits a random time and tries again later.

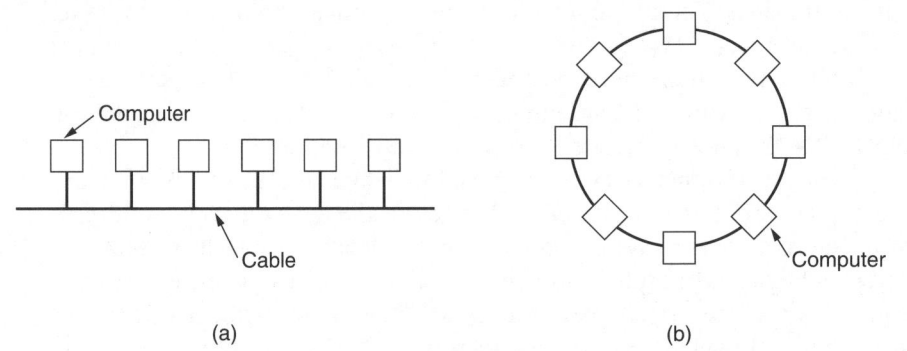

(a)   (b)

Figure 1-7. Two broadcast networks. (a) Bus. (b) Ring.

A second type of broadcast system is the ring. In a ring, each bit propagates around on its own, not waiting for the rest of the packet to which it belongs. Typically, each bit circumnavigates the entire ring in the time it takes to transmit a few bits, often before the complete packet has even been transmitted. As with all other broadcast systems, some rule is needed for arbitrating simultaneous accesses to the ring. Various methods, such as having the machines take turns, are in use. IEEE 802.5 (the IBM token ring), is a ring-based LAN operating at 4 and 16 Mbps. FDDI is another example of a ring network.

Broadcast networks can be further divided into static and dynamic, depending on how the channel is allocated. A typical static allocation would be to divide time into discrete intervals and use a round-robin algorithm, allowing each machine to broadcast only when its time slot comes up. Static allocation wastes channel capacity when a machine has nothing to say during its allocated slot, so most systems attempt to allocate the channel dynamically (i.e., on demand).

Dynamic allocation methods for a common channel are either centralized or decentralized. In the centralized channel allocation method, there is a single entity, for example, a bus arbitration unit, which determines who goes next. It might do this by accepting requests and making a decision according to some internal algorithm. In the decentralized channel allocation method, there is no central entity; each machine must decide for itself whether to transmit. You might think that this always leads to chaos, but it does not. Later we will study many algorithms designed to bring order out of the potential chaos.

1.2.2 Metropolitan Area Networks

A **metropolitan area network**, or **MAN**, covers a city. The best-known example of a MAN is the cable television network available in many cities. This system grew from earlier community antenna systems used in areas with poor over-the-air television reception. In these early systems, a large antenna was placed on top of a nearby hill and signal was then piped to the subscribers' houses.

At first, these were locally-designed, ad hoc systems. Then companies began jumping into the business, getting contracts from city governments to wire up an entire city. The next step was television programming and even entire channels designed for cable only. Often these channels were highly specialized, such as all news, all sports, all cooking, all gardening, and so on. But from their inception until the late 1990s, they were intended for television reception only.

Starting when the Internet attracted a mass audience, the cable TV network operators began to realize that with some changes to the system, they could provide two-way Internet service in unused parts of the spectrum. At that point, the cable TV system began to morph from a way to distribute television to a metropolitan area network. To a first approximation, a MAN might look something like the system shown in Fig. 1-8. In this figure we see both television signals and Internet being fed into the centralized **head end** for subsequent distribution to people's homes. We will come back to this subject in detail in Chap. 2.

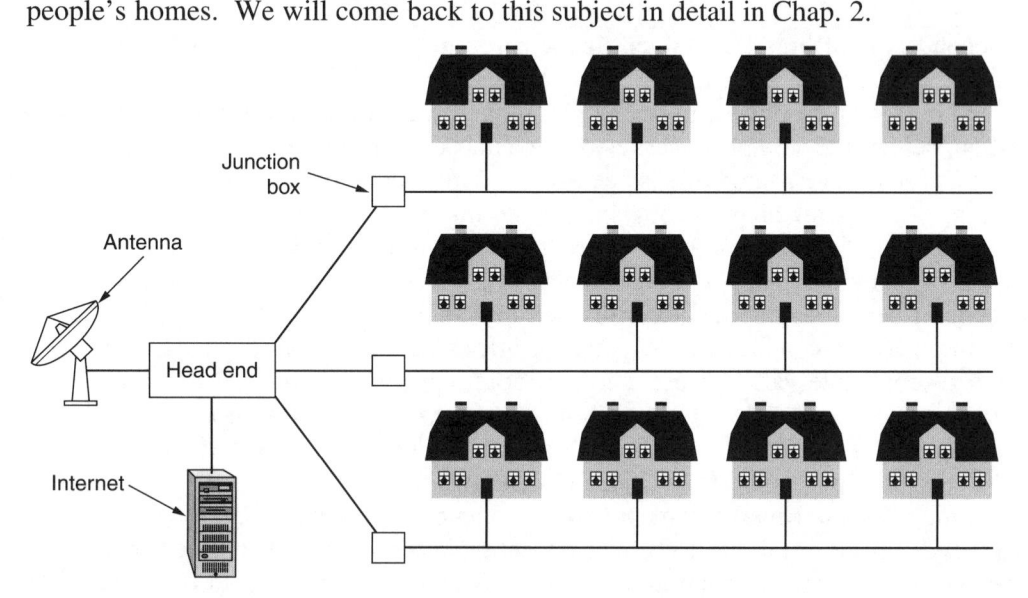

Figure 1-8. A metropolitan area network based on cable TV.

Cable television is not the only MAN. Recent developments in high-speed wireless Internet access resulted in another MAN, which has been standardized as IEEE 802.16. We will look at this area in Chap. 2.

1.2.3 Wide Area Networks

A **wide area network**, or **WAN**, spans a large geographical area, often a country or continent. It contains a collection of machines intended for running user (i.e., application) programs. We will follow traditional usage and call these machines **hosts**. The hosts are connected by a **communication subnet**, or just **subnet** for short. The hosts are owned by the customers (e.g., people's personal computers), whereas the communication subnet is typically owned and operated by a telephone company or Internet service provider. The job of the subnet is to carry messages from host to host, just as the telephone system carries words from speaker to listener. Separation of the pure communication aspects of the network (the subnet) from the application aspects (the hosts), greatly simplifies the complete network design.

In most wide area networks, the subnet consists of two distinct components: transmission lines and switching elements. **Transmission lines** move bits between machines. They can be made of copper wire, optical fiber, or even radio links. **Switching elements** are specialized computers that connect three or more transmission lines. When data arrive on an incoming line, the switching element must choose an outgoing line on which to forward them. These switching computers have been called by various names in the past; the name **router** is now most commonly used. Unfortunately, some people pronounce it "rooter" and others have it rhyme with "doubter." Determining the correct pronunciation will be left as an exercise for the reader. (Note: the perceived correct answer may depend on where you live.)

In this model, shown in Fig. 1-9, each host is frequently connected to a LAN on which a router is present, although in some cases a host can be connected directly to a router. The collection of communication lines and routers (but not the hosts) form the subnet.

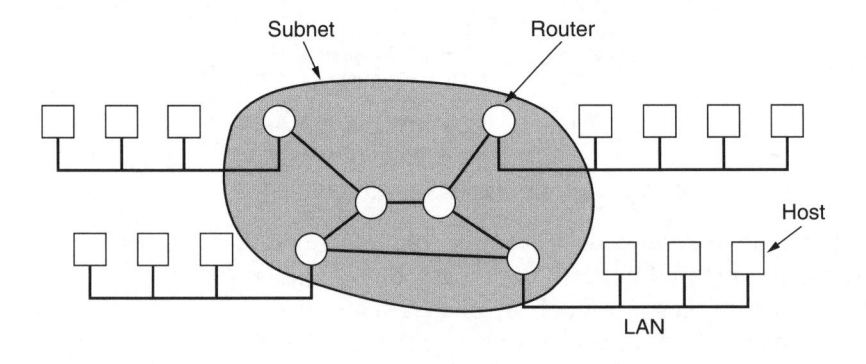

Figure 1-9. Relation between hosts on LANs and the subnet.

A short comment about the term "subnet" is in order here. Originally, its **only** meaning was the collection of routers and communication lines that moved packets from the source host to the destination host. However, some years later, it also acquired a second meaning in conjunction with network addressing (which we will discuss in Chap. 5). Unfortunately, no widely-used alternative exists for its initial meaning, so with some hesitation we will use it in both senses. From the context, it will always be clear which is meant.

In most WANs, the network contains numerous transmission lines, each one connecting a pair of routers. If two routers that do not share a transmission line wish to communicate, they must do this indirectly, via other routers. When a packet is sent from one router to another via one or more intermediate routers, the packet is received at each intermediate router in its entirety, stored there until the required output line is free, and then forwarded. A subnet organized according to this principle is called a **store-and-forward** or **packet-switched** subnet. Nearly all wide area networks (except those using satellites) have store-and-forward subnets. When the packets are small and all the same size, they are often called **cells**.

The principle of a packet-switched WAN is so important that it is worth devoting a few more words to it. Generally, when a process on some host has a message to be sent to a process on some other host, the sending host first cuts the message into packets, each one bearing its number in the sequence. These packets are then injected into the network one at a time in quick succession. The packets are transported individually over the network and deposited at the receiving host, where they are reassembled into the original message and delivered to the receiving process. A stream of packets resulting from some initial message is illustrated in Fig. 1-10.

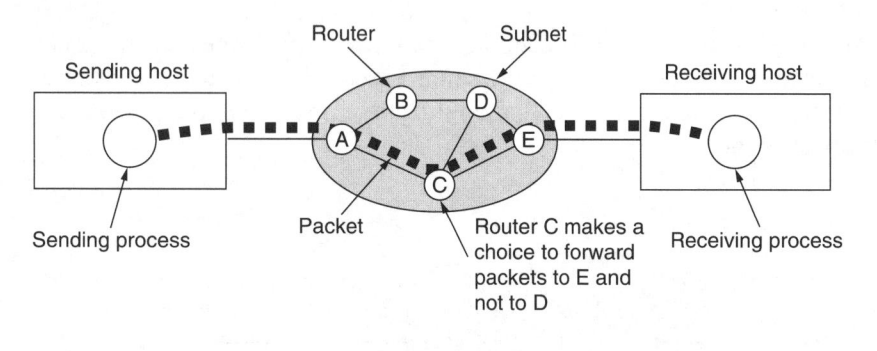

Figure 1-10. A stream of packets from sender to receiver.

In this figure, all the packets follow the route *ACE*, rather than *ABDE* or *ACDE*. In some networks all packets from a given message *must* follow the same route; in others each packet is routed separately. Of course, if *ACE* is the best route, all packets may be sent along it, even if each packet is individually routed.

Routing decisions are made locally. When a packet arrives at router *A*, it is up to *A* to decide if this packet should be sent on the line to *B* or the line to *C*. How *A* makes that decision is called the **routing algorithm**. Many of them exist. We will study some of them in detail in Chap. 5.

Not all WANs are packet switched. A second possibility for a WAN is a satellite system. Each router has an antenna through which it can send and receive. All routers can hear the output *from* the satellite, and in some cases they can also hear the upward transmissions of their fellow routers *to* the satellite as well. Sometimes the routers are connected to a substantial point-to-point subnet, with only some of them having a satellite antenna. Satellite networks are inherently broadcast and are most useful when the broadcast property is important.

1.2.4 Wireless Networks

Digital wireless communication is not a new idea. As early as 1901, the Italian physicist Guglielmo Marconi demonstrated a ship-to-shore wireless telegraph, using Morse Code (dots and dashes are binary, after all). Modern digital wireless systems have better performance, but the basic idea is the same.

To a first approximation, wireless networks can be divided into three main categories:

1. System interconnection.

2. Wireless LANs.

3. Wireless WANs.

System interconnection is all about interconnecting the components of a computer using short-range radio. Almost every computer has a monitor, keyboard, mouse, and printer connected to the main unit by cables. So many new users have a hard time plugging all the cables into the right little holes (even though they are usually color coded) that most computer vendors offer the option of sending a technician to the user's home to do it. Consequently, some companies got together to design a short-range wireless network called **Bluetooth** to connect these components without wires. Bluetooth also allows digital cameras, headsets, scanners, and other devices to connect to a computer by merely being brought within range. No cables, no driver installation, just put them down, turn them on, and they work. For many people, this ease of operation is a big plus.

In the simplest form, system interconnection networks use the master-slave paradigm of Fig. 1-11(a). The system unit is normally the master, talking to the mouse, keyboard, etc., as slaves. The master tells the slaves what addresses to use, when they can broadcast, how long they can transmit, what frequencies they can use, and so on. We will discuss Bluetooth in more detail in Chap. 4.

The next step up in wireless networking are the wireless LANs. These are systems in which every computer has a radio modem and antenna with which it can communicate with other systems. Often there is an antenna on the ceiling that the machines talk to, as shown in Fig. 1-11(b). However, if the systems are close enough, they can communicate directly with one another in a peer-to-peer configuration. Wireless LANs are becoming increasingly common in small offices and

Figure 1-11. (a) Bluetooth configuration. (b) Wireless LAN.

homes, where installing Ethernet is considered too much trouble, as well as in older office buildings, company cafeterias, conference rooms, and other places. There is a standard for wireless LANs, called **IEEE 802.11**, which most systems implement and which is becoming very widespread. We will discuss it in Chap. 4.

The third kind of wireless network is used in wide area systems. The radio network used for cellular telephones is an example of a low-bandwidth wireless system. This system has already gone through three generations. The first generation was analog and for voice only. The second generation was digital and for voice only. The third generation is digital and is for both voice and data. In a certain sense, cellular wireless networks are like wireless LANs, except that the distances involved are much greater and the bit rates much lower. Wireless LANs can operate at rates up to about 50 Mbps over distances of tens of meters. Cellular systems operate below 1 Mbps, but the distance between the base station and the computer or telephone is measured in kilometers rather than in meters. We will have a lot to say about these networks in Chap. 2.

In addition to these low-speed networks, high-bandwidth wide area wireless networks are also being developed. The initial focus is high-speed wireless Internet access from homes and businesses, bypassing the telephone system. This service is often called local multipoint distribution service. We will study it later in the book. A standard for it, called IEEE 802.16, has also been developed. We will examine the standard in Chap. 4.

Almost all wireless networks hook up to the wired network at some point to provide access to files, databases, and the Internet. There are many ways these connections can be realized, depending on the circumstances. For example, in Fig. 1-12(a), we depict an airplane with a number of people using modems and seat-back telephones to call the office. Each call is independent of the other ones. A much more efficient option, however, is the flying LAN of Fig. 1-12(b). Here each seat comes equipped with an Ethernet connector into which passengers can plug their computers. A single router on the aircraft maintains a radio link with some router on the ground, changing routers as it flies along. This configuration is just a traditional LAN, except that its connection to the outside world happens to be a radio link instead of a hardwired line.

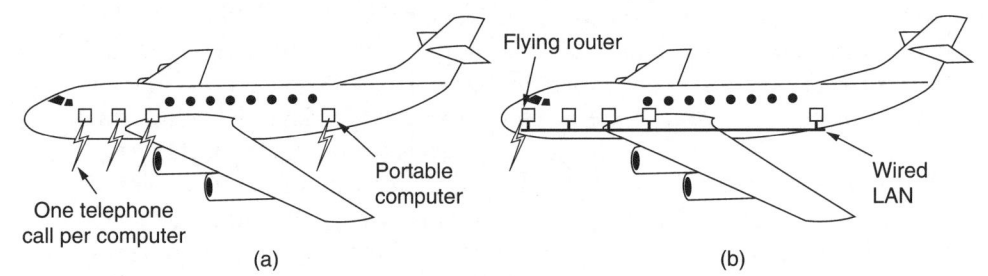

Figure 1-12. (a) Individual mobile computers. (b) A flying LAN.

Many people believe wireless is the wave of the future (e.g., Bi et al., 2001; Leeper, 2001; Varshey and Vetter, 2000) but at least one dissenting voice has been heard. Bob Metcalfe, the inventor of Ethernet, has written: "Mobile wireless computers are like mobile pipeless bathrooms—portapotties. They will be common on vehicles, and at construction sites, and rock concerts. My advice is to wire up your home and stay there" (Metcalfe, 1995). History may record this remark in the same category as IBM's chairman T.J. Watson's 1945 explanation of why IBM was not getting into the computer business: "Four or five computers should be enough for the entire world until the year 2000."

1.2.5 Home Networks

Home networking is on the horizon. The fundamental idea is that in the future most homes will be set up for networking. Every device in the home will be capable of communicating with every other device, and all of them will be accessible over the Internet. This is one of those visionary concepts that nobody asked for (like TV remote controls or mobile phones), but once they arrived nobody can imagine how they lived without them.

Many devices are capable of being networked. Some of the more obvious categories (with examples) are as follows:

1. Computers (desktop PC, notebook PC, PDA, shared peripherals).

2. Entertainment (TV, DVD, VCR, camcorder, camera, stereo, MP3).

3. Telecommunications (telephone, mobile telephone, intercom, fax).

4. Appliances (microwave, refrigerator, clock, furnace, airco, lights).

5. Telemetry (utility meter, smoke/burglar alarm, thermostat, babycam).

Home computer networking is already here in a limited way. Many homes already have a device to connect multiple computers to a fast Internet connection. Networked entertainment is not quite here, but as more and more music and movies can be downloaded from the Internet, there will be a demand to connect stereos and televisions to it. Also, people will want to share their own videos with friends and family, so the connection will need to go both ways. Telecommunications gear is already connected to the outside world, but soon it will be digital and go over the Internet. The average home probably has a dozen clocks (e.g., in appliances), all of which have to be reset twice a year when daylight saving time (summer time) comes and goes. If all the clocks were on the Internet, that resetting could be done automatically. Finally, remote monitoring of the home and its contents is a likely winner. Probably many parents would be willing to spend some money to monitor their sleeping babies on their PDAs when they are eating out, even with a rented teenager in the house. While one can imagine a separate network for each application area, integrating all of them into a single network is probably a better idea.

Home networking has some fundamentally different properties than other network types. First, the network and devices have to be easy to install. The author has installed numerous pieces of hardware and software on various computers over the years, with mixed results. A series of phone calls to the vendor's help-desk typically resulted in answers like (1) Read the manual, (2) Reboot the computer, (3) Remove all hardware and software except ours and try again, (4) Download the newest driver from our Web site, and if all else fails, (5) Reformat the hard disk and then reinstall Windows from the CD-ROM. Telling the purchaser of an Internet refrigerator to download and install a new version of the refrigerator's operating system is not going to lead to happy customers. Computer users are accustomed to putting up with products that do not work; the car-, television-, and refrigerator-buying public is far less tolerant. They expect products to work for 100% from the word go.

Second, the network and devices have to be foolproof in operation. Air conditioners used to have one knob with four settings: OFF, LOW, MEDIUM, and HIGH. Now they have 30-page manuals. Once they are networked, expect the chapter on security alone to be 30 pages. This will be beyond the comprehension of virtually all the users.

Third, low price is essential for success. People will not pay a $50 premium for an Internet thermostat because few people regard monitoring their home temperature from work that important. For $5 extra, it might sell, though.

Fourth, the main application is likely to involve multimedia, so the network needs sufficient capacity. There is no market for Internet-connected televisions that show shaky movies at 320×240 pixel resolution and 10 frames/sec. Fast Ethernet, the workhorse in most offices, is not good enough for multimedia. Consequently, home networks will need better performance than that of existing office networks and at lower prices before they become mass market items.

Fifth, it must be possible to start out with one or two devices and expand the reach of the network gradually. This means no format wars. Telling consumers to buy peripherals with IEEE 1394 (FireWire) interfaces and a few years later retracting that and saying USB 2.0 is the interface-of-the-month is going to make consumers skittish. The network interface will have to remain stable for many years; the wiring (if any) will have to remain stable for decades.

Sixth, security and reliability will be very important. Losing a few files to an e-mail virus is one thing; having a burglar disarm your security system from his PDA and then plunder your house is something quite different.

An interesting question is whether home networks will be wired or wireless. Most homes already have six networks installed: electricity, telephone, cable television, water, gas, and sewer. Adding a seventh one during construction is not difficult, but retrofitting existing houses is expensive. Cost favors wireless networking, but security favors wired networking. The problem with wireless is that the radio waves they use are quite good at going through fences. Not everyone is overjoyed at the thought of having the neighbors piggybacking on their Internet connection and reading their e-mail on its way to the printer. In Chap. 8 we will study how encryption can be used to provide security, but in the context of a home network, security has to be foolproof, even with inexperienced users. This is easier said than done, even with highly sophisticated users.

In short, home networking offers many opportunities and challenges. Most of them relate to the need to be easy to manage, dependable, and secure, especially in the hands of nontechnical users, while at the same time delivering high performance at low cost.

1.2.6 Internetworks

Many networks exist in the world, often with different hardware and software. People connected to one network often want to communicate with people attached to a different one. The fulfillment of this desire requires that different, and frequently incompatible networks, be connected, sometimes by means of machines called **gateways** to make the connection and provide the necessary translation, both in terms of hardware and software. A collection of interconnected networks is called an **internetwork** or **internet**. These terms will be used in a generic sense, in contrast to the worldwide Internet (which is one specific internet), which we will always capitalize.

A common form of internet is a collection of LANs connected by a WAN. In fact, if we were to replace the label "subnet" in Fig. 1-9 by "WAN," nothing else in the figure would have to change. The only real technical distinction between a subnet and a WAN in this case is whether hosts are present. If the system within the gray area contains only routers, it is a subnet; if it contains both routers and hosts, it is a WAN. The real differences relate to ownership and use.

Subnets, networks, and internetworks are often confused. Subnet makes the most sense in the context of a wide area network, where it refers to the collection of routers and communication lines owned by the network operator. As an analogy, the telephone system consists of telephone switching offices connected to one another by high-speed lines, and to houses and businesses by low-speed lines. These lines and equipment, owned and managed by the telephone company, form the subnet of the telephone system. The telephones themselves (the hosts in this analogy) are not part of the subnet. The combination of a subnet and its hosts forms a network. In the case of a LAN, the cable and the hosts form the network. There really is no subnet.

An internetwork is formed when distinct networks are interconnected. In our view, connecting a LAN and a WAN or connecting two LANs forms an internetwork, but there is little agreement in the industry over terminology in this area. One rule of thumb is that if different organizations paid to construct different parts of the network and each maintains its part, we have an internetwork rather than a single network. Also, if the underlying technology is different in different parts (e.g., broadcast versus point-to-point), we probably have two networks.

1.3 NETWORK SOFTWARE

The first computer networks were designed with the hardware as the main concern and the software as an afterthought. This strategy no longer works. Network software is now highly structured. In the following sections we examine the software structuring technique in some detail. The method described here forms the keystone of the entire book and will occur repeatedly later on.

1.3.1 Protocol Hierarchies

To reduce their design complexity, most networks are organized as a stack of **layers** or **levels**, each one built upon the one below it. The number of layers, the name of each layer, the contents of each layer, and the function of each layer differ from network to network. The purpose of each layer is to offer certain services to the higher layers, shielding those layers from the details of how the offered services are actually implemented. In a sense, each layer is a kind of virtual machine, offering certain services to the layer above it.

This concept is actually a familiar one and used throughout computer science, where it is variously known as information hiding, abstract data types, data encapsulation, and object-oriented programming. The fundamental idea is that a particular piece of software (or hardware) provides a service to its users but keeps the details of its internal state and algorithms hidden from them.

Layer n on one machine carries on a conversation with layer n on another machine. The rules and conventions used in this conversation are collectively known as the layer *n* protocol. Basically, a **protocol** is an agreement between the communicating parties on how communication is to proceed. As an analogy, when a woman is introduced to a man, she may choose to stick out her hand. He, in turn, may decide either to shake it or kiss it, depending, for example, on whether she is an American lawyer at a business meeting or a European princess at a formal ball. Violating the protocol will make communication more difficult, if not completely impossible.

A five-layer network is illustrated in Fig. 1-13. The entities comprising the corresponding layers on different machines are called **peers**. The peers may be processes, hardware devices, or even human beings. In other words, it is the peers that communicate by using the protocol.

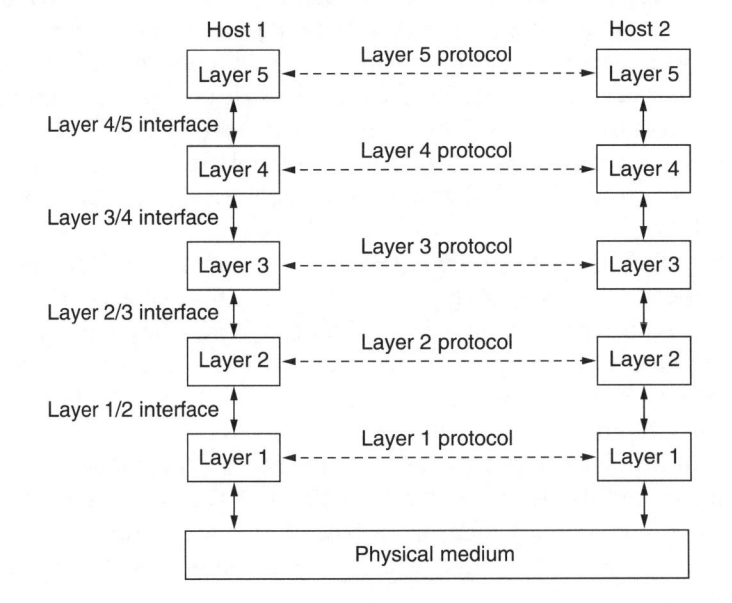

Figure 1-13. Layers, protocols, and interfaces.

In reality, no data are directly transferred from layer *n* on one machine to layer *n* on another machine. Instead, each layer passes data and control information to the layer immediately below it, until the lowest layer is reached. Below layer 1 is the **physical medium** through which actual communication occurs. In Fig. 1-13, virtual communication is shown by dotted lines and physical communication by solid lines.

Between each pair of adjacent layers is an **interface**. The interface defines which primitive operations and services the lower layer makes available to the upper one. When network designers decide how many layers to include in a network and what each one should do, one of the most important considerations is defining clean interfaces between the layers. Doing so, in turn, requires that each layer perform a specific collection of well-understood functions. In addition to minimizing the amount of information that must be passed between layers, clear-cut interfaces also make it simpler to replace the implementation of one layer with a completely different implementation (e.g., all the telephone lines are replaced by satellite channels) because all that is required of the new implementation is that it offer exactly the same set of services to its upstairs neighbor as the old implementation did. In fact, it is common that different hosts use different implementations.

A set of layers and protocols is called a **network architecture**. The specification of an architecture must contain enough information to allow an implementer to write the program or build the hardware for each layer so that it will correctly obey the appropriate protocol. Neither the details of the implementation nor the specification of the interfaces is part of the architecture because these are hidden away inside the machines and not visible from the outside. It is not even necessary that the interfaces on all machines in a network be the same, provided that each machine can correctly use all the protocols. A list of protocols used by a certain system, one protocol per layer, is called a **protocol stack**. The subjects of network architectures, protocol stacks, and the protocols themselves are the principal topics of this book.

An analogy may help explain the idea of multilayer communication. Imagine two philosophers (peer processes in layer 3), one of whom speaks Urdu and English and one of whom speaks Chinese and French. Since they have no common language, they each engage a translator (peer processes at layer 2), each of whom in turn contacts a secretary (peer processes in layer 1). Philosopher 1 wishes to convey his affection for *oryctolagus cuniculus* to his peer. To do so, he passes a message (in English) across the 2/3 interface to his translator, saying "I like rabbits," as illustrated in Fig. 1-14. The translators have agreed on a neutral language known to both of them, Dutch, so the message is converted to "Ik vind konijnen leuk." The choice of language is the layer 2 protocol and is up to the layer 2 peer processes.

The translator then gives the message to a secretary for transmission, by, for example, fax (the layer 1 protocol). When the message arrives, it is translated into French and passed across the 2/3 interface to philosopher 2. Note that each protocol is completely independent of the other ones as long as the interfaces are not changed. The translators can switch from Dutch to say, Finnish, at will, provided that they both agree, and neither changes his interface with either layer 1 or layer 3. Similarly, the secretaries can switch from fax to e-mail or telephone without disturbing (or even informing) the other layers. Each process may add some information intended only for its peer. This information is not passed upward to the layer above.

Now consider a more technical example: how to provide communication to the top layer of the five-layer network in Fig. 1-15. A message, M, is produced by an application process running in layer 5 and given to layer 4 for transmission.

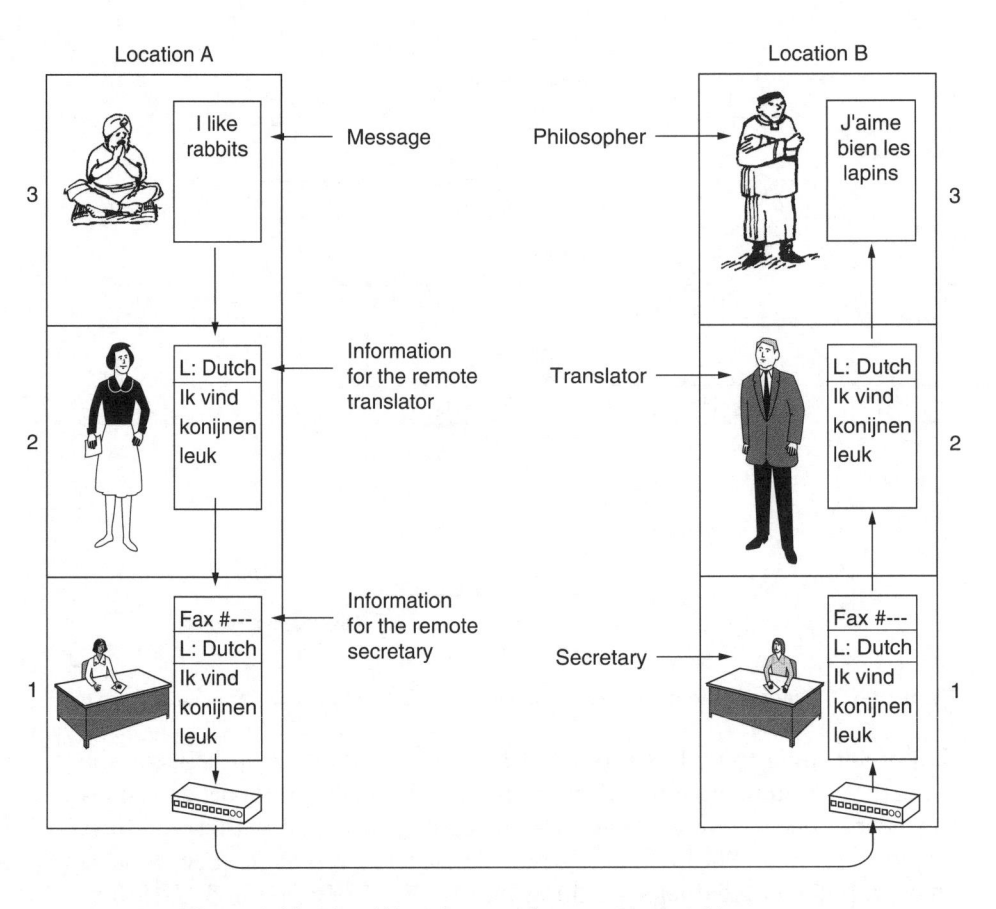

Figure 1-14. The philosopher-translator-secretary architecture.

Layer 4 puts a **header** in front of the message to identify the message and passes the result to layer 3. The header includes control information, such as sequence numbers, to allow layer 4 on the destination machine to deliver messages in the right order if the lower layers do not maintain sequence. In some layers, headers can also contain sizes, times, and other control fields.

In many networks, there is no limit to the size of messages transmitted in the layer 4 protocol, but there is nearly always a limit imposed by the layer 3 protocol. Consequently, layer 3 must break up the incoming messages into smaller units, packets, prepending a layer 3 header to each packet. In this example, M is split into two parts, M_1 and M_2.

Layer 3 decides which of the outgoing lines to use and passes the packets to layer 2. Layer 2 adds not only a header to each piece, but also a trailer, and gives the resulting unit to layer 1 for physical transmission. At the receiving machine the message moves upward, from layer to layer, with headers being stripped off as it progresses. None of the headers for layers below n are passed up to layer n.

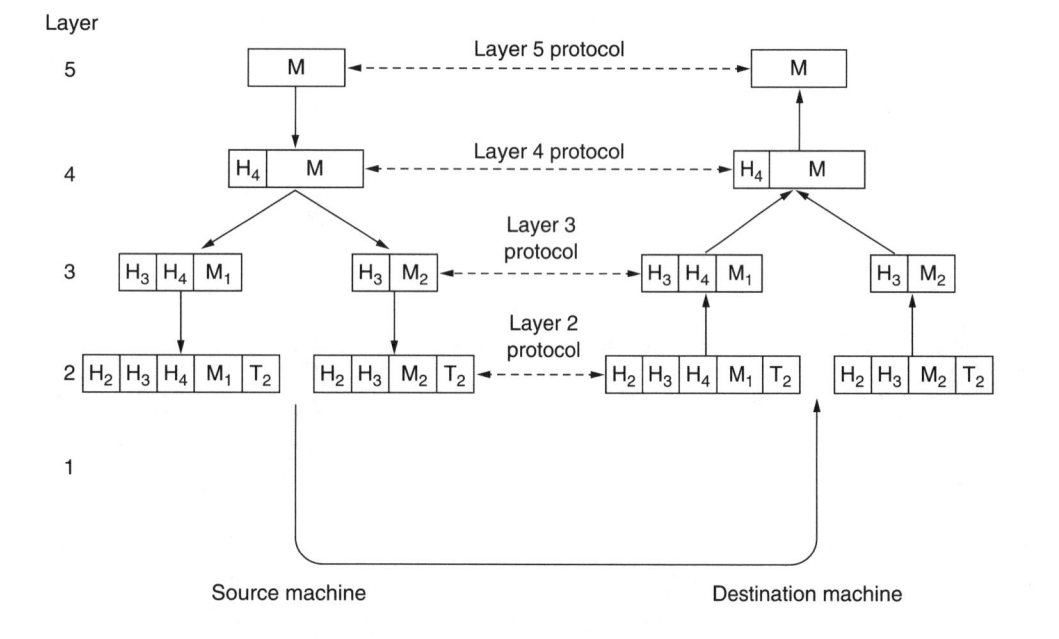

Figure 1-15. Example information flow supporting virtual communication in layer 5.

The important thing to understand about Fig. 1-15 is the relation between the virtual and actual communication and the difference between protocols and interfaces. The peer processes in layer 4, for example, conceptually think of their communication as being "horizontal," using the layer 4 protocol. Each one is likely to have a procedure called something like *SendToOtherSide* and *GetFromOtherSide*, even though these procedures actually communicate with lower layers across the 3/4 interface, not with the other side.

The peer process abstraction is crucial to all network design. Using it, the unmanageable task of designing the complete network can be broken into several smaller, manageable design problems, namely, the design of the individual layers.

Although Sec. 1.3 is called "Network Software," it is worth pointing out that the lower layers of a protocol hierarchy are frequently implemented in hardware or firmware. Nevertheless, complex protocol algorithms are involved, even if they are embedded (in whole or in part) in hardware.

1.3.2 Design Issues for the Layers

Some of the key design issues that occur in computer networks are present in several layers. Below, we will briefly mention some of the more important ones.

Every layer needs a mechanism for identifying senders and receivers. Since a network normally has many computers, some of which have multiple processes, a means is needed for a process on one machine to specify with whom it wants to talk. As a consequence of having multiple destinations, some form of **addressing** is needed in order to specify a specific destination.

Another set of design decisions concerns the rules for data transfer. In some systems, data only travel in one direction; in others, data can go both ways. The protocol must also determine how many logical channels the connection corresponds to and what their priorities are. Many networks provide at least two logical channels per connection, one for normal data and one for urgent data.

Error control is an important issue because physical communication circuits are not perfect. Many error-detecting and error-correcting codes are known, but both ends of the connection must agree on which one is being used. In addition, the receiver must have some way of telling the sender which messages have been correctly received and which have not.

Not all communication channels preserve the order of messages sent on them. To deal with a possible loss of sequencing, the protocol must make explicit provision for the receiver to allow the pieces to be reassembled properly. An obvious solution is to number the pieces, but this solution still leaves open the question of what should be done with pieces that arrive out of order.

An issue that occurs at every level is how to keep a fast sender from swamping a slow receiver with data. Various solutions have been proposed and will be discussed later. Some of them involve some kind of feedback from the receiver to the sender, either directly or indirectly, about the receiver's current situation. Others limit the sender to an agreed-on transmission rate. This subject is called **flow control**.

Another problem that must be solved at several levels is the inability of all processes to accept arbitrarily long messages. This property leads to mechanisms for disassembling, transmitting, and then reassembling messages. A related issue is the problem of what to do when processes insist on transmitting data in units that are so small that sending each one separately is inefficient. Here the solution is to gather several small messages heading toward a common destination into a single large message and dismember the large message at the other side.

When it is inconvenient or expensive to set up a separate connection for each pair of communicating processes, the underlying layer may decide to use the same connection for multiple, unrelated conversations. As long as this **multiplexing** and **demultiplexing** is done transparently, it can be used by any layer. Multiplexing is needed in the physical layer, for example, where all the traffic for all connections has to be sent over at most a few physical circuits.

When there are multiple paths between source and destination, a route must be chosen. Sometimes this decision must be split over two or more layers. For example, to send data from London to Rome, a high-level decision might have to be made to transit France or Germany based on their respective privacy laws. Then a low-level decision might have to made to select one of the available circuits based on the current traffic load. This topic is called **routing**.

1.3.3 Connection-Oriented and Connectionless Services

Layers can offer two different types of service to the layers above them: connection-oriented and connectionless. In this section we will look at these two types and examine the differences between them.

Connection-oriented service is modeled after the telephone system. To talk to someone, you pick up the phone, dial the number, talk, and then hang up. Similarly, to use a connection-oriented network service, the service user first establishes a connection, uses the connection, and then releases the connection. The essential aspect of a connection is that it acts like a tube: the sender pushes objects (bits) in at one end, and the receiver takes them out at the other end. In most cases the order is preserved so that the bits arrive in the order they were sent.

In some cases when a connection is established, the sender, receiver, and subnet conduct a **negotiation** about parameters to be used, such as maximum message size, quality of service required, and other issues. Typically, one side makes a proposal and the other side can accept it, reject it, or make a counterproposal.

In contrast, **connectionless service** is modeled after the postal system. Each message (letter) carries the full destination address, and each one is routed through the system independent of all the others. Normally, when two messages are sent to the same destination, the first one sent will be the first one to arrive. However, it is possible that the first one sent can be delayed so that the second one arrives first.

Each service can be characterized by a **quality of service**. Some services are reliable in the sense that they never lose data. Usually, a reliable service is implemented by having the receiver acknowledge the receipt of each message so the sender is sure that it arrived. The acknowledgement process introduces overhead and delays, which are often worth it but are sometimes undesirable.

A typical situation in which a reliable connection-oriented service is appropriate is file transfer. The owner of the file wants to be sure that all the bits arrive correctly and in the same order they were sent. Very few file transfer customers would prefer a service that occasionally scrambles or loses a few bits, even if it is much faster.

Reliable connection-oriented service has two minor variations: message sequences and byte streams. In the former variant, the message boundaries are preserved. When two 1024-byte messages are sent, they arrive as two distinct 1024-byte messages, never as one 2048-byte message. In the latter, the connection is simply a stream of bytes, with no message boundaries. When 2048 bytes arrive at the receiver, there is no way to tell if they were sent as one 2048-byte message, two 1024-byte messages, or 2048 1-byte messages. If the pages of a book are sent over a network to a phototypesetter as separate messages, it might be important to preserve the message boundaries. On the other hand, when a user logs into a remote server, a byte stream from the user's computer to the server is all that is needed. Message boundaries are not relevant.

As mentioned above, for some applications, the transit delays introduced by acknowledgements are unacceptable. One such application is digitized voice traffic. It is preferable for telephone users to hear a bit of noise on the line from time to time than to experience a delay waiting for acknowledgements. Similarly, when transmitting a video conference, having a few pixels wrong is no problem, but having the image jerk along as the flow stops to correct errors is irritating.

Not all applications require connections. For example, as electronic mail becomes more common, electronic junk is becoming more common too. The electronic junk-mail sender probably does not want to go to the trouble of setting up and later tearing down a connection just to send one item. Nor is 100 percent reliable delivery essential, especially if it costs more. All that is needed is a way to send a single message that has a high probability of arrival, but no guarantee. Unreliable (meaning not acknowledged) connectionless service is often called **datagram service**, in analogy with telegram service, which also does not return an acknowledgement to the sender.

In other situations, the convenience of not having to establish a connection to send one short message is desired, but reliability is essential. The **acknowledged datagram service** can be provided for these applications. It is like sending a registered letter and requesting a return receipt. When the receipt comes back, the sender is absolutely sure that the letter was delivered to the intended party and not lost along the way.

Still another service is the **request-reply service**. In this service the sender transmits a single datagram containing a request; the reply contains the answer. For example, a query to the local library asking where Uighur is spoken falls into this category. Request-reply is commonly used to implement communication in the client-server model: the client issues a request and the server responds to it. Figure 1-16 summarizes the types of services discussed above.

	Service	Example
Connection-oriented	Reliable message stream	Sequence of pages
	Reliable byte stream	Remote login
	Unreliable connection	Digitized voice
Connection-less	Unreliable datagram	Electronic junk mail
	Acknowledged datagram	Registered mail
	Request-reply	Database query

Figure 1-16. Six different types of service.

The concept of using unreliable communication may be confusing at first. After all, why would anyone actually prefer unreliable communication to reliable communication? First of all, reliable communication (in our sense, that is, acknowledged) may not be available. For example, Ethernet does not provide reliable communication. Packets can occasionally be damaged in transit. It is up to higher protocol levels to deal with this problem. Second, the delays inherent in providing a reliable service may be unacceptable, especially in real-time applications such as multimedia. For these reasons, both reliable and unreliable communication coexist.

1.3.4 Service Primitives

A service is formally specified by a set of **primitives** (operations) available to a user process to access the service. These primitives tell the service to perform some action or report on an action taken by a peer entity. If the protocol stack is located in the operating system, as it often is, the primitives are normally system calls. These calls cause a trap to kernel mode, which then turns control of the machine over to the operating system to send the necessary packets.

The set of primitives available depends on the nature of the service being provided. The primitives for connection-oriented service are different from those of connectionless service. As a minimal example of the service primitives that might be provided to implement a reliable byte stream in a client-server environment, consider the primitives listed in Fig. 1-17.

Primitive	Meaning
LISTEN	Block waiting for an incoming connection
CONNECT	Establish a connection with a waiting peer
RECEIVE	Block waiting for an incoming message
SEND	Send a message to the peer
DISCONNECT	Terminate a connection

Figure 1-17. Five service primitives for implementing a simple connection-oriented service.

These primitives might be used as follows. First, the server executes LISTEN to indicate that it is prepared to accept incoming connections. A common way to implement LISTEN is to make it a blocking system call. After executing the primitive, the server process is blocked until a request for connection appears.

Next, the client process executes CONNECT to establish a connection with the server. The CONNECT call needs to specify who to connect to, so it might have a parameter giving the server's address. The operating system then typically sends a packet to the peer asking it to connect, as shown by (1) in Fig. 1-18. The client process is suspended until there is a response. When the packet arrives at the server, it is processed by the operating system there. When the system sees that the packet is requesting a connection, it checks to see if there is a listener. If so, it does two things: unblocks the listener and sends back an acknowledgement (2). The arrival of this acknowledgement then releases the client. At this point the client and server are both running and they have a connection established. It is important to note that the acknowledgement (2) is generated by the protocol code itself, not in response to a user-level primitive. If a connection request arrives and there is no listener, the result is undefined. In some systems the packet may be queued for a short time in anticipation of a LISTEN.

The obvious analogy between this protocol and real life is a customer (client) calling a company's customer service manager. The service manager starts out by being near the telephone in case it rings. Then the client places the call. When the manager picks up the phone, the connection is established.

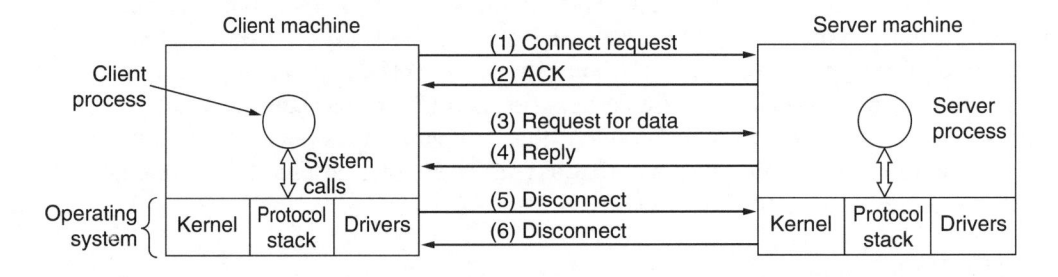

Figure 1-18. Packets sent in a simple client-server interaction on a connection-oriented network.

The next step is for the server to execute RECEIVE to prepare to accept the first request. Normally, the server does this immediately upon being released from the LISTEN, before the acknowledgement can get back to the client. The RECEIVE call blocks the server.

Then the client executes SEND to transmit its request (3) followed by the execution of RECEIVE to get the reply.

The arrival of the request packet at the server machine unblocks the server process so it can process the request. After it has done the work, it uses SEND to return the answer to the client (4). The arrival of this packet unblocks the client, which can now inspect the answer. If the client has additional requests, it can make them now. If it is done, it can use DISCONNECT to terminate the connection. Usually, an initial DISCONNECT is a blocking call, suspending the client and sending a packet to the server saying that the connection is no longer needed (5). When the server gets the packet, it also issues a DISCONNECT of its own, acknowledging the client and releasing the connection. When the server's packet (6) gets back to the client machine, the client process is released and the connection is broken. In a nutshell, this is how connection-oriented communication works.

Of course, life is not so simple. Many things can go wrong here. The timing can be wrong (e.g., the CONNECT is done before the LISTEN), packets can get lost, and much more. We will look at these issues in great detail later, but for the moment, Fig. 1-18 briefly summarizes how client-server communication might work over a connection-oriented network.

Given that six packets are required to complete this protocol, one might wonder why a connectionless protocol is not used instead. The answer is that in a perfect world it could be, in which case only two packets would be needed: one for the request and one for the reply. However, in the face of large messages in either direction (e.g., a megabyte file), transmission errors, and lost packets, the situation changes. If the reply consisted of hundreds of packets, some of which could be lost during transmission, how would the client know if some pieces were missing? How would the client know whether the last packet actually received was really the last packet sent? Suppose that the client wanted a second file. How could it tell packet 1 from the second file from a lost packet 1 from the first file that suddenly found its way to the client? In short, in the real world, a simple request-reply protocol over an unreliable network is often inadequate. In Chap. 3 we will study a variety of protocols in detail that overcome these and other problems. For the moment, suffice it to say that having a reliable, ordered byte stream between processes is sometimes very convenient.

1.3.5 The Relationship of Services to Protocols

Services and protocols are distinct concepts, although they are frequently confused. This distinction is so important, however, that we emphasize it again here. A *service* is a set of primitives (operations) that a layer provides to the layer above it. The service defines what operations the layer is prepared to perform on behalf of its users, but it says nothing at all about how these operations are implemented. A service relates to an interface between two layers, with the lower layer being the service provider and the upper layer being the service user.

A *protocol*, in contrast, is a set of rules governing the format and meaning of the packets, or messages that are exchanged by the peer entities within a layer. Entities use protocols to implement their service definitions. They are free to change their protocols at will, provided they do not change the service visible to their users. In this way, the service and the protocol are completely decoupled.

In other words, services relate to the interfaces between layers, as illustrated in Fig. 1-19. In contrast, protocols relate to the packets sent between peer entities on different machines. It is important not to confuse the two concepts.

An analogy with programming languages is worth making. A service is like an abstract data type or an object in an object-oriented language. It defines operations that can be performed on an object but does not specify how these operations are implemented. A protocol relates to the *implementation* of the service and as such is not visible to the user of the service.

Many older protocols did not distinguish the service from the protocol. In effect, a typical layer might have had a service primitive SEND PACKET with the

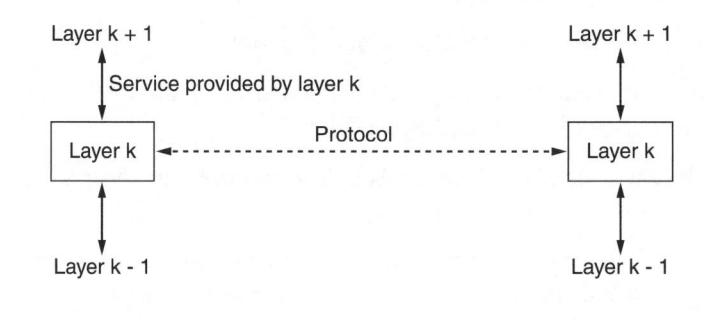

Figure 1-19. The relationship between a service and a protocol.

user providing a pointer to a fully assembled packet. This arrangement meant that all changes to the protocol were immediately visible to the users. Most network designers now regard such a design as a serious blunder.

1.4 REFERENCE MODELS

Now that we have discussed layered networks in the abstract, it is time to look at some examples. In the next two sections we will discuss two important network architectures, the OSI reference model and the TCP/IP reference model. Although the *protocols* associated with the OSI model are rarely used any more, the *model* itself is actually quite general and still valid, and the features discussed at each layer are still very important. The TCP/IP model has the opposite properties: the model itself is not of much use but the protocols are widely used. For this reason we will look at both of them in detail. Also, sometimes you can learn more from failures than from successes.

1.4.1 The OSI Reference Model

The OSI model (minus the physical medium) is shown in Fig. 1-20. This model is based on a proposal developed by the International Standards Organization (ISO) as a first step toward international standardization of the protocols used in the various layers (Day and Zimmermann, 1983). It was revised in 1995 (Day, 1995). The model is called the **ISO OSI (Open Systems Interconnection) Reference Model** because it deals with connecting open systems—that is, systems that are open for communication with other systems. We will just call it the OSI model for short.

The OSI model has seven layers. The principles that were applied to arrive at the seven layers can be briefly summarized as follows:

1. A layer should be created where a different abstraction is needed.

2. Each layer should perform a well-defined function.

3. The function of each layer should be chosen with an eye toward defining internationally standardized protocols.

4. The layer boundaries should be chosen to minimize the information flow across the interfaces.

5. The number of layers should be large enough that distinct functions need not be thrown together in the same layer out of necessity and small enough that the architecture does not become unwieldy.

Below we will discuss each layer of the model in turn, starting at the bottom layer. Note that the OSI model itself is not a network architecture because it does not specify the exact services and protocols to be used in each layer. It just tells what each layer should do. However, ISO has also produced standards for all the layers, although these are not part of the reference model itself. Each one has been published as a separate international standard.

The Physical Layer

The **physical layer** is concerned with transmitting raw bits over a communication channel. The design issues have to do with making sure that when one side sends a 1 bit, it is received by the other side as a 1 bit, not as a 0 bit. Typical questions here are how many volts should be used to represent a 1 and how many for a 0, how many nanoseconds a bit lasts, whether transmission may proceed simultaneously in both directions, how the initial connection is established and how it is torn down when both sides are finished, and how many pins the network connector has and what each pin is used for. The design issues here largely deal with mechanical, electrical, and timing interfaces, and the physical transmission medium, which lies below the physical layer.

The Data Link Layer

The main task of the **data link layer** is to transform a raw transmission facility into a line that appears free of undetected transmission errors to the network layer. It accomplishes this task by having the sender break up the input data into **data frames** (typically a few hundred or a few thousand bytes) and transmit the frames sequentially. If the service is reliable, the receiver confirms correct receipt of each frame by sending back an **acknowledgement frame**.

Another issue that arises in the data link layer (and most of the higher layers as well) is how to keep a fast transmitter from drowning a slow receiver in data. Some traffic regulation mechanism is often needed to let the transmitter know

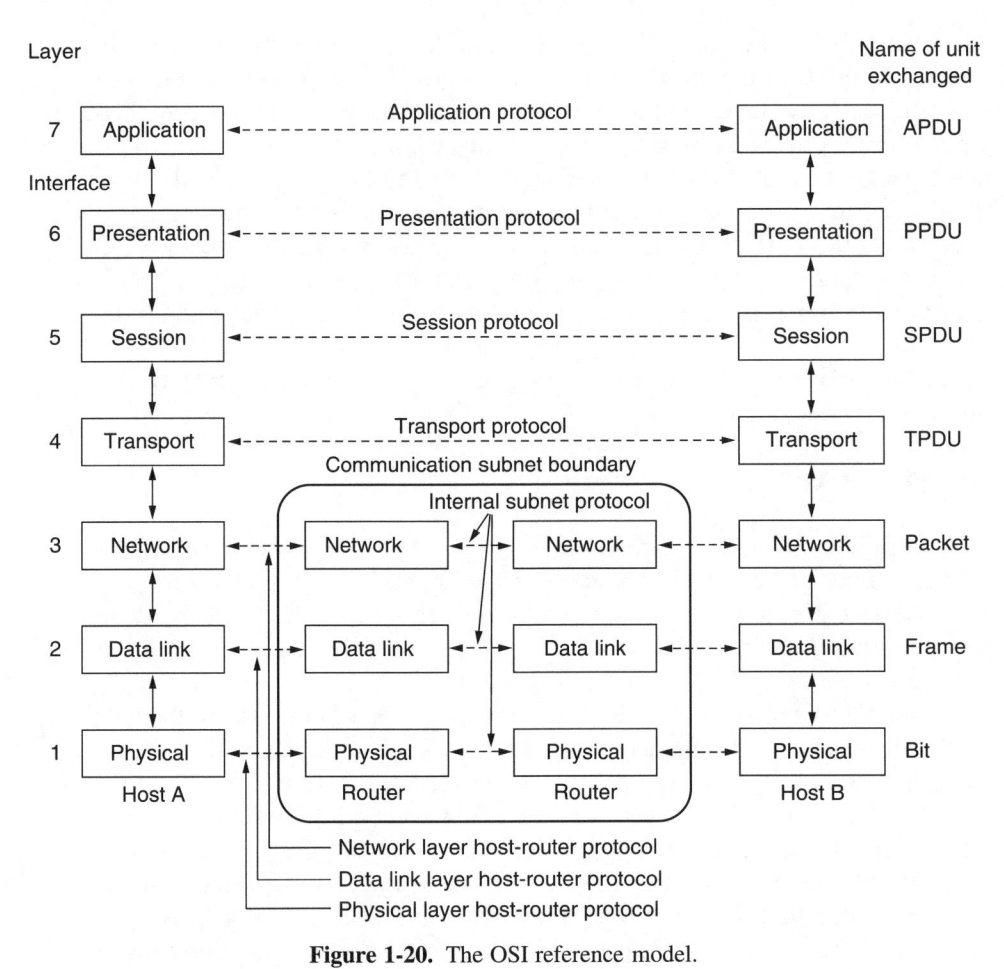

Figure 1-20. The OSI reference model.

how much buffer space the receiver has at the moment. Frequently, this flow regulation and the error handling are integrated.

Broadcast networks have an additional issue in the data link layer: how to control access to the shared channel. A special sublayer of the data link layer, the medium access control sublayer, deals with this problem.

The Network Layer

The **network layer** controls the operation of the subnet. A key design issue is determining how packets are routed from source to destination. Routes can be based on static tables that are "wired into" the network and rarely changed. They can also be determined at the start of each conversation, for example, a terminal session (e.g., a login to a remote machine). Finally, they can be highly dynamic, being determined anew for each packet, to reflect the current network load.

If too many packets are present in the subnet at the same time, they will get in one another's way, forming bottlenecks. The control of such congestion also belongs to the network layer. More generally, the quality of service provided (delay, transit time, jitter, etc.) is also a network layer issue.

When a packet has to travel from one network to another to get to its destination, many problems can arise. The addressing used by the second network may be different from the first one. The second one may not accept the packet at all because it is too large. The protocols may differ, and so on. It is up to the network layer to overcome all these problems to allow heterogeneous networks to be interconnected.

In broadcast networks, the routing problem is simple, so the network layer is often thin or even nonexistent.

The Transport Layer

The basic function of the **transport layer** is to accept data from above, split it up into smaller units if need be, pass these to the network layer, and ensure that the pieces all arrive correctly at the other end. Furthermore, all this must be done efficiently and in a way that isolates the upper layers from the inevitable changes in the hardware technology.

The transport layer also determines what type of service to provide to the session layer, and, ultimately, to the users of the network. The most popular type of transport connection is an error-free point-to-point channel that delivers messages or bytes in the order in which they were sent. However, other possible kinds of transport service are the transporting of isolated messages, with no guarantee about the order of delivery, and the broadcasting of messages to multiple destinations. The type of service is determined when the connection is established. (As an aside, an error-free channel is impossible to achieve; what people really mean by this term is that the error rate is low enough to ignore in practice.)

The transport layer is a true end-to-end layer, all the way from the source to the destination. In other words, a program on the source machine carries on a conversation with a similar program on the destination machine, using the message headers and control messages. In the lower layers, the protocols are between each machine and its immediate neighbors, and not between the ultimate source and destination machines, which may be separated by many routers. The difference between layers 1 through 3, which are chained, and layers 4 through 7, which are end-to-end, is illustrated in Fig. 1-20.

The Session Layer

The session layer allows users on different machines to establish **sessions** between them. Sessions offer various services, including **dialog control** (keeping track of whose turn it is to transmit), **token management** (preventing two parties from attempting the same critical operation at the same time), and **synchroniza-tion** (checkpointing long transmissions to allow them to continue from where they were after a crash).

The Presentation Layer

Unlike lower layers, which are mostly concerned with moving bits around, the **presentation layer** is concerned with the syntax and semantics of the information transmitted. In order to make it possible for computers with different data representations to communicate, the data structures to be exchanged can be defined in an abstract way, along with a standard encoding to be used "on the wire." The presentation layer manages these abstract data structures and allows higher-level data structures (e.g., banking records), to be defined and exchanged.

The Application Layer

The **application layer** contains a variety of protocols that are commonly needed by users. One widely-used application protocol is **HTTP (HyperText Transfer Protocol)**, which is the basis for the World Wide Web. When a browser wants a Web page, it sends the name of the page it wants to the server using HTTP. The server then sends the page back. Other application protocols are used for file transfer, electronic mail, and network news.

1.4.2 The TCP/IP Reference Model

Let us now turn from the OSI reference model to the reference model used in the grandparent of all wide area computer networks, the ARPANET, and its successor, the worldwide Internet. Although we will give a brief history of the ARPANET later, it is useful to mention a few key aspects of it now. The ARPANET was a research network sponsored by the DoD (U.S. Department of Defense). It eventually connected hundreds of universities and government installations, using leased telephone lines. When satellite and radio networks were added later, the existing protocols had trouble interworking with them, so a new reference architecture was needed. Thus, the ability to connect multiple networks in a seamless way was one of the major design goals from the very beginning. This architecture later became known as the **TCP/IP Reference Model**, after its two primary protocols. It was first defined in (Cerf and Kahn, 1974). A later perspective is given in (Leiner et al., 1985). The design philosophy behind the model is discussed in (Clark, 1988).

Given the DoD's worry that some of its precious hosts, routers, and internetwork gateways might get blown to pieces at a moment's notice, another major goal was that the network be able to survive loss of subnet hardware, with existing conversations not being broken off. In other words, DoD wanted connections to remain intact as long as the source and destination machines were functioning, even if some of the machines or transmission lines in between were suddenly put out of operation. Furthermore, a flexible architecture was needed since applications with divergent requirements were envisioned, ranging from transferring files to real-time speech transmission.

The Internet Layer

All these requirements led to the choice of a packet-switching network based on a connectionless internetwork layer. This layer, called the **internet layer**, is the linchpin that holds the whole architecture together. Its job is to permit hosts to inject packets into any network and have them travel independently to the destination (potentially on a different network). They may even arrive in a different order than they were sent, in which case it is the job of higher layers to rearrange them, if in-order delivery is desired. Note that "internet" is used here in a generic sense, even though this layer is present in the Internet.

The analogy here is with the (snail) mail system. A person can drop a sequence of international letters into a mail box in one country, and with a little luck, most of them will be delivered to the correct address in the destination country. Probably the letters will travel through one or more international mail gateways along the way, but this is transparent to the users. Furthermore, that each country (i.e., each network) has its own stamps, preferred envelope sizes, and delivery rules is hidden from the users.

The internet layer defines an official packet format and protocol called **IP** (**Internet Protocol**). The job of the internet layer is to deliver IP packets where they are supposed to go. Packet routing is clearly the major issue here, as is avoiding congestion. For these reasons, it is reasonable to say that the TCP/IP internet layer is similar in functionality to the OSI network layer. Figure 1-21 shows this correspondence.

The Transport Layer

The layer above the internet layer in the TCP/IP model is now usually called the **transport layer**. It is designed to allow peer entities on the source and destination hosts to carry on a conversation, just as in the OSI transport layer. Two end-to-end transport protocols have been defined here. The first one, **TCP** (**Transmission Control Protocol**), is a reliable connection-oriented protocol that allows a byte stream originating on one machine to be delivered without error on any other machine in the internet. It fragments the incoming byte stream into discrete messages and passes each one on to the internet layer. At the destination, the receiving TCP process reassembles the received messages into the output stream. TCP also handles flow control to make sure a fast sender cannot swamp a slow receiver with more messages than it can handle.

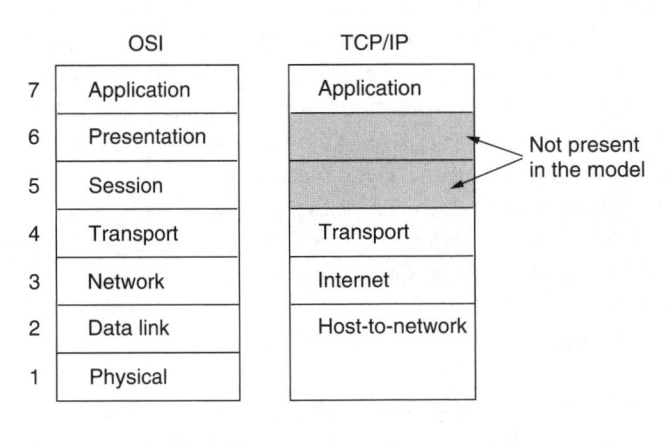

Figure 1-21. The TCP/IP reference model.

The second protocol in this layer, **UDP (User Datagram Protocol)**, is an unreliable, connectionless protocol for applications that do not want TCP's sequencing or flow control and wish to provide their own. It is also widely used for one-shot, client-server-type request-reply queries and applications in which prompt delivery is more important than accurate delivery, such as transmitting speech or video. The relation of IP, TCP, and UDP is shown in Fig. 1-22. Since the model was developed, IP has been implemented on many other networks.

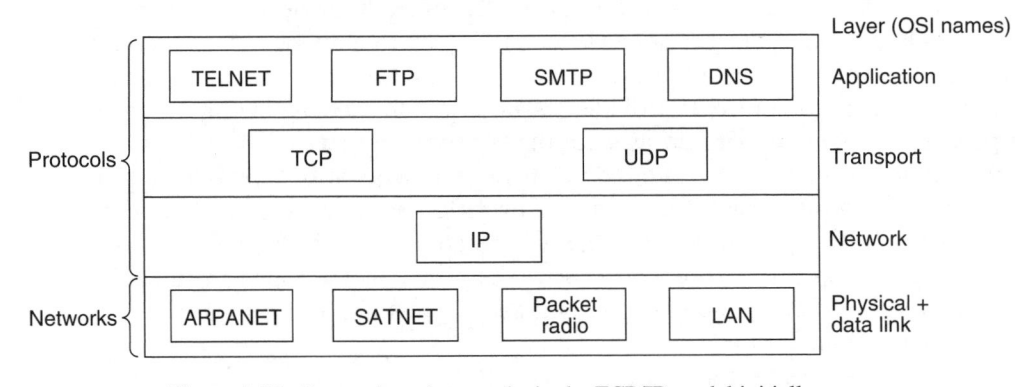

Figure 1-22. Protocols and networks in the TCP/IP model initially.

The Application Layer

The TCP/IP model does not have session or presentation layers. No need for them was perceived, so they were not included. Experience with the OSI model has proven this view correct: they are of little use to most applications.

On top of the transport layer is the **application layer**. It contains all the higher-level protocols. The early ones included virtual terminal (TELNET), file transfer (FTP), and electronic mail (SMTP), as shown in Fig. 1-22. The virtual terminal protocol allows a user on one machine to log onto a distant machine and work there. The file transfer protocol provides a way to move data efficiently from one machine to another. Electronic mail was originally just a kind of file transfer, but later a specialized protocol (SMTP) was developed for it. Many other protocols have been added to these over the years: the Domain Name System (DNS) for mapping host names onto their network addresses, NNTP, the protocol for moving USENET news articles around, and HTTP, the protocol for fetching pages on the World Wide Web, and many others.

The Host-to-Network Layer

Below the internet layer is a great void. The TCP/IP reference model does not really say much about what happens here, except to point out that the host has to connect to the network using some protocol so it can send IP packets to it. This protocol is not defined and varies from host to host and network to network. Books and papers about the TCP/IP model rarely discuss it.

1.4.3 A Comparison of the OSI and TCP/IP Reference Models

The OSI and TCP/IP reference models have much in common. Both are based on the concept of a stack of independent protocols. Also, the functionality of the layers is roughly similar. For example, in both models the layers up through and including the transport layer are there to provide an end-to-end, network-independent transport service to processes wishing to communicate. These layers form the transport provider. Again in both models, the layers above transport are application-oriented users of the transport service.

Despite these fundamental similarities, the two models also have many differences. In this section we will focus on the key differences between the two reference models. It is important to note that we are comparing the *reference models* here, not the corresponding *protocol stacks*. The protocols themselves will be discussed later. For an entire book comparing and contrasting TCP/IP and OSI, see (Piscitello and Chapin, 1993).

Three concepts are central to the OSI model:

1. Services.

2. Interfaces.

3. Protocols.

Probably the biggest contribution of the OSI model is to make the distinction between these three concepts explicit. Each layer performs some services for the layer above it. The *service* definition tells what the layer does, not how entities above it access it or how the layer works. It defines the layer's semantics.

A layer's *interface* tells the processes above it how to access it. It specifies what the parameters are and what results to expect. It, too, says nothing about how the layer works inside.

Finally, the peer *protocols* used in a layer are the layer's own business. It can use any protocols it wants to, as long as it gets the job done (i.e., provides the offered services). It can also change them at will without affecting software in higher layers.

These ideas fit very nicely with modern ideas about object-oriented programming. An object, like a layer, has a set of methods (operations) that processes outside the object can invoke. The semantics of these methods define the set of services that the object offers. The methods' parameters and results form the object's interface. The code internal to the object is its protocol and is not visible or of any concern outside the object.

The TCP/IP model did not originally clearly distinguish between service, interface, and protocol, although people have tried to retrofit it after the fact to make it more OSI-like. For example, the only real services offered by the internet layer are SEND IP PACKET and RECEIVE IP PACKET.

As a consequence, the protocols in the OSI model are better hidden than in the TCP/IP model and can be replaced relatively easily as the technology changes. Being able to make such changes is one of the main purposes of having layered protocols in the first place.

The OSI reference model was devised *before* the corresponding protocols were invented. This ordering means that the model was not biased toward one particular set of protocols, a fact that made it quite general. The downside of this ordering is that the designers did not have much experience with the subject and did not have a good idea of which functionality to put in which layer.

For example, the data link layer originally dealt only with point-to-point networks. When broadcast networks came around, a new sublayer had to be hacked into the model. When people started to build real networks using the OSI model and existing protocols, it was discovered that these networks did not match the required service specifications (wonder of wonders), so convergence sublayers had to be grafted onto the model to provide a place for papering over the differences. Finally, the committee originally expected that each country would have one network, run by the government and using the OSI protocols, so no thought was given to internetworking. To make a long story short, things did not turn out that way.

With TCP/IP the reverse was true: the protocols came first, and the model was really just a description of the existing protocols. There was no problem with the protocols fitting the model. They fit perfectly. The only trouble was that the *model* did not fit any other protocol stacks. Consequently, it was not especially useful for describing other, non-TCP/IP networks.

Turning from philosophical matters to more specific ones, an obvious difference between the two models is the number of layers: the OSI model has seven layers and the TCP/IP has four layers. Both have (inter)network, transport, and application layers, but the other layers are different.

Another difference is in the area of connectionless versus connection-oriented communication. The OSI model supports both connectionless and connection-oriented communication in the network layer, but only connection-oriented communication in the transport layer, where it counts (because the transport service is visible to the users). The TCP/IP model has only one mode in the network layer (connectionless) but supports both modes in the transport layer, giving the users a choice. This choice is especially important for simple request-response protocols.

1.4.4 A Critique of the OSI Model and Protocols

Neither the OSI model and its protocols nor the TCP/IP model and its protocols are perfect. Quite a bit of criticism can be, and has been, directed at both of them. In this section and the next one, we will look at some of these criticisms. We will begin with OSI and examine TCP/IP afterward.

At the time the second edition of this book was published (1989), it appeared to many experts in the field that the OSI model and its protocols were going to take over the world and push everything else out of their way. This did not happen. Why? A look back at some of the lessons may be useful. These lessons can be summarized as:

1. Bad timing.

2. Bad technology.

3. Bad implementations.

4. Bad politics.

Bad Timing

First let us look at reason one: bad timing. The time at which a standard is established is absolutely critical to its success. David Clark of M.I.T. has a theory of standards that he calls the *apocalypse of the two elephants*, which is illustrated in Fig. 1-23.

This figure shows the amount of activity surrounding a new subject. When the subject is first discovered, there is a burst of research activity in the form of discussions, papers, and meetings. After a while this activity subsides, corporations discover the subject, and the billion-dollar wave of investment hits.

It is essential that the standards be written in the trough in between the two "elephants." If the standards are written too early, before the research is finished, the subject may still be poorly understood; the result is bad standards. If they are written too late, so many companies may have already made major investments in

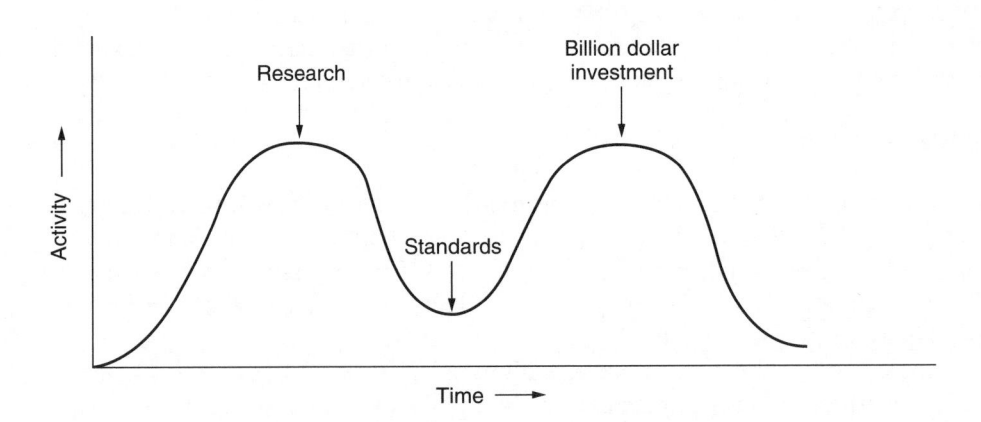

Figure 1-23. The apocalypse of the two elephants.

different ways of doing things that the standards are effectively ignored. If the interval between the two elephants is very short (because everyone is in a hurry to get started), the people developing the standards may get crushed.

It now appears that the standard OSI protocols got crushed. The competing TCP/IP protocols were already in widespread use by research universities by the time the OSI protocols appeared. While the billion-dollar wave of investment had not yet hit, the academic market was large enough that many vendors had begun cautiously offering TCP/IP products. When OSI came around, they did not want to support a second protocol stack until they were forced to, so there were no initial offerings. With every company waiting for every other company to go first, no company went first and OSI never happened.

Bad Technology

The second reason that OSI never caught on is that both the model and the protocols are flawed. The choice of seven layers was more political than technical, and two of the layers (session and presentation) are nearly empty, whereas two other ones (data link and network) are overfull.

The OSI model, along with the associated service definitions and protocols, is extraordinarily complex. When piled up, the printed standards occupy a significant fraction of a meter of paper. They are also difficult to implement and inefficient in operation. In this context, a riddle posed by Paul Mockapetris and cited in (Rose, 1993) comes to mind:

Q: What do you get when you cross a mobster with an international standard?
A: Someone who makes you an offer you can't understand.

In addition to being incomprehensible, another problem with OSI is that some functions, such as addressing, flow control, and error control, reappear again and again in each layer. Saltzer et al. (1984), for example, have pointed out that to be effective, error control must be done in the highest layer, so that repeating it over and over in each of the lower layers is often unnecessary and inefficient.

Bad Implementations

Given the enormous complexity of the model and the protocols, it will come as no surprise that the initial implementations were huge, unwieldy, and slow. Everyone who tried them got burned. It did not take long for people to associate "OSI" with "poor quality." Although the products improved in the course of time, the image stuck.

In contrast, one of the first implementations of TCP/IP was part of Berkeley UNIX and was quite good (not to mention, free). People began using it quickly, which led to a large user community, which led to improvements, which led to an even larger community. Here the spiral was upward instead of downward.

Bad Politics

On account of the initial implementation, many people, especially in academia, thought of TCP/IP as part of UNIX, and UNIX in the 1980s in academia was not unlike parenthood (then incorrectly called motherhood) and apple pie.

OSI, on the other hand, was widely thought to be the creature of the European telecommunication ministries, the European Community, and later the U.S. Government. This belief was only partly true, but the very idea of a bunch of government bureaucrats trying to shove a technically inferior standard down the throats of the poor researchers and programmers down in the trenches actually developing computer networks did not help much. Some people viewed this development in the same light as IBM announcing in the 1960s that PL/I was the language of the future, or DoD correcting this later by announcing that it was actually Ada.

1.4.5 A Critique of the TCP/IP Reference Model

The TCP/IP model and protocols have their problems too. First, the model does not clearly distinguish the concepts of service, interface, and protocol. Good software engineering practice requires differentiating between the specification and the implementation, something that OSI does very carefully, and TCP/IP does not. Consequently, the TCP/IP model is not much of a guide for designing new networks using new technologies.

Second, the TCP/IP model is not at all general and is poorly suited to describing any protocol stack other than TCP/IP. Trying to use the TCP/IP model to describe Bluetooth, for example, is completely impossible.

Third, the host-to-network layer is not really a layer at all in the normal sense of the term as used in the context of layered protocols. It is an interface (between the network and data link layers). The distinction between an interface and a layer is crucial, and one should not be sloppy about it.

Fourth, the TCP/IP model does not distinguish (or even mention) the physical and data link layers. These are completely different. The physical layer has to do with the transmission characteristics of copper wire, fiber optics, and wireless communication. The data link layer's job is to delimit the start and end of frames and get them from one side to the other with the desired degree of reliability. A proper model should include both as separate layers. The TCP/IP model does not do this.

Finally, although the IP and TCP protocols were carefully thought out and well implemented, many of the other protocols were ad hoc, generally produced by a couple of graduate students hacking away until they got tired. The protocol implementations were then distributed free, which resulted in their becoming widely used, deeply entrenched, and thus hard to replace. Some of them are a bit of an embarrassment now. The virtual terminal protocol, TELNET, for example, was designed for a ten-character per second mechanical Teletype terminal. It knows nothing of graphical user interfaces and mice. Nevertheless, 25 years later, it is still in widespread use.

In summary, despite its problems, the OSI *model* (minus the session and presentation layers) has proven to be exceptionally useful for discussing computer networks. In contrast, the OSI *protocols* have not become popular. The reverse is true of TCP/IP: the *model* is practically nonexistent, but the *protocols* are widely used. Since computer scientists like to have their cake and eat it, too, in this book we will use a modified OSI model but concentrate primarily on the TCP/IP and related protocols, as well as newer ones such as 802, SONET, and Bluetooth. In effect, we will use the hybrid model of Fig. 1-24 as the framework for this book.

5	Application layer
4	Transport layer
3	Network layer
2	Data link layer
1	Physical layer

Figure 1-24. The hybrid reference model to be used in this book.

1.5 EXAMPLE NETWORKS

The subject of computer networking covers many different kinds of networks, large and small, well known and less well known. They have different goals, scales, and technologies. In the following sections, we will look at some examples, to get an idea of the variety one finds in the area of computer networking.

We will start with the Internet, probably the best known network, and look at its history, evolution, and technology. Then we will consider ATM, which is often used within the core of large (telephone) networks. Technically, it is quite different from the Internet, contrasting nicely with it. Next we will introduce Ethernet, the dominant local area network. Finally, we will look at IEEE 802.11, the standard for wireless LANs.

1.5.1 The Internet

The Internet is not a network at all, but a vast collection of different networks that use certain common protocols and provide certain common services. It is an unusual system in that it was not planned by anyone and is not controlled by anyone. To better understand it, let us start from the beginning and see how it has developed and why. For a wonderful history of the Internet, John Naughton's (2000) book is highly recommended. It is one of those rare books that is not only fun to read, but also has 20 pages of *ibid.*'s and *op. cit.*'s for the serious historian. Some of the material below is based on this book.

Of course, countless technical books have been written about the Internet and its protocols as well. For more information, see, for example, (Maufer, 1999).

The ARPANET

The story begins in the late 1950s. At the height of the Cold War, the DoD wanted a command-and-control network that could survive a nuclear war. At that time, all military communications used the public telephone network, which was considered vulnerable. The reason for this belief can be gleaned from Fig. 1-25(a). Here the black dots represent telephone switching offices, each of which was connected to thousands of telephones. These switching offices were, in turn, connected to higher-level switching offices (toll offices), to form a national hierarchy with only a small amount of redundancy. The vulnerability of the system was that the destruction of a few key toll offices could fragment the system into many isolated islands.

Around 1960, the DoD awarded a contract to the RAND Corporation to find a solution. One of its employees, Paul Baran, came up with the highly distributed and fault-tolerant design of Fig. 1-25(b). Since the paths between any two switching offices were now much longer than analog signals could travel without distortion, Baran proposed using digital packet-switching technology throughout the system. Baran wrote several reports for the DoD describing his ideas in detail. Officials at the Pentagon liked the concept and asked AT&T, then the U.S. national telephone monopoly, to build a prototype. AT&T dismissed Baran's ideas out of hand. The biggest and richest corporation in the world was not about to allow some young whippersnapper tell it how to build a telephone system. They said Baran's network could not be built and the idea was killed.

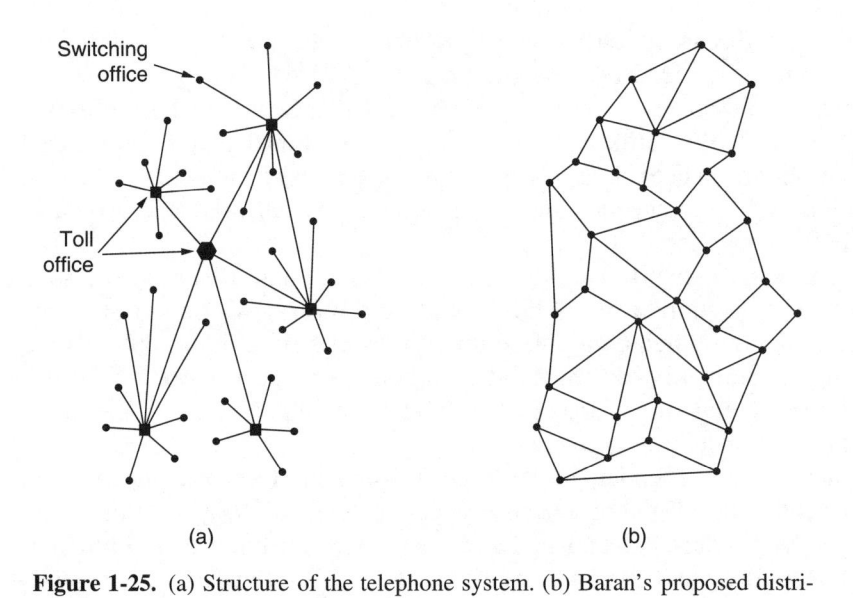

Switching
office

Toll
office

(a)   (b)

Figure 1-25. (a) Structure of the telephone system. (b) Baran's proposed distributed switching system.

Several years went by and still the DoD did not have a better command-and-control system. To understand what happened next, we have to go back to October 1957, when the Soviet Union beat the U.S. into space with the launch of the first artificial satellite, Sputnik. When President Eisenhower tried to find out who was asleep at the switch, he was appalled to find the Army, Navy, and Air Force squabbling over the Pentagon's research budget. His immediate response was to create a single defense research organization, **ARPA**, the **Advanced Research Projects Agency**. ARPA had no scientists or laboratories; in fact, it had nothing more than an office and a small (by Pentagon standards) budget. It did its work by issuing grants and contracts to universities and companies whose ideas looked promising to it.

For the first few years, ARPA tried to figure out what its mission should be, but in 1967, the attention of ARPA's then director, Larry Roberts, turned to networking. He contacted various experts to decide what to do. One of them, Wesley Clark, suggested building a packet-switched subnet, giving each host its own router, as illustrated in Fig. 1-10.

After some initial skepticism, Roberts bought the idea and presented a somewhat vague paper about it at the ACM SIGOPS Symposium on Operating System Principles held in Gatlinburg, Tennessee in late 1967 (Roberts, 1967). Much to Roberts' surprise, another paper at the conference described a similar system that had not only been designed but actually implemented under the direction of Donald Davies at the National Physical Laboratory in England. The NPL system was not a national system (it just connected several computers on the NPL campus), but it demonstrated that packet switching could be made to work. Furthermore, it cited Baran's now discarded earlier work. Roberts came away from Gatlinburg determined to build what later became known as the **ARPANET**.

The subnet would consist of minicomputers called **IMPs** (**Interface Message Processors**) connected by 56-kbps transmission lines. For high reliability, each IMP would be connected to at least two other IMPs. The subnet was to be a datagram subnet, so if some lines and IMPs were destroyed, messages could be automatically rerouted along alternative paths.

Each node of the network was to consist of an IMP and a host, in the same room, connected by a short wire. A host could send messages of up to 8063 bits to its IMP, which would then break these up into packets of at most 1008 bits and forward them independently toward the destination. Each packet was received in its entirety before being forwarded, so the subnet was the first electronic store-and-forward packet-switching network.

ARPA then put out a tender for building the subnet. Twelve companies bid for it. After evaluating all the proposals, ARPA selected BBN, a consulting firm in Cambridge, Massachusetts, and in December 1968, awarded it a contract to build the subnet and write the subnet software. BBN chose to use specially modi-fied Honeywell DDP-316 minicomputers with 12K 16-bit words of core memory as the IMPs. The IMPs did not have disks, since moving parts were considered unreliable. The IMPs were interconnected by 56-kbps lines leased from telephone companies. Although 56 kbps is now the choice of teenagers who cannot afford ADSL or cable, it was then the best money could buy.

The software was split into two parts: subnet and host. The subnet software consisted of the IMP end of the host-IMP connection, the IMP-IMP protocol, and a source IMP to destination IMP protocol designed to improve reliability. The original ARPANET design is shown in Fig. 1-26.

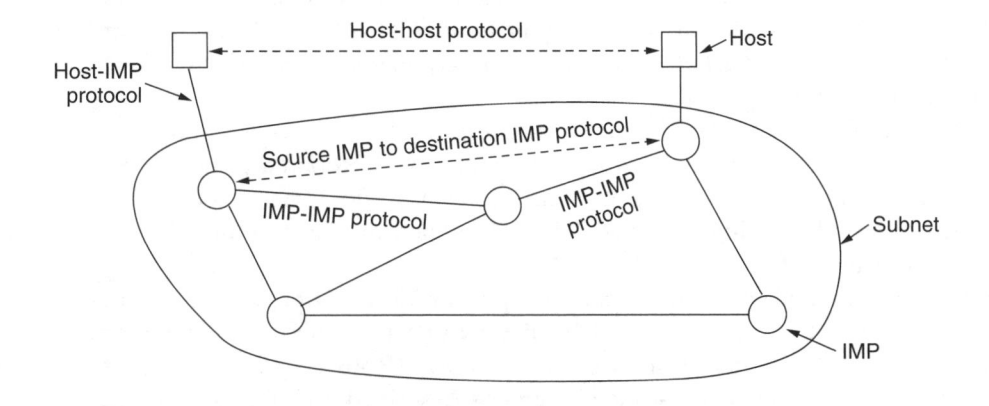

Figure 1-26. The original ARPANET design.

Outside the subnet, software was also needed, namely, the host end of the host-IMP connection, the host-host protocol, and the application software. It soon became clear that BBN felt that when it had accepted a message on a host-IMP wire and placed it on the host-IMP wire at the destination, its job was done.

Roberts had a problem: the hosts needed software too. To deal with it, he convened a meeting of network researchers, mostly graduate students, at Snowbird, Utah, in the summer of 1969. The graduate students expected some network expert to explain the grand design of the network and its software to them and then to assign each of them the job of writing part of it. They were astounded when there was no network expert and no grand design. They had to figure out what to do on their own.

Nevertheless, somehow an experimental network went on the air in December 1969 with four nodes: at UCLA, UCSB, SRI, and the University of Utah. These four were chosen because all had a large number of ARPA contracts, and all had different and completely incompatible host computers (just to make it more fun). The network grew quickly as more IMPs were delivered and installed; it soon spanned the United States. Figure 1-27 shows how rapidly the ARPANET grew in the first 3 years.

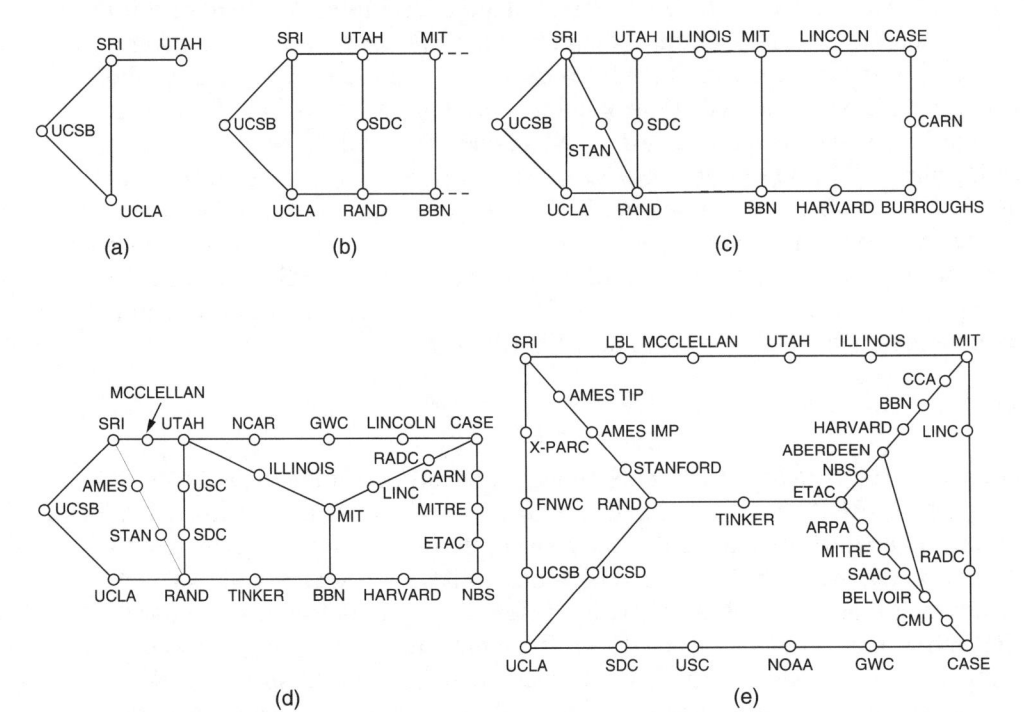

Figure 1-27. Growth of the ARPANET. (a) December 1969. (b) July 1970. (c) March 1971. (d) April 1972. (e) September 1972.

In addition to helping the fledgling ARPANET grow, ARPA also funded research on the use of satellite networks and mobile packet radio networks. In one now famous demonstration, a truck driving around in California used the packet radio network to send messages to SRI, which were then forwarded over the ARPANET to the East Coast, where they were shipped to University College in London over the satellite network. This allowed a researcher in the truck to use a computer in London while driving around in California.

This experiment also demonstrated that the existing ARPANET protocols were not suitable for running over multiple networks. This observation led to more research on protocols, culminating with the invention of the TCP/IP model and protocols (Cerf and Kahn, 1974). TCP/IP was specifically designed to handle communication over internetworks, something becoming increasingly important as more and more networks were being hooked up to the ARPANET.

To encourage adoption of these new protocols, ARPA awarded several contracts to BBN and the University of California at Berkeley to integrate them into Berkeley UNIX. Researchers at Berkeley developed a convenient program interface to the network (sockets) and wrote many application, utility, and management programs to make networking easier.

The timing was perfect. Many universities had just acquired a second or third VAX computer and a LAN to connect them, but they had no networking software. When 4.2BSD came along, with TCP/IP, sockets, and many network utilities, the complete package was adopted immediately. Furthermore, with TCP/IP, it was easy for the LANs to connect to the ARPANET, and many did.

During the 1980s, additional networks, especially LANs, were connected to the ARPANET. As the scale increased, finding hosts became increasingly expensive, so **DNS (Domain Name System)** was created to organize machines into domains and map host names onto IP addresses. Since then, DNS has become a generalized, distributed database system for storing a variety of information related to naming. We will study it in detail in Chap. 7.

NSFNET

By the late 1970s, NSF (the U.S. National Science Foundation) saw the enormous impact the ARPANET was having on university research, allowing scientists across the country to share data and collaborate on research projects. However, to get on the ARPANET, a university had to have a research contract with the DoD, which many did not have. NSF's response was to design a successor to the ARPANET that would be open to all university research groups. To have something concrete to start with, NSF decided to build a backbone network to connect its six supercomputer centers, in San Diego, Boulder, Champaign, Pittsburgh, Ithaca, and Princeton. Each supercomputer was given a little brother, consisting of an LSI-11 microcomputer called a **fuzzball**. The fuzzballs were connected with 56-kbps leased lines and formed the subnet, the same hardware technology as the ARPANET used. The software technology was different however: the fuzzballs spoke TCP/IP right from the start, making it the first TCP/IP WAN.

NSF also funded some (eventually about 20) regional networks that connected to the backbone to allow users at thousands of universities, research labs, libraries, and museums to access any of the supercomputers and to communicate with one another. The complete network, including the backbone and the regional networks, was called **NSFNET**. It connected to the ARPANET through a link between an IMP and a fuzzball in the Carnegie-Mellon machine room. The first NSFNET backbone is illustrated in Fig. 1-28.

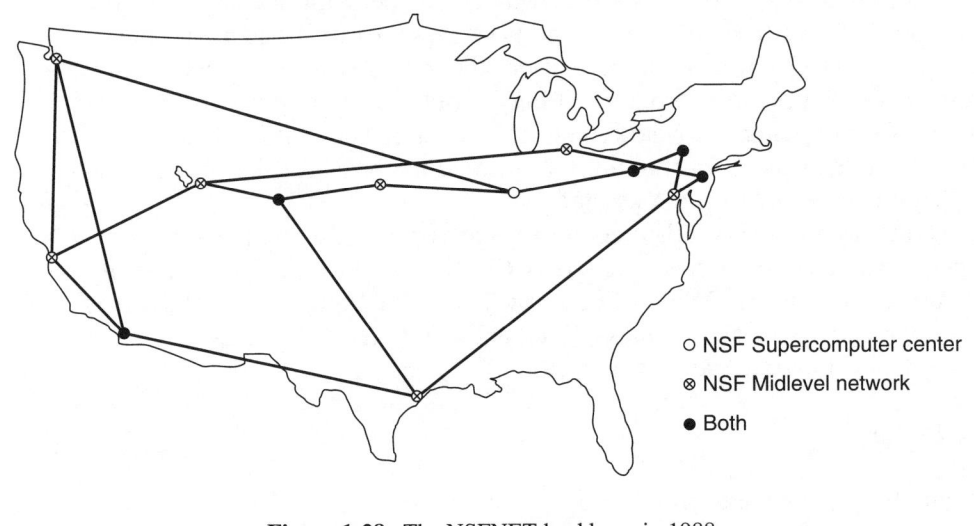

○ NSF Supercomputer center

⊗ NSF Midlevel network

● Both

Figure 1-28. The NSFNET backbone in 1988.

NSFNET was an instantaneous success and was overloaded from the word go. NSF immediately began planning its successor and awarded a contract to the Michigan-based MERIT consortium to run it. Fiber optic channels at 448 kbps were leased from MCI (since merged with WorldCom) to provide the version 2 backbone. IBM PC-RTs were used as routers. This, too, was soon overwhelmed, and by 1990, the second backbone was upgraded to 1.5 Mbps.

As growth continued, NSF realized that the government could not continue financing networking forever. Furthermore, commercial organizations wanted to join but were forbidden by NSF's charter from using networks NSF paid for. Consequently, NSF encouraged MERIT, MCI, and IBM to form a nonprofit corporation, **ANS (Advanced Networks and Services)**, as the first step along the road to commercialization. In 1990, ANS took over NSFNET and upgraded the 1.5-Mbps links to 45 Mbps to form **ANSNET**. This network operated for 5 years and was then sold to America Online. But by then, various companies were offering commercial IP service and it was clear the government should now get out of the networking business.

To ease the transition and make sure every regional network could communicate with every other regional network, NSF awarded contracts to four different network operators to establish a **NAP** (**Network Access Point**). These operators were PacBell (San Francisco), Ameritech (Chicago), MFS (Washington, D.C.), and Sprint (New York City, where for NAP purposes, Pennsauken, New Jersey counts as New York City). Every network operator that wanted to provide backbone service to the NSF regional networks had to connect to all the NAPs.

This arrangement meant that a packet originating on any regional network had a choice of backbone carriers to get from its NAP to the destination's NAP. Consequently, the backbone carriers were forced to compete for the regional networks' business on the basis of service and price, which was the idea, of course. As a result, the concept of a single default backbone was replaced by a commercially-driven competitive infrastructure. Many people like to criticize the Federal Government for not being innovative, but in the area of networking, it was DoD and NSF that created the infrastructure that formed the basis for the Internet and then handed it over to industry to operate.

During the 1990s, many other countries and regions also built national research networks, often patterned on the ARPANET and NSFNET. These included EuropaNET and EBONE in Europe, which started out with 2-Mbps lines and then upgraded to 34-Mbps lines. Eventually, the network infrastructure in Europe was handed over to industry as well.

Internet Usage

The number of networks, machines, and users connected to the ARPANET grew rapidly after TCP/IP became the only official protocol on January 1, 1983. When NSFNET and the ARPANET were interconnected, the growth became exponential. Many regional networks joined up, and connections were made to networks in Canada, Europe, and the Pacific.

Sometime in the mid-1980s, people began viewing the collection of networks as an internet, and later as the Internet, although there was no official dedication with some politician breaking a bottle of champagne over a fuzzball.

The glue that holds the Internet together is the TCP/IP reference model and TCP/IP protocol stack. TCP/IP makes universal service possible and can be compared to the adoption of standard gauge by the railroads in the 19th century or the adoption of common signaling protocols by all the telephone companies.

What does it actually mean to be on the Internet? Our definition is that a machine is on the Internet if it runs the TCP/IP protocol stack, has an IP address, and can send IP packets to all the other machines on the Internet. The mere ability to send and receive electronic mail is not enough, since e-mail is gatewayed to many networks outside the Internet. However, the issue is clouded somewhat by the fact that millions of personal computers can call up an Internet service provider using a modem, be assigned a temporary IP address, and send IP packets to other Internet hosts. It makes sense to regard such machines as being on the Internet for as long as they are connected to the service provider's router.

Traditionally (meaning 1970 to about 1990), the Internet and its predecessors had four main applications:

1. **E-mail**. The ability to compose, send, and receive electronic mail has been around since the early days of the ARPANET and is enormously popular. Many people get dozens of messages a day and consider it their primary way of interacting with the outside world, far outdistancing the telephone and snail mail. E-mail programs are available on virtually every kind of computer these days.

2. **News**. Newsgroups are specialized forums in which users with a common interest can exchange messages. Thousands of newsgroups exist, devoted to technical and nontechnical topics, including computers, science, recreation, and politics. Each newsgroup has its own etiquette, style, and customs, and woe betide anyone violating them.

3. **Remote login**. Using the telnet, rlogin, or ssh programs, users anywhere on the Internet can log on to any other machine on which they have an account.

4. **File transfer**. Using the FTP program, users can copy files from one machine on the Internet to another. Vast numbers of articles, databases, and other information are available this way.

Up until the early 1990s, the Internet was largely populated by academic, government, and industrial researchers. One new application, the **WWW** (**World Wide Web**) changed all that and brought millions of new, nonacademic users to the net. This application, invented by CERN physicist Tim Berners-Lee, did not change any of the underlying facilities but made them easier to use. Together with the Mosaic browser, written by Marc Andreessen at the National Center for Supercomputer Applications in Urbana, Illinois, the WWW made it possible for a site to set up a number of pages of information containing text, pictures, sound, and even video, with embedded links to other pages. By clicking on a link, the user is suddenly transported to the page pointed to by that link. For example, many companies have a home page with entries pointing to other pages for product information, price lists, sales, technical support, communication with employees, stockholder information, and more.

Numerous other kinds of pages have come into existence in a very short time, including maps, stock market tables, library card catalogs, recorded radio programs, and even a page pointing to the complete text of many books whose copyrights have expired (Mark Twain, Charles Dickens, etc.). Many people also have personal pages (home pages).

Much of this growth during the 1990s was fueled by companies called **ISPs** (**Internet Service Providers**). These are companies that offer individual users at home the ability to call up one of their machines and connect to the Internet, thus gaining access to e-mail, the WWW, and other Internet services. These companies signed up tens of millions of new users a year during the late 1990s, completely changing the character of the network from an academic and military playground to a public utility, much like the telephone system. The number of Internet users now is unknown, but is certainly hundreds of millions worldwide and will probably hit 1 billion fairly soon.

Architecture of the Internet

In this section we will attempt to give a brief overview of the Internet today. Due to the many mergers between telephone companies (telcos) and ISPs, the waters have become muddied and it is often hard to tell who is doing what. Consequently, this description will be of necessity somewhat simpler than reality. The big picture is shown in Fig. 1-29. Let us examine this figure piece by piece now.

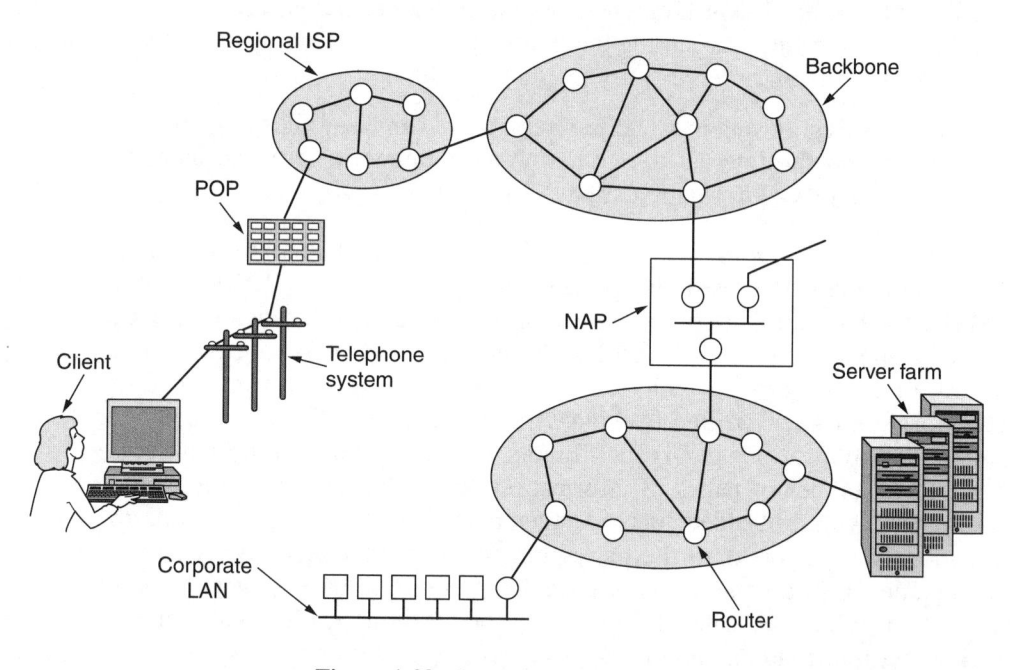

Figure 1-29. Overview of the Internet.

A good place to start is with a client at home. Let us assume our client calls his or her ISP over a dial-up telephone line, as shown in Fig. 1-29. The modem is a card within the PC that converts the digital signals the computer produces to analog signals that can pass unhindered over the telephone system. These signals are transferred to the ISP's **POP (Point of Presence)**, where they are removed from the telephone system and injected into the ISP's regional network. From this point on, the system is fully digital and packet switched. If the ISP is the local telco, the POP will probably be located in the telephone switching office where the telephone wire from the client terminates. If the ISP is not the local telco, the POP may be a few switching offices down the road.

The ISP's regional network consists of interconnected routers in the various cities the ISP serves. If the packet is destined for a host served directly by the ISP, the packet is delivered to the host. Otherwise, it is handed over to the ISP's backbone operator.

At the top of the food chain are the major backbone operators, companies like AT&T and Sprint. They operate large international backbone networks, with thousands of routers connected by high-bandwidth fiber optics. Large corporations and hosting services that run server farms (machines that can serve thousands of Web pages per second) often connect directly to the backbone. Backbone operators encourage this direct connection by renting space in what are called **carrier hotels**, basically equipment racks in the same room as the router to allow short, fast connections between server farms and the backbone.

If a packet given to the backbone is destined for an ISP or company served by the backbone, it is sent to the closest router and handed off there. However, many backbones, of varying sizes, exist in the world, so a packet may have to go to a competing backbone. To allow packets to hop between backbones, all the major backbones connect at the NAPs discussed earlier. Basically, a NAP is a room full of routers, at least one per backbone. A LAN in the room connects all the routers, so packets can be forwarded from any backbone to any other backbone. In addition to being interconnected at NAPs, the larger backbones have numerous direct connections between their routers, a technique known as **private peering**. One of the many paradoxes of the Internet is that ISPs who publicly compete with one another for customers often privately cooperate to do private peering (Metz, 2001).

This ends our quick tour of the Internet. We will have a great deal to say about the individual components and their design, algorithms, and protocols in subsequent chapters. Also worth mentioning in passing is that some companies have interconnected all their existing internal networks, often using the same technology as the Internet. These **intranets** are typically accessible only within the company but otherwise work the same way as the Internet.

1.5.2 Connection-Oriented Networks: X.25, Frame Relay, and ATM

Since the beginning of networking, a war has been going on between the people who support connectionless (i.e., datagram) subnets and the people who support connection-oriented subnets. The main proponents of the connectionless subnets come from the ARPANET/Internet community. Remember that DoD's original desire in funding and building the ARPANET was to have a network that would continue functioning even after multiple direct hits by nuclear weapons wiped out numerous routers and transmission lines. Thus, fault tolerance was high on their priority list; billing customers was not. This approach led to a connectionless design in which every packet is routed independently of every other packet. As a consequence, if some routers go down during a session, no harm is done as long as the system can reconfigure itself dynamically so that subsequent packets can find some route to the destination, even if it is different from that which previous packets used.

The connection-oriented camp comes from the world of telephone companies. In the telephone system, a caller must dial the called party's number and wait for a connection before talking or sending data. This connection setup establishes a route through the telephone system that is maintained until the call is terminated. All words or packets follow the same route. If a line or switch on the path goes down, the call is aborted. This property is precisely what the DoD did not like about it.

Why do the telephone companies like it then? There are two reasons:

1. Quality of service.

2. Billing.

By setting up a connection in advance, the subnet can reserve resources such as buffer space and router CPU capacity. If an attempt is made to set up a call and insufficient resources are available, the call is rejected and the caller gets a kind of busy signal. In this way, once a connection has been set up, the connection will get good service. With a connectionless network, if too many packets arrive at the same router at the same moment, the router will choke and probably lose packets. The sender will eventually notice this and resend them, but the quality of service will be jerky and unsuitable for audio or video unless the network is very lightly loaded. Needless to say, providing adequate audio quality is something telephone companies care about very much, hence their preference for connections.

The second reason the telephone companies like connection-oriented service is that they are accustomed to charging for connect time. When you make a long distance call (or even a local call outside North America) you are charged by the minute. When networks came around, they just automatically gravitated toward a model in which charging by the minute was easy to do. If you have to set up a connection before sending data, that is when the billing clock starts running. If there is no connection, they cannot charge for it.

Ironically, maintaining billing records is very expensive. If a telephone company were to adopt a flat monthly rate with unlimited calling and no billing or record keeping, it would probably save a huge amount of money, despite the increased calling this policy would generate. Political, regulatory, and other factors weigh against doing this, however. Interestingly enough, flat rate service exists in other sectors. For example, cable TV is billed at a flat rate per month, no matter how many programs you watch. It could have been designed with pay-per-view as the basic concept, but it was not, due in part to the expense of billing (and given the quality of most television, the embarrassment factor cannot be totally discounted either). Also, many theme parks charge a daily admission fee for unlimited rides, in contrast to traveling carnivals, which charge by the ride.

That said, it should come as no surprise that all networks designed by the telephone industry have had connection-oriented subnets. What is perhaps surprising, is that the Internet is also drifting in that direction, in order to provide a better quality of service for audio and video, a subject we will return to in Chap. 5. But now let us examine some connection-oriented networks.

X.25 and Frame Relay

Our first example of a connection-oriented network is **X.25**, which was the first public data network. It was deployed in the 1970s at a time when telephone service was a monopoly everywhere and the telephone company in each country expected there to be one data network per country—theirs. To use X.25, a computer first established a connection to the remote computer, that is, placed a telephone call. This connection was given a connection number to be used in data transfer packets (because multiple connections could be open at the same time). Data packets were very simple, consisting of a 3-byte header and up to 128 bytes of data. The header consisted of a 12-bit connection number, a packet sequence number, an acknowledgement number, and a few miscellaneous bits. X.25 networks operated for about a decade with mixed success.

In the 1980s, the X.25 networks were largely replaced by a new kind of network called **frame relay**. The essence of frame relay is that it is a connection-oriented network with no error control and no flow control. Because it was connection-oriented, packets were delivered in order (if they were delivered at all). The properties of in-order delivery, no error control, and no flow control make frame relay akin to a wide area LAN. Its most important application is interconnecting LANs at multiple company offices. Frame relay enjoyed a modest success and is still in use in places today.

Asynchronous Transfer Mode

Yet another, and far more important, connection-oriented network is **ATM** (**Asynchronous Transfer Mode**). The reason for the somewhat strange name is that in the telephone system, most transmission is synchronous (closely tied to a clock), and ATM is not.

ATM was designed in the early 1990s and launched amid truly incredible hype (Ginsburg, 1996; Goralski, 1995; Ibe, 1997; Kim et al., 1994; and Stallings, 2000). ATM was going to solve all the world's networking and telecommunications problems by merging voice, data, cable television, telex, telegraph, carrier pigeon, tin cans connected by strings, tom-toms, smoke signals, and everything else into a single integrated system that could do everything for everyone. It did not happen. In large part, the problems were similar to those we described earlier concerning OSI, that is, bad timing, technology, implementation, and politics. Having just beaten back the telephone companies in round 1, many in the Internet community saw ATM as Internet versus the Telcos: the Sequel. But it really was not, and this time around even diehard datagram fanatics were aware that the Internet's quality of service left a lot to be desired. To make a long story short, ATM was much more successful than OSI, and it is now widely used deep within the telephone system, often for moving IP packets. Because it is now mostly used by carriers for internal transport, users are often unaware of its existence, but it is definitely alive and well.

ATM Virtual Circuits

Since ATM networks are connection-oriented, sending data requires first sending a packet to set up the connection. As the setup packet wends its way through the subnet, all the routers on the path make an entry in their internal tables noting the existence of the connection and reserving whatever resources are needed for it. Connections are often called **virtual circuits**, in analogy with the physical circuits used within the telephone system. Most ATM networks also support **permanent virtual circuits**, which are permanent connections between two (distant) hosts. They are similar to leased lines in the telephone world. Each connection, temporary or permanent, has a unique connection identifier. A virtual circuit is illustrated in Fig. 1-30.

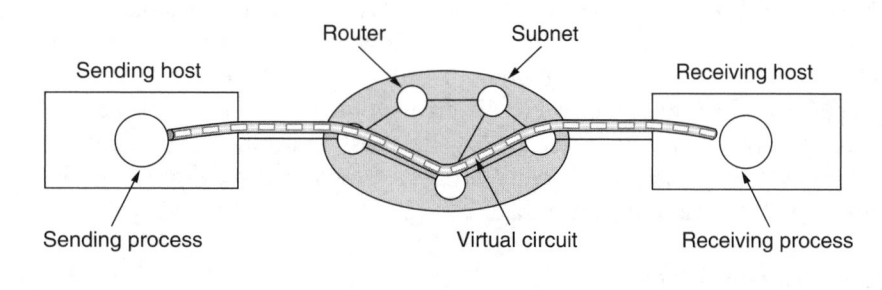

Figure 1-30. A virtual circuit.

Once a connection has been established, either side can begin transmitting data. The basic idea behind ATM is to transmit all information in small, fixed-size packets called **cells**. The cells are 53 bytes long, of which 5 bytes are header and 48 bytes are payload, as shown in Fig. 1-31. Part of the header is the connection identifier, so the sending and receiving hosts and all the intermediate routers can tell which cells belong to which connections. This information allows each router to know how to route each incoming cell. Cell routing is done in hardware, at high speed. In fact, the main argument for having fixed-size cells is that it is easy to build hardware routers to handle short, fixed-length cells. Variable-length

IP packets have to be routed by software, which is a slower process. Another plus of ATM is that the hardware can be set up to copy one incoming cell to multiple output lines, a property that is required for handling a television program that is being broadcast to many receivers. Finally, small cells do not block any line for very long, which makes guaranteeing quality of service easier.

All cells follow the same route to the destination. Cell delivery is not guaranteed, but their order is. If cells 1 and 2 are sent in that order, then if both arrive, they will arrive in that order, never first 2 then 1. But either or both of them can be lost along the way. It is up to higher protocol levels to recover from lost cells. Note that although this guarantee is not perfect, it is better than what the Internet provides. There packets can not only be lost, but delivered out of order as well. ATM, in contrast, guarantees never to deliver cells out of order.

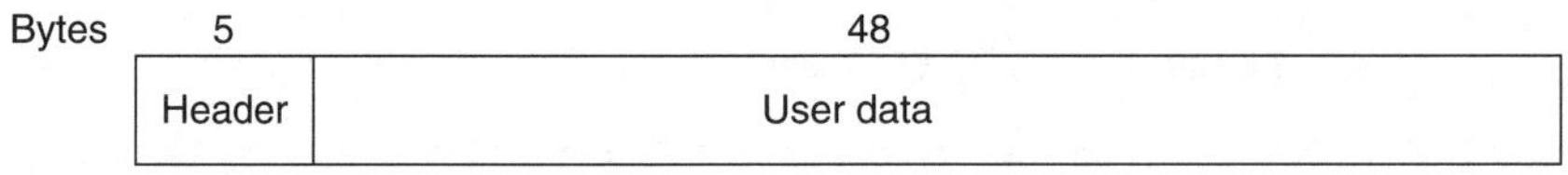

Bytes   5   48

Header	User data

Figure 1-31. An ATM cell.

ATM networks are organized like traditional WANs, with lines and switches (routers). The most common speeds for ATM networks are 155 Mbps and 622 Mbps, although higher speeds are also supported. The 155-Mbps speed was chosen because this is about what is needed to transmit high definition television. The exact choice of 155.52 Mbps was made for compatibility with AT&T's SONET transmission system, something we will study in Chap. 2. The 622 Mbps speed was chosen so that four 155-Mbps channels could be sent over it.

The ATM Reference Model

ATM has its own reference model, different from the OSI model and also different from the TCP/IP model. This model is shown in Fig. 1-32. It consists of three layers, the physical, ATM, and ATM adaptation layers, plus whatever users want to put on top of that.

The physical layer deals with the physical medium: voltages, bit timing, and various other issues. ATM does not prescribe a particular set of rules but instead says that ATM cells can be sent on a wire or fiber by themselves, but they can also be packaged inside the payload of other carrier systems. In other words, ATM has been designed to be independent of the transmission medium.

The **ATM layer** deals with cells and cell transport. It defines the layout of a cell and tells what the header fields mean. It also deals with establishment and release of virtual circuits. Congestion control is also located here.

Because most applications do not want to work directly with cells (although some may), a layer above the ATM layer has been defined to allow users to send

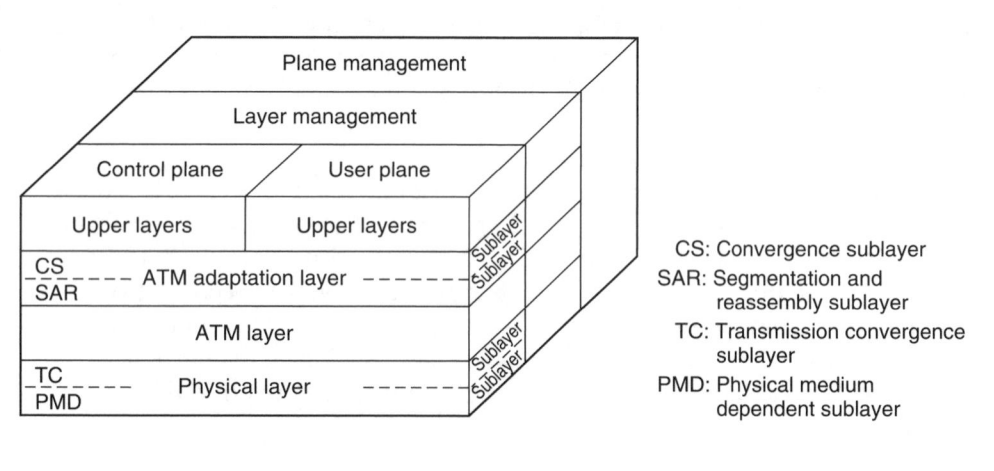

Figure 1-32. The ATM reference model.

packets larger than a cell. The ATM interface segments these packets, transmits the cells individually, and reassembles them at the other end. This layer is the **AAL (ATM Adaptation Layer)**.

Unlike the earlier two-dimensional reference models, the ATM model is defined as being three-dimensional, as shown in Fig. 1-32. The **user plane** deals with data transport, flow control, error correction, and other user functions. In contrast, the **control plane** is concerned with connection management. The layer and plane management functions relate to resource management and interlayer coordination.

The physical and AAL layers are each divided into two sublayers, one at the bottom that does the work and a convergence sublayer on top that provides the proper interface to the layer above it. The functions of the layers and sublayers are given in Fig. 1-33.

The **PMD (Physical Medium Dependent)** sublayer interfaces to the actual cable. It moves the bits on and off and handles the bit timing. For different carriers and cables, this layer will be different.

The other sublayer of the physical layer is the **TC (Transmission Convergence)** sublayer. When cells are transmitted, the TC layer sends them as a string of bits to the PMD layer. Doing this is easy. At the other end, the TC sublayer gets a pure incoming bit stream from the PMD sublayer. Its job is to convert this bit stream into a cell stream for the ATM layer. It handles all the issues related to telling where cells begin and end in the bit stream. In the ATM model, this functionality is in the physical layer. In the OSI model and in pretty much all other networks, the job of framing, that is, turning a raw bit stream into a sequence of frames or cells, is the data link layer's task.

As we mentioned earlier, the ATM layer manages cells, including their generation and transport. Most of the interesting aspects of ATM are located here. It is a mixture of the OSI data link and network layers; it is not split into sublayers.

OSI layer	ATM layer	ATM sublayer	Functionality
3/4	AAL	CS	Providing the standard interface (convergence)
		SAR	Segmentation and reassembly
2/3	ATM		Flow control Cell header generation/extraction Virtual circuit/path management Cell multiplexing/demultiplexing
2	Physical	TC	Cell rate decoupling Header checksum generation and verification Cell generation Packing/unpacking cells from the enclosing envelope Frame generation
1		PMD	Bit timing Physical network access

Figure 1-33. The ATM layers and sublayers, and their functions.

The AAL layer is split into a **SAR (Segmentation And Reassembly)** sublayer and a **CS (Convergence Sublayer)**. The lower sublayer breaks up packets into cells on the transmission side and puts them back together again at the destination. The upper sublayer makes it possible to have ATM systems offer different kinds of services to different applications (e.g., file transfer and video on demand have different requirements concerning error handling, timing, etc.).

As it is probably mostly downhill for ATM from now on, we will not discuss it further in this book. Nevertheless, since it has a substantial installed base, it will probably be around for at least a few more years. For more information about ATM, see (Dobrowski and Grise, 2001; and Gadecki and Heckart, 1997).

1.5.3 Ethernet

Both the Internet and ATM were designed for wide area networking. However, many companies, universities, and other organizations have large numbers of computers that must be connected. This need gave rise to the local area network. In this section we will say a little bit about the most popular LAN, Ethernet.

The story starts out in pristine Hawaii in the early 1970s. In this case, "pristine" can be interpreted as "not having a working telephone system." While not being interrupted by the phone all day long makes life more pleasant for vacationers, it did not make life more pleasant for researcher Norman Abramson and his colleagues at the University of Hawaii who were trying to connect users on remote islands to the main computer in Honolulu. Stringing their own cables under the Pacific Ocean was not in the cards, so they looked for a different solution.

The one they found was short-range radios. Each user terminal was equipped with a small radio having two frequencies: upstream (to the central computer) and downstream (from the central computer). When the user wanted to contact the computer, it just transmitted a packet containing the data in the upstream channel. If no one else was transmitting at that instant, the packet probably got through and was acknowledged on the downstream channel. If there was contention for the upstream channel, the terminal noticed the lack of acknowledgement and tried again. Since there was only one sender on the downstream channel (the central computer), there were never collisions there. This system, called ALOHANET, worked fairly well under conditions of low traffic but bogged down badly when the upstream traffic was heavy.

About the same time, a student named Bob Metcalfe got his bachelor's degree at M.I.T. and then moved up the river to get his Ph.D. at Harvard. During his studies, he was exposed to Abramson's work. He became so interested in it that after graduating from Harvard, he decided to spend the summer in Hawaii working with Abramson before starting work at Xerox PARC (Palo Alto Research Center). When he got to PARC, he saw that the researchers there had designed and built what would later be called personal computers. But the machines were isolated. Using his knowledge of Abramson's work, he, together with his colleague David Boggs, designed and implemented the first local area network (Metcalfe and Boggs, 1976).

They called the system **Ethernet** after the *luminiferous ether*, through which electromagnetic radiation was once thought to propagate. (When the 19th century British physicist James Clerk Maxwell discovered that electromagnetic radiation could be described by a wave equation, scientists assumed that space must be filled with some ethereal medium in which the radiation was propagating. Only after the famous Michelson-Morley experiment in 1887 did physicists discover that electromagnetic radiation could propagate in a vacuum.)

The transmission medium here was not a vacuum, but a thick coaxial cable (the ether) up to 2.5 km long (with repeaters every 500 meters). Up to 256 machines could be attached to the system via transceivers screwed onto the cable. A cable with multiple machines attached to it in parallel is called a **multidrop cable**. The system ran at 2.94 Mbps. A sketch of its architecture is given in Fig. 1-34. Ethernet had a major improvement over ALOHANET: before transmitting, a computer first listened to the cable to see if someone else was already transmitting. If so, the computer held back until the current transmission finished. Doing so avoided interfering with existing transmissions, giving a much higher efficiency. ALOHANET did not work like this because it was impossible for a terminal on one island to sense the transmission of a terminal on a distant island. With a single cable, this problem does not exist.

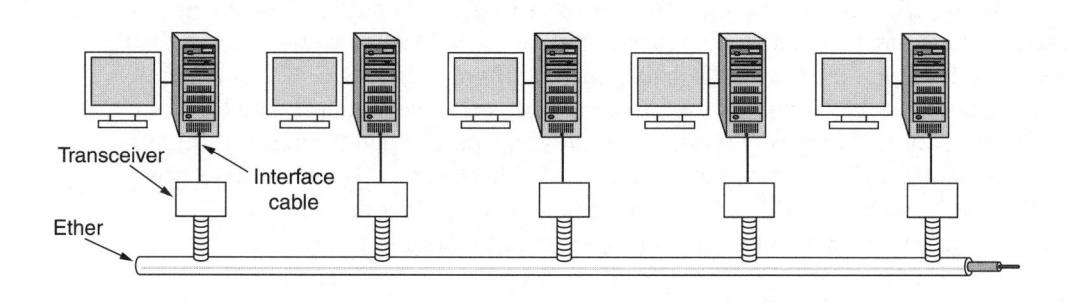

Figure 1-34. Architecture of the original Ethernet.

Despite the computer listening before transmitting, a problem still arises: what happens if two or more computers all wait until the current transmission completes and then all start at once? The solution is to have each computer listen during its own transmission and if it detects interference, jam the ether to alert all senders. Then back off and wait a random time before retrying. If a second collision happens, the random waiting time is doubled, and so on, to spread out the competing transmissions and give one of them a chance to go first.

The Xerox Ethernet was so successful that DEC, Intel, and Xerox drew up a standard in 1978 for a 10-Mbps Ethernet, called the **DIX standard**. With two minor changes, the DIX standard became the IEEE 802.3 standard in 1983.

Unfortunately for Xerox, it already had a history of making seminal inventions (such as the personal computer) and then failing to commercialize on them, a story told in *Fumbling the Future* (Smith and Alexander, 1988). When Xerox showed little interest in doing anything with Ethernet other than helping standardize it, Metcalfe formed his own company, 3Com, to sell Ethernet adapters for PCs. It has sold over 100 million of them.

Ethernet continued to develop and is still developing. New versions at 100 Mbps, 1000 Mbps, and still higher have come out. Also the cabling has improved, and switching and other features have been added. We will discuss Ethernet in detail in Chap. 4.

In passing, it is worth mentioning that Ethernet (IEEE 802.3) is not the only LAN standard. The committee also standardized a token bus (802.4) and a token ring (802.5). The need for three more-or-less incompatible standards has little to do with technology and everything to do with politics. At the time of standardization, General Motors was pushing a LAN in which the topology was the same as Ethernet (a linear cable) but computers took turns in transmitting by passing a short packet called a **token** from computer to computer. A computer could only send if it possessed the token, thus avoiding collisions. General Motors announced that this scheme was essential for manufacturing cars and was not prepared to budge from this position. This announcement notwithstanding, 802.4 has basically vanished from sight.

Similarly, IBM had its own favorite: its proprietary token ring. The token was passed around the ring and whichever computer held the token was allowed to transmit before putting the token back on the ring. Unlike 802.4, this scheme, standardized as 802.5, is still in use at some IBM sites, but virtually nowhere outside of IBM sites. However, work is progressing on a gigabit version (802.5v), but it seems unlikely that it will ever catch up with Ethernet. In short, there was a war between Ethernet, token bus, and token ring, and Ethernet won, mostly because it was there first and the challengers were not as good.

1.5.4 Wireless LANs: 802.11

Almost as soon as notebook computers appeared, many people had a dream of walking into an office and magically having their notebook computer be connected to the Internet. Consequently, various groups began working on ways to accomplish this goal. The most practical approach is to equip both the office and the notebook computers with short-range radio transmitters and receivers to allow them to communicate. This work rapidly led to wireless LANs being marketed by a variety of companies.

The trouble was that no two of them were compatible. This proliferation of standards meant that a computer equipped with a brand X radio would not work in a room equipped with a brand Y base station. Finally, the industry decided that a wireless LAN standard might be a good idea, so the IEEE committee that standardized the wired LANs was given the task of drawing up a wireless LAN standard. The standard it came up with was named 802.11. A common slang name for it is **WiFi**. It is an important standard and deserves respect, so we will call it by its proper name, 802.11.

The proposed standard had to work in two modes:

1. In the presence of a base station.

2. In the absence of a base station.

In the former case, all communication was to go through the base station, called an **access point** in 802.11 terminology. In the latter case, the computers would just send to one another directly. This mode is now sometimes called **ad hoc networking**. A typical example is two or more people sitting down together in a room not equipped with a wireless LAN and having their computers just communicate directly. The two modes are illustrated in Fig. 1-35.

The first decision was the easiest: what to call it. All the other LAN standards had numbers like 802.1, 802.2, 802.3, up to 802.10, so the wireless LAN standard was dubbed 802.11. The rest was harder.

In particular, some of the many challenges that had to be met were: finding a suitable frequency band that was available, preferably worldwide; dealing with the fact that radio signals have a finite range; ensuring that users' privacy was

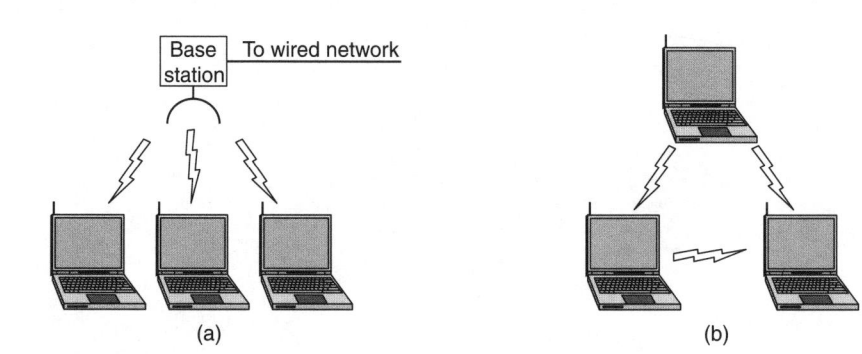

Figure 1-35. (a) Wireless networking with a base station. (b) Ad hoc networking.

maintained; taking limited battery life into account; worrying about human safety (do radio waves cause cancer?); understanding the implications of computer mobility; and finally, building a system with enough bandwidth to be economically viable.

At the time the standardization process started (mid-1990s), Ethernet had already come to dominate local area networking, so the committee decided to make 802.11 compatible with Ethernet above the data link layer. In particular, it should be possible to send an IP packet over the wireless LAN the same way a wired computer sent an IP packet over Ethernet. Nevertheless, in the physical and data link layers, several inherent differences with Ethernet exist and had to be dealt with by the standard.

First, a computer on Ethernet always listens to the ether before transmitting. Only if the ether is idle does the computer begin transmitting. With wireless LANs, that idea does not work so well. To see why, examine Fig. 1-36. Suppose that computer A is transmitting to computer B, but the radio range of A's transmitter is too short to reach computer C. If C wants to transmit to B it can listen to the ether before starting, but the fact that it does not hear anything does not mean that its transmission will succeed. The 802.11 standard had to solve this problem.

The second problem that had to be solved is that a radio signal can be reflected off solid objects, so it may be received multiple times (along multiple paths). This interference results in what is called **multipath fading**.

The third problem is that a great deal of software is not aware of mobility. For example, many word processors have a list of printers that users can choose from to print a file. When the computer on which the word processor runs is taken into a new environment, the built-in list of printers becomes invalid.

The fourth problem is that if a notebook computer is moved away from the ceiling-mounted base station it is using and into the range of a different base station, some way of handing it off is needed. Although this problem occurs with cellular telephones, it does not occur with Ethernet and needed to be solved. In

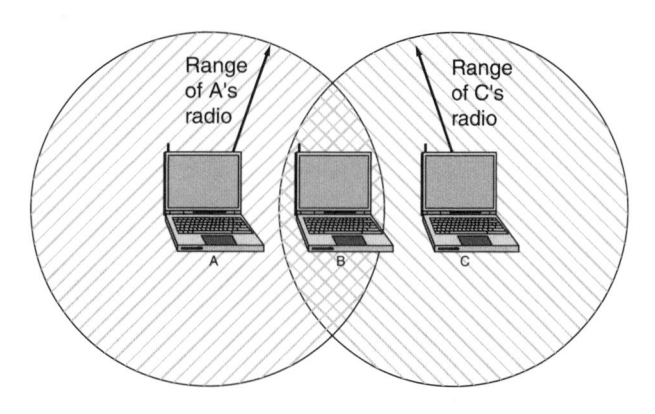

Figure 1-36. The range of a single radio may not cover the entire system.

particular, the network envisioned consists of multiple cells, each with its own base station, but with the base stations connected by Ethernet, as shown in Fig. 1-37. From the outside, the entire system should look like a single Ethernet. The connection between the 802.11 system and the outside world is called a **portal**.

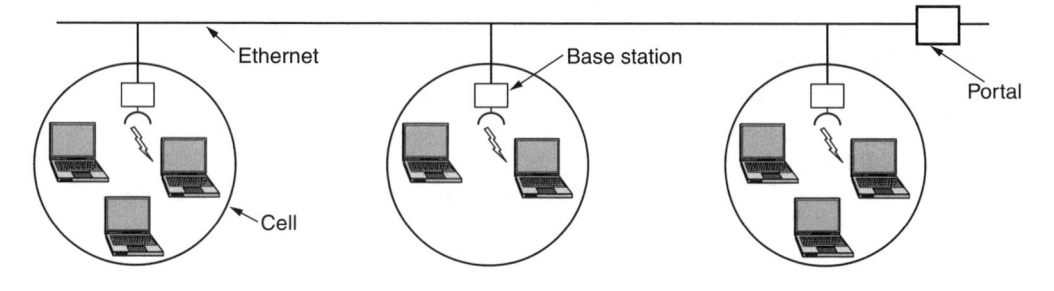

Figure 1-37. A multicell 802.11 network.

After some work, the committee came up with a standard in 1997 that addressed these and other concerns. The wireless LAN it described ran at either 1 Mbps or 2 Mbps. Almost immediately, people complained that it was too slow, so work began on faster standards. A split developed within the committee, resulting in two new standards in 1999. The 802.11a standard uses a wider frequency band and runs at speeds up to 54 Mbps. The 802.11b standard uses the same frequency band as 802.11, but uses a different modulation technique to achieve 11 Mbps. Some people see this as psychologically important since 11 Mbps is faster than the original wired Ethernet. It is likely that the original 1-Mbps 802.11 will die off quickly, but it is not yet clear which of the new standards will win out.

To make matters even more complicated than they already were, the 802 committee has come up with yet another variant, 802.11g, which uses the modulation technique of 802.11a but the frequency band of 802.11b. We will come back to 802.11 in detail in Chap. 4.

That 802.11 is going to cause a revolution in computing and Internet access is now beyond any doubt. Airports, train stations, hotels, shopping malls, and universities are rapidly installing it. Even upscale coffee shops are installing 802.11 so that the assembled yuppies can surf the Web while drinking their lattes. It is likely that 802.11 will do to the Internet what notebook computers did to computing: make it mobile.

1.6 NETWORK STANDARDIZATION

Many network vendors and suppliers exist, each with its own ideas of how things should be done. Without coordination, there would be complete chaos, and users would get nothing done. The only way out is to agree on some network standards.

Not only do standards allow different computers to communicate, but they also increase the market for products adhering to the standard. A larger market leads to mass production, economies of scale in manufacturing, VLSI implementations, and other benefits that decrease price and further increase acceptance. In the following sections we will take a quick look at the important, but little-known, world of international standardization.

Standards fall into two categories: de facto and de jure. **De facto** (Latin for "from the fact") standards are those that have just happened, without any formal plan. The IBM PC and its successors are de facto standards for small-office and home computers because dozens of manufacturers chose to copy IBM's machines very closely. Similarly, UNIX is the de facto standard for operating systems in university computer science departments.

De jure (Latin for "by law") standards, in contrast, are formal, legal standards adopted by some authorized standardization body. International standardization authorities are generally divided into two classes: those established by treaty among national governments, and those comprising voluntary, nontreaty organizations. In the area of computer network standards, there are several organizations of each type, which are discussed below.

1.6.1 Who's Who in the Telecommunications World

The legal status of the world's telephone companies varies considerably from country to country. At one extreme is the United States, which has 1500 separate, privately owned telephone companies. Before it was broken up in 1984, AT&T, at that time the world's largest corporation, completely dominated the scene. It provided telephone service to about 80 percent of America's telephones, spread throughout half of its geographical area, with all the other companies combined servicing the remaining (mostly rural) customers. Since the breakup, AT&T continues to provide long-distance service, although now in competition with other companies. The seven Regional Bell Operating Companies that were split off from AT&T and numerous independents provide local and cellular telephone service. Due to frequent mergers and other changes, the industry is in a constant state of flux.

Companies in the United States that provide communication services to the public are called **common carriers**. Their offerings and prices are described by a document called a **tariff**, which must be approved by the Federal Communications Commission for the interstate and international traffic and by the state public utilities commissions for intrastate traffic.

At the other extreme are countries in which the national government has a complete monopoly on all communication, including the mail, telegraph, telephone, and often, radio and television. Most of the world falls in this category. In some cases the telecommunication authority is a nationalized company, and in others it is simply a branch of the government, usually known as the **PTT** (**Post, Telegraph & Telephone** administration). Worldwide, the trend is toward liberalization and competition and away from government monopoly. Most European countries have now (partially) privatized their PTTs, but elsewhere the process is still slowly gaining steam.

With all these different suppliers of services, there is clearly a need to provide compatibility on a worldwide scale to ensure that people (and computers) in one country can call their counterparts in another one. Actually, this need has existed for a long time. In 1865, representatives from many European governments met to form the predecessor to today's **ITU** (**International Telecommunication Union**). Its job was standardizing international telecommunications, which in those days meant telegraphy. Even then it was clear that if half the countries used Morse code and the other half used some other code, there was going to be a problem. When the telephone was put into international service, ITU took over the job of standardizing telephony (pronounced te-LEF-ony) as well. In 1947, ITU became an agency of the United Nations.

ITU has three main sectors:

1. Radiocommunications Sector (ITU-R).

2. Telecommunications Standardization Sector (ITU-T).

3. Development Sector (ITU-D).

ITU-R is concerned with allocating radio frequencies worldwide to the competing interest groups. We will focus primarily on ITU-T, which is concerned with telephone and data communication systems. From 1956 to 1993, ITU-T was known as **CCITT**, an acronym for its French name: Comité Consultatif International Télégraphique et Téléphonique. On March 1, 1993, CCITT was reorganized to make it less bureaucratic and renamed to reflect its new role. Both ITU-T and

CCITT issued recommendations in the area of telephone and data communications. One still frequently runs into CCITT recommendations, such as CCITT X.25, although since 1993 recommendations bear the ITU-T label.

ITU-T has four classes of members:

1. National governments.

2. Sector members.

3. Associate members.

4. Regulatory agencies.

ITU-T has about 200 governmental members, including almost every member of the United Nations. Since the United States does not have a PTT, somebody else had to represent it in ITU-T. This task fell to the State Department, probably on the grounds that ITU-T had to do with foreign countries, the State Department's specialty. There are approximately 500 sector members, including telephone companies (e.g., AT&T, Vodafone, WorldCom), telecom equipment manufacturers (e.g., Cisco, Nokia, Nortel), computer vendors (e.g., Compaq, Sun, Toshiba), chip manufacturers (e.g., Intel, Motorola, TI), media companies (e.g., AOL Time Warner, CBS, Sony), and other interested companies (e.g., Boeing, Samsung, Xerox). Various nonprofit scientific organizations and industry consortia are also sector members (e.g., IFIP and IATA). Associate members are smaller organizations that are interested in a particular Study Group. Regulatory agencies are the folks who watch over the telecom business, such as the U.S. Federal Communications Commission.

ITU-T's task is to make technical recommendations about telephone, telegraph, and data communication interfaces. These often become internationally recognized standards, for example, V.24 (also known as EIA RS-232 in the United States), which specifies the placement and meaning of the various pins on the connector used by most asynchronous terminals and external modems.

It should be noted that ITU-T recommendations are technically only suggestions that governments can adopt or ignore, as they wish (because governments are like 13-year-old boys—they do not take kindly to being given orders). In practice, a country that wishes to adopt a telephone standard different from that used by the rest of the world is free to do so, but at the price of cutting itself off from everyone else. This might work for North Korea, but elsewhere it would be a real problem. The fiction of calling ITU-T standards "recommendations" was and is necessary to keep nationalist forces in many countries placated.

The real work of ITU-T is done in its 14 Study Groups, often as large as 400 people. There are currently 14 Study Groups, covering topics ranging from telephone billing to multimedia services. In order to make it possible to get anything at all done, the Study Groups are divided into Working Parties, which are in turn divided into Expert Teams, which are in turn divided into ad hoc groups. Once a bureaucracy, always a bureaucracy.

Despite all this, ITU-T actually gets things done. Since its inception, it has produced close to 3000 recommendations occupying about 60,000 pages of paper. Many of these are widely used in practice. For example, the popular V.90 56-kbps modem standard is an ITU recommendation.

As telecommunications completes the transition started in the 1980s from being entirely national to being entirely global, standards will become increasingly important, and more and more organizations will want to become involved in setting them. For more information about ITU, see (Irmer, 1994).

1.6.2 Who's Who in the International Standards World

International standards are produced and published by **ISO (International Standards Organization**[†]), a voluntary nontreaty organization founded in 1946. Its members are the national standards organizations of the 89 member countries. These members include ANSI (U.S.), BSI (Great Britain), AFNOR (France), DIN (Germany), and 85 others.

ISO issues standards on a truly vast number of subjects, ranging from nuts and bolts (literally) to telephone pole coatings [not to mention cocoa beans (ISO 2451), fishing nets (ISO 1530), women's underwear (ISO 4416) and quite a few other subjects one might not think were subject to standardization]. Over 13,000 standards have been issued, including the OSI standards. ISO has almost 200 Technical Committees, numbered in the order of their creation, each dealing with a specific subject. TC1 deals with the nuts and bolts (standardizing screw thread pitches). TC97 deals with computers and information processing. Each TC has subcommittees (SCs) divided into working groups (WGs).

The real work is done largely in the WGs by over 100,000 volunteers worldwide. Many of these "volunteers" are assigned to work on ISO matters by their employers, whose products are being standardized. Others are government officials keen on having their country's way of doing things become the international standard. Academic experts also are active in many of the WGs.

On issues of telecommunication standards, ISO and ITU-T often cooperate (ISO is a member of ITU-T) to avoid the irony of two official and mutually incompatible international standards.

The U.S. representative in ISO is **ANSI (American National Standards Institute**), which despite its name, is a private, nongovernmental, nonprofit organization. Its members are manufacturers, common carriers, and other interested parties. ANSI standards are frequently adopted by ISO as international standards.

The procedure used by ISO for adopting standards has been designed to achieve as broad a consensus as possible. The process begins when one of the

---

† For the purist, ISO's true name is the International Organization for Standardization.

national standards organizations feels the need for an international standard in some area. A working group is then formed to come up with a **CD** (**Committee Draft**). The CD is then circulated to all the member bodies, which get 6 months to criticize it. If a substantial majority approves, a revised document, called a **DIS** (**Draft International Standard**) is produced and circulated for comments and voting. Based on the results of this round, the final text of the **IS** (**International Standard**) is prepared, approved, and published. In areas of great controversy, a CD or DIS may have to go through several versions before acquiring enough votes, and the whole process can take years.

NIST (**National Institute of Standards and Technology**) is part of the U.S. Department of Commerce. It used to be the National Bureau of Standards. It issues standards that are mandatory for purchases made by the U.S. Government, except for those of the Department of Defense, which has its own standards.

Another major player in the standards world is **IEEE** (**Institute of Electrical and Electronics Engineers**), the largest professional organization in the world. In addition to publishing scores of journals and running hundreds of conferences each year, IEEE has a standardization group that develops standards in the area of electrical engineering and computing. IEEE's 802 committee has standardized many kinds of LANs. We will study some of its output later in this book. The actual work is done by a collection of working groups, which are listed in Fig. 1-38. The success rate of the various 802 working groups has been low; having an 802.x number is no guarantee of success. But the impact of the success stories (especially 802.3 and 802.11) has been enormous.

1.6.3 Who's Who in the Internet Standards World

The worldwide Internet has its own standardization mechanisms, very different from those of ITU-T and ISO. The difference can be crudely summed up by saying that the people who come to ITU or ISO standardization meetings wear suits. The people who come to Internet standardization meetings wear jeans (except when they meet in San Diego, when they wear shorts and T-shirts).

ITU-T and ISO meetings are populated by corporate officials and government civil servants for whom standardization is their job. They regard standardization as a Good Thing and devote their lives to it. Internet people, on the other hand, prefer anarchy as a matter of principle. However, with hundreds of millions of people all doing their own thing, little communication can occur. Thus, standards, however regrettable, are sometimes needed.

When the ARPANET was set up, DoD created an informal committee to oversee it. In 1983, the committee was renamed the **IAB** (**Internet Activities Board**) and was given a slighter broader mission, namely, to keep the researchers involved with the ARPANET and the Internet pointed more-or-less in the same direction, an activity not unlike herding cats. The meaning of the acronym "IAB" was later changed to **Internet Architecture Board**.

Number	Topic
802.1	Overview and architecture of LANs
802.2 ↓	Logical link control
802.3 *	Ethernet
802.4 ↓	Token bus (was briefly used in manufacturing plants)
802.5	Token ring (IBM's entry into the LAN world)
802.6 ↓	Dual queue dual bus (early metropolitan area network)
802.7 ↓	Technical advisory group on broadband technologies
802.8 †	Technical advisory group on fiber optic technologies
802.9 ↓	Isochronous LANs (for real-time applications)
802.10 ↓	Virtual LANs and security
802.11 *	Wireless LANs
802.12 ↓	Demand priority (Hewlett-Packard's AnyLAN)
802.13	Unlucky number. Nobody wanted it
802.14 ↓	Cable modems (defunct: an industry consortium got there first)
802.15 *	Personal area networks (Bluetooth)
802.16 *	Broadband wireless
802.17	Resilient packet ring

Figure 1-38. The 802 working groups. The important ones are marked with *. The ones marked with ↓ are hibernating. The one marked with † gave up and disbanded itself.

Each of the approximately ten members of the IAB headed a task force on some issue of importance. The IAB met several times a year to discuss results and to give feedback to the DoD and NSF, which were providing most of the funding at this time. When a standard was needed (e.g., a new routing algorithm), the IAB members would thrash it out and then announce the change so the graduate students who were the heart of the software effort could implement it. Communication was done by a series of technical reports called **RFCs** (**Request For Comments**). RFCs are stored on-line and can be fetched by anyone interested in them from *www.ietf.org/rfc*. They are numbered in chronological order of creation. Over 3000 now exist. We will refer to many RFCs in this book.

By 1989, the Internet had grown so large that this highly informal style no longer worked. Many vendors by then offered TCP/IP products and did not want to change them just because ten researchers had thought of a better idea. In the summer of 1989, the IAB was reorganized again. The researchers were moved to the **IRTF** (**Internet Research Task Force**), which was made subsidiary to IAB, along with the **IETF** (**Internet Engineering Task Force**). The IAB was repopulated with people representing a broader range of organizations than just the research community. It was initially a self-perpetuating group, with members serving for a 2-year term and new members being appointed by the old ones. Later, the **Internet Society** was created, populated by people interested in the Internet. The Internet Society is thus in a sense comparable to ACM or IEEE. It is governed by elected trustees who appoint the IAB members.

The idea of this split was to have the IRTF concentrate on long-term research while the IETF dealt with short-term engineering issues. The IETF was divided up into working groups, each with a specific problem to solve. The chairmen of these working groups initially met as a steering committee to direct the engineering effort. The working group topics include new applications, user information, OSI integration, routing and addressing, security, network management, and standards. Eventually, so many working groups were formed (more than 70) that they were grouped into areas and the area chairmen met as the steering committee.

In addition, a more formal standardization process was adopted, patterned after ISOs. To become a **Proposed Standard**, the basic idea must be completely explained in an RFC and have sufficient interest in the community to warrant consideration. To advance to the **Draft Standard** stage, a working implementation must have been rigorously tested by at least two independent sites for at least 4 months. If the IAB is convinced that the idea is sound and the software works, it can declare the RFC to be an Internet Standard. Some Internet Standards have become DoD standards (MIL-STD), making them mandatory for DoD suppliers. David Clark once made a now-famous remark about Internet standardization consisting of "rough consensus and running code."

1.7 METRIC UNITS

To avoid any confusion, it is worth stating explicitly that in this book, as in computer science in general, metric units are used instead of traditional English units (the furlong-stone-fortnight system). The principal metric prefixes are listed in Fig. 1-39. The prefixes are typically abbreviated by their first letters, with the units greater than 1 capitalized (KB, MB, etc.). One exception (for historical reasons) is kbps for kilobits/sec. Thus, a 1-Mbps communication line transmits 10^6 bits/sec and a 100 psec (or 100 ps) clock ticks every 10^{-10} seconds. Since milli and micro both begin with the letter "m," a choice had to be made. Normally, "m" is for milli and "μ" (the Greek letter mu) is for micro.

It is also worth pointing out that for measuring memory, disk, file, and database sizes, in common industry practice, the units have slightly different meanings. There, kilo means 2^{10} (1024) rather than 10^3 (1000) because memories are always a power of two. Thus, a 1-KB memory contains 1024 bytes, not 1000 bytes. Similarly, a 1-MB memory contains 2^{20} (1,048,576) bytes, a 1-GB memory contains 2^{30} (1,073,741,824) bytes, and a 1-TB database contains 2^{40}

Exp.	Explicit	Prefix	Exp.	Explicit	Prefix
10^{-3}	0.001	milli	10^3	1,000	Kilo
10^{-6}	0.000001	micro	10^6	1,000,000	Mega
10^{-9}	0.000000001	nano	10^9	1,000,000,000	Giga
10^{-12}	0.000000000001	pico	10^{12}	1,000,000,000,000	Tera
10^{-15}	0.000000000000001	femto	10^{15}	1,000,000,000,000,000	Peta
10^{-18}	0.000000000000000001	atto	10^{18}	1,000,000,000,000,000,000	Exa
10^{-21}	0.000000000000000000001	zepto	10^{21}	1,000,000,000,000,000,000,000	Zetta
10^{-24}	0.000000000000000000000001	yocto	10^{24}	1,000,000,000,000,000,000,000,000	Yotta

Figure 1-39. The principal metric prefixes.

(1,099,511,627,776) bytes. However, a 1-kbps communication line transmits 1000 bits per second and a 10-Mbps LAN runs at 10,000,000 bits/sec because these speeds are not powers of two. Unfortunately, many people tend to mix up these two systems, especially for disk sizes. To avoid ambiguity, in this book, we will use the symbols KB, MB, and GB for 2^{10}, 2^{20}, and 2^{30} bytes, respectively, and the symbols kbps, Mbps, and Gbps for 10^3, 10^6, and 10^9 bits/sec, respectively.

1.8 OUTLINE OF THE REST OF THE BOOK

This book discusses both the principles and practice of computer networking. Most chapters start with a discussion of the relevant principles, followed by a number of examples that illustrate these principles. These examples are usually taken from the Internet and wireless networks since these are both important and very different. Other examples will be given where relevant.

The book is structured according to the hybrid model of Fig. 1-24. Starting with Chap. 2, we begin working our way up the protocol hierarchy beginning at the bottom. The second chapter provides some background in the field of data communication. It covers wired, wireless, and satellite transmission systems. This material is concerned with the physical layer, although we cover only the architectural rather than the hardware aspects. Several examples of the physical layer, such as the public switched telephone network, mobile telephones, and the cable television network are also discussed.

Chapter 3 discusses the data link layer and its protocols by means of a number of increasingly complex examples. The analysis of these protocols is also covered. After that, some important real-world protocols are discussed, including HDLC (used in low- and medium-speed networks) and PPP (used in the Internet).

Chapter 4 concerns the medium access sublayer, which is part of the data link layer. The basic question it deals with is how to determine who may use the network next when the network consists of a single shared channel, as in most LANs and some satellite networks. Many examples are given from the areas of wired LANs, wireless LANs (especially Ethernet), wireless MANs, Bluetooth, and satellite networks. Bridges and data link switches, which are used to connect LANs, are also discussed here.

Chapter 5 deals with the network layer, especially routing, with many routing algorithms, both static and dynamic, being covered. Even with good routing algorithms though, if more traffic is offered than the network can handle, congestion can develop, so we discuss congestion and how to prevent it. Even better than just preventing congestion is guaranteeing a certain quality of service. We will discuss that topic as well here. Connecting heterogeneous networks to form internetworks leads to numerous problems that are discussed here. The network layer in the Internet is given extensive coverage.

Chapter 6 deals with the transport layer. Much of the emphasis is on connection-oriented protocols, since many applications need these. An example transport service and its implementation are discussed in detail. The actual code is given for this simple example to show how it could be implemented. Both Internet transport protocols, UDP and TCP, are covered in detail, as are their performance issues. Issues concerning wireless networks are also covered.

Chapter 7 deals with the application layer, its protocols and applications. The first topic is DNS, which is the Internet's telephone book. Next comes e-mail, including a discussion of its protocols. Then we move onto the Web, with detailed discussions of the static content, dynamic content, what happens on the client side, what happens on the server side, protocols, performance, the wireless Web, and more. Finally, we examine networked multimedia, including streaming audio, Internet radio, and video on demand.

Chapter 8 is about network security. This topic has aspects that relate to all layers, so it is easiest to treat it after all the layers have been thoroughly explained. The chapter starts with an introduction to cryptography. Later, it shows how cryptography can be used to secure communication, e-mail, and the Web. The book ends with a discussion of some areas in which security hits privacy, freedom of speech, censorship, and other social issues collide head on.

Chapter 9 contains an annotated list of suggested readings arranged by chapter. It is intended to help those readers who would like to pursue their study of networking further. The chapter also has an alphabetical bibliography of all references cited in this book.

The author's Web site at Prentice Hall:

http://www.prenhall.com/tanenbaum

has a page with links to many tutorials, FAQs, companies, industry consortia, professional organizations, standards organizations, technologies, papers, and more.

1.9 SUMMARY

Computer networks can be used for numerous services, both for companies and for individuals. For companies, networks of personal computers using shared servers often provide access to corporate information. Typically they follow the client-server model, with client workstations on employee desktops accessing powerful servers in the machine room. For individuals, networks offer access to a variety of information and entertainment resources. Individuals often access the Internet by calling up an ISP using a modem, although increasingly many people have a fixed connection at home. An up-and-coming area is wireless networking with new applications such as mobile e-mail access and m-commerce.

Roughly speaking, networks can be divided up into LANs, MANs, WANs, and internetworks, with their own characteristics, technologies, speeds, and niches. LANs cover a building and operate at high speeds. MANs cover a city, for example, the cable television system, which is now used by many people to access the Internet. WANs cover a country or continent. LANs and MANs are unswitched (i.e., do not have routers); WANs are switched. Wireless networks are becoming extremely popular, especially wireless LANs. Networks can be interconnected to form internetworks.

Network software consists of protocols, which are rules by which processes communicate. Protocols are either connectionless or connection-oriented. Most networks support protocol hierarchies, with each layer providing services to the layers above it and insulating them from the details of the protocols used in the lower layers. Protocol stacks are typically based either on the OSI model or on the TCP/IP model. Both have network, transport, and application layers, but they differ on the other layers. Design issues include multiplexing, flow control, error control, and others. Much of this book deals with protocols and their design.

Networks provide services to their users. These services can be connection-oriented or connectionless. In some networks, connectionless service is provided in one layer and connection-oriented service is provided in the layer above it.

Well-known networks include the Internet, ATM networks, Ethernet, and the IEEE 802.11 wireless LAN. The Internet evolved from the ARPANET, to which other networks were added to form an internetwork. The present Internet is actually a collection of many thousands of networks, rather than a single network. What characterizes it is the use of the TCP/IP protocol stack throughout. ATM is widely used inside the telephone system for long-haul data traffic. Ethernet is the most popular LAN and is present in most large companies and universities. Finally, wireless LANs at surprisingly high speeds (up to 54 Mbps) are beginning to be widely deployed.

To have multiple computers talk to each other requires a large amount of standardization, both in the hardware and software. Organizations such as the ITU-T, ISO, IEEE, and IAB manage different parts of the standardization process.

PROBLEMS

1. Imagine that you have trained your St. Bernard, Bernie, to carry a box of three 8mm tapes instead of a flask of brandy. (When your disk fills up, you consider that an emergency.) These tapes each contain 7 gigabytes. The dog can travel to your side, wherever you may be, at 18 km/hour. For what range of distances does Bernie have a higher data rate than a transmission line whose data rate (excluding overhead) is 150 Mbps?

2. An alternative to a LAN is simply a big timesharing system with terminals for all users. Give two advantages of a client-server system using a LAN.

3. The performance of a client-server system is influenced by two network factors: the bandwidth of the network (how many bits/sec it can transport) and the latency (how many seconds it takes for the first bit to get from the client to the server). Give an example of a network that exhibits high bandwidth and high latency. Then give an example of one with low bandwidth and low latency.

4. Besides bandwidth and latency, what other parameter is needed to give a good characterization of the quality of service offered by a network used for digitized voice traffic?

5. A factor in the delay of a store-and-forward packet-switching system is how long it takes to store and forward a packet through a switch. If switching time is 10 μsec, is this likely to be a major factor in the response of a client-server system where the client is in New York and the server is in California? Assume the propagation speed in copper and fiber to be 2/3 the speed of light in vacuum.

6. A client-server system uses a satellite network, with the satellite at a height of 40,000 km. What is the best-case delay in response to a request?

7. In the future, when everyone has a home terminal connected to a computer network, instant public referendums on important pending legislation will become possible. Ultimately, existing legislatures could be eliminated, to let the will of the people be expressed directly. The positive aspects of such a direct democracy are fairly obvious; discuss some of the negative aspects.

8. A collection of five routers is to be connected in a point-to-point subnet. Between each pair of routers, the designers may put a high-speed line, a medium-speed line, a low-speed line, or no line. If it takes 100 ms of computer time to generate and inspect each topology, how long will it take to inspect all of them?

9. A group of $2^n - 1$ routers are interconnected in a centralized binary tree, with a router at each tree node. Router i communicates with router j by sending a message to the root of the tree. The root then sends the message back down to j. Derive an approximate expression for the mean number of hops per message for large n, assuming that all router pairs are equally likely.

10. A disadvantage of a broadcast subnet is the capacity wasted when multiple hosts attempt to access the channel at the same time. As a simplistic example, suppose that

Higher National in Computing

time is divided into discrete slots, with each of the n hosts attempting to use the channel with probability p during each slot. What fraction of the slots are wasted due to collisions?

11. What are two reasons for using layered protocols?

12. The president of the Specialty Paint Corp. gets the idea to work with a local beer brewer to produce an invisible beer can (as an anti-litter measure). The president tells her legal department to look into it, and they in turn ask engineering for help. As a result, the chief engineer calls his counterpart at the other company to discuss the technical aspects of the project. The engineers then report back to their respective legal departments, which then confer by telephone to arrange the legal aspects. Finally, the two corporate presidents discuss the financial side of the deal. Is this an example of a multilayer protocol in the sense of the OSI model?

13. What is the principal difference between connectionless communication and connection-oriented communication?

14. Two networks each provide reliable connection-oriented service. One of them offers a reliable byte stream and the other offers a reliable message stream. Are these identical? If so, why is the distinction made? If not, give an example of how they differ.

15. What does "negotiation" mean when discussing network protocols? Give an example.

16. In Fig. 1-19, a service is shown. Are any other services implicit in this figure? If so, where? If not, why not?

17. In some networks, the data link layer handles transmission errors by requesting damaged frames to be retransmitted. If the probability of a frame's being damaged is p, what is the mean number of transmissions required to send a frame? Assume that acknowledgements are never lost.

18. Which of the OSI layers handles each of the following:
    (a) Dividing the transmitted bit stream into frames.
    (b) Determining which route through the subnet to use.

19. If the unit exchanged at the data link level is called a frame and the unit exchanged at the network level is called a packet, do frames encapsulate packets or do packets encapsulate frames? Explain your answer.

20. A system has an n-layer protocol hierarchy. Applications generate messages of length M bytes. At each of the layers, an h-byte header is added. What fraction of the network bandwidth is filled with headers?

21. List two ways in which the OSI reference model and the TCP/IP reference model are the same. Now list two ways in which they differ.

22. What is the main difference between TCP and UDP?

23. The subnet of Fig. 1-25(b) was designed to withstand a nuclear war. How many bombs would it take to partition the nodes into two disconnected sets? Assume that any bomb wipes out a node and all of the links connected to it.

24. The Internet is roughly doubling in size every 18 months. Although no one really knows for sure, one estimate put the number of hosts on it at 100 million in 2001. Use

these data to compute the expected number of Internet hosts in the year 2010. Do you believe this? Explain why or why not.

25. When a file is transferred between two computers, two acknowledgement strategies are possible. In the first one, the file is chopped up into packets, which are individually acknowledged by the receiver, but the file transfer as a whole is not acknowledged. In the second one, the packets are not acknowledged individually, but the entire file is acknowledged when it arrives. Discuss these two approaches.

26. Why does ATM use small, fixed-length cells?

27. How long was a bit on the original 802.3 standard in meters? Use a transmission speed of 10 Mbps and assume the propagation speed in coax is 2/3 the speed of light in vacuum.

28. An image is 1024 × 768 pixels with 3 bytes/pixel. Assume the image is uncompressed. How long does it take to transmit it over a 56-kbps modem channel? Over a 1-Mbps cable modem? Over a 10-Mbps Ethernet? Over 100-Mbps Ethernet?

29. Ethernet and wireless networks have some similarities and some differences. One property of Ethernet is that only one frame at a time can be transmitted on an Ethernet. Does 802.11 share this property with Ethernet? Discuss your answer.

30. Wireless networks are easy to install, which makes them inexpensive since installation costs usually far overshadow equipment costs. Nevertheless, they also have some disadvantages. Name two of them.

31. List two advantages and two disadvantages of having international standards for network protocols.

32. When a system has a permanent part and a removable part (such as a CD-ROM drive and the CD-ROM), it is important that the system be standardized, so that different companies can make both the permanent and removable parts and everything still works together. Give three examples outside the computer industry where such international standards exist. Now give three areas outside the computer industry where they do not exist.

33. Make a list of activities that you do every day in which computer networks are used. How would your life be altered if these networks were suddenly switched off?

34. Find out what networks are used at your school or place of work. Describe the network types, topologies, and switching methods used there.

35. The *ping* program allows you to send a test packet to a given location and see how long it takes to get there and back. Try using *ping* to see how long it takes to get from your location to several known locations. From thes data, plot the one-way transit time over the Internet as a function of distance. It is best to use universities since the location of their servers is known very accurately. For example, *berkeley.edu* is in Berkeley, California, *mit.edu* is in Cambridge, Massachusetts, *vu.nl* is in Amsterdam, The Netherlands, *www.usyd.edu.au* is in Sydney, Australia, and *www.uct.ac.za* is in Cape Town, South Africa.

36. Go to IETF's Web site, *www.ietf.org*, to see what they are doing. Pick a project you like and write a half-page report on the problem and the proposed solution.

37. Standardization is very important in the network world. ITU and ISO are the main official standardization organizations. Go to their Web sites, *www.itu.org* and *www.iso.org*, respectively, and learn about their standardization work. Write a short report about the kinds of things they have standardized.

38. The Internet is made up of a large number of networks. Their arrangement determines the topology of the Internet. A considerable amount of information about the Internet topology is available on line. Use a search engine to find out more about the Internet topology and write a short report summarizing your findings.

Notes

Notes

Notes